CRIME AND JUSTICE ADMINISTRATION

ALVIN W. COHN
Administration of Justice Services

J. B. Lippincott Company
Philadelphia
New York / San Jose / Toronto

ISBN 0-397-47344-3

Library of Congress Catalog Card Number

Printed in the United States of America

1 3 5 7 9 8 6 4 2

Library of Congress Cataloging in Publication Data

Cohn, Alvin W
  Crime and justice administration.

  Bibliography: p.
  Includes index.
  1. Crime and criminals. 2. Criminal justice,
Administration of. I. Title.
  HV6025.C57   364   76-798
  ISBN 0-397-47344-3

3/16/77 *pul·* 9.95

For Sara, Felicia, and Meredith

Those who hold power over the destinies of others must balance that power with justice. Those who control the administration of justice must temper that control with compassion. Those who are just and compassionate know the true meaning of humanity.

pREfACE

Crime and Justice Administration is a book designed for the student of criminology and criminal justice. It is primarily a descriptive work which outlines the major themes, subjects, programs, practices, and procedures associated with efforts at crime definition, control, and prevention in the United States. It is a beginning text, but one written to enable the reader to appreciate and to understand some of the major dilemmas and concepts involved in the theory and practice of crime control and prevention.

Quotations from the works of major theorists and others appear liberally throughout the text. These are designed to acquaint the student with some of the significant contributors to the literature of criminology and to give some notion of the substance of their work. In this way, the major figures speak for themselves, rather than appearing less distinctly in summaries and syntheses. The words of such notable writers as Tappan, Sutherland, Cressey, Barnes, Teeters, Korn, Geis, Schrag, Empey, Matza, Sellin,

Wolfgang, and Schur, among many others, have been left intact wherever it was appropriate to do so.

This book does not attempt to deal with all of the issues, concerns, practices, programs, policies, theories, procedures, and controversies in criminology or criminal justice administration. No book could possibly satisfy such a mandate. However, the author has attempted to deal with some of the primary questions, and has dealt with others within the limitations of space. Obviously, in such an undertaking, what is important to some may appear to have been subordinated to other matter. However, it is hoped that the author's choices have, on the whole, been reasonable ones, and that readers will find few serious omissions or biases.

Initially, this book was planned with the expectation that it would serve as an introductory text for both criminology and criminal justice administration. In the first chapter, the relationship between the subject matter of these two areas is examined. However, as the manuscript developed, it became apparent that a judicious mix of criminological theory and data and criminal justice practices and procedures within the confines of a relatively short book would be difficult, if not impossible, to achieve. For this reason, it was decided to "tilt" toward criminal justice administration, though in the author's opinion, the final product serves the needs of both subject areas with, once more, allowances for its obvious limitations.

Criminal justice texts tend to be heavily law enforcement oriented and are frequently without any substantive analyses of theories and concepts related to crime, criminality, and criminal behavior. In contrast, many criminology texts are similarly oriented toward their traditional concern with theories of causation and depictions of the meaning and significance of criminal behavior. Criminology texts, however, generally deal with the processes of social control and sometimes justice administration, while criminal justice texts seldom explore such issues as causation, corrections, or non-police-oriented dilemmas associated with crime control—omissions which, in some degree, limit their usefulness.

There will be no attempt in this volume to correct these imbalances. However, a conscious decision has been made to include as many issues as possible with which a beginning student should have some familiarity. Thus, while this is primarily an introduction to criminal justice administration, considerable attention has been given to such subjects as the meaning and significance of causation and of crime data, the concept of punishment, the scope and significance of the correctional process, the meaning of justice, the new thrust of "critical criminology," sometimes called "radical criminology," and, throughout most of the chapters, an historical review of programs and services as they have developed into the "nonsystem" of criminal justice that we have in contemporary America.

Chapter 1 presents an overview of criminology and criminal justice, making the point that, to date, our efforts at crime control have resulted in failure. Chapter 2, "Crime, Criminals, and Criminal Law," examines the nature of crime, who commits what crimes, and the meaning of criminal law. Chapter 3, "Crime Data Overview," looks at the nature of crime data and the problem of collecting meaningful information about the extent of crime in our society. Chapters 4 and 5 examine, in traditional fashion, the various categories of crimes and criminal behaviors while also describing what is meant by person and property offenses, as well as several special offender categories, including the professional and organized criminal, the sexual psychopath, and the political criminal.

Chapter 6, "Causation Overview," explores the nature and meaning of causation and its relation to our understanding processes of social control, while Chapter 7 reviews many of the significant causal theories associated with crime and delinquency. The latter chapter also discusses the historical development of criminological theory, from the Preclassical, Classical, and Neoclassical, to Positive orientations. In Chapter 8, "Criminal Justice Overview," the actual processes for handling an offender are reviewed, from the time of arrest through postconviction remedies to discharge or release from the system. Chapters 9 and 10 deal with "Police" and "Courts" respectively, including their historical development and contemporary practices.

Chapters 11 through 16, in effect, deal with the correctional process, with Chapter 11, "Corrections Overview," detailing the author's views on why corrections has failed to "correct" those under its supervision. Chapter 12, "Punishment," provides an historical analysis of the various methods and reasons for criminal punishment. Chapter 13, "Juvenile Justice," describes the system used to deal with dependent, neglected, and delinquent youths in the United States and some of the current issues associated with juvenile justice programming, including diversion. Chapters 14, 15, and 16 deal with "Probation," "Prisons," and "Parole," respectively, with each discussed not only in terms of their historical developments, but their contemporary programs and practices as well.

Several persons have contributed significantly to the writing of this book and especially several of its chapters. Patrick Langan worked intensively in researching the chapter on Punishment and provided a great deal of the form which the chapter finally took. Philip Lynn worked on the "Crime Data Overview" chapter, as well as the sections detailing the various offense categories in Chapters 4 and 5. His diligence in researching these materials was of great help in putting these three chapters together. Richard Casey demonstrated his command of the literature in summarizing the materials for Chapter 7, "Causal Theories." I very much appreciate their effort, concern, assistance, talent, and friendship, but assume full responsibility for the final form of those and all other chapters in the book.

I appreicate the assistance, patience, and concern of A. Richard Heffron at J.B. Lippincott Co. His encouragement and valuable suggestions helped to provide direction to the author. I am grateful to Ms. Jiggs Umlauf for her skillful typing. To Mark Blessington and Emilio Viano I owe a special debt of gratitude. They reviewed the manuscript and made valuable suggestions regarding substance and format.

I am most indebted to my wife, Sara, who not only demonstrated great concern and patience while the "author was at work," but who quite willingly read the manuscript as it was being prepared and made valuable contributions toward its readability.

Finally, I would like to express the hope that as the student reads this book, he or she will not only understand, but will be able to act upon that understanding when reminded that *Today is almost yesterday; tomorrow will soon be today!*

Alvin W. Cohn
January, 1976

AckNOWlEdGMENTS

A number of materials contained in Chapter 8, "Criminal Justice Overview," originally appeared in an article by the author, "Training in the Criminal Justice Nonsystem," which was published in *Federal Probation,* June, 1974. The author also published many of the ideas contained in Chapter 1, "Introduction," and Chapter 13, "Juvenile Justice," in a book co-authored with Emilio Viano, *Social Problems and Criminal Justice,* published by Nelson-Hall Publishers, Chicago, in 1975. In addition, the following authors and publishers granted permission to reprint material from their publications:

Clark and Marshall, *A Treatise on the Law of Crimes,* 6th Edition, published by Callaghan and Company, 6141 North Cicero Avenue, Chicago, Illinois 60646. Reprinted with permission.

David Dressler, *Practice and Theory of Probation and Parole,* 2nd Edition. Copyright © 1959 by Columbia University Press. Reprinted by permission of Columbia University Press.

Mabel A. Elliott, *Crime and Modern Society.*

CONTENTS

iNTROduCTiON

The Failure of Crime Control

> A rather heavy bill of indictment is to be drawn
> against criminal procedure in the United States,
> or against the legal machinery available for the
> apprehension and prosecution of offenders. Crim-
> inal law in dealing with those who violate it should
> be characterized by accuracy and celerity of
> operations and by certainty of results; justice
> should proceed in orderly fashion, with dispatch
> and with efficiency. In the United States such is
> far from being the case. Criminal law in this coun-
> try is wanting in a number of respects for its
> successful or proper functioning.

These are the words of Harry Best, who wrote
them in 1930 (p. 529), but who could have written them in the 1970s. Criminal justice in the
United States today is neither efficient in its
administration nor effective in managing the
crime problem. Its goals are unclear, its procedures sometimes are without respect for due

process, its management is frequently devoid of leadership, and the clients and communities supposedly served by the system more often than not receive mediocre services.

And yet, there is a degree of imaginative programming, competent personnel, increased education and training, and heightened concern, all of which are probably beginning to have some impact on efficiency and effectiveness. It appears that crime is probably tolerated at greater levels today than ever before in our history, either because there is so much of it, or citizens have learned to accommodate themselves to its increase. While crimes of violence and others known as offenses against the person are abhorred, we have come to realize that, to a certain extent, crime is healthy and normal for a progressive and free society (Durkheim, 1950). That is not to say that we like murder or rape or vehicle theft, but it is to say that without a certain degree of freedom, there could be no crime. In a repressive society, deviance is not tolerated. In a civilized society, crime can represent disenchantment, feelings of oppression, aimlessness, and discontentment with the status quo. It can represent, as we learned in the 1960s at the height of the civil rights movement, that without crime, significant change in governmental structures and implementation of the rights of citizens may not come about, or if they do, will happen much too slowly.

Historically, concern in the United States for the effects of crime and delinquency, their impact on society, and the processes for control have received varying degrees of attention. But today citizens are both alarmed and frightened, and in many political campaigns we have observed that candidates for office have suggested that crime is the number one problem in the country. In 1968, the Joint Commission on Correctional Manpower and Training commissioned Louis Harris and Associates to survey the public attitudes on crime. Their report, *The Public Looks at Crime and Corrections* (1968:1), could read as a current statement:

> The public feels that our society has not been able to deal successfully with the problem of crime. There is a sense of disappointment in what has been accomplished through law enforcement, the courts, and corrections. . . . There is little hope for the future unless some change occurs.

Certainly, as Clarence Schrag (1971:1) has noted, "American justice is in turmoil." An historical pattern of neglect has necessitated major changes, some of which have been addressed by the Law Enforcement Assistance Administration of the U.S. Department of Justice. However, criminologists such as Schrag not only lament the failure of the system to curtail crime, they also indict the system in terms of its operational inefficiencies (Schrag, 1971:1): "There is evidence that instead of preventing crime, the system of justice—as it is now embodied in our police, courts, and correctional agencies—*is a significant factor in crime causation*" (emphasis added).

The average citizen, although disenchanted with the system, may nonetheless view as workable the simple progression of a crime's commission followed by its offender's arrest, conviction, and punishment. But, for several reasons, that process is probably more the exception than the rule. Complainants in white collar crimes and victimless crimes generally do not want to prosecute. Victims of many predatory crimes, such as rape, burglary, and assault, do not always report such offenses. Lack of law enforcement personnel often precludes effective investigation when offenses are reported. Frequently, when crimes are investigated, not enough evidence is obtained to bring an alleged suspect to trial. Prosecutors and judges, feeling overworked and in a hurry, screen out many cases or otherwise engage in bargaining justice, which adds significantly to the dropout rate in the system. The correctional system is overburdened and consequently unable to effectively reduce recidivism rates among those under its control and supervision.

The inefficiency, ineffectiveness, and burgeoning caseloads for police, courts, and corrections add up to a network of services basically unable to deal with the crime problem. Increased technology, scientific developments, more manpower, diversion from the system of minor offenders and selected juveniles, decriminalization of some laws, more training and education, and some improvements in organizational management conceivably have helped. Collectively, however, they and other developments have been insufficient to reduce the effects of the social problem of crime.

Dealing with crime and delinquency in the United States is a pervasive, complex, and difficult social problem (Viano and Cohn, 1975:245). The extent of crime in the country and the controversy over the figures used to measure its extent become subjects of great importance for social planners and policy makers. Crime and delinquency are *probably* on the rise, especially if one reads the *Uniform*

Crime Reports of the Federal Bureau of Investigation, but we cannot be certain or precise as to what these rates are. This is so, as we shall discuss in several forthcoming chapters, because all crime is not reported, some crime which is reported is not recorded, and many offenders who are apprehended for the violation of laws are, for several reasons, discharged, dismissed, or otherwise dropped out of the system. The debates over these issues, however, obviously do not satisfy the victims or potential victims who remain just as concerned about the safety of their persons or property.

Criminology as a Discipline

Concern about the problems of criminal justice administration has centered, in part, on classes of crimes and the reasons some people are unable or unwilling to live according to the norms of society. All sorts of people think about the causes of crime: novelists, philosophers, policemen, physiologists, psychologists, burglars, and judges. Each in some way has made some kind of contribution to an understanding of the problem, but none alone nor all collectively have resolved the problem. Concepts of cause related to such issues as genetics, economics, cultural values, criminal associations, education, recreation, and family life have been espoused, but none seems to answer the question, Why?

People have been writing about crime and its causes from various perspectives and disciplines for many centuries, but it is the discipline of criminology that accepts as its primary responsibility the blending of all issues, concerns, beliefs, and variables that may be associated with crime and its causation and control. Korn (1966:2) describes it this way:

> ...Criminology is the field which focuses on the distinctive problems created by society's overt refusal to tolerate certain forms of behavior it has generated in certain of its members. The problems posed by these imponderables range from the moral to the philosophical to the practical and technical, from the ideological and political to the managerial and administrative. What makes their (criminologists') study particularly intriguing to the adventurous mind is the fact that not one of them has been solved.

The criminologist's role, then, rests on the classical touchstones of science: explain, predict, and control. His mission is to understand the problems of crime and delinquency, and through theory and practice, help society deal with the problems as they evolve, become defined, and are understood.

Consensus over boundaries of the discipline of criminology has not been reached. While schools of law and medicine offer an accepted nucleus of subjects, this is not so where criminology is taught. What police, the courts, and correctional students need to learn produces more disagreement than agreement; yet schools and programs have been proliferating in recent years. Besides disagreement over such fundamentals as causation, prevention, treatment, and control, criminologists cannot agree on how criminal justice services relate to criminology nor how the various concepts ought to be practiced.

Henslin (1972:1) suggests:

> A major theme running through the writings of those who have expressed themselves on this matter is that criminologists have been overly preoccupied with offenders, to the neglect of more basic, and potentially more fruitful, concerns . . . especially analysis of how law comes into being, the process by which particular behaviors come to be labelled as criminal . . . (and) on the analysis of the conditions under which criminal law develops such that particular *behaviors* (in contrast to individuals exhibiting particular behaviors) come to be proscribed by law.

Criminology and Criminal Justice

The two terms of criminology and criminal justice are frequently used interchangeably by writers and, perhaps, the way they are used is more an academic problem than a real one. Some argue that criminology is primarily concerned with theory related to causation of crime and conceptual issues related to the manner in which society reacts to crime. Some maintain that criminal justice is the pragmatic concern of the actual processes utilized to administer and control crime and criminals. Criminology is viewed as an academic issue, while criminal justice is seen in operational terms, that is, the actual agencies which are found in the criminal justice system. Some maintain that the question can be answered in terms of research interests: that criminology focuses on purely theoretical concerns, while criminal justice is directed toward administrative matters.

Reflecting a legal and sociological perspective, from which

much of criminology has developed, Sutherland and Cressey (1974:3) state:

> Criminology is the body of knowledge regarding delinquency and crime as social phenomena. It includes within its scope the processes of making laws, of breaking laws, and of reacting toward the breaking of laws . . . (and it) consists of three principal divisions, as follows: (a) the sociology of law . . .; (b) criminal etiology . . .; and (c) penology. . . . The objective of criminology is the development of a body of general and verified principles and of other types of knowledge regarding this process of law, crime, and reaction to crime.

In *Introduction to the Criminal Justice System* (1972:1), Kerper states, "The criminal justice system is the institution charged with direct responsibility for the prevention and control of crime." By implication, she is defining the parameters of the field, which appear to be quite distinct from Sutherland and Cressey's definition of criminology. Newman (1975:x) looks at both and concludes:

> Criminal justice is mostly concerned with the decision process in the crime control agencies of police, prosecutors' offices, trial courts, and correctional facilities, and in programs like probation and parole. Thus the effectiveness or dysfunction of criminal justice intervention may be tested against, and in turn test, hypotheses and theories of crime causation proposed by criminologists. . . .
> The distinction in research focus between the criminological emphasis on causal factors in contrast to research into operational reality and effectiveness of criminal justice agencies has sometimes been viewed as merely a difference between "pure" and "applied" research. . . . Criminal justice is not applied criminology . . .

In the last analysis, until criminology or criminal justice administration becomes a "professional" discipline, like medicine or law, with its own body of knowledge and distinct method for educating those who want to enter the field, the differences between the two will remain more of an academic issue than a practical one. Universities will continue to develop their own curricula, based on their beliefs as to what is proper to be taught. Police and correctional training academies will continue to develop and instruct based on agency needs and desires, but will probably continue to be more pragmatic than theoretical. And it will probably remain true for many years to come that criminologists graduating from schools with sociological, psychological, and/or legal frames of reference will find themselves teaching, researching, and administering, along with graduates of programs primarily concerned with criminal justice management and administration. In the future, there may be more of a blending of the two orientations, as a distinct body of knowledge develops, and as research interests coincide and merge. At the present time, there is no more than an overlap of concerns.

Historical Developments in Crime Control

The historical analysis of efforts to define crime and societal reaction to it is fascinating, but complex, and is subject to considerable speculation and interpretation. This is especially so since it has only been in the last several hundred years that we have had accurate documentation about the feelings, beliefs, laws, and practices of various societies. Thus, any apparent reconstruction of official policies and programs, prior to then, can only be piecemeal and probably incomplete. Korn and McCorkle (1965) not only concur in the above, they also suggest that the credibility of much that is documented needs to be questioned.

Conceptions of crime and its control, of deviance and social order, are the results of human responsiveness to changes in experience, needs, knowledge, technology, institutions, and physical and intellectual resources. Schrag (1971:10) says:

> ... in spite of the current clamor about disorder and alienation the capability of implementing man's ideas seems always to be increasing. The goals of crime control, therefore, are not simply to produce uniformity of conduct but to anticipate and, so far as possible, to direct or manage the processes of social change. If the task is more difficult today than before, it is largely because of the increasing disparities in people's beliefs, interests, practices, and resources.

Man has not always been humane or concerned with the welfare of others in society, especially those who were the deviants: the sick, the infirm, the criminal, the mentally ill or incapable. In fact, information available now indicates that until only a few hundred years ago it was commonly believed that such deviants were possessed by the devil or other demons and could be saved only by means of exorcism—that is, by driving such evil spirits out of the body of the deviate. Consequently, severe physical punishments, including flogging, branding, stoning, and execution were regarded as proper and natural forms of revenge. Relatives of the victim, or the victim himself, originally controlled physical punishment, but later the responsibility fell on government. This change from blood feuds and other forms of personal revenge probably occurred as rulers recognized that only government assumption of responsibility for revenge could possibly control or prevent outbreaks of hostilities among offenders, victims, clans, and/or other interested parties.

This age of revenge or private vengeance has been referred to as the Preclassical period in criminology. Marked by demonology and other unscientific ideas, it was an age when retaliation was the primary method for controlling crime and criminals. Many people believe that retaliation still enters significantly into criminal justice practices today, and that it reflects the public's endorsement of repressive measures, especially for politically unpopular offenders and those who commit heinous offenses, such as child molestation or forcible rape.

An age of reason ushered in the Classical period of criminology during the late 18th and early 19th centuries. Several philosophies, especially in the areas of law, government responsibility, and man's conception of man, significantly influenced the development of new ways to control crime and criminals. Physical punishment became unpopular and prisons became the primary correctional device. The emerging philosophies of hedonism and rationalism, the increasing popularity of contract theories of government (which detailed the relationship between government and the governed), and the growing evidence, according to some, of the essential interdependence of men, all helped to support prisons as the ideal way of correcting criminals. Since it was believed that man had free will, needed pleasure, and wanted to avoid pain, it was thought that criminal behavior could be controlled by defining crimes precisely and detailing the punishments that would occur as a result of their violation.

At this time also, the industrial age became a force in society, especially in Europe, where cities began to emerge and urbanism became the predominant way of life. Economics were based on industrial production instead of agriculture, populations shifted, and the cities not only grew, they became crowded.

In an effort to establish a fair, equitable, and rational system of justice, punishments were graded by law according to the perceived severity of the offenses committed. Framers of this philosophy hoped that the penalty as the offender and society perceived it would be at least equal to the rewards of the crime. Precise punishments were fixed by law, and judges no longer had complete discretion to do as they wanted. Once an offender was found guilty his fate was sealed. "Let the punishment fit the crime" became the motto of the criminal justice system.

Police and courts were expected to enforce the law without question or option; they were to ensure the certainty of punishment. In short, reformers thought that all persons in society certainly had to know that "crime does not pay!" The process was to have no exceptions. However, in time the very young and the insane were legally exempted from prosecution and unequivocal punishments (a time often referred to as the Neoclassical period of criminology).

During this period in Classical criminology, the crime, or the offense, received primary emphasis; the law was paramount. But during the late 19th century, several persons began to suggest that man was not completely a free agent, being so thoroughly hedonistic that he sought pleasure all the time. Instead, they argued, the only way to control crime was to look at the offender and attempt to find out precisely why he committed deviant acts. Such knowledge, they argued, would allow society to be truly able to control crime, especially since the offender could be treated and potential offenders prevented, or deterred, from engaging in criminal behavior. The new era has been called the age of reform but is more popularly referred to as Positive criminology.

Cities continued to predominate and industrial production was even more the basis for the world's expanding economies. Then, too, Freud's psychoanalytic theories gained acceptance, so reformers argued that if the causes of deviant behavior were not understood, "crime" could not be cured. Cure, then, became the primary process for controlling crime and delinquency in society.

Sutherland and Cressey (1974:356) summarize the reasons for this shift from retribution to precise forms of punishment and then to rehabilitation. They state:

> The official policy of individualized treatment for offenders developed out of the positive school's arguments against the practice of attempting to im-

pose uniform punishments . . . It was, and is, argued that policies calling for uniform punishments are as obviously ineffective as would be a policy calling for uniform treatment of all medical patients, no matter what their ailments. This led some persons to advocate that the type of punishment be adapted to the individual offender; even today "individualization" is sometimes used to refer to a system for imposing punishments. However, as the treatment reaction has increased in popularity, "individualization" has come to designate a treatment process . . . [involving] expert diagnosis . . . and expert therapy.

Justice, Criminology, and Radicalism

Justice, Aristotle once remarked, is a special virtue in that its possessor benefits his fellow members of society rather than himself. While the concept of justice is complicated and subject to many interpretations, both in theory and practice, it very simply may be defined as giving each person what is that person's due. According to Rawls (1971), justice can be viewed *as* fairness, although the two terms cannot be treated synonymously. Justice is not equality, for the latter term means nothing more than treating each person the same as every other. Justice can never be administered equally to all persons, especially since we have come to realize and accept that people are different and individually unique.

If Aristotle is correct, however, then what we have developed as a way of life in Western society is based on the notion that *sharing* constitutes the fundamental element of our associations, especially from a political point of view. Through sharing and citizenship (Wolin, 1975:31), we give each person a claim to rights, immunities, and advantages. Participation means the sharing in common deliberation over matters of general concern. Nozick in his book, *Anarchy, State, and Utopia* (Wolin, 1975:31) states the following:

> Individuals have rights and there are things no persons or group may do to them (without violating their rights). . . . The fundamental question of political philosophy . . . is whether there should be any state at all . . . the fact of our separate existences (means that) there is no moral outweighing of one of our lives by others so as to lead to a greater overall social good. There is no justified sacrifice of some of us for others.

Radical criminologists today maintain that traditional definitions of crime exclude behavior which is not defined legally as "crime," such as imperialism, exploitation, racism, and sexism. Further, they argue that there is much behavior which is not typically prosecuted, such as tax evasion, price fixing, consumer fraud, and government corruption (Platt, 1974:1). They also suggest that some of the most serious crimes against the people have been neglected, as the American Friends Service Committee (1971:10–11) points out:

> Actions that clearly ought to be labeled "criminal" because they bring the greatest harm to the greatest number, are in fact, accomplished officially by agencies of government. The overwhelming number of murders in this century has been committed by governments in wartime. Hundreds of unlawful killings by police go unprosecuted each year. The largest forceful acquisitions of property in the United States has been the theft of lands guaranteed by treaty to Indian tribes, thefts sponsored by the government. The largest number of dislocations, tantamount to kidnapping—the evacuation and internment of Japanese-Americans during World War II—was carried out by the government with the approval of the courts. Civil rights demonstrators, struggling to exercise their constitutional rights, have been repeatedly beaten and harassed by police and sheriffs. And in the Vietnam war America has violated its Constitution and international law.

Herman and Julia Schwendinger (1970) propose that a radical perspective defines crime as a violation of politically defined human rights, including the rights to food, shelter, human dignity, and a right to self-determination. However, it may be argued that if criminologists confine their research inquiries *only* to the state and the legal machinery which deals with criminals, we will become as lopsided in our investigations of the causes of crime and criminality, and their control, as the radical criminologists claim others have always been. That is, since the development of Positive criminology, where we have looked to control crime and criminality by investigating the offender, our concerns have been geared so much to an analysis of *criminal behavior*, that we have overlooked the possible institutional and organizational precipitant of that behavior. Our overemphasis on seeking that elusive *cause* of crime and delinquency, as Schrag (1971:1) has indicated, and the best way to "cure" it, has detained us from realizing that the criminal justice system in America may itself be a ". . . significant factor in crime causation."

Sykes (1974:212) chooses to refer to this new movement in criminology as "critical" rather than radical. He ponders: "Is critical criminology valid? The question is really an unanswerable one—because what we are confronted with is not so much a body of precise, systematic theoretical propositions as a viewpoint, a perspective, or an orientation . . ." However, he goes on to state (1974:213):

> . . . I think it can be argued that "critical criminology" holds out the promise of having a profound. impact on our thinking about crime and society. . . . It makes us examine how the legal apparatus designed for the control of crime takes on a life of its own. . . . It directs needed attention to the relationship between the political order and nonconformity, . . . the relationship between the individual and the state. And it impels us, once again, to analyze equality before the law as a basic element of a democratic society.

In their book *The New Criminology*, Taylor, Walton, and Young (1973:282), espouse a radical theme and state:

> It has often been argued . . . that for Durkheim *crime* was a normal social fact . . . For us, as for Marx and for other new criminologists, *deviance* is normal—in the sense that men are now consciously involved (in the prisons that are contemporary society and in the real prisons) in asserting their human diversity. . . . The task is to create a society in which the facts of human diversity, whether personal, organic, or social, are not subject to the power to criminalize.

They go on to suggest that (1973:278):

> A criminology which is to be adequate to an understanding of these developments, and which will be able to bring politics back into the discussion of what were previously technical issues, will need to deal with the society as a totality. This 'new' criminology will in fact be an *old* criminology, in that it will face the same problems that were faced by the classical social theories.

Pressures for Change

Change is an inevitable, if not irresistible, consequence of human interaction. As societies grow and prosper, there is a desire to replace old customs with new traditions. But the road to change is frequently a difficult one, full of rocks and pitfalls, never straight, and only occasionally marked. Who shall guide the traveler is not an easy decision, for we can never be certain always where it is we want or need to go. In the administration of criminal justice, the fact that we have no consensual goals—even though we think we want to control crime—makes change a difficult process to engineer. The general citizenry has been unwilling to involve itself in matters pertaining to criminal justice and justice officials have been reluctant to involve citizens. The consequence has been that the various pushes and pulls, within and without the system, have been insufficient to bring about meaningful and effective change.

One push or pull, the move toward reintegration of offenders into society, is a sound one, but it tends to neglect two significant problems. One is that there are too many laws on the books, many of which are unenforceable, and others which simply are not enforced, which increases the numbers of offenders in our society. Decriminalization is discussed frequently, but it has not taken hold as a viable means for reducing crime. Admittedly, such crimes as sexual behavior among consenting adults, public intoxication, and abortion are being removed from the criminal codes, but there are many other areas of human activity that also need to be considered, such as drug addiction and gambling.

The second problem is that where there have been efforts to involve communities in policy development in this reintegration effort, or in what has been loosely described as "community control," criminal justice officials, along with their political superiors, have done what they could to diminish impact and influence. Burgess *et al.*, (1937:8–28) discuss attempts at community involvement in "The Chicago Area Project." Waskow (1969:4–7), among others, reports on efforts to control the police. Mobilization for Youth was a grand dream of some to deal with delinquency, while the Office of Economic Opportunity was created to eradicate poverty. All of these programs and efforts attempted to involve the community in dealing with its own problems, but all were demeaned when citizens appeared to have developed too much power and voice in their own destinies.

The National Advisory Commission on Criminal Justice Standards and Goals, in its summary publication, *A National Strategy to Reduce Crime* (1973:38) states:

> Citizens should actively participate in activities to control crime in their community, and criminal justice agencies should actively encourage citizen participation.

Of course, what must be safeguarded is that citizens do not form vigilante groups, lynch mobs, or other associations for greater coercion or repression than now exists. But if, by working together, criminal justice agencies, victims, communities, and offenders can bring about better definitions of what crime is, and fair and just procedures for bringing about control over those crimes which are consensually agreed to be reprehensible, then the democratic society for which we have longed can possibly become a reality insofar as criminal justice is concerned.

In *Radical Nonintervention: Rethinking the Delinquency Problem*, Professor Edwin Schur argues that any attempts to bring about change in the nature or extent of crime in our society should focus not so much on the offender (in the positivistic tradition), but upon the structure of the criminal justice system and how it might contribute to the creation and maintenance of crime. He (1973:237) also notes:

> All available evidence indicates that crime in America will not effectively be reduced until we make basic changes in the structure and quality of American life. Respect for law and order will not be restored until respect for the nature of our society is restored. Our confrontation with crime cannot be successful if we persist in viewing it as a battle with some alien force. Since America's crime problems are largely of our own creation, we have it well within our power to modify them and to bring them within reasonable control.

References

American Friends Service Committee
    1971   Struggle for Justice. New York: Hill and Wang.
Best, Harry
    1930   Crime and the Criminal Law in the United States. New York: Mcmillan Co.
Burgess, Ernest W., J.D. Lohman, and C.R. Shaw
    1937   "The Chicago Area Project." In Marjorie Bell, ed. Coping with Crime. New York: The National Probation Association: 8–28.
Durkheim, Emile
    1950   Rules of Sociological Method. 8th ed. Trans. by S.H. Solvay and J.H. Mueller. Ed. by G.E.G. Catlin. Glencoe, Illinois: Free Press.
Henslin, James M.
    1972   "Toward Refocusing Criminology." Paper presented at the 1972 Inter-American Congress of Criminology. Caracas, Venezuela. (Mimeo.)
Joint Commission on Correctional Manpower and Training
    1968   The Public Looks at Crime and Corrections. Washington, D.C.: JCCMT.

Kerper, Hazel B.
1972   Introduction to the Criminal Justice System. St. Paul, Minnesota:
West Publishing Co.
Korn, Richard R.
1966   "A Framework for Problem-Solving in Criminology." Berkeley,
California: School of Criminology, University of California.
(Mimeo.)
Korn, Richard R. and Lloyd W. McCorkle
1965   Criminology and Penology. New York: Holt, Rinehart and Win-
ston.
National Advisory Commission on Criminal Justice Standards and Goals
1973   A National Strategy to Reduce Crime. Washington, D.C.: U.S.
Government Printing Office.
Newman, Donald J.
1975   Introduction to Criminal Justice. Philadelphia: J.B. Lippincott Co.
Platt, Tony
1974   "Prospects for a Radical Criminology in the United States."
Crime and Social Justice 1 (Spring, Summer):2-10.
Rawls, John
1971   A Theory of Justice. Cambridge, Massachusetts: Harvard Univer-
sity Press.
Schrag, Clarence
1971   Crime and Justice: American Style. Rockville, Maryland: National
Institute of Mental Health, Center for Studies of Crime and De-
linquency.
Schur, Edwin
1973   Radical Nonintervention: Rethinking the Delinquency Problem.
Englewood Cliffs, New Jersey: Prentice-Hall.
Schwendinger, Herman and Julia
1970   "Defenders of Order or Guardians of Human Rights?" Issues in
Criminology 5 (Summer) 2:123-157.
Sutherland, Edwin H. and Donald R. Cressey
1974   Criminology. 9th ed. Philadelphia: J.B. Lippincott Co.
Sykes, Gresham M.
1974   "The Rise of Critical Criminology." Journal of Criminal Law and
Criminology 65 (June) 2:206-213.
Taylor, Ian, Paul Walton, and Jock Young
1973   The New Criminology—For a Social Theory of Deviance. New
York: Harper and Row, Publishers.
Viano, Emilio and Alvin W. Cohn
1975   Social Problems and Criminal Justice. Chicago: Nelson-Hall.
Waskow, Arthur I.
1969   "Community Control of the Police." Trans-Action (December):
4-7.
Wolin, Sheldon S.
1975   Book Review, Anarchy, State, and Utopia, by Robert Nozick.
New York Times Book Review, May 11, 1975:31.

CHAPTER 2

CRIME, CRIMINALS, ANd CRIMINAL LAW

The Criminal Code

Every society has its own system of rules, regulations, and traditions by which the conduct of its members is governed. In some societies, these may be loose, flexible, and informal. In others, the form of social control is formalized into strict codes of behavior. In our society, for example, public opinion, custom, and morality do influence our behavior, but more formalized codes of conduct and behavioral expectations are spelled out in laws. In a very simple delineation, those laws pertaining to adult criminal behavior are contained in the criminal code. Laws which relate to civil conduct, generally, are called torts. Laws for juveniles are found in a juvenile code.

The criminal code of any community is basically concerned with acts—or omissions—which are viewed as offenses against the community rather than offenses against the persons or groups harmed. This is a change from earlier concepts where all offenses were against the person or group, which resulted in blood feuds, clan fights, or individual acts of vengeance. From a very simple point of view, this is the basic distinction today between violations of the criminal and civil codes. In criminal cases, the state always initiates prosecution as the plaintiff or injured party. Furthermore, when punishment is pronounced, it is always exacted by and on behalf of the state. In civil cases, the person or group who alleges harm initiates and carries through the action in court. If there is a judgment against the defendant, it is always rendered on behalf of the injured party. Distinctions between civil and criminal breaches of the law are not always clear-cut, especially since some civil offenses carry criminal penalties—such as violations of some federal regulatory agencies' laws and provisions.

While most of us, if not all, have at one time or another violated the criminal code, many of us have never been apprehended or convicted for such violations. And since we were never adjudicated in a court of law, it is doubtful that we were ever stigmatized as criminals. Furthermore, what constitutes a crime in one jurisdiction may not be a crime in another. "Blue Laws" against Sunday sales is an example. Further, what may be a crime at one time may not be a crime at a later date. Prohibition serves as an example.

What we are confronted with is not only the interrelationship between the definitions of crime and criminals, but the definitions of each of these terms. On the surface it would appear that any act which is in violation of the criminal code is a crime and that anyone who commits such an act is a criminal. These definitions, however, are too simple and ignore some fundamental issues which criminologists and legal scholars have pondered for many years.

Definitions

In a classic work called *A Treatise on the Law of Crimes*, by Clark and Marshall, as revised by Wingersky (1958:79), a crime is defined as:

> ... any act or omission prohibited by public law for the protection of the public, and made punishable by the state in a judicial proceeding in its own name. It is a public wrong, as distinguished from a mere private wrong or civil injury to an individual.

Citing the eminent legal authority Blackstone, Wingersky (1958:89) goes on to state that a crime is in reality nothing more than a public wrong, which is defined as "a breach and violation of the public rights and duties due to the whole community, considered as a community, in its social aggregate capacity."

Tappan (1960:3) comments on the difficulty of defining crime and asserts that this has been due to the fact that definitions are formulated "by authorities of significantly different training and orientation." After considerable discussion concerning the issues, he goes on to give a "legal" definition of crime (1960:10):

> Crime is an intentional act or omission in violation of criminal law (statutory and case law), committed without defense or justification, and sanctioned by the state as a felony or misdemeanor.

Elliott (1952:13–14) states that crime is a legal problem and defines it as:

> ... any act, or failure to act, which is forbidden or prescribed by law, the failure to abide by such law being punishable by fine, imprisonment, banishment, death, or other punitive treatment, as the particular state may prescribe.

Sutherland and Cressey (1974:4) are not as precise in their definition, for they link the concepts of crime, criminal behavior, and criminal law together. They state:

> Criminal behavior is behavior in violation of the criminal law ... it is not a crime unless it is prohibited by the criminal law ... (which) is defined conventionally as a body of specific rules regarding human conduct which have been promulgated by political authority, which apply uniformly to all members of the classes to which the rules refer, and which are enforced by punishment administered by the state. The characteristics which distinguish this body of rules ... from other rules are ... *politicality, specificity, uniformity*, and *penal sanction.*

Korn and McCorkle (1965:45) believe that it is not possible to define crime unless the concept of criminal is clarified, which in their opinion is a *status* assigned to an actor:

> A person is assigned the status of a criminal when he is adjudged to be punishable by the authorities in continuous political control over the territory in which he is.

Accordingly, their definition omits references to such issues as law, the criminal code, or the breaking of the law. Korn and McCorkle assert that this is so because frequently people are often adjudicated and punished in the absence of laws or under laws that were not "legal" or appropriate, because the innocent are sometimes punished, and the guilty are not always detected: "This latter category of actual but undetected violators may be called offenders-in-fact and ought not to be confused with the class of *criminals-by-adjudication*." They go on to explain that the phrase "authorities in continuous political control" is used in order to exclude those punishments where a group seizes power illegally, such as vigilantes.

With the above in mind, Korn and McCorkle (1965:46) define crime as flowing from the definition of criminal:

> A crime is an act or omission ascribed to a person when he is punished by the authorities in continuous political control over the territory in which he is.

Once again, there is an absence of any reference to laws or codes, and they suggest that an act is not a crime until an offender is caught, tried, and punished. They make the following four points in defending their position:

> 1. Some people are exempt from conviction and punishment even though conviction and punishment follows such acts if committed by others. Examples in this case are children under the statutory age and those who are judged legally insane.
> 2. Some people convicted of crimes are released without punishment due to procedural issues—thereby removing the status of criminal from the actor.
> 3. There are many unrepealed laws which go unenforced.
> 4. It is not possible to always predict the conditions or circumstances under which an apparent violation of the law will lead to conviction and punishment.

It would appear on the surface that more is being made about the problem of defining crime and criminal than is necessary. Some would say that a crime has been committed, even though we may not be certain who the criminal is. In most cases this is true, but not always. For example, if one finds a body and there appears to be evidence of murder, one would assume that a crime had been committed. But, suppose the assailant is found and he insists that it was justifiable homicide—that is, he claims that he killed the victim out of self-defense. In this situation, of course, a court will have to determine if it indeed was murder or if it was self-defense. In the first instance, the assailant is likely to be found guilty, adjudicated, and punished by appropriate authorities. But, if the court finds that it was justifiable or defensible, the assailant would be freed, for then no crime had been committed.

Although some social scientists have tended to view crime as a problem of anti-social behavior or even behavior which appears to be in opposition to the prevailing social order, it does not seem possible or practical to define crime without some kind of reference to the legal order of the society in which the definition is made. In effect, while many things may be described as crimes and many people labeled as criminals, an act cannot possibly be a crime nor a person a criminal unless the behavior of an actor is viewed legally and appropriately as a violation of a specific law contained in a specific criminal code. This means that while all crimes probably can be viewed as anti-social behavior, all anti-social behavior is not designated as crime by society.

As a consequence of the above, it appears most reasonable to define *a crime as an intentional act or omission in violation of a specific criminal law made punishable by the state in the name of the public and which is sanctioned in a judicial proceeding.* This definition does not deal with all of the qualifications raised by Korn and McCorkle, but it does respond to the criteria of politicality, specificity, and penal sanction raised by Sutherland and Cressey. The latter authors' concern for *uniformity* must be assumed in this definition; that is, all classes of people are subject to the same laws and sanctions equally, even though the realities of criminal justice administration are frequently otherwise.

This definition also takes into consideration a fundamental point raised by Tappan; namely, there must be a concurrence of "act" and "intent" before a crime has been committed or a "criminal" found guilty of such an act. Tappan (1960:10–11) discusses this issue and states:

> It is a basic principle of the Anglo-American system as well as most other systems of justice that neither an act alone nor an intent alone is sufficient to constitute a crime; the two must concur to establish criminal responsi-

> bility, for it would be futile and dangerous for the state to attempt to
> punish individuals merely for a subjective state of mind, so difficult to
> determine with certainty, or for conduct engaged in by mistake.

For someone to be criminally liable, that person must engage in some
kind of behavior or otherwise show some kind of outward manifestation. There must be some kind of action or inaction which is specifically proscribed before it can be viewed as a crime. Criminal
behavior, however, also includes failure to act where there is a positive
duty, such as the failure to report a crime or submit evidence to proper
authorities.

Act and Intent

Criminal intent, or *mens rea* (guilty or evil mind), is a difficult
concept, both in terms of its meaning and its application. Wingersky
(1958:239) cites an explanation written by Judge Learned Hand in
1941:

> Ordinarily one is not guilty of a crime unless he is aware of the existence
> of all those facts which make his conduct criminal. That awareness is all
> that is meant by the *mens rea*, the "criminal intent," necessary to guilt, as
> distinct from the additional specific intent required in certain instances . . .
> and even this general intent is not always necessary.

A criminal intent may be inferred as a result of the facts of the
case or as a matter of law, especially in instances of negligence. As a
result of negligent driving, for example, a person can be convicted of
manslaughter if someone is accidentally killed. In this instance, there
is legal concurrence of act and intent, for the driver of a vehicle is
responsible for maintaining that vehicle and for driving according to
the standards of the law. To be criminally liable when there is an
omission to act, a person must be under a legal duty to act and the
omission must be willful or due to "culpable negligence." This applies, for example, to parents legally responsible for dependent
children or to railroad switchmen who are entrusted with the responsibility of switching railroad tracks.

A person cannot be found guilty as a result of an act or of an
intent alone; both must be present before guilt can be established;
furthermore, there must be concurrence of act and intent. It would

be exceedingly dangerous to live in a society where one could be punished for his thoughts. One is not culpable merely for wishing someone else dead; but one can be found guilty if and when this intent is translated into some demonstrable action that eventually takes place. In court, it must be proved that the harm which befell a victim was actually caused by the wrongful act and that the actual harm was intended.

Common law doctrine holds that if I chase someone with a knife intending to kill that person and my intended victim falls and sustains a mortal injury to his head, I would not be technically culpable for I did not intend death to occur in that manner. Many legislatures, however, as Korn and McCorkle (1965:105) point out, have not taken kindly to this common law principle and have attempted to modify it by statute. They add, "In most jurisdictions today, a death or injury unintentionally inflicted in the course of another felony is made punishable as if it were deliberate. Thus, a robber who accidentally kills a bystander with a wild shot is held guilty of murder even though he clearly lacked any intention to shoot that person." This kind of statutory culpability is frequently referred to as "felony murder."

Criminal Responsibility

The notion of *mens rea* is an essential ingredient to the plea of insanity in criminal court trials. It also serves as the basis by which the feebleminded, insane, and very young children are "excused" from culpability. In the latter instance, the law assumes that a very young child is simply incapable of forming criminal intent. As a consequence, every juvenile code spells out the minimum age of responsibility. In most jurisdictions, this age is somewhere between 6 and 8, but for all practical purposes, one who is younger than 10 rarely is dealt with officially as a delinquent.

The greatest controversy over the plea of insanity is that of determining actual criminal responsibility. If an offender is alleged to have been legally insane at the time that a harmful act took place, that person is relieved of culpability of having committed the criminal act. The problem which arises is how the court determines whether indeed the accused was incapable of criminal intent at the time the act took place. The problem is made more difficult because neither judges nor psychiatrists can reach consensus on the definition of "legal insanity" nor agree on the best "test" for such a determination.

The basic Anglo-American rule testing criminal responsibility is the M'Naghten rule or the knowledge of right and wrong test. In 1843 Daniel M'Naghten, thinking that he had assassinated the Prime Minister of England, actually shot and killed the Prime Minister's secretary, Edward Drummond. When M'Naghten was acquitted on the grounds of insanity, there was such a public uproar that Parliament initiated an investigation by asking the 15 Chief Justices of England to define the legal rules on criminal responsibility. Their conclusion, known as the M'Naghten Rules, has tended to survive both in England and the United States, even though court decisions have altered the rules in some jurisdictions. The basic rule reads as follows:

> To establish defence on the ground of insanity, it must be clearly proved that, at the time of committing the act, the party accused was labouring under such a defect of reason, from disease of the mind, as not to know the nature and quality of the act he was doing: or, if he did know it, that he did not know he was doing what was wrong. The mode of putting the latter part of the question to the jury on these occasions has generally been, whether the accused *at the time of doing the act knew the difference between right and wrong*. (Emphasis added.)

This became the "right and wrong" test and popularly has been translated to mean that an accused is mentally competent if he is able to cooperate intellectually in the preparation of his own defense. Some years later, the "Irresistible Impulse" clause was added to the basic rules, but it does not materially change them from being a "cognitive" test for criminal responsibility—a test of the defendant's capability to *know* and *understand* the difference between right and wrong.

The M'Naghten Rules became popularly adopted in most jurisdictions in the United States soon after their acceptance in England, but scholars have been unable to determine the reason for their popularity or why they have tenaciously remained as the primary test. In fact, as long ago as 1925, the noted criminologist Sheldon Glueck (p. 157) wrote:

... there is nothing inherently sacred in the origin of these tests (M'Naghten), nothing absolutely authoritative, nothing very consistent in them, and no very good reasons why they should not be changed.

Dr. Bernard Diamond, a noted authority on the concept of criminal responsibility, states (1964:46–54) that one of the reasons many psychiatrists reject the M'Naghten Rules is because they require a moral judgment on the part of the physician, ". . . a judgment outside his professional training, experience and competence."

In 1869, New Hampshire rejected the M'Naghten formula. There, the court ruled that there could be no fixed rule testing the criminal responsibility of a mentally ill defendant. Instead, the court held that it was up to the jury to decide whether the defendant was suffering from a mental defect or disease and whether the criminal act was the *result* of the defect or disease. No other state was willing to adopt such a procedure that was behaviorally oriented rather than cognitive until 1954, when the U.S. District Court of Appeals for the District of Columbia handed down the famous Durham decision. Diamond states (1964:50):

> In this landmark of medical jurisprudence, Judge David L. Bazelon accepted the principle of the New Hampshire rule of 1869 and held that the M'Naghten formula must be replaced by a rule which is "simply that an accused is not criminally responsible if his unlawful act was the product of mental disease or defect."

Most states did not adopt the "product" test because of the uncertainty of the definitions of "mental disease or defect," and "product."

The American Law Institute, in cooperation with the American Bar Association and other legal organizations, developed a Model Penal Code in which the following rule of criminal responsibility is contained (1955):

> (1) A person is not responsible for his criminal conduct if at the time of such conduct as a result of mental disease or defect he lacks substantial capacity to appreciate the criminality of his conduct or to conform his conduct to the requirements of the law. (2) The terms "mental disease or defect" do not include an abnormality manifested only by repeated criminal or otherwise antisocial conduct.

Psychiatrists have tended to object to section two of the ALI formula on the basis that it is not proper to legislate definitions as to what is or is not "mental disease or defect." They argue that such definitions are medical not legislative issues. In 1961, the Third Circuit U.S. Court of Appeals, through Judge John Biggs, Jr., issued the Currens decision. Judge Biggs attempted to deal with the concerns of the psychiatrists and issued the following rule:

> The jury must be satisfied that at the time of committing the prohibited act the defendant, as a result of mental disease or defect, lacked substantial capacity to conform his conduct to the requirements of the law which he is alleged to have violated.

Diamond believes that the Currens rule is among the most advanced concepts yet proposed and that its legal reasoning is perfect (1964:52):

> If a defendant for any mental abnormality whatsoever is incapable of behaving in a law-abiding manner, then he does not possess the *mens rea* (the guilty mind) requisite for the imposition of criminal sanctions. He should be treated as sick and not punished as bad by society.

Diamond goes on to suggest, however, that the Currens rule may work well in the federal system where there are relatively few criminal cases, but that the use of the formula in the states would empty approximately 50 percent of all prisons, for the prisoners would be found not guilty by reason of insanity.

As a consequence, he has suggested that a viable test would be that of "diminished responsibility," where an offender would be charged only with that offense for which he was intellectually and behaviorally capable of committing. If the mental state of the offender, for example, was such that he could not premeditate a murder but nonetheless murdered someone, he might be charged with manslaughter instead. He believes (1961), nonetheless, that a psychiatrist has an important function to perform in the criminal trial itself, which disagrees with another noted forensic psychiatrist, Dr. Philip Roche (1958). Roche argues that a psychiatrist should not take any part in a judicial proceeding to determine guilt and responsibility. Instead, he suggests that psychiatrists should work with other behavioral scientists only *after* the defendant has been found guilty and then as a member of a board of experts to determine what should be done with the guilty person.

This, of course, is similar to the concept of the indeterminate sentence, which holds that professionals or clinicians, not the court, should decide how long an offender should be institutionalized or remain under official supervision. Many authorities hold that this concept, as it has been implemented over the years, has not worked and in fact tends to violate the constitutional right of due process. It has not worked many claim, simply because we do not know the best methods for diagnosing and treating persons who engage in criminal behavior, and because most offenders would rather do "straight time" according to fixed sentences (terms) than wait for release according to the "best judgment" of officials in correctional agencies.

As is obvious from the above discussion, legal and forensic scholars are unable to reach any consensus on the best approach to dealing with the mentally incompetent offender. The various rules which have recently been promulgated have had some impact on judicial proceedings, but, for the most part, the M'Naghten Rules remain the most popular. To some, it would seem to be making more out of the issue than is necessary, for, in the last analysis, the primary issue is that of determining what should happen to a mentally ill offender, not how to judge an offender's competency. Whether the answer is imprisonment or hospitalization is a debatable issue and unfortunately it appears that the solution is not readily forthcoming.

Classification of Crimes and Criminals

Mala In Se and Mala Prohibita

Over the years, societies have struggled with methods of classifying crimes and criminals. By and large, modern civilizations have dealt with this issue primarily in terms of seriousness. At the root of this probably is the distinction made between offenses *mala in se* and *mala prohibita*. The former refer to those acts which are wrong in and of themselves because they violate natural law. Laws classified as *mala prohibita* are those dealing with created offenses—behaviors which are legislatively prohibited by statute. All serious common law offenses are classed as *mala in se*, to which, according to Wingersky

(1958:102), are added all breaches of the public peace or order, injuries to person or property, outrages upon public decency or good morals, and willful and corrupt breaches of official duty. Further, "Acts *mala prohibita* include any act forbidden by statute, but not otherwise punishable by the state as a wrong."

It is not always clear as to the distinction between the two concepts. Blackstone (Wingersky, 1958:79–80), for example, defines *mala prohibita* as offenses against the municipal law and not against the law of nature, and he goes on to state:

> It is clear, that the right of punishing crimes against the law of nature, as murder and the like, is in a state of mere nature vested in every individual. For it must be vested in somebody; otherwise the laws of nature would be vain and fruitless, if none were empowered to put them in execution: and if that power is vested in any *one*, it must also be vested in *all* mankind; since all are by nature equal.

Wingersky (1958:81) discusses the difficulty in separating the two kinds of offenses with this succinct observation:

> As the community becomes structured, growing in population, communication, and complexity, both internally and externally, more rules for controlling behavior are framed and adopted by the community, and successive human legislators. *Both sets of rules merge and are used for regulating conduct*. The core of the problem lies in discovering the source of these rules, and the method and reasoning for promulgating them. Thus, murder was punished before a formal human legislative body enacted what is currently called a statute.

Misdemeanors and Felonies

Closely related to the above classification is that of dividing offenses into *misdemeanor* and *felony* categories, which simply distinguishes between crimes according to their seriousness. A misdemeanor is generally a minor offense and one that is punishable by no more than a $1,000 fine and/or one year of imprisonment, generally in a local institution. A felony is the more serious of the two and may result in incarceration for a term of one year or more, including a life sentence in a state or federal prison. According to the *Uniform Crime Reports* of the Federal Bureau of Investigation, the most serious felonies are those which are "indexed," and include the seven of murder, forcible rape, robbery, aggravated assault, burglary, larceny-theft, and motor vehicle theft. These Crime Index Offenses were selected to measure crime in the United States ". . . because of the inherent seriousness of the criminal act and/or because the volume of such offenses caused a serious problem for law enforcement" (FBI, 1973: vi).

Almost all the traditional felonies, as well as some crimes classified as misdemeanors, generally have sprung from the *mala in se* classification because they have been viewed as being against the law of nature and inherently evil. The *mala prohibita* offenses, which are wrong merely because the state has condemned the behavior, may lack as much moral reprehensibility and are consequently seen as less serious offenses. These, for the most part, are misdemeanors. Tappan (1960:19) discusses the difficulty of always being able to distinguish between the two categories:

> Many people criticize the classification of crimes into the felony and misdemeanor categories on the ground that there is no meaningful dividing line between the two and that, very commonly, conduct that in one state would be a felony is a misdemeanor elsewhere and vice versa. Absurdities appear frequently where a crime is divided into grades, part of which are felonies, part misdemeanors. The felonious criminal is often allowed to plead to a misdemeanor in such a case.

An example of an offense that is viewed in some jurisdictions as a felony and in others as a misdemeanor is that of possession of marijuana. An example of an offense that is typically graded into both categories is that of theft, with the dividing line based on the value of the stolen property. In this latter example, one aspect that leads to confusion is the proper method for determining the value of the item: wholesale or retail price, purchase or fair market value price?

Except for extreme cases, legislatures can only classify crimes in an arbitrary way. That is, while murder is seen as morally reprehensible and littering as not much more than a nuisance, the preponderance of criminal behavior is not always so easily classified into felonies and misdemeanors. Furthermore, changing values of society frequently place lawmakers in the position of being in what is commonly called a "legislative lag." Legislators are frequently unwilling to take a stand publicly and are often busy legislating in other areas. Consequently, criminal codes are not easily changed nor changed as quickly as vested interest groups would like them to be. In recent years, this has led the courts to intervene in this process, much to the consternation of some groups. Examples in which courts, through case or procedural law,* have rendered decisions which amount to new law, involve such issues as abortion, drug abuse, and various civil rights problems such as school desegregation.

Sutherland and Cressey (1974:17) suggest that the simple classification of crimes into misdemeanors and felonies has led to an objection that the classification is also used to categorize criminals:

> It is assumed that misdemeanants are less dangerous and more susceptible to rehabilitative measures than felons. But it is quite fallacious to judge either dangerousness or the probability of reformation from one act, for an individual may commit a misdemeanor one week, a felony the second week, and a misdemeanor the third. The acts do not represent changes in his character or changes in his dangerousness ... (Furthermore) thousands of persons charged with committing felonies successfully arrange to have the charge reduced to a misdemeanor, and the distinction between the two classes of offense is lost. Consequently there seems to be good reason to abandon this classification.

Behavior Classification

Aside from the legalistic approach of describing and defining crimes as discussed above, some people have attempted to develop classifications based upon the personalities and/or behavior of the "criminal." This *personalistic* approach appears to have as many faults and problems as the *legalistic* approach and, according to some, focuses too much on the individual, at the expense of the law and societal demands. It received its greatest impetus when Lombroso developed his scheme of the "born criminal"—one who behaved as he did because he had no free will and was unable to alter his hereditary destiny. In the years since Lombroso and even today, many psychologists and sociologists have attempted to develop classifications or typologies of behavior. One of the vestiges of this attempt has been our ongoing concern with the violent offender, especially when he engages in person offenses.

*Case or procedural laws are, in actuality, the decisions rendered by courts regarding specific case situations. They are tantamount to law and must be adhered to as any other laws. Substantive laws on the other hand, are enacted by legislative bodies, such as legislatures and city councils, and constitute the body of statutes normally contained in a criminal code.

The legalistic and personalistic approaches are not too dissimilar in terms of their underlying philosophy. The former suggests that the definition of a crime implies a definition of the person who commits it. Those who argue the personalistic approach invert that reasoning by suggesting that a certain type of person commits a certain type of crime (Korn and McCorkle, 1965:145). These authors suggest that two other models have been developed: classification by life organization or by criminal career, but the two are not always distinguishable. In essence, both are concerned with the commitment offenders have to engaging in criminal behavior, how professional they are in their criminal life styles, and the degree of socialization of each offender in terms of living "crime free" lives.

Clinard and Quinney (1967) also focus on behavior systems in an effort to classify criminal behavior patterns. They analyze types of crimes as a basis for their typology construction. They state (1967:14) that "Criminal behavior systems are constructed types that serve as a means by which concrete occurrences can be compared and understood within a system of characteristics that underlie the types." In effect, they not only attempt to classify criminal behavior, they provide a model by which the behavior can be understood in relation to causation.

Clinard and Quinney (1967:14–18) have developed eight types of criminal behaviors based on four distinct characteristics: (1) the criminal career of the offender, (2) the extent to which the behavior has group support, (3) correspondence between criminal behavior and legitimate behavior patterns, and (4) societal reaction. The meaning of each of these categories of characteristics follows:

1. *Criminal Career of Offender*: the extent to which criminal behavior is a part of the offender's career, including concept of self as a criminal and extent to which criminal behavior has become part of the offender's life style.

2. *Group Support of Criminal Behavior*: the extent to which the criminal behavior of the offender is supported and encouraged by other members of the group to which the offender belongs, including group values and beliefs as well as various social roles.

3. *Correspondence between Criminal Behavior and Legitimate Behavior Patterns*: the extent to which the type of criminal behavior is consistent with legitimate patterns of behavior in the society, including the degree to which the actual criminal behavior is in conflict with the social values of the majority in society.

FIGURE 2.1 Typology of Criminal Behavior Systems

Classification Characteristics	1 Violent Personal Crime	2 Occasional Property Crime	3 Occupational Crime	4 Political Crime	5 Public Order Crime	6 Conventional Crime	7 Organized Crime	8 Professional Crime
Criminal Career of the Offender	*Low* Crime not part of offender's career; usually does not conceive of self as criminal	*Low* Little or no criminal self-concept; does not identify with crime	*Low* No criminal self-concept; occasionally violates the law; part of one's legitimate work; accepts conventional values of society	*Low* Usually no criminal self-concept; violates the law out of conscience; attempts to change society or correct perceived injustices; desire for a better society	*Medium* Confused self-concept; vacillation in identification with crime	*Medium* Income supplemented through crimes of gain; often a youthful activity; vacillation in self-concept; partial commitment to a criminal subculture	*High* Crime pursued as a livelihood; criminal self-concept; progression in crime; isolation from larger society	*High* Crime pursued as a livelihood; criminal self-concept; status in the world of crime; commitment to world of professional criminals
Group Support of Criminal Behavior	*Low* Little or no group support; offenses committed for personal reasons; some support in subcultural norms	*Low* Little group support; individual offenses	*Medium* Some groups may tolerate offenses; offender integrated in groups	*High* Group support; association with persons of same values; behavior reinforced by group	*Medium* Partial support for behavior from some groups; considerable association with other offenders	*High* Behavior supported by group norms; status achieved in groups; Principal association with other offenders	*High* Business associations in crime; behavior prescribed by the groups; integration of the person into the group	*High* Associations primarily with other offenders; status gained in criminal offenses; behavior prescribed by group norms
Correspondence between Criminal Behavior and Legitimate Behavior Patterns	*Low* Violation of values on life and personal safety	*Low* Violation of value on private property	*High* Behavior corresponds to pursuit of business activity; "sharp" practices respected; "buyer beware" philosophy; hands off policy	*Medium* Some toleration of protest and dissent, short of revolution; dissent periodically regarded as a threat (in times of national unrest)	*Medium* Some forms required by legitimate society; some are economic activities	*Medium* Consistent with goals on economic success; inconsistent with sanctity of private property; behavior not consistent with expectations of adolescence and young adulthood	*Medium* Illegal services received by legitimate society; economic risk values; large-scale control also employed in legitimate society	*Medium* Engaged in an occupation; skill respected; survival because of cooperation from legitimate society; law-abiding persons often accomplices

	High	Medium	Low	High	Medium	High	Medium	Medium
Societal Reaction	Capital punishment; long imprisonment	Arrest; jail; short imprisonment, probation	Indifference; monetary penalties, revocation of license to practice, seizure of product or injunction	Strong disapproval; regarded as threat to society; prison	Arrest; jail; prison; probation	Arrest; jail; probation; institutionalization; parole; rehabilitation	Considerable public toleration; arrest and sentence when detected; often not visible to society; immunity through politicians and law officers	Rarely strong societal reaction, most cases "fixed"
Legal Categories of Crime	Murder, assault, forcible rape, child molesting	Some auto theft, shoplifting, check forgery, vandalism	Embezzlement, fraudulent sales, false advertising, fee splitting, violation of labor practice laws, antitrust violations, black market activity, prescription violation	Treason, sedition, espionage, sabotage, radicalism, military draft violations, war collaboration, various protests defined as criminal	Drunkenness, vagrancy, disorderly conduct, prostitution, homosexuality, gambling, traffic violation, drug addiction	Robbery, larceny, burglary, gang theft	Racketeering, organized prostitution and commercialized vice, control of drug traffic, organized gambling	Confidence games, shoplifting, pickpocketing, forgery, counterfeiting

*Source: Marshal B. Clinard & Richard Quinney. Criminal Behavior Systems: A Typology. New York: Holt, Rinehart and Winston. 1967: 16–17.

4. *Societal Reaction*: the extent to which society reacts to the criminal behavior, including informal reactions such as disapproval, as well as formal reactions such as by segments of the criminal justice system.

The eight types of criminal behavior include:

1. Violent Personal Crime
2. Occasional Property Crime
3. Occupational Crime
4. Political Crime
5. Public Order Crime
6. Conventional Crime
7. Organized Crime
8. Professional Crime

These eight categories together with the four basic characteristics are contained in the paradigm (Figure 2.1) as constructed by Clinard and Quinney. The paradigm also includes the various legal categories of crimes which fall under the eight classifications.

Who Is the Criminal?

Considerable attention has been given in this chapter to the definitions of crime and criminals, as well as ways by which one can categorize laws and the behaviors of offenders. While the Clinard and Quinney model appears to have great relevance for future study and application, we agree with Gibbons (1968:43), who states:

> ... the criminologist should be free to contrive his own classifications of offenders or of crimes which cut across existing legal labels, combine several specific legally defined offenses into a single category, sort some offenders charged with a related but different offense, or define careers in criminality by assembling particular offenses into *patterns* of conduct.

When we attempt to bring some order out of the chaos of knowledge, experiences, beliefs, and expectations surrounding the criminal and the crimes he commits, we are struck not only with the overwhelming nature of the subject matter itself, but with the myriad of approaches by scholars of differing orientations. Notwithstanding the increasing amount of information we are obtaining about unreported and self-disclosed crime, the criminologist, for the most part, must confine his studies to those who have been apprehended and convicted. Further, it appears inescapable that regardless of orientation, what the criminal law is at any given time dictates in large measure what criminality is at that same time.

In a classic article entitled "Who Is the Criminal?" Tappan (1947:96–102) addresses this issue:

> Only those are criminals who have been selected by a clear substantive and a careful adjective law, such as obtains in our courts. The unconvicted offenders of whom the criminologist may wish to take cognizance are an important but unselected group; it has no specific membership presently ascertainable. Sociologists may strive, as does the legal profession, to perfect measures for more complete and accurate ascertainment of offenders, but it is futile simply to rail against a machinery of justice which is, and to a large extent must inevitably remain, something less than entirely accurate or efficient.

This is not to suggest that criminologists, lawyers, researchers, and practitioners should not work together in order to achieve greater effectiveness in the network of criminal justice services. Nor is it to suggest that methods should not be attempted to obtain reliable information about offenders who are not apprehended. Instead, it is to suggest that there is a great deal of work yet to be done to understand crime and criminality, especially as forms of deviance which society prohibits.

How we develop and enforce laws, define certain behaviors as criminal, determine who the criminal is, and understand why certain people commit offenses in violation of public sentiment, are among the significant issues which must be addressed. We agree with Durkheim (1950:65–73) when he suggests that crime is normal and healthy for a free society and we agree that our present society must learn how to tolerate greater levels of deviance, but we cannot be certain where that threshold ought to be in a free society.

Laws change over time and place and we always have deviants who violate laws. What this society cannot afford, as the Watergate scandal proved and civil libertarians have maintained for decades, is a dual system of laws: one applicable for the rich or powerful, who tend to escape the rigors of the law, and one for the poor or disenfranchised who are suppressed by the law. Everyone should be subject to the same laws and similarly held accountable when these laws are violated.

References

American Law Institute
  1955   Model Penal Code 4.01 (1) Tent. Draft No. 4.
Clinard, Marshal B. and Richard Quinney
  1967   Criminal Behavior Systems: A typology. New York: Holt, Rine-
          hart and Winston.
Diamond, Bernard L.
  1964   "Psychiatry and the Criminal: Rules of Criminal Responsibility
          of the Mentally Ill." Forensic Medicine 36 (August) 2:46–54.

  1961   "Criminal Responsibility of the Mentally Ill." Stanford Law Re-
          view 14:59–86.
Durkheim, Emile
  1950   "The Normal and the Pathological." In Rules of Sociological
          Method. 8th ed. Trans. by S.A. Solvay and J.H. Mueller. Ed. by
          G.E.G. Catlin. Glencoe, Illinois: The Free Press.
Elliott, Mabel A.
  1952   Crime in Modern Society. New York: Harper and Brothers.
Federal Bureau of Investigation
  1973   Uniform Crime Reports: Crime in the United States. Wash-
          ington, D.C.: U.S. Government Printing Office.
Gibbons, Don G.
  1968   Society, Crime, and Criminal Careers. Englewood Cliffs, New
          Jersey: Prentice-Hall.
Glueck, Sheldon, S.
  1925   Mental Disorder and the Criminal Law. Boston: Little, Brown
          and Co.
Korn, Richard R. and Lloyd W. McCorkle
  1965   Criminology and Penology. New York: Holt, Rinehart and
          Winston.
Roche, Philip Q.
  1958   The Criminal Mind: A Study of Communication Between the
          Criminal Law and Psychiatry. New York: Farrar, Straus and
          Cudahy.
Sutherland, Edwin H. and Donald R. Cressey
  1974   Criminology. 9th ed. Philadelphia: J.B. Lippincott Co.
Tappan, Paul W.
  1960   Crime, Justice and Correction. New York: McGraw-Hill.

  1947   "Who is the Criminal?" American Sociological Review 12 (Feb-
          ruary):96–102.
Wingersky, Melvin F.
  1958   A Treatise on the Law of Crimes (Clark and Marshall). 6th rev. ed.
          Chicago: Callaghan and Co.

CHAPTER 3

CRIME dATA OVERVIEW

Concern for Crime Data

Crime in the United States has clearly become
one of the nation's most pressing concerns.
A Gallup Poll conducted in late 1974, for example, showed that people rank the crime "problem" as their number three concern, topped only
by the energy crisis and unemployment. Public
fear of crime is also apparent by such factors as
the increasing sale of personal and home security
devices and the continuing attention to the issue
by the mass media. One popular news magazine
attempted to sum up overall public attitudes on
the problem of crime by stating that "spreading
throughout this country is a feeling of frustration that borders on despair" (*U.S. News and
World Report*, 1974:30).

Crime statistics, as any statistics in general,
are not always as easy to characterize as these
apparent bleak conclusions might seem to indicate. Numerous factors are involved in criminal
justice administration and in social processes

which ultimately transform people and their actions into crime statistics. It is not a simple nor easily understood problem. Former District of Columbia Police Chief Jerry V. Wilson points out that the public does not distinguish very well between overall crime statistics or rates and the various forms of crime which make up those totals (*Washington Post*, November 15, 1974:A27). He indicates that while murder is most often emphasized by the media, most murders are the result of quarrels between spouses rather than the result of attacks by strangers. The fear of crime as a result of murder statistics, therefore, might be more appropriately directed toward friends and relatives than toward those on the streets. Most interesting, as noted by this former police administrator, is the recognition that "to obtain legislative and budgetary resources, the police must persuade both legislators and the general public that crime is bad and is likely to worsen." Creating solutions to the crime problem and reducing crime could, he emphasizes, inevitably result in reduced need for law enforcement services.

Such examples are not meant to say that crime rates and trends are more fiction than reality, but rather that such statistics are produced within a complex social fabric that is all too frequently overlooked by, or not presented to, the general public. The same problem is not uncommon within the framework of the criminal justice system itself. Conclusions as to the success of police, court, and correctional practices are frequently based on sketchy notions about their actual impact on crime and on incomplete data.

To the student of criminology, as well as to many criminal justice administrators, the issue of crime statistics is frequently dull and seemingly difficult to comprehend. The value and utility of crime data are often ignored or only casually considered in an effort to get on to the more "concrete" issues. Moreover, few personnel associated with criminal justice administration are competent to manage and interpret crime data.

Many authorities claim that this lack of attention to basic results is one of the reasons why criminal justice agencies have been hard pressed to prove their effectiveness. Planning, programming, and budgeting decisions rely heavily upon the accuracy of feedback data on what is being accomplished by an agency or department. Crime data are an essential element in that overall feedback system. In order to make the best use of this type of information, one must understand how crime data are generated, as well as the value and limitations which must be placed on them.

How are Crime Data Generated?

Traditionally, the level of crime in the United States has been gauged by way of statistics compiled yearly by the Federal Bureau of Investigation and reported in the *Uniform Crime Reports* (UCR). Over the years as well as today, these statistics have been used as a barometer for measuring the relative increase or decrease in overall as well as specific crime categories. The "Crime Index" is the measurement unit of the UCR and is the result of known serious offenses (including homicide, forcible rape, robbery, aggravated assault, burglary, larceny-theft, and auto theft) reported to the FBI by a majority of local law enforcement agencies throughout the country. In 1973, for example, over 6,600 police agencies covering 93 percent of the total national population reported crime data to the UCR. But, with all these data which are available, it is necessary to acquire an understanding of their meaning and limitations before they can be meaningfully interpreted. A number of factors may operate to confound or otherwise reduce the accuracy of crime reports.

As previously indicated, crime data in general and the UCR in particular reflect only those offenses which are *known and reported* by the police. Certainly the police are in a position to, and occasionally do, observe crimes being committed. Yet, the largest majority of crimes which become known to law enforcement agencies are due to citizen reporting. Black and Reiss (1967), in an analysis of 5,360 calls for service in three large metropolitan police forces, found that about 81 percent were citizen initiated. The volume of crimes which eventually finds its way into local and national police statistics is, under these conditions, extremely dependent upon the public's willingness and ability to report offenses. Yet, intuition dictates and professional surveys verify that a great number of criminal offenses are not reported to the police.

Reasons for Crime Nonreporting

Specific attention will be paid later to an explanation of survey data on hidden or the so-called "dark figure" of crime and delinquency. At this point, it may be helpful to note some of the reasons why crime is frequently not reported.

1. In many cases persons may simply not realize that a crime is being committed.

This is the case, for example, in crimes where the victim is too young or otherwise unable to realize the nature of the actions being perpetrated against him. Traffic violations and violations of local ordinances and statutes are frequently committed without any knowledge that an offense has occurred. The loss of property may often signal that a crime has been committed or it may only involve property that has been misplaced or simply lost. Store proprietors are continuously plagued with short inventories. In such cases they must justify whether the shortage is due to simple loss or damage, shoplifting, or employee pilferage. Such determinations are extremely difficult to make and are frequently resolved internally rather than by notifying a law enforcement agency. However the reporting of theft of any kind seems to be increasing throughout the country.

2. Some offenses may not involve any apparent victim who could report the crime.

While a corporation or company may clearly be victimized through theft, embezzlement, or other means, such crimes do not involve the type of personal victimization which generally results in alerting law enforcement agencies.

The illicit use or possession of drugs, or other prohibited substances, while clearly in violation of the law, has no clear victimization involved. One may argue in the case of these so-called "victimless crimes" that the victim and the law violator are the same person. But, unless an outside party chooses to report the offense or the offense is detected by the police, most violations of this nature go unreported.

And, too, who is the victim in cases of littering, vandalism of public property, and similar matters? While the public at large stands to lose when such acts are committed, we can assume the vast majority go unreported. Even when given the physical evidence of such destruction, law enforcement officials generally will be unable to determine whether the act involved one or more offenses or offenders.

3. When there is a victim involved, many offenses still go unreported.

TABLE 3.1. Victim Survey Results—Reasons Given by Crime Victims for Not Reporting Incident, 1965-1966 (In percent)

Reasons for not notifying police	Mentioned at all	Most important
Did not want to take time	13	6
Did not want to harm offender	12	7
Afraid of reprisal	5	2
Was private, not criminal, affair	41	26
Police couldn't do anything about matter	58	36
Police wouldn't want to be bothered	28	8
Didn't know how or if they should notify police	6	1
Too confused or upset to notify police	6	2
Not sure if real offenders would be caught	31	12
Fear of insurance cancellation	1	0
Total	–	100
N	(1,017)	(906)

Source: Ennis, Philip H. "Criminal Victimization in the United States. Field Surveys II. A Report of a National Survey." President's Commission on Law Enforcement and Administration of Justice. Washington, D.C.: U.S. Government Printing Office, 1967:44.

According to field surveys conducted in 1967 for the President's Crime Commission (Ennis, 1967:44) and depicted in Table 3.1, the most prevalent reason for not reporting crime involves the feeling that the report would serve no useful purpose.

Understandably, this feeling is most often evident in cases where the loss or damage is relatively minor and/or hard to trace. As might be expected, the more serious the offense, the more likely it will be reported, even though there is substantial variation in reporting among the most serious offenses. Aside from murder, car theft is an "index" or major crime category which is most frequently *reported to and recorded by police.* Compensation for loss through insurance claims, in this instance, is of course a significant incentive to reporting.

In addition, some individuals, whether victims or witnesses, do not wish to become involved in the law enforcement process. Among some minorities, and perhaps among the wealthy this unwillingness to become involved with police agencies is rather deeply ingrained within the social structure. In such social settings, it also may be the case that certain crimes are viewed with more tolerance than throughout the general surrounding society. Certain activities may not always be viewed as crime. Sexual behavior, drug use, and gambling may be socially approved and are not likely to be reported as crimes. Nonetheless, where there is evidence of crime, many do report it to the police, in spite of their misgivings about "getting involved."

The fear of involvement often takes other forms. Rape victims, for example, often refrain from reporting the offense due to the assumed insensitivity on the part of the law enforcement agencies for the victims of such criminal acts. The increasing use of rape "hotlines," victim advocates, and community ombudsmen for specialized handling of these victims has revealed that a great number of these crimes remains unreported.

Other "victims" may also be *willing participants* in illegal acts. Homosexuality, prostitution, and gambling are examples of proscribed acts which are relatively common, but which typically go unreported because there is no "unwilling" victim in the traditional sense of the word.

Reporting and Recording of Crime

Even when crime is *reported* to law enforcement agencies, there is no certainty that it will be *recorded* as such by police officers or the police agency.

The 1967 national survey of victimization previously noted indicated that there is a substantial discrepancy between the number of index crimes (i.e., homicide, forcible rape, robbery, aggravated assault, burglary, larceny-theft, and auto theft) that are reported to the police and the number of offenses subsequently recorded. While there are many differences between the recording rates for the various types of offenses, overall police figures show substantially fewer offenses than actually reported by the survey sample.

The reasons for not recording crime vary just as those which have been cited for not reporting crime. By and large, however, the national study reveals that in many cases police do not record because they either do not respond to calls, they do not regard the incident as a crime, or they simply ignore some calls.

As well, it must be recognized that some law enforcement departments, like other criminal justice agencies, work under substantial economic constraints. Under such circumstances, resources must be allocated in the most prudent manner possible. Total recording, as total enforcement, is neither economically nor practically possible. Under such circumstances offenses of greatest severity and those of political interest receive the bulk of enforcement attention, and lesser violations are more likely to be handled informally, or not handled at all.

Since the mid-1960s, alternatives to arrest have also become more prevalent. Citations in lieu of arrest for minor violations, direct referrals to social agencies, and the use of Youth Service Bureaus, for example, are some of the mechanisms that are being increasingly used in place of formal police processing. This diversion process is, of course, a desirable alternative to arrest for certain types of offenses, but it does not account for all the differences between *reported* and *unrecorded* crime, and is a negative factor in the development of accurate crime data.

The "Shrinkage" Effect

As we have seen so far in our discussion of the problems associated with crime data, the process of applying definitions is a crucial consideration. In order for a crime statistic to be developed, criminal activity is not the only factor which is involved. Individuals must become aware of the criminal activity either as victims or as witnesses, and most importantly, *decide to define it* as criminal behavior.

The youth who steals an apple from the corner grocer produces a potential "delinquent" statistic. Yet, for purposes of crime accounting, no crime was committed if the grocer decides that the offense was not serious enough to report to the police. Both the grocer and the youth may be well aware of the fact that a minor theft has been committed. But in order for the act to be recorded as minor theft, many other factors that transpire between the grocer and the youth have to be considered.

A great deal of research has been conducted on the social and interpersonal factors which tend to heighten or detract from one's chances of becoming a criminal or delinquent. And, once an individual has been arrested and recorded as an offender by the police, what is the nature of the decision-making process that fosters or detracts from his/her chances of going on through the criminal justice system to trial, conviction, and sentencing?

As Quinney (1970), Goldman (1963), and numerous other authorities suggest, the commission of illegal behavior, no matter how serious, is not always enough in itself to ensure that a formal police, court, or prison sanction will be imposed. Numerous other factors are involved even where the nature of the offense is the same.

In our simple example of the grocery store theft, chances are that the youth would be released by the grocer with only a reprimand and the incident forgotten. On the other hand, if the youth is belligerent, has the appearances of being a "rowdy," is a member of a social or racial minority, and/or is not familiar to the grocer, there is a likelihood that the grocer will decide to define the act more seriously by calling for the police. This is what Quinney (1970) has referred to as the "social reality of crime." That is, crime exists only to the extent that it is so defined by people who have the defining power or prerogative, from the time of the illegal behavior to the point of conviction by a court. [See also Goldman (1963) and Lohman et al., (1965) for additional discussions regarding differential treatment of offenders based on demographic factors.]

Figure 3.1 reveals that the largest numerical shrinkage occurs at the initial stages of the defining process; that is, where the decision is made concerning notification of police, whether or not the police respond, interpret the incident as a crime, and/or actually make an arrest.

The implication of this large shrinkage effect will become more clearly apparent later in this chapter as we discuss who the criminals and delinquents are, and the utility of the UCR "Crime Index." At present it may suffice to note that the shrinkage effect makes it extremely difficult to establish accurately changes in actual crime levels between years and between various parts of the country. This is due to the fact that we are using only a small proportion of actual crime data in order to make those estimates. The same can be said of attempts to generalize about the characteristics of all offenders based on the small percentage that ultimately are supervised by correctional authorities.

Many researchers relate attempts to estimate offenses and offenders to the attempt to estimate the size and construction of an iceberg. That is, only part of what exists is observable. The question in criminological terms becomes one of how accurately can we estimate the "dark figure" of crime, since not all crime is observable. In this respect, some significant contemporary research has been con-

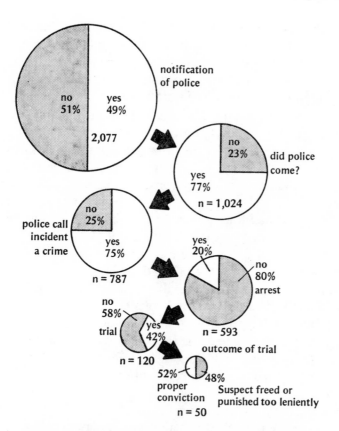

Figure 3-1. Victim Survey Results–Police Notification and
Judicial Outcome of Victimization, 1965-1966.
Source: Philip H. Ennis. "Criminal Victimization in the United
States. Field Survey II. A Report of a National Survey,"
President's Commission on Law Enforcement and Administra-
tion of Justice. Washington, D.C.: U.S. Government Printing
Office, 1967, p. 68.

ducted, which will be reported later. First, it is necessary to explore
the volume, trends, and rates of crime as they are reported to and
recorded by the nation's law enforcement agencies.

Reported Crimes

In 1930, the FBI initiated the Uniform Crime Reporting Program (UCR) in order to gain a better understanding of the crime
problem. Since that date, increasing numbers of local and state law

enforcement agencies voluntarily have been compiling and submitting crime data to the UCR program, which are published annually. Presently, a majority of all law enforcement agencies contribute to the program, although this varies from state to state depending in large measure upon the nature of the state's law enforcement network.

Reporting is performed in a standardized manner in order to promote general accuracy, uniformity, and comparability of data. In order to overcome the differences in definitions between state legal codes, standard crime act definitions were established. Also, seven criminal acts were selected for purposes of measuring serious crime in the United States. These seven crimes, as previously enumerated are known as the Crime Index or "Part I" offenses. All other offenses are placed in a second or "Part II" classification.

Tables 3.2 and 3.3 provide a general summary of UCR data for each Index Crime between 1933 and 1972.* As is clearly evident, both property and violent recorded crime rates have risen over the past 40 years per 100,000 population. Violent crime has risen to over twice its 1933 rate while property crime has risen nearly four times over the same period. Even when one takes into account the population at risk (i.e., persons vulnerable to these offenses) which has changed over the years, these trends are still readily apparent.

Property and violent crime will be discussed at some length in following chapters as will other forms of criminal activity. At present, however, the published general trends in crime help to provide a useful overall perspective.

For example, Table 3.4 provides some insight into the general volume, nature, and distribution of known serious offenses by regions in the United States. It appears from these data that the Western states are among the highest in both the occurrence of property and violent crime followed by the North Central, Northeastern, and Southern states respectively. The total index of crime for each region, however, does not reflect the difference in the composition of criminal offenses, which can be more clearly seen in the breakdown of offenses in Table 3.4. Obviously, the composition of crime is crucial to an understanding of the severity of crime in any given area. This cannot be understood by using or comparing total crime indices alone.

*The reader is cautioned against over-generalizations which might accrue from these data since the UCR reporting and recording systems have been altered over the years, as have definitions of certain crimes.

TABLE 3.2. Property Crime, 1933–1972, By Type (Reported Rates)
(Rate per 100,000 population)

Year	Total, Three Property Crimes	Burglary	Larceny, $50 and Over	Motor Vehicle Theft
1933	673.2	360.8	61.6	250.8
1934	602.1	316.6	62.0	223.5
1935	519.6	266.4	62.2	191.0
1936	484.2	260.1	60.1	164.0
1937	494.9	271.5	58.9	164.5
1938	475.9	273.7	59.6	142.6
1939	475.6	284.2	57.6	133.8
1940	471.5	285.7	54.1	131.7
1941	471.2	270.5	61.0	139.7
1942	432.9	236.3	74.3	122.3
1943	464.4	240.5	87.3	136.6
1944	489.5	244.6	96.1	148.8
1945	582.1	288.0	116.4	177.7
1946	594.8	304.2	130.2	160.5
1947	560.8	298.4	136.1	126.3
1948	552.1	296.2	141.9	114.0
1949	555.5	315.7	132.0	107.8
1950	558.9	312.1	135.8	111.0
1951	583.5	304.0	153.3	126.2
1952	653.9	325.7	192.5	135.7
1953	681.8	346.6	194.8	140.4
1954	697.3	368.9	196.9	131.5
1955	671.5	343.4	192.5	135.6
1956	724.5	359.9	210.0	154.6
1957	792.9	396.5	229.6	166.8
1958	855.5	439.0	248.9	167.6
1959	851.3	432.3	250.8	168.2
1960	966.7	502.1	282.9	181.7
1961	984.2	512.3	289.5	182.4
1962	1,033.3	528.2	309.1	196.0
1963	1,128.5	568.8	344.7	215.0
1964	1,254.7	625.9	383.4	245.4
1965	1,317.5	653.2	409.7	254.6
1966	1,452.9	710.7	457.7	284.5
1967	1,675.6	814.2	530.3	331.1
1968	1,944.8	918.1	637.3	389.4
1969	2,157.6	968.9	756.6	432.1
1970	2,386.1	1,071.2	861.2	453.7
1971	2,514.0	1,148.3	909.2	456.5
1972	2,431.8	1,126.1	882.6	423.1

Source: Federal Bureau of Investigation. Uniform Crime Reports for the United States. Annual issues and unpublished data.

TABLE 3.3. Violent Crime, 1933–1972 By Type (Reported Rates)
(Rate per 100,000 population)

Year	Total, Four Violent Crimes	Murder and Nonnegligent Manslaughter	Forcible Rape	Robbery	Aggravated Assault
1933	176.8	7.7	3.9	108.8	56.4
1934	150.9	6.1	4.2	86.0	54.6
1935	133.9	7.0	4.7	70.7	51.5
1936	122.1	7.1	5.4	57.8	51.8
1937	123.7	7.0	5.7	61.7	49.3
1938	120.0	6.6	4.8	60.7	47.9
1939	117.9	6.6	5.6	56.1	49.6
1940	114.7	6.6	5.5	53.6	49.0
1941	112.3	6.5	5.7	49.5	50.6
1942	113.3	6.5	6.1	46.6	54.1
1943	109.2	5.6	7.5	44.6	51.5
1944	114.4	5.6	8.0	43.5	57.3
1945	131.6	5.9	8.9	54.1	62.7
1946	142.2	6.9	8.7	59.4	67.2
1947	140.2	6.2	8.6	55.8	69.6
1948	136.3	6.0	7.7	51.8	70.8
1949	138.4	5.4	7.3	54.8	70.9
1950	132.7	5.3	7.3	48.5	71.6
1951	128.0	5.1	7.6	46.8	68.5
1952	139.3	5.3	7.2	51.4	75.4
1953	145.5	5.2	7.3	54.9	78.1
1954	146.8	4.9	6.9	57.5	77.5
1955	136.3	4.8	8.1	48.1	75.3
1956	136.8	4.8	8.5	46.6	76.9
1957	141.1	4.7	8.5	49.5	78.4
1958	148.0	4.7	9.4	54.9	79.0
1959	147.1	4.8	9.4	51.2	81.7
1960	159.5	5.0	9.5	59.9	85.1
1961	156.8	4.7	9.3	58.0	84.7
1962	160.9	4.6	9.4	59.4	87.6
1963	166.7	4.5	9.3	61.5	91.4
1964	188.7	4.9	11.1	67.8	104.9
1965	198.1	5.1	12.0	71.2	109.8
1966	217.7	5.6	13.1	80.3	118.8
1967	250.5	6.1	13.8	102.1	128.5
1968	295.3	6.8	15.7	130.9	141.8
1969	325.1	7.3	18.2	147.3	152.3
1970	360.7	7.8	18.5	171.4	163.0
1971	392.7	8.5	20.3	187.1	176.8
1972	397.7	8.9	22.3	179.9	186.6

Source: Federal Bureau of Investigation. Uniform Crime Reports for the United States. Annual issues and unpublished data.

TABLE 3.4. Crime Rate by Region, 1973
(Rate per 100,000 inhabitants)

Crime Index Offenses	Northeastern States	North Central States	Southern States	Western States
Total	3,738.5	3,922.2	3,636.8	5,801.5
Violent	453.8	353.3	411.8	461.4
Property	3,284.7	3,568.9	3,225.1	5,340.1
Murder	7.6	7.6	12.9	7.8
Forcible rape	19.1	22.3	23.8	35.4
Robbery	253.7	166.8	141.6	183.5
Aggravated assault	173.4	156.7	233.4	234.6
Burglary	1,123.8	1,040.4	1,117.4	1,766.1
Larceny-theft	1,579.3	2,132.0	1,792.2	3,032.3
Auto theft	581.6	396.6	315.4	541.7

Source: Federal Bureau of Investigation. Uniform Crime Reports for the United States, 1973:2.

For example, any area or region that has a preponderance of murder and a low auto theft rate may have the same crime index as a region or area that exhibits many auto thefts and few murders. Most people would say that the crime "problem" is more serious in the first case, although this is not reflected in the total crime index. Caution therefore must be employed in comparing crime rates between areas of the country until greater understanding of the nature of the problem is obtained.

Notwithstanding potential problems in making gross comparisons, several other trends can be noted. For example, in addition to being on the increase, both violent crime and property crime appear to be most prevalent in communities with the largest populations. As Figure 3.2 indicates, there is an apparent difference between the rates of violent crime in communities with populations of over 250,000 and those under 10,000. The differences are somewhat less distinct however between communities with 50,000 or fewer inhabitants. A much more distinct difference is noted in Figure 3.3 when property crimes between the various sized communities are compared. Reasons for this trend will be more fully discussed in the following chapters. In the present context it may suffice to say that criminologists have long noted the apparent relationship between highly concentrated and mobile populations and higher rates of crime on all levels.

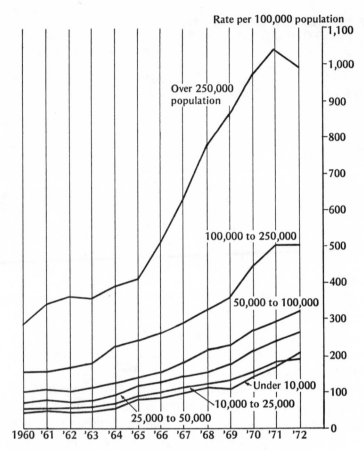

Figure 3-2. Violent Crime by Size of Community, 1960-1972.
Source: Executive Office of the President: Office of Management and
Budget. *Social Indicators, 1973.* Washington, D.C.: U.S. Government
Printing Office, 1973, p. 45.

The victims of crime are not evenly distributed across the entire
population but tend to exhibit a marked difference in terms of their
vulnerability. Regarding violent crime, Tables 3.5 and 3.6 indicate
that those most often victimized are individuals from minority races
and particularly females of Negro and other racial minorities, as well
as younger persons, and those from lower income brackets. Property
crime presents a rather similar picture of victimization. Here again
survey data (Ennis, 1967 and U.S. Dept. of Justice, 1974) indicate
that minorities, in both racial and socio-economic terms, most often
fall victim to crime.

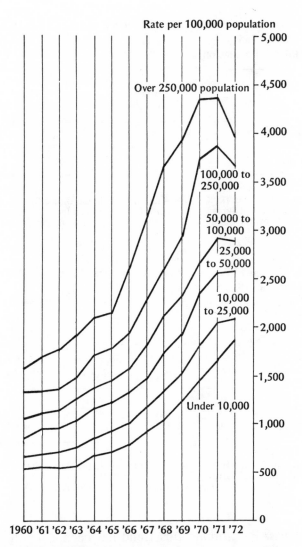

Rate per 100,000 population

Over 250,000 population

100,000 to
250,000

50,000 to
100,000

25,000
to 50,000

10,000
to 25,000

Under 10,000

1960 '61 '62 '63 '64 '65 '66 '67 '68 '69 '70 '71 '72

Figure 3-3. Property Crime, by Size of Community: 1960–
1972. (Reported Rates)
Source: Executive Office of the President: Office of Management and Budget. *Social Indicators, 1973.* Washington,
D.C.: U.S. Government Printing Office, 1973, p. 45.

The social migration trends of the past 40 years have tended to
reinforce the pattern of crime and victimization which has been
noted. Increased movement of low income, social, and ethnic minorities from rural to urban areas has helped to increase the rate of crime

TABLE 3.5. Victims of Forcible Rape, Robbery, and Aggravated Assault,
by Race and Sex, 1965
(Rate per 100,000 population)

Crime	White		Negro and Other Races	
	Male	Female	Male	Female
Forcible rape	(X)	50	(X)	193
Robbery	97	43	174	270
Aggravated assault	297	71	305	386

X Not applicable.

Source: Ennis, Philip H. "Criminal Victimization in the United States. Field Surveys
II. A Report of a National Survey." President's Commission on Law Enforcement and
Administration of Justice. Washington, D.C.: U.S. Government Printing Office, 1967:33.

TABLE 3.6. Victims of Forcible Rape, Robbery, and Aggravated Assault,
by Age and Income, 1965
(Rate per 100,000 population)

Crime	Age			Total Family Income	
	10 to 29 Years	30 to 49 Years	50 Years and Over	Under $6,000	$6,000 and Over
Forcible rape	148	75	(NA)	59	13
Robbery	113	143	102	141	43
Aggravated Assault	368	234	114	282	183

NA Not available

Source: Ennis, Philip H. "Criminal Victimization in the United States. Field Surveys
II. A Report of a National Survey." President's Commission on Law Enforcement and
Administration of Justice. Washington, D.C.: U.S. Government Printing Office, 1967:33.

in urban areas. Reinforcing this trend has been a simultaneous and
commonly noted "flight" of the more wealthy white majority from
urban and inner-city areas to the suburbs.

The fear of crime on the part of the victim as well as society in
general has apparently also risen as the data in Figure 3.4 indicate.
These data were collected from national surveys conducted at specific
points in time over an eight-year period as part of a Gallup poll. The
level of fear between the sexes and the various community sizes reflects to a degree the relative victimization rates of these groups. Yet
it is impossible to judge by these scales whether the level of fear is

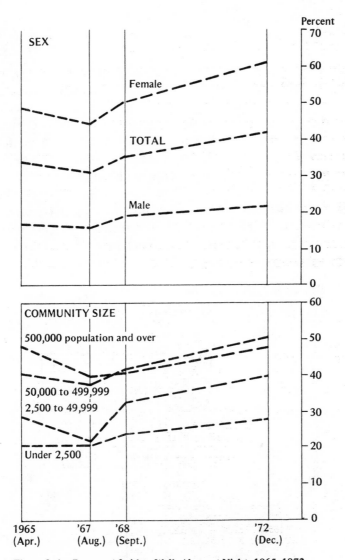

Figure 3-4. Persons Afraid to Walk Alone at Night, 1965-1972, by Sex and Community Size
Source: American Institute of Public Opinion, Princeton, New Jersey. (As reproduced in *Social Indicators, 1973,* op. cit., p. 58).

warranted in relationship to those rates of victimization. In any event, it seems apparent that fear of crime has become a prominent part of our society, especially in terms of political and urban planning activities.

Victim Demography

The criminal, unlike the victim, is more elusive and less easy to describe in terms of common social or demographic characteristics. As has been noted, what is known about the criminal as well as the delinquent is based on that minority of criminals who become known to and are arrested by the police. For example, to expand on the data previously described, Figure 3.5 shows the percentage of crime cleared by arrest in 1973 for all crimes known to the police and reported that year to the UCR. There is a striking difference between the clearance rates for violent as opposed to property crimes. The range is from the high 81 percent clearance rate for negligent manslaughter to the low 16 percent clearance rate for auto thefts. With a majority of known offenders eluding arrest, not to mention trial and

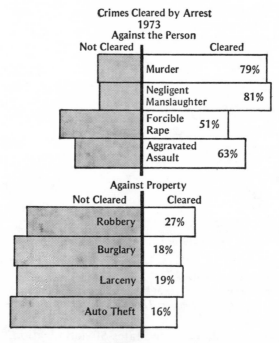

Figure 3-5. Crimes Cleared by Arrest, 1973.
Source: Federal Bureau of Investigation. *Crime in the United States—1973.* Washington, D.C.: U.S. Government Printing Office, 1973, p. 2.

conviction, conclusions on the nature of the criminal should be approached cautiously, particularly in the realm of property offenses.

Survey data (National Commission on the Causes and Prevention of Violence, 1967) indicate that violent crime offenders are most frequently young males from minority racial groups. Until 1972 very little cumulative data had been compiled on offenders in state and local institutions in terms of their socio-economic characteristics. The first nationwide attempt to assess the socio-economic characteristics of a large segment of the nation's incarcerated population was conducted in 1972 by the U.S. Bureau of Census. Rather than focusing simply on the volume and flow of inmates into and out of the nation's jails, the study surveyed the inmates and their backgrounds. While some 55 percent of those incarcerated in these jails were awaiting trial, overall survey findings (U.S. Bureau of Census, 1971:1-2) reveal that·

> Approximately 95 percent of all inmates were male, and about 6 in 10 were less than 30 years of age. During the year preceding their admission, almost half earned an income below that defined by the U.S. Government as poverty level for persons without dependents. About two out of every five were unemployed at the time of admission, and roughly 20 percent of the employed had worked on a part-time basis only. Approximately half the inmates had never been married and slightly more than half reported to have no dependents. Black inmates comprised a proportion of the jail population much higher than the proportion of blacks in the total U.S. population. By geographical region, the South had a larger share of the total inmate population than the North Central region, the Northeast, and the West, although the West had a slightly higher ratio of inmates to inhabitants ... On the average, blacks were much more likely than whites to have been charged with offenses involving violence against persons.

Delinquency Data

Official delinquency statistics have been severely criticized over the past 30 years as a result of "hidden delinquency" findings. Official statistics, as will be noted later, are even more biased in the realm of juvenile delinquency than they are in the area of adult crime. Known delinquents, as adults, are over-represented by minorities, poorly educated or slow learners, and those from generally poor socio-economic environments. Hidden delinquency studies, starting with

Porterfield (1943), have shown that these juveniles have the greatest likelihood of being referred to and convicted by the courts. Official statistics do tell us, however, that known juvenile delinquents, regardless of socio-economic class, account for a greater proportion of police arrests, particularly for violent crimes, than ever before.

For example, in 1973, persons under the age of 18 accounted for 26 percent of all police arrests in the nation, according to UCR data. For the period 1968–1973, juveniles accounted for a 10 percent increase in arrests for property crime and a 53 percent increase in violent crime. Of the persons who were arrested by the police, 42 percent were young persons and were referred to juvenile courts. Between 1968–1973, arrests for young females under 18 increased 35 percent while arrests for young males under 18 rose 10 percent. (See Chapter 13 for additional discussion on this issue.)

With the foregoing official crime rates and statistics in mind, one must ask how closely these data reflect the *actual* level and nature of crime in society. A substantial amount of information recently has been developed in attempts to make valid judgments on this "dark figure" of crime issue.

Dark Figure of Crime

Two basic approaches have been utilized in order to establish actual levels of crime. The "self-report" forms of research attempt to estimate crime and delinquency by identifying criminal acts that individuals from a general population sample admit to having performed. The "victimization" study, on the other hand, approaches the problem from the reverse point of view by asking a general population sample whether or not they have been victims of a crime. Each type of survey has its own particular usage and shortcomings.

The self-report study is most useful in calculating the *number of offenders and the volume of offenses which each individual commits*. These types of surveys, however, are difficult to complete effectively with large sample populations simply because such information is difficult to generate other than through fairly controlled circumstances. The surveys are most often used, therefore, on smaller samples of individuals in conjunction with attempts to measure the effectiveness of various types of preventive or control programs or projects.

One representative study of this type was conducted by Erickson and Empey (1963:456) on a sample of boys in Utah. The random sample included only males aged 15–17, of which four subsamples were selected: 50 high school boys who had never been to court, 30 who had been to court once, 50 repeat offenders who were on probation, and 50 incarcerated offenders. Each boy was interviewed personally and asked whether he had committed any of 22 different acts which ranged in severity from grand larceny to defying parents or smoking.

The researchers found that three offenses were most common: minor theft, traffic violations, and the purchase and drinking of alcohol. In more than 9 times out of 10, most offenses went undetected and unacted upon by authorities, particularly those of a minor nature. In the more serious offense categories, such as grand larceny, auto theft, breaking and entering, etc., about 8 out of 10 offenses went undetected and 9 out of 10 did not result in court action. These findings are interesting in themselves, but the self-report study also reveals that the sample of delinquents committed a disproportionately larger number of offenses than those in the nondelinquent sample. A substantially large number of illegal acts, therefore, appear not only to be undetected or not prosecuted, but are lodged in a small sample of repeat offenders rather than equally distributed over a given population.

Despite these findings, this and similar self-report studies have severe methodological limitations. As Hood and Sparks (1970:20) state:

> (These studies) . . . give us only a very imprecise estimate of the dark figure. Their main drawbacks, for this purpose, are that so far the investigators have never taken a representative sample of an area for which there are comparable police statistics, nor have they asked their respondents about delinquencies committed within a specific time period. If these things were done the results could be compared with the total number of offenses actually reported to or discovered by the police in the same period. All that current self-report studies can show is the proportion of respondents who admit crimes who are also known to the police.

As opposed to self-report studies, studies of victimization are more adaptable to large survey research. Information involving *an individual's victimization* is more likely to be elicited because it lacks the "punitive" implications associated with perpetrating a crime. Research of this type, of course, is subject to errors of memory or judgment on the part of the victim and must be administered carefully in order to ensure the validity and uniformity of answers. Yet, studies of victimization provide us with the greatest measure of information on the dark figure of crime. While these studies reveal the overall volume and nature of criminal acts, unlike the self-report studies, they cannot reveal the *numbers* of different offenders who are responsible for those crimes. As well, victimization studies are not as accurate in estimating crimes where there is no apparent victimization such as in cases of illegal drug usage and possession, illicit sexual behavior, or business crime. This is also the case where the victim cannot be identified or interviewed easily such as in the case of crimes against businesses or child abuse. Nevertheless, the application of victimization survey techniques is a relatively recent and generally promising technique for the estimation of the dark figure.

Comparative Crime Data

In 1966, the National Opinion Research Center (NORC) conducted a survey of victims of crime for the President's Crime Commission (Ennis, 1967). NORC contacted a representative sample of 10,000 households in the continental United States and interviewed an adult in each household to determine whether anyone had been victimized in the past 12 months. Victims who were identified in this fashion were then interviewed.

In general, the study revealed that only about one-half of the major crimes that were committed were known to the police as reported in the UCR. According to survey figures, approximately 20 percent of all U.S. households had been victims of serious crimes in 1966. Table 3.7 reveals the victim survey estimates of the incidence of Part I and Part II offenses, by offense and urbanization.

Table 3.8 provides a comparison of UCR Part I crime data with those generated through the NORC sample.

Overall, the survey data indicate a higher volume of crime, the only exceptions being homicide and vehicle theft. The discrepancies between homicide and auto theft statistics are generally accounted for by sampling errors and problems in victim reporting. While rape appears to be almost four times as frequent as police reports indicate,

TABLE 3.7. Victim Survey Estimates of the Incidence of Part I and Part II
Offenses, by Offense and Urbanization, 1965-1966 (Per 100,000 population)
NOTE: The victim survey data in this table were generated from a survey of
victims of crime conducted by the National Opinion Research Center (NORC)
for the President's Commission on Law Enforcement and Administration of
Justice. In 1966 a representative sample of 10,000 households in the continental
United States was contacted and an adult in each household was interviewed to
determine whether anyone in the household had been victimized in the past
twelve months; victims identified in this fashion were then interviewed, generating the NORC sample data in this table.

Note well that this source apparently uses Part I as synonymous with the
Federal Bureau of Investigation's index offenses; Part I offenses, as used by the
FBI, contain some of the offenses listed herein as Part II offenses.

Crime	Central Parts of Metropoli- tan Areas	Suburban Parts of Metropoli- tan Areas	Non- metropolitan Areas
Part I total	2,860	2,347	1,267
Homicide	0	0	8
Forcible rape	83	38	8
Robbery	207	95	0
Aggravated assault	293	286	110
Burglary	1,335	839	727
Larceny ($50+)	704	810	346
Vehicle theft	238	279	68
Part II total	4,792	5,214	2,949
Simple assault	569	467	203
Larceny (-$50)	1,532	1,840	1,056
Auto offense	435	591	313
Malicious mischief or arson	1,190	1,382	684
Counterfeiting or forgery	31	48	51
Fraud	217	334	220
Consumer fraud	135	133	110
Other sex	207	133	93
Family	331	191	118
Other victimization	145	95	101
Total	7,652	7,561	4,216
N	(9,661)	(10,491)	(11,837)

Source: Ennis, Philip H. "Criminal Victimization in the United States. Field Surveys
II. A Report of a National Survey." President's Commission on Law Enforcement and
Administration of Justice. Washington, D.C.: U.S. Government Printing Office, 1967:24.

TABLE 3.8. Incidence of Part I Offenses—A Comparison of Victim Survey Estimates and Uniform Crime Reports of Offenses Known, by Offense, United States, 1965–1966

	NORC Sample Estimated Rate per 100,000 Population	"Uniform Crime[a] Reports, 1965" Total per 100,000 Population	"Uniform Crime[b] Reports, 1965" (Individual or Residential Rates) per 100,000 Population
Homicide	3.0	5.1	5.1
Forcible rape	42.5	11.6	11.6
Robbery	94.0	61.4	61.4
Aggravated assault	218.3	106.6	106.6
Burglary	949.1	605.3	296.6
Larceny ($50+)	606.5	393.3	267.4
Vehicle theft	206.2	251.0	[c]226.0
Total	2,119.6	1,434.3	974.7
N	32,966	–	–

[a] "Crime in the United States, 1965 Uniform Crime Reports," Table 1, p. 51.

[b] "Crime in the United States, 1965 Uniform Crime Reports," Table 14, p. 105, shows for burglary and larcenies the number of residential and individual crimes. The overall rate per 100,000 population is therefore reduced by the proportion of these crimes that occurred to individuals. Since all robberies to individuals were included in the NORC sample regardless of whether the victim was acting as an individual or as part of an organization, the total UCR figures were used as comparison.

[c] The reduction of the UCR auto theft rate by 10 percent is based on the figures of the Automobile Manufacturers Association ("Automobile Facts and Figures," 1966), showing 10 percent of all cars owned by leasing-rental agencies and private and governmental fleets. The Chicago Police Department's auto theft personnel confirmed that about 7–10 percent of stolen cars recovered were from fleet and rental sources and other nonindividually owned sources.

Source: Ennis, Philip H. "Criminal Victimization in the United States. Field Surveys II. A Report of a National Survey." President's Commission on Law Enforcement and Administration of Justice. Washington, D.C.: U.S. Government Printing Office, 1967:8.

and robbery about 50 percent greater, on the whole the study indicates that there is at least twice as much major crime as is known to the police.

The NORC study provides somewhat different findings in terms of the regional distribution of crime than data available through the UCR. Table 3.9 indicates that while aggravated assaults are highest in the South, according to the UCR, the survey shows a higher comparative rate in the West. Conversely, the UCR indicates that robbery is high in the North Central and Western regions, but the survey

TABLE 3.9. Comparison (Standardized for Differences in Population Across Regions) of UCR and NORC Estimated Percentages of Index Offenses Occurring in Each Geographic Region, by Offense*

Crime	Northeast		North Central		South		West		Sums Across Four Regions	
	NORC	UCR	NORC	UCR	NORC	UCR	NORC	UCR	NORC	UCR
Homicide	0.00	18.37	0.00	18.91	100.00	41.62	0.00	21.08	100.00 (10)	99.98 (19)
Forcible rape	14.53	17.59	24.41	23.38	27.90	22.71	33.13	36.30	99.97 (172)	99.98 (45)
Robbery	34.32	18.47	20.98	31.63	11.85	18.26	32.83	31.63	99.98 (405)	99.99 (241)
Aggravated assault	17.61	19.04	25.02	20.38	18.58	33.41	38.77	27.14	99.98 (931)	99.97 (404)
Burglary	18.90	19.92	25.00	20.71	21.94	22.71	34.15	36.64	99.99 (3947)	99.98 (2442)
Larceny ($50+)	19.00	23.35	23.52	20.40	23.60	19.57	33.86	36.66	99.98 (2525)	99.98 (1563)
Vehicle theft	30.08	25.85	18.39	23.05	10.38	17.55	41.12	33.52	99.97 (924)	99.97 (1018)
Index total	20.55	21.77	23.68	21.50	20.61	21.57	35.16	35.16	100.00 (8914)	100.00 (5732)

Source: Ennis, Philip H. "Criminal Victimization in the United States. Field Surveys II. A Report of a National Survey." President's Commission on Law Enforcement and Administration of Justice. Washington, D.C.: 1967. Derived from Table 9.

*Numbers in parentheses are the respective "rate totals" across the four geographic regions.

matches robbery rates in the North Central and South, and provides a rate three times as large as that of the UCR in the Northeast.

The NORC sample does tend to confirm the belief that crime is more prevalent in areas of larger and more densely crowded populations. That is, there is more crime in the central city than in surrounding suburban areas.

National Crime Panel

A recent comprehensive victimization survey, conducted by the National Crime Panel, found that there were 16.7 million rapes, robberies, aggravated assaults, and serious thefts during the first half of 1973. Victims, however, said they had *reported* only 5.3 million crimes and only 3.9 million found their way into the UCR. Conducted for the Law Enforcement Assistance Administration (LEAA) of the U.S. Department of Justice in 1974 by the U.S. Bureau of Census, the survey staff conducted detailed personal interviews from a random sample of 60,000 households and 15,000 businesses in the 50 states and the District of Columbia.

Of the total number of victimizations reported, about 57 percent involved individuals, 39 percent were associated with households, and about four percent concerned businesses, as Table 3.10 indicates.

Personal larceny was most frequently reported in the survey population and made up over 40 percent of all victimizations. In all, personal larceny was about three times more prevalent than personal crimes of violence which include rape, robbery, and assault. In examining robbery and assault more closely, the Crime Panel found that injury was involved in about one-half of these cases.

The Crime Panel report also reveals that in cases of violent crime a majority of 65 percent involve persons who are strangers to each other. In cases of robbery this also obtains, for 84 percent of the sample reports a similar stranger-to-stranger relationship. Rape, robbery, and assault are crimes that have been referred to as "high fear" crimes in large measure because of this victim-offender relationship. Community attitude or fear of crime is largely based on perceptions of the extent of these types of crimes and the Crime Panel survey provides reliable data which have been developed on this victim-offender relationship.

TABLE 3.10. Percent Distribution of Victimization, by Type of Crime

Type of Crime	Percent	
All crimes	100.0	
Crimes against persons	56.6	
Rape		0.5
Robbery		3.1
Assault		11.7
Personal larceny		41.3
Crimes against households	39.2	
Burglary		16.6
Household larceny		19.4
Motor vehicle theft		3.2
Crimes against businesses	4.2	
Burglary		3.6
Robbery		0.6

Source: U.S. Department of Justice. Criminal Victimization In the United States, January–June 1973. Vol. 1, Nov. 1974.

The survey also confirms some of the data previously available on the nature of the victim. Black males, who have the highest victimization rates (85 per 1,000), are followed by white males (74 per 1,000). Contrary to the NORC data, black and white females are far less frequently victimized than males and there is no apparent difference between the female groups in terms of personal victimization.

The younger age groups between 12 and 19 have the highest rates of victimization. Robbery, assault, and larceny are very high comparatively in this age grouping and drop off sharply after age 25. Marital status of victims seems to parallel that of age with single males having the highest rate for all personal crime victimizations and those who are widowed the lowest.

Personal crimes of violence are more frequent among the lowest income categories of individuals while larceny is highest among those in the highest income categories. Blacks in lower income categories have a somewhat greater likelihood of being victims of violent crime than their white counterparts. But, by and large, one's economic status appears to be a greater determinant of potential victimization than race. For example, whether black or white, one is more likely to be a victim of violent crime when in a low economic status and more likely to be a victim of personal larceny when in a high economic status.

Household larceny is the most common of three household crimes and accounts for about 50 percent. Burglary accounts for about 42 percent of such offenses and auto theft about 8 percent of all crimes against households. Renters are also more likely to be victims of these three categories of crime than homeowners. Black households are, at the same time, more susceptible to burglary and larceny than white households.

The Future for Crime Data

The Crime Panel study in general indicates that anywhere from three to four times as much crime is being committed as is reported in the UCR. This information is not only interesting, it is highly useful in defining the actual severity of the crime problem. However, what this and the previous NORC victimization study cannot tell us is how much the dark figure of crime has increased or decreased over time. This information will only be available once similar studies are completed and comparisons are made. Comparisons of this type will be valuable in telling us what progress is being made in crime reduction. These comparisons will also help to determine whether increases in known offenses are due to increases in the actual volume of crime or merely to increases in the reporting of crime.

Many individuals also claim that increases in known crime in the recent past are due to improvements in our ability to apprehend offenders, as well as increased willingness of citizens to report offenses. If this is the case, then increases in the level of known crimes which have received so much publicity may be totally or at least in part due to the apparent success rather than failure in the use of crime countermeasures.

Moreover, some theoreticians claim that the crime "problem" is in part self-perpetuated. That is, as we are more successful in counteracting crime and apprehending criminals, known crime (i.e., UCR) increases. As a result, public anxiety over crime increases, additional countermeasures are introduced, and even more crime is revealed. In effect, this self-perpetuating phenomenon does not show that crime is increasing, but that more of the dark figure of crime is being unearthed.

To what extent these and other contentions hold true will be

TABLE 3.11. Comparison of Victim Survey Estimates and Uniform Crime Reports, Frequency Profile, Part I Crimes, 1965–1966

| Crime | NORC Sample | | Uniform Crime Reports 1965 |
	Percent of all Part I Crimes Known	Percent of all Crimes Reported to Police	
Homicide	0.1	0.2	0.5
Forcible rape	2.0	2.3	1.2
Robbery	4.4	4.6	6.3
Aggravated assault	10.3	10.4	10.9
Burglary	44.9	41.6	30.5
Larceny (+$50)	28.6	27.5	27.4
Vehicle theft	9.7	13.4	23.2
Total	100.0	100.0	100.0

Source: Ennis, Philip H. "Criminal Victimization in the United States. Field Surveys II. A Report of a National Survey." President's Commission on Law Enforcement and Administration of Justice. Washington, D.C.: U.S. Government Printing Office, 1967:13.

revealed over the coming years as more of the Crime Panel Surveys are completed and additional studies conducted. In the interim, we should not totally discount the utility of the UCR, for the UCR and other reports of known crime provide us with much useful information for planning and related purposes, notwithstanding their apparent limitations.

Hindelang (1974) is at least one researcher who claims that the UCR provides a "crude approximation" of the relative occurrence and distribution of offenses. He notes, for example, as shown in Table 3.11, that the NORC victim survey and the UCR provide a rather close relative comparison of the incidence of serious crimes.

While there are several points of substantial divergence, the two data sources provide near perfect agreement in rank ordering of the offenses.

Whether or not these comparisons will hold true over time will have to be tested as additional studies are completed. And, utilized jointly, both victim surveys and reports of known offenses can be more precise in delineating the extent and composition of crime.

References

Black, Donald J. and Albert J. Reiss, Jr.
    1967   "Patterns of Behavior in Police and Citizen Transactions." In the President's Commission on Law Enforcement and Administration of Justice. Studies in Crime and Law Enforcement in Major Metropolitan Areas. Field Surveys III. Vol. 2. Washington, D.C.: U.S. Government Printing Office.

Ennis, Philip H.
    1967   "Criminal Victimization in the United States." In the President's Commission on Law Enforcement and Administration of Justice. A Report of a National Survey. Field Surveys II. Washington, D.C.: U.S. Government Printing Office.

Erickson, Maynard L. and LaMar T. Empey
    1963   "Court Records, Undetected Delinquency, and Decision-Making." Journal of Criminal Law, Criminology and Police Science 54 (December) 4:456–469.

Executive Office of the President
    1973   Social Indicators—1973. Washington, D.C.: U.S. Government Printing Office.

Federal Bureau of Investigation
    1973   Uniform Crime Reports—1973. Washington, D.C.: U.S. Government Printing Office.

Goldman, Nathan
    1963   Differential Selection of Juvenile Offenders for Court Appearance. New York: National Council on Crime and Delinquency.

Hindelang, Michael J. et al.
    1973   Sourcebook of Criminal Justice Statistics: 1973: Washington, D.C.: U.S. Government Printing Office.

    1974   "The Uniform Crime Reports Revisited." Journal of Criminal Justice 2:1–17.

Hood, Roger and Richard Sparks
    1970   Key Issues in Criminology. New York: McGraw-Hill Book Co.

National Commission on the Causes and Prevention of Violence
    1969   Crime of Violence. Staff Report. Vol. 11. Washington, D.C.: U.S. Government Printing Office.

Lohman, Joseph D., A. Wahl, and R.M. Carter
    1965-67 The San Francisco Project. Research Reports 1–12. Berkeley, California: School of Criminology, University of California.

Porterfield, Austin L.
    1943   "Delinquency and Its Outcome in Court and College." American Journal of Sociology 49 (November):199–208.

Quinney, Richard
    1970   The Social Reality of Crime. Boston: Little, Brown and Co.

U.S. Bureau of Census
  1972   Survey of Inmates of Local Jails. Advance Report. Washington, D.C.: U.S. Government Printing Office.
U.S. Department of Justice
  1974   Criminal Victimization in the United States: January–June, 1973. Vol. I. November. Washington, D.C. Law Enforcement Assistance Administration.
U.S. News and World Report
  1974   "The Losing Battle Against Crime in America." December 16: 30–48.
The Washington Post.
  1974   "Changing the Crime Count." November 5:A27.

CHAPTER 4

pERSON ANd pROpERTy offENSES

Introduction

The foregoing chapter has provided an overview of the nature and prevalence of crime and criminals as well as a perspective for the interpretation of crime statistics and patterns. The overview will serve as a base for examining property and person offender categories of crimes in this and the following chapter.

In particular, one should note that most of what is known about criminal offenses and the offender population is based primarily on data that have been compiled through the apprehension of offenders. Additionally, as we will see, offenses vary greatly in terms of their vulnerability or risk of detection. For example, murder is frequently detected, larceny by check less often. What is known about crime and criminals, consequently, reflects the actions, decisions, and capabilities of law enforcement and other criminal justice agencies as well as the nature of criminal actions, offenders, and victims.

The difficulty in obtaining complete and accurate data of this type is a many faceted problem not only from theoretical but also from operational points of view. As we will see, for example, the cost of crime is often of a very practical significance where victim compensation is involved. The cost of crime, however, is frequently difficult or impossible to measure—particularly where loss of life or of physical capabilities is concerned. Crime panels set up to establish the costs of particular offenses to the victim have consequently attempted to utilize alternative frames of reference from which to approach the problem. Murder, as an example, may be viewed not only as a loss to the victim's family for which support was provided, but also as a loss to the community in terms of productivity over an average lifetime. Certainly from this perspective the problem of obtaining sufficient amounts and types of data upon which to make reasonable judgments becomes much more complex.

Where data are available, there is also the potential problem of its appropriate utilization. Most often, data become available in a myriad of formats and quantities particularly where the number of possible elements and areas of inquiry are as limitless as they appear to be in the field of criminology. Data which have been generated on offenses and offenders historically have been subjected to a number of classification systems, all of which are attempts to establish *patterns* or *models* by which crime data can be better described and understood.

Previously, we examined several of these classification systems or typologies which have been used as frames of reference for studying both the offense and the offender. It became apparent from that discussion that basic criminological data can be manipulated and reorganized in a number of ways which provide additional perspectives or insights into the subject matter. But all of these have their shortcomings. Consequently, criminologists continue to develop new ways by which available data can be organized in order to increase and enhance knowledge.

The typology developed by Clinard and Quinney (1967) is one useful approach that has been suggested. Under this typological "system," the authors suggest that criminal offenses and offenders can be segregated into eight different types. These range from what they refer to as "occasional property crimes," such as auto theft, to "professional crimes," such as extortion or confidence games.

Yet, even with this relatively large number of individual types or classifications, there is a substantial degree of overlap. For example, the aforementioned could easily be interchanged categorically, based upon the nature of the offender, his method of operation, or his criminal skill level. "Public order crime" such as prostitution, and organized crime such as racketeering, are also relatively interchangeable. In the case of prostitution, classification is based on whether the woman is operating as an individual or whether she is part of a criminal hierarchy or "syndicate."

Attempts to categorize, type, classify or otherwise segregate criminal offenses and/or offenders are continuously beset by problems of definition and conceptual organization. However, the discussion of crime and criminals in this and the following chapter is intended to provide some of the basic data upon which most typological systems are based. In this sense, the classification system used is primarily of a descriptive nature.

For purposes of presentation, the present chapter basically utilizes the FBI's *Uniform Crime Report* model since this tends to be a primary source of raw data regarding offenses and offenders and their classifications—especially person and property offender categories.

The following chapter, Chapter 5, brings additional perspective to the subject by examining so-called "special offenses categories." In essence, these are offenses which are dealt with in special judicial or administrative manners. Moreover, they are categories of offenders—such as the sexual psychopath, drug offenders, political, or organized criminals—which typically are recognized and which generally elicit particular types of public response.

Personal Crime

The FBI limits its coverage of personal crime or "crimes of violence" to murder, forcible rape, robbery, and aggravated assault, each of which will be discussed in turn. In overview, however, a number of factors tend to form a common linkage through all these violent crimes, much of which becomes known as a result of surveys conducted by the National Crime Panel (1974). Since the NCP data represent the first in a series of such surveys, profiles of trends and rates must remain primarily a product of information contained in the *Uniform Crime Reports* (Federal Bureau of Investigation: 1974, for the year 1973).

Overall, violent crime as calculated by the UCR in 1973 accounted for approximately one in every nine Part I offenses. While it accounts for a smaller volume of offenses as compared to property crime, it has risen at a 40 percent rate over the period 1968 to 1973, or nearly twice the rate of known property offenses.

Of the four violent crimes, assault is the most prevalent with over 416,000 reported to the police nationwide in 1973, and robbery the second most prevalent with nearly 383,000 reported during the same period. An examination of the NCP data, however (omitting murder), suggests that the difference in degree of violence between these two offenses is significant: assault has a rate of 13 per 1,000 population as compared to 4 per 1,000 for robbery. In both cases, the less serious kinds of offenses within these categories, such as attempted robbery or robbery without injury, were much more prevalent than the more serious kinds of categories, such as murder.

NCP data also provide some of the first concise information on the victim-offender relationship involving violent crime, as presented in Table 4.1. For the first six months of 1973, about two-thirds of all personal crimes of violence were committed by strangers. Referred to as "stranger-to-stranger" crime, this is the prime source of public fear involving crime and has elicited the greatest political and bureaucratic response.

Robbery, whether it did or did not involve injury, involved the greatest amount of stranger-to-stranger relationships, while assault, which is the most common of the violent crimes, is much less likely to have involved a stranger. This was most frequently the case, in fact, where the assault actually resulted in injury. In the same sense, as we will discuss later, murder was most frequently committed by friends or acquaintances.

Generally, blacks are more likely than whites and males are more likely than females to be the victims of personal crime. As well, the highest rate of personal victimization involved both male and female youth ranging in age from 12 to 19, with a successively declining rate as one's age increased. Although some differences existed with regard to specific types of offenses, the risk of having been a victim of personal crime dropped off sharply after age 25.

As one might expect, family income had a relationship to rates of victimization. In the NCP data, for example, families with annual incomes below $3,000 had the highest victimization rates while those with incomes of more than $15,000 annually had the lowest rates. Not only were blacks generally more susceptible to violent crime, but

TABLE 4.1. Victimization Rates, Crimes of Violence Against Persons, first half and second quarter of 1973, by relationship between victim and offender
(Rate per 1,000 population age 12 and over)

Type of Victimization	Stranger		Nonstranger	
	First Half of 1973 (January–June)	Second Quarter of 1973 (April–June)	First Half of 1973 (January–June)	Second Quarter of 1973 (April–June)
Crimes of violence	11.2	5.6	6.0	3.2
Rape and attempted rape	0.4	0.2	0.1	0.1
Robbery	3.0	1.3	0.6	0.3
Robbery and attempted robbery with injury	1.0	0.4	0.2	0.1
From serious assault	0.6	0.3	0.1	(B)
From minor assault	0.4	0.1	0.1	(B)
Robbery without injury	1.1	0.5	0.2	0.1
Attempted robbery without injury	0.9	0.3	0.2	0.1
Assault	7.9	4.1	5.3	2.8
Aggravated assault	3.3	1.8	1.9	1.1
With injury	0.9	0.5	0.7	0.4
Attempted assault with weapon	2.4	1.3	1.1	0.6
Simple assault	4.6	2.4	3.5	1.8
With injury	1.0	0.5	1.0	0.5
Attempted assault without weapon	3.7	1.8	2.5	1.3
Total population age 12 and over	161,502,000	161,808,000	161,502,000	161,808,000

NOTE: In general, small differences between any two figures in this table are not statistically significant because of sampling. Detail may not add to total shown because of rounding. The population figure for January through June is based on a statistical average for these six months centering on April 1. The figure, therefore, is usually smaller than that for April through June, which is based on a statistical average centering on May 15.

B Rate not shown because estimated number of victimizations in this category was too small to be statistically reliable.

Source: National Crime Panel. "Criminal Victimization in the United States, January–June, 1973." Vol. 1, November. Washington, D.C.: U.S. Government Printing Office. 1974:15.

blacks in both low and high family income categories were more likely to be victimized than were whites with the same characteristics.

The general pattern which emerges here, which will be discussed throughout this and the following chapter, is that the disadvantaged, disenfranchised, and minority group member is disproportionately both victim and offender. While the fear of violent crime is real, its impact is much more apparent among these groups of individuals than it is among the white majority in the population. In the next four sections we will examine the violent crimes more closely in an attempt to highlight these and related trends.

Murder

Murder is defined as the willful killing by one person of another. Deaths caused by negligence, suicide, or accident are not considered as murder. Neither are justifiable homicides, such as the killing of a felon by a police officer in the line of duty, or the defensive killing of an individual by a citizen in an attempt to protect life and property.

Between 1968 and 1973, increases in both the numbers and rates of murders were the lowest among the crimes of violence, according to the UCR (1974). The 18,550 murders nationwide in 1973 represented a 42 percent increase in the volume of this offense and a 35 percent rate increase per 100,000 persons over that of 1968. While violent crime is frequently depicted as murder, particularly in the mass media, murder comprised only 2 percent of all violent crimes in 1973 and only one-half of one percent of all Crime Index offenses.

While the large metropolitan areas, and particularly the core cities, have the highest murder rates, the total volume of murder, as other offense categories, is increasing more rapidly in the suburban areas. In 1973, for example, cities of 250,000 or more population experienced a murder rate of 20.7 per 100,000 persons or a 5 percent increase over the previous year; while the suburban areas reported a 5.1 rate per 100,000 persons and a 9 percent increase over the same period.

In order to provide the basis for a more complete analysis of murder, UCR police reporting agencies provide supplemental data on the circumstances of the crime. The murder victim, as in the case of other violent crimes, is disproportionately male and black, between the ages of 20 and 29. In nearly 7 of 10 cases of murder in 1973, the act was committed by a firearm, with 53 percent of all murders committed specifically by a handgun. The next most frequently used weapon involved a knife or similar weapon, which was utilized in about one in every five instances.

Murder is typically considered to be a crime of passion or an impulsive act. As such, it is generally not within the range of offenses that law enforcement considers subject to meaningful prevention and control measures, except for gun registration. In 1973, for instance, murder within the family made up one-fourth of all such offenses, about half of which involved the killing of one spouse by another. Felony murder is classified in the UCR as murder committed in the course of other felonies, such as burglary, or in such cases as gangland slayings. Felony murders comprised 29 percent of all murders in 1973, over 50 percent of which were committed in connection with robbery offenses.

As a result of the frequent overt nature of the act and the fact that in many cases there is no attempt at concealment, murder is the most frequently cleared (by arrest) of all Part I offenses. In 1973, 79 percent of all murders were cleared, although this was a drop from the 86 percent clearance rate of 1968. Over 45 percent of the individuals arrested for murder were under age 25. Youth and young adults comprise a large portion of those arrested for this and other forms of violent crime as exemplified by the 59 percent increase in the number of persons under 18 years of age who were arrested for murder between 1968 and 1973.

Rape

Rape, under definitions applied in the UCR, is the carnal knowledge of a female through the use of force or the threat of force. Assault to rape is also included, although statutory rape without force is not included in this accounting system.

Over the five-year period between 1968 and 1973, both the volume and rate of forcible rape climbed faster than any other violent crime, even though it comprised less than six percent of all crimes of violence and less than one percent of the total Crime Index offenses. While increases in the offense were noticeable in all areas of the country, the large cities accounted for disproportionately more of the total volume.

In 1973, the risk rate of females in 58 of the nation's largest cities was about 100 per 100,000 individuals, while the same rates calculated in the city and county were a contrasting 35 and 25 per 100,000 females respectively.

These rates and trends reflect only a proportion of the actual offenses, especially since rape has been traditionally recognized as an offense which is most often under-reported. This may be due in part to victim fear or embarrassment or to a host of other reasons. Both the NORC victimization survey conducted in 1967 and the NCP data of 1973 report substantial unreporting of up to one-fourth the actual levels of occurrence. However, the present trend may be toward increased reporting particularly due to the work and efforts of such agencies as hotlines and victim advocacy centers which provide needed support for the rape victim.

Individuals arrested for this offense are most frequently young and between 16 and 24 years of age. Most often rape is considered to be an offense committed by a stranger, yet this is generally not the case. Due to the large-scale unreporting of this offense and for a number of probable social and cultural reasons, this and other misconceptions have developed around this offense. Amir (1971), in a study of 646 cases of rape in Philadelphia, provides some of the first structured research that has been done in the field and refutes many traditional beliefs about rape.

For example, Amir concluded that rape was committed primarily within races, between individuals who were acquainted, most often in the woman's own home, and with apparent lack of violence. Drinking was involved in only one-third of the offenses studied; and over two-thirds of the offenses involved two or more offenders with the same victim. Of particular significance, Amir's work places the victim-offender relationship in sharper focus. He noted, for example, that victims may have been partially responsible for their victimization either consciously or by default: over 50 percent of the study victims admitted they failed to resist their attacker in any way and about 40 percent either had police records or dubious "reputations."

It is important to note that Amir's work is an example of American criminologists' recent interest in the study of victimology—or the victim-offender relationship. In the offense of rape, as well as other criminal acts, a number of social factors interact which are part of the pattern of causation, many of which are not related to the offender. In studying the nature of crime, one must examine the "dynamics" or the process of the situation rather than simply the nature of the offender or the criminal act by itself. Unfortunately, systematic research similar to that of Amir's has not been done in relationship to most other types of offenses.

Robbery

Robbery is the stealing or taking of anything of value from a person by force or violence or through the threat of violence. Assault to rob and attempted robbery are included in this category. Robbery is committed in the presence of the victim and sometimes results in injury to the victim.

Between 1968 and 1973, reported robbery rose 46 percent while the rate per 100,000 inhabitants rose 39 percent. In 1973, this accounted for nearly 383,000 offenses throughout the United States or about 44 percent of all reported crimes of violence. Geographically, the Northeastern sector accounted for the largest proportion of these offenses throughout the country.

As in other offenses, robbery has become increasingly more evident in suburban areas. While core cities experienced a two percent decrease in robbery in 1973, the suburban areas surrounding these cities reported a 10 percent increase. Nevertheless, large cities over 250,000 population still accounted for the bulk of robberies, or nearly two-thirds of the total for this offense category in 1973. This translated into a victimization rate of 571 per 100,000 in the cities as opposed to rates of 76 and 18 per 100,000 for the suburban and rural areas respectively.

In 1973, 66 percent of all reported robberies involved the use of some form of weapon, typically a handgun, and one-half of all robberies were perpetrated on the streets. Robberies committed without a weapon involved muggings or other forms of personal violence. Between 1968 and 1973, armed robbery increased 60 percent as compared to 24 percent for strong-arm robbery. By-and-large, street robbery is an offense that most typifies the types of "high fear" crime that citizens, legislators, communities, and other agencies react to most strongly. The viciousness and frequent brutality of these acts are the primary reason for that fear.

While street robbery takes a heavy toll from the victim and the community, this type of offense is not increasing as rapidly as other varieties, such as the robbery of stores and residences. Between 1968 and 1973, these increased 167 percent and 64 percent respectively.

During the same period bank robberies increased 37 percent, with an average dollar loss in 1973 of $4,653 per offense.

The cost of crime will be discussed later in this chapter, but it is to be noted at this point that robbery is the type of offense that is frequently difficult to measure in terms of loss. In 1973, the estimated loss of property in reported robbery alone reached $100 million. NORC data (Ennis, 1967), based on the relationship of reported to unreported personal loss, conservatively estimated the actual loss to individuals to be closer to $200 million. According to the same source, as presented in Table 4.2, robberies accounted for the greatest net dollar value loss (i.e., gross loss minus recovered loss) among these four Part I crimes. A more complete view of loss due to robbery will be made later as we discuss its effects on business.

In terms of the incidence of robbery per 100,000 persons, the most likely victims are black males between 30 and 40 years of age who have low incomes. In addition to these findings, NORC data also reveal that females with similar characteristics are nearly as likely as males to be subjects of robbery.

The physical aspect required of much robbery makes it an "easier" crime for younger offenders. In 1973, for example, 76 percent of persons arrested for robbery were under 25 years of age and 56 percent were under 21. In addition, 63 percent were black and only 7 percent were women. However, this must be considered a highly biased finding since only 27 percent of all known robberies in 1973 were cleared by arrests. We do not know the racial or sexual characteristics of those who were not apprehended.

Aggravated Assault

As defined by the FBI's UCR program, aggravated assault is an unlawful attack by one person upon another for the purpose of inflicting severe bodily injury usually accompanied by the use of a weapon or other means likely to produce death or serious bodily harm. Attempts to inflict death or injury are not distinguished in the accounting of this crime.

Aggravated assault rose 47 percent in volume and at a 40 percent increase in rate between 1968 and 1973. In 1973, aggravated assault comprised 48 percent of the reported crimes of violence or 416,270 individual offenses throughout the country. Regionally, the

TABLE 4.2. Victim Survey Estimates of Mean Dollar Losses From Part I and Part II Crimes, by Offense, 1965–1966

Crime	Gross Loss	Recovery	Net Loss	Number of Cases[a]
Part I:				
Robbery	$274	$4	$271	(19)
Burglary	191	20	170	(238)
Grand larceny	160	51	109	(204)
Vehicle theft	1,141	982	159	(59)
Mean for Part I crimes			149	
Part II:				
Petty larceny	21	6	15	(391)
Auto offense	376	217	159	(133)
Malicious mischief	120	18	102	(237)
Counterfeiting and forgery	[323]	[0]	[323]	(9)
Fraud	906	150	756	(69)
Consumer fraud	99	20	78	(32)
Mean for Part II crimes			128	

[a] Attempted crimes are removed from the base.

Source: Ennis, Philip H. "Criminal Victimization in the United States. Field Surveys II. A Report of a National Survey." President's Commission on Law Enforcement and Administration of Justice. Washington, D.C.: U.S. Government Printing Office, 1967:16.

South had the highest incidence with 37 percent of the total, followed by the North Central states, with 22 percent of the total.

Suburban areas accounted for the greatest increase in the volume of offenses, 14 percent, as compared to only a 1 percent increase in cities with over 250,000 population. As in the case of other violent crime, the large cities accounted for the bulk of reported offenses and the greater victimization rates. During 1973, major metropolitan areas experienced a rate of 360 victims per 100,000 population, with the rates in the suburban and rural areas at 150 and 110 respectively.

In terms of the nature and circumstances of aggravated assault, it is quite similar to that of murder. That is, a large percentage of these acts occurs within the family or between friends or neighbors. Assaults are generally not a planned or calculated act as injuries inflicted in robbery are, but are most often the result of unforeseen circumstances, flights of temper, or uncontrolled anger. As such, like murder, there is very little in the way of meaningful prevention that law enforcement agencies can realistically attempt or accomplish. Even under these circumstances, NORC data indicate that about 65 percent of these offenses are reported to authorities, but less than one-half appear in official statistics. Where family and acquaintances are involved, there is the tendency to avoid formal notification of police.

Of those assaults reported in 1973, about 26 percent involved the use of a firearm and another 50 percent were almost equally distributed between the use of a knife or an object that could be classified as a dangerous weapon. The remainder of the offenses involved personal weapons such as fists or feet. Over the five-year period from 1968 to 1973, the use of such personal weapons rose 83 percent, while the use of firearms rose 63 percent.

In 1973, 63 percent of all reported aggravated assaults were cleared by arrest, which is in keeping with high clearance rates for several other personal crimes. While the nature of offenders tends to follow that of other violent crimes, the distinctions between age, sex, race, and socio-economic levels are less clearly defined.

Property Crime

While violent crime frequently has severe personal impact on the lives of victims, certainly a much larger number of individual lives are in some way touched by property crime. Of the 8.6 million reported Part I crimes committed in the United States in 1973, 90 percent involved property offenses (UCR, 1974). Property crime, however, did not increase as rapidly as crimes against persons. Between 1968 and 1973 the volume of burglary, larceny-theft, and auto theft increased only 28 percent, with an associated rate increase of 22 percent. Of these three offenses, larceny accounted for the largest volume of crime, followed by burglary, and then auto theft. Larceny alone accounted for 50 percent of all reported Part I crime in 1973, burglary about 30 percent, and auto theft just less than 10 percent of the total.

In addition to their volume, property offenses can also be differentiated from violent crimes on the basis of their clearance rates. For example, in 1973, only 16 to 18 percent of all property crime was cleared by police arrests as compared to between 51 and 81 percent involving various violent offenses. Low clearance rates in these areas of crime may be an indication of the operational limitations of law enforcement agencies in respect to the magnitude of property offenses.

The 1973 UCR, for example, points out that on the average there is a reported larceny approximately every 7 seconds, a burglary every 12 seconds, and an auto theft every 34 seconds, every minute, every day. However, NCP data revealed that of these three approximations, only reported auto theft nears the actual numbers of offenses committed. This is probably due to insurance companies' demands. Depending upon geographic location, settings, and other factors, the level of unreported property crime can reach up to four times that which is actually reported, according to the NCP victimization data. Household larceny was, for example, the most frequently reported of the household crimes in the NCP sample, accounting for about 50 percent of the total offenses. Burglary was the next most frequent, with 42 percent of the total, and auto theft third with about 9 percent.

Demographic characteristics of victims of property crime are similar to those associated with victims of violent crime. Age, for example, is related to the incidence of property offenses with the younger heads of households experiencing the greatest volume of both burglary and larceny. Renters are more likely than homeowners to be victims of burglary, larceny, and auto theft. This is especially true for black renters. Among homeowners, blacks continue to be more victimized than whites for the same offenses. (U.S. Department of Justice, 1974)

The highest rate of burglary occurred in households with the lowest incomes and the lowest rate occurred in households with annual incomes between $10,000 and $15,000. In both larceny and auto theft, the lowest income households tended to have the lowest rates of victimization, whether headed by blacks or whites. Larceny was more prevalent than burglary among white households with annual incomes in excess of $3,000 and burglary more prevalent than larceny among black households with annual incomes less than $10,000. Black households were, in fact, burglarized at a higher rate than white households. In terms of auto theft, higher income households had a higher victimization rate, with black households having a higher rate than white families similarly situated.

Burglary was the most prevalent of the commercial crimes, having made up about 85 percent of the sample of businesses. While

TABLE 4.3. Rate of Burglaries per 100 Businesses, All Businesses and Retail Trade Only, by Community Location, 1967.

NOTE: The data on burglary rates per 100 businesses were generated in a survey of business victimization and loss from crime. This survey was undertaken by Albert J. Reiss for the Small Business Administration in 1968–1969. The sample used in the survey was drawn from 1966 tax returns filed by all businesses for 1965 (except agriculture, forestry, and fishery businesses). One of every 1,400 tax returns was designed to be selected. The sampling frame was stratified by type of business ownership and size of gross receipts. The final, usable sample—after deletions for businesses going out of business by 1968 and for nonusable interview and questionnaire returns—was 5,056 businesses.

Also to be noted are certain definitions particular to this table. "Ghetto," a type of community location, refers to an area which qualifies as an "urban slum." Retail trade businesses refer to one major industry grouping in the sample. Others were mining and contract construction; manufacturing; transportation, communication, and utilities; wholesale trade; finance, insurance, and real estate; and services.

Community Location	All Businesses	Retail Trade Only
Ghetto	69	97
Central city nonghetto	38	37
Suburban	29	28
10,000 to 50,000	22	25
2,500 to 10,000	12	12
Under 2,500 and rural	16	13
Location not reported	30	48
All businesses	27	27

Source: U.S. Department of Commerce. Small Business Administration. "Crime Against Small Business." 1969:75.

the NCP data did not deal with community characteristics and business crime, the U.S. Department of Commerce provides some insights as revealed in Tables 4.3 and 4.4. As one might expect, the pattern of commercial victimization follows the general demographic pattern of crime distribution.

The specific pattern and trends of the three Part I property crimes are discussed separately in the following sections.

Burglary

Burglary is the unlawful entry of a structure (sometimes called "breaking-and-entering") with intent to commit a crime. Force does

TABLE 4.4. Rate of Robberies per 100 Businesses, All Businesses and Retail Trade Only, by Community Location, 1967

Community Location	All Businesses	Retail Trade Only
Ghetto	23	19
Central city nonghetto	6	6
Suburban	2	3
10,000 to 50,000	4	5
2,500 to 10,000	3	8
Under 2,500 and rural	4	3
Location not reported	1	0
All businesses	5	5

Source: U.S. Department of Commerce. Small Business Administration. "Crime Against Small Business." 1969:76.

not have to be used in the commission of the act. In cases where larceny is committed in the course of burglary, it is not counted as a separate offense.

Of the two-and-one-half million burglaries committed in 1973, about 35 percent were committed in cities with over 250,000 population. From another perspective, the victimization rate in these areas was nearly twice that of the suburbs and between three and four times that of the rural areas. While the rate of burglary has tended to increase faster in the suburbs than in the city, this is not as noticeable as in the case of other property offenses previously examined.

Burglary rates have tended to be highest in the Western states and, like several other offense categories, lowest in the North Central states. However, the Southern states, which are generally associated with violent crime, have experienced one of the largest increases in burglary.

Between 1968 and 1973, residential burglary committed during the daytime rose 56 percent, which was higher than any other category, and nighttime residential burglaries had a 52 percent increase. Nonresidential burglary, however, rose only 27 percent over the same period while the same offense committed during nighttime hours remained constant. In 1973, 75 percent of these burglaries involved forced entry.

In 1973, nighttime burglary comprised over 61 percent of all burglaries, which has obvious implications for law enforcement agencies in terms of prevention and control. The nature of the crime is such that it occurs in areas both of wealth and/or opportunity, and involves both professional and amateur offenders. Low clearance rates for the offense suggest that the "professional," who possesses substantial skills, is probably the least likely to be apprehended. In any event, individuals who were apprehended were overwhelmingly young—perhaps the most inexperienced. In 1973, persons under 25 accounted for 84 percent of all arrests for burglary in the nation, and those under 18 accounted for 54 percent of the total. Whites made up about twice the number of arrests as blacks.

Table 4.3 reveals that next to robbery, burglary precipitates the greatest net loss among the property offenses. In 1973, this amounted to $856 million dollars in valuables that were reported stolen. This, of course, would be substantially higher were all unreported offenses known.

While this will be dealt with later, it should be remembered that burglary also has a substantial economic impact on business. In 1967–1968, the Small Business Administration estimated the loss to be $958 million nationwide (see Table 4.4). It would appear that the UCR unavoidably but grossly underestimated the impact of this type of burglary. For example, since 1968 the UCR has registered a 27 percent increase in reported nonresidential burglaries but established their 1973 dollar loss at only $313 million or $645 million less than SBA's 1967–1968 estimates.

Larceny

The UCR program classifies larceny-theft as the unlawful taking or stealing of property or articles without the use of force, violence, or fraud. This classification covers a wide variety of thefts to include such common varieties as thefts of bicycles and auto accessories, plus shoplifting and pocket picking, but excludes such offenses as embezzlement, confidence games, and forgery.

Larceny is by far the most pervasive of all crimes against property. In 1973, these offenses accounted for 50 percent of all reported crime in the nation, up 25 percent over the previous five years.

Of all Part I property crimes, larceny reflects the least difference in the rate of victimization between city and suburbs, but a striking contrast between city and rural areas. In 1973, the victimization rate for cities was 2,652 per 100,000 population with corresponding suburban and rural rates of 1,952 and 678 respectively. The nature and distribution of reported offenses in these three areas for the year 1973 is presented in Table 4.5.

In general, the nature of reported thefts appears relatively similar in each of these three areas, although pocket picking and purse snatching are less prevalent in the suburban areas. Theft from autos and auto parts theft consistently make up a large portion of all larceny, with the distribution of various types of theft remaining relatively constant over time.

The clearance rate for larceny has been relatively low, as in other forms of property crime. The volume of offenses in itself presents a major obstacle to adequate enforcement and control. The nature of the offense is also a major contributing factor in that offenses are generally the result of opportunities or circumstances presenting themselves and involve considerable subterfuge.

Recognizing the relative inadequacy of law enforcement agencies in this area, many citizens probably refrain from reporting these offenses to the authorities. The NORC victimization survey, for example, estimated that no more than 60 percent of all larceny over $50 was reported to the police.

Just as the volume of this crime is not accurately known, the

TABLE 4.5. Larceny Analysis, 1973
(Percent distribution)

		Area		
Classification	Total United States	Cities over 250,000	Suburban	Rural
Pocket-picking	1.0	2.1	0.4	0.3
Purse-snatching	2.2	4.0	0.9	0.4
Shoplifting	10.8	11.3	7.5	3.8
From autos (except accessories)	17.4	18.6	16.2	15.3
Auto accessories	16.0	18.8	17.1	11.2
Bicycles	16.9	11.7	17.3	5.3
From buildings	16.8	17.8	13.9	16.4
From coin-operated machines	1.3	1.0	1.4	1.3
All others	17.6	14.7	25.3	46.0
Total	100.0	100.0	100.0	100.0

Source: Federal Bureau of Investigation. Uniform Crime Reports–1973. Washington, D.C.: U.S. Government Printing Office. 1974:24.

total value of stolen property is also unknown. Nevertheless, in 1973, based on what was known, the UCR placed an approximate value of $603 million on the value of all goods stolen.

Juveniles and young adults increasingly have accounted for a large percentage of all arrests for this offense. In 1979, individuals under 21 years of age comprised two-thirds of all those arrested, and 48 percent were under 18. In terms of sex, females made up 32 percent of all arrests for larceny in 1973, which represented a higher involvement in this offense for females than in any other Part I crime.

Auto Theft

Auto theft is the unlawful stealing of or attempt to steal a motor vehicle and includes cases where vehicles are stolen and abandoned or taken for so-called joy rides. This does not include unauthorized use where one has ready access to the vehicle. Auto theft is the least prevalent of all property crime and has amounted to the smallest increases in both volume and rate. Between 1967 and 1973, reported offenses for auto theft increased 19 percent with the rate at 13 per 100,000 population.

As with other offenses, the large cities have the highest rate of victimization. In 1973, that rate was 978 offenses per 100,000 persons, while the suburban and rural areas experienced substantially lower rates of 307 and 83 per 100,000 respectively. One must realize, of course, that the volume and rate of the offense depends more upon the number of autos available within a population area than upon the population itself. In terms of "autos at risk" nationwide, for example, one in every 138 registered vehicles was stolen in 1973. This rate was highest in the Northeastern sector of the country and lowest in the South.

Auto theft is clearly a problem which is associated with high-density population areas. It is also the case that most auto theft involves young offenders. Relatively few cases are cleared and the number of arrests for auto theft reflects this fact. In 1973, for example, 56 percent of individuals arrested for this offense were under 18 years of age, and 74 percent were under 21 years of age. Females accounted for 14 percent of these arrests and whites for 66 percent of the total.

While auto theft is infrequently solved, it is nonetheless the most frequently reported of all property crimes, particularly due to insurance involvement in claims. For this reason, even though the victim's loss is substantial, a large percentage of that loss is recouped through insurance coverage. Nevertheless, the UCR indicated that the average value of autos stolen was $1,095 in 1973.

Costs of Crime

Our discussion to this point has revolved around the incidence and impact of all Part I crimes reported through the UCR. This approach has been utilized because these offenses are commonly recognized as "major" offense categories. As a result, data have been routinely compiled along these lines together with their various incidence, rates, and trends.

Yet there are offenses that can be considered as "major" crimes but which are not treated by the UCR. For example, the so-called "white collar" crimes of embezzlement and business theft as well as such organized crime enterprises as prostitution, narcotics, and gambling have an enormous impact on society.

In large measure, failure to treat these offenses within the UCR's major crime categories may be due to the fact that they are less visible to the general public as well as to the authorities. As a result, solutions are not as frequently attainable in these areas of crime. In addition, the general public often has a different emotional reaction and philosophical view of these and other similar offenses.

Organized crime, for example, provides many illicit goods and services that are desired by segments of society but which cannot always be purchased through legitimate channels. The social impact of these offenses, such as prostitution, drugs, and gambling, is also generally difficult to measure as compared to the more personalized forms of violent and property crime.

White collar crime, at the same time, is often hard to visualize as "crime" to many people. Employee theft, for instance, is sometimes rationalized on the basis that the company can absorb the loss or will not miss it, or that the employee is only compensating himself because the company is unfair in one way or another, or that insurance will cover the losses anyway.

Discussion of the general substance and nature of these and

other offenses will be saved for the next chapter. In the present context, however, it is imperative that they be incorporated in an attempt to assess the cost of crime.

As we have noted, the Part I crime classifications do not tell the whole story in terms of the cost of crime. In fact, of the seven crimes with the greatest economic impact, as developed by the President's Crime Commission (1967), only two, willful homicide and larceny over $50 (reported and unreported), were included in the Crime Index. In effect, therefore, an examination of the cost of crime only *begins* with the offenses classified by the UCR.

As we noted in the introduction to this chapter, the problems of placing a price tag on crime have both conceptual as well as practical implications. One such conceptual framework was developed and employed by the Wickersham Commission (U.S. National Commission on Law Observance and Enforcement, 1931) in one of the only comprehensive analyses of the costs of crime in the United States.

A less comprehensive yet practical overview of the nation's crime costs was presented in the President's Crime Commission Report (1967), *Crime and Its Impact: An Assessment.** While the study is based on data developed for 1965, it still remains as one of the most recent and thorough approaches to the subject and a responsible focal point for viewing the overall nature and relative impact of the cost of crime. The relative economic impact of crime and related expenditures as developed by the President's Crime Commission are presented in Figure 4.1. For the year 1965, it was calculated that with all aspects of crime considered, the cost to society was nearly $30 billion. Of that figure, Part I crime as reported by the UCR accounted for only about four percent, or about the same as unreported commercial theft alone.

Of all areas of crime, those dealing with illegal goods and services constituted the greatest percentage. Narcotics, loan sharking, prostitution, drugs, alcohol, and gambling, which comprise this category, are typically offenses which are associated with organized crime. The second most expensive of direct crime costs involves property offenses such as commercial theft and fraud. Among the indirect costs of crime, those associated with the support of law enforce-

---

*See particularly Chapter 3, "The Economic Impact of Crime," (p. 42).

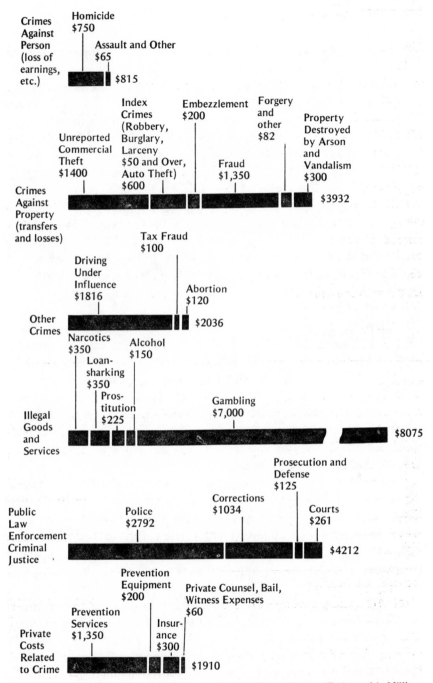

Figure 4-1. Economic Impact of Crimes and Related Expenditures. (Estimated in Millions of Dollars)

Source: President's Commission on Law Enforcement and Administration of Justice. Task Force Report: *Crime and Its Impact—An Assessment*. Washington, D.C.: U.S. Government Printing Office, 1967, p. 44.

ment services are greatest, followed by costs within the correctional system.

One of the most useful aspects of the Crime Commission's study in addition to its comprehensive perspective is the approach which it utilized in efforts to calculate the total economic implications of crime. For example, rather than viewing traffic offenses solely from the perspective of property damage, it considered such factors as the cost of medical treatment for victims, the loss in wages where injury was a factor, and the overhead expenditures that are accounted for in insurance claims. In terms of Part I Crime, willful homicide represented an economic loss to the community by the loss of a productive worker, the consequent loss of tax revenues, and a loss to the victim's family and dependents in terms of support. In the case of assault and nonfatal violent crime, one can routinely expect such associated expenses as hospitalization, loss of wages, insurance overhead, and possible court litigation.

Viewing the costs of specific crime in this more systematic manner is also applied to an analysis of all crime costs to society, whether direct or indirect. In this way, not only are there expenses incurred with each offense, but there are those which derive their basis from the very fact that crime exists. Law enforcement services which provide prevention, apprehension, and service functions, prosecutorial and defense services, judicial operations, and correctional agencies, require substantial budgets for the processing of suspects and convicted offenders.

As well, there are other costs which are related to crime. Private police service, for example, has become a major industry in the United States, particularly in recent years with the increased use of such police agencies by commercial enterprises. Private residences and businesses also expend considerable amounts for security and alarm equipment. Finally, where imprisonment is required, the offender is not only an economic liability to the taxpayer but represents a loss to the community through lost productivity, wages, and tax revenues.

Notwithstanding its attempts to conduct a comprehensive analysis, the President's Crime Commission recognized the numerous inadequacies of crime data for the development of a truly accurate picture of the economics of crime. While it determined, for example, that gambling is the most expensive crime for the public, it also recognized that gambling is rarely reported to the police and therefore its costs cannot be estimated reliably.

Because of the ambiguity and lack of sound data in this and other crime classifications, estimates of crime costs can and do vary substantially. While this is true today, it is somewhat less pronounced than in 1967 (when the Crime Commission reports were released) due to recent victimization surveys and the addition of several other data collection sources on crime and associated factors.

The National Bomb Data Center, as an example, now processes all information and reports of bombings or bomb threats. Similarly, the National Fire Protection Association processes data on incendiary fires or arson. In the latter case, the Association estimated that the loss due to these fires in 1971 was $233 million or over 10 percent of all fire damage (Moll, 1974:7). This provides a poor comparison with the Commission's estimate of $74 million, even considering the fact that the Commission's report was developed on the basis of data that were six years older. In any event, it is apparent that data continue to accumulate, particularly as public interest in crime and its effects increases. This is in part reflected by increased mass media attention to the subject. While the research methodology in these cases is not always explicit, it does provide additional perspectives on the issue.

An NBC-TV program in 1975 explored the costs of white collar crime to the public. Its report concluded that employee theft in 1974 alone cost American consumers over $6 billion. It was estimated that five cents on each dollar of sales was needed to cover the costs of theft and protection; bribes and kickbacks between retailers and salespersons cost at least another two to three cents per dollar of sales.

In a comprehensive study of crime in America, the Economic Unit of *U.S. News and World Report* (1974:32) portrayed a somewhat similar picture based on data from government and industry. As illustrated in Figure 4.2, this analysis placed the total crime bill in the United States at nearly $90 billion. This was up from its 1970 study which pegged the cost at $51 billion.

As reported by the President's Crime Commission, gambling is by far the most costly of all crime categories. In combination, organized crime and business and property losses account for two of every three dollars of expense to the public for crime. Interestingly enough, drunken driving, in terms of lost wages, medical costs, and property damage, costs more than all homicides and assaults. In all, the *U.S. News and World Report* study estimated that the total crime

COST OF CRIME—	NEARLY $90 BILLION A YEAR Estimates of economic impact of crime per year—	
TOTAL TAKE BY ORGANIZED CRIME FROM ILLEGAL GOODS AND SERVICES $37.2 BIL.	Gambling	$30.0 BIL.
	Narcotics	$5.2 BIL.
	Hijacked goods	$1.5 BIL.
	Interest from loan sharking	$0.5 BIL.
CRIMES AGAINST PROPERTY AND BUSINESS (excluding organized crime) $21.3 BIL.	Embezzlement, fraud, forgery	$7.0 BIL.
	"Kickbacks" paid by businesses	$5.0 BIL.
	Unreported business thefts	$5.0 BIL.
	Robbery, burglary, theft, shoplifting	$3.0 BIL.
	Vandalism, arson	$1.3 BIL.
OTHER CRIMES $9.5 BIL.	Homicides, assaults (loss of earnings, medical costs)	$3.0 BIL.
	Drunken driving (wage loss, medical costs of victims, property damage)	$6.5 BIL.
LAW ENFORCEMENT COSTS $14.6 BIL.	Police (federal, state, local)	$8.6 BIL.
	Penal system	$3.2 BIL.
	Court system	$2.8 BIL.
PRIVATE CRIME-FIGHTING COSTS (cost of services and equipment)		$6.0 BIL.

TOTAL CRIME EXPENSE $88.6 BIL.

Figure 4-2. Total Crime Expense.
Source: U.S. News and World Report. "Special Section: Crime, A High Price Tag That Everybody Pays." December 16, 1974, p. 32. Estimates based on data from government and industry.

bill cost each man, woman, and child in the United States $420 in 1974.

While these and other data are, of course, estimates, they at least indicate that the magnitude and relative impact of crime costs are extremely high—even higher than we had previously believed. As in all data on the volume and nature of crime, however, their exact dimensions and effects cannot be determined totally until a more precise understanding of the hidden factors of crime can be made. Unfortunately, in terms of the costs of crime, such important areas as organized crime and crimes against business are not adequately covered in current victimization or crime reporting studies. Until a more accurate means of gauging these crimes can be developed, a great deal of speculation will invariably be involved in such analyses, and we can do no more than make approximations or "reasonable" guesses about their extent, costs, and societal impact.

References

Amir, Menachem
    1971   Patterns of Forcible Rape. Chicago: University of Chicago Press.
Clinard, Marshall and Richard Quinney
    1967   Criminal Behavior Systems: A Typology. New York: Holt, Rinehart and Winston.
Ennis, Philip H.
    1967   "Criminal Victimization in the United States. Field Surveys II. A Report of a National Survey." President's Commission on Law Enforcement and Administration of Justice. Washington, D.C.: U.S. Government Printing Office.
Federal Bureau of Investigation
    1974   Uniform Crime Reports—Crime in the United States—1973. Washington, D.C.: U.S. Government Printing Office.
Moll, Kendall D.
    1974   Arson, Vandalism, and Violence: Law Enforcement Problems Affecting Fire Departments. Washington, D.C.: U.S. Government Printing Office.
NBC-TV
    1975   "White Collar Rip-Off." Telecast June 1, 1975.
National Crime Panel
    1974   Criminal Victimization in the United States, January–June, 1973. Vol. 1, November. Washington, D.C.: U.S. Government Printing Office.
President's Commission on Law Enforcement and Administration of Justice

1967   Task Force Report: Crime and Its Impact—An Assessment. Washington, D.C.: U.S. Government Printing Office.

U.S. Department of Commerce
1969   Crime Against Small Business. Washington, D.C.: U.S. Government Printing Office.

U.S. National Commission on Law Observance and Enforcement (Wickersham Commission)
1931   Report on the Cost of Crime. Washington, D.C.: U.S. Government Printing Office.

U.S. News and World Report
1974   "Special Section: Crime, A High Price Tag that Everybody Pays." December 16:32.

chapter 5

special offenses categories

Special Categories

We have previously discussed the volume and nature of crime as it is officially revealed in the seven Uniform Crime Reporting categories. It should be clear from that discussion that the volume and rate of official crime appears to be increasing, both for property and violent crimes.

We also raised the question of whether the UCR presents a *complete* picture of the scope and impact of crime in the United States. An examination of this issue from a "costs of crime" frame of reference reveals that the FBI Uniform Crime Reports, in fact, reflects only a *small percentage* of the overall amount of crime. Those which are recorded generally are those which have the most direct and noticeable impact upon the victim. Consequently, they are also the offenses which are often reported and dramatized by newspapers, television, and other mass media.

Bank robbers, for example, receive considerable attention, yet the perpetrator inside the bank, who by fraud or embezzlement takes many times that of the robber, usually receives less attention. The so-called "white collar" crimes are among a number of offense categories that have come to receive special judicial or administrative handling and typically are regarded from different perspectives by the public.

In this chapter we will examine a number of such special crime classifications, including white collar, the political, and organized criminals. Similarly, we will briefly examine several special offender categories—such as the sex offender, the "psychopathic" criminal, and the public inebriate, most of whom receive individual attention from various community-based agencies and resources.

White Collar Crime

Edwin Sutherland first called attention to the white collar criminal as one who is responsible for a large number of offenses in the business and professional environment, but who typically goes undetected (Sutherland, 1940:1–12). The label of white collar crime has come to be a very general term which has been applied to many different offenses, ranging from fraud and misrepresentation to price fixing and computer crime.

Aside from the offenses themselves, a general element which conceptually holds these crimes together is the nature of the offender himself. Characteristically, the white collar criminal possesses all of the signs of success and respectability, and is frequently a highly respected member of the community. This fact alone often makes it difficult to deal with the while collar criminal as a "criminal," even when his misdeeds have been exposed to the public. The more prominent and influential the individual is, the more likely it is that he will go unprosecuted, or if prosecuted, it will be for a reduced offense.

White collar crime is often glamorized in American folklore. Many "Hollywood" films tend to demonstrate the social acceptance of crimes committed by wit or deceit. "The Music Man," "Paper Moon," and "The Sting" portray the confidence man in various capacities, but all have an underlying sense of unconventional respectability.

From another perspective, the white collar criminal is more readily associated with "middle class" values, less as a "common criminal," and consequently less likely to be labeled the latter in official or unofficial ways. In essence, the white collar criminal exhibits the same criminal behavior as the "blue collar criminal" but he generally benefits by a better address, education, and legal counsel. However, as we noted in the previous chapter, the "price" which he exacts from the general public can be well in excess of that which can be attributed to the seven major crime category offenders. While the individual street offender may cause substantial harm to the person or property of his victim, the white collar criminal frequently sets in motion an offense that impacts an infinitely larger number of individuals.

Yet, official criminal sanctions for white collar crimes have not generally reflected this impact which these crimes have on society. While the Sherman Antitrust Act, for example, was enacted in 1890, it lay dormant for nearly 70 years until General Electric, Westinghouse, and 27 other electrical manufacturers were convicted of a major price-fixing conspiracy in 1961.* Even so, in relatively few cases have convictions of corporations or their executive officers resulted in sentences of incarceration. They sometimes receive very heavy fines, but they seldom go to prison. In large measure, this leniency is the result of overall social attitudes toward the offense, including a general ignorance of its impact and pervasiveness. Since no single agency, such as the FBI, has the responsibility to report on this and other special offense categories, the public is generally left to establish for itself the relative significance of these crimes.

As has been noted, white collar crime can take a larger number of forms depending upon availability and opportunity. Recent additions to the pool of such offenses include computer crime and Medicare fraud. In the former case, portable telephone computer access terminals are being used illicitly to "enter" and manipulate programs and data bases to the advantage of the offender. The computer in a financial institution in this way may be utilized to issue checks or change funds from one account to another. In similar manner, inventory control systems may be manipulated and merchandise transferred if one has sufficient and appropriate knowledge of techniques. Medicare fraud is an example of recent innovation in white collar crime. In such cases, patients may be systematically referred

---

*See, for example, Richard A. Smith, "The Incredible Electrical Conspiracy." In Donald Cressey and David Ward (eds.), _Delinquency, Crime, and Social Process._ New York: Harper and Row Publishers. 1969:884-912.

between a number of physicians and fees charged even though none of the specific services of these physicians may be appropriate.

Medicare fraud is but a specific example of the much broader area of fraud which involves methods of obtaining money or property by cheating or false pretenses. It is likely that many individuals could provide examples of acts in this area to which they have fallen victim. No doubt, this is one of the most prevalent of the white collar crimes. Most of these acts are not reported, primarily as a result of shame or embarrassment. NORC surveys of households in this respect indicate that only about one-sixth of the number of frauds are actually reported to authorities (Reiss, 1967:119). The study also indicates that about 40 percent of businesses accepting checks have experienced some problem in terms of "bad checks," yet only a small percentage of businesses actually report these as criminal offenses.

The President's Crime Commission Report, *Crime and Its Impact* (1967:50), itemizes several other areas in which fraud is frequently found. Mail fraud, for example, is estimated to have cost the public as much as $500 million in 1965, with no more than $3.2 million actually recovered.

Securities frauds, as reported by the Securities and Exchange Commission, are also of substantial proportion, ranging from $24 million to $58 million annually at the time of the Crime Commission Report. Similarly, the Food and Drug Administration conservatively estimated that at least $500 million is spent annually on worthless or extravagantly misrepresented drugs and therapeutic devices. Other fraudulent enterprises and their associated annual public expenses, as reported by the Crime Commission, include the home repair and improvement business, amounting from $500 million to $1 billion; automobile repair frauds, $100 million; phoney charity solicitations, $150 million; and credit card fraud, $20 million annually.

These are only a few of the types of fraudulent enterprises and schemes which annually extract additional tens of millions of dollars from the public. Additionally, if one were to consider the impact of criminal tax fraud from its general perspective, the financial implications nationwide probably would be of immense proportions.

Embezzlement is another type of offense that typically is employed by the white collar criminal. As in other areas of this kind of crime, the exact numbers and costs are nearly impossible to establish.

On the one hand, the embezzler is often very shrewd and typically aided in this capacity by virtue of the fact that he is dealing in an enterprise with which he is completely familiar. Common targets of these offenders, such as savings and loan associations and banking institutions, are also not always willing to treat these offenses criminally due to a fear that they may harm the businesses' reputations. As a result, many offenses that are detected are handled informally through such means as restitution for corporate loss, through dismissal, or forced resignation.

Employee theft is an even more widespread form of business crime, although the individual offense may not typically be as sophisticated or as economically noteworthy as that of embezzlement. Inventory and stock shortages that cannot be accounted for through such means as breakage, loss, or spoilage are commonly confronted in all areas of business and industry. The distribution of these losses between the various common sources of loss and those due to shoplifting, employee theft, or embezzlement are, of course, difficult if not impossible to determine. Large business operations are becoming more sophisticated and elaborate in inventory protection, but the true amounts and kinds of losses are still difficult to detail.

As a result of discussions with industry and security experts, the Crime Commission estimated that about 75 to 80 percent of all losses are due to some type of dishonesty (*Crime and Its Impact*, 1967:48). One of the nation's largest private security firms estimates the annual national loss due to employee theft alone to be $6 billion. (NBC-TV, 1975). The pervasiveness of the offense is reflected in NBC's additional estimate that 7 in every 10 employees have in some way dishonestly taken funds, goods, or benefits from their employers.

The extent of retail losses due to shoplifting and employee theft is certainly unclear. Shoplifting has traditionally been cited by businesses as a primary factor in inventory shrinkages, particularly in department stores where goods are readily available to the customer. The President's Crime Commission surveys of neighborhood businesses (Reiss, 1967:103) indicated 47 percent of all businesses reported some measure of shoplifting loss. The extent of shoplifting is a matter of guesswork and based on the numbers of those apprehended; it can never be more than a calculated estimate on the part of retail store operators. Nonetheless, the Task Force Report, *Crime and Its Impact* (1967:48) expressed the belief that employee theft far exceeds that which can be attributed to shoplifting, with estimates on the former running as high as 75 to 80 percent of all losses.

Losses due to theft in the nonretail business areas are subject to even greater imprecision in knowledge and information. Wholesale businesses, for example, have placed the shrinkage of their inventories as high as five percent of sales (Ross, 1961:140–143), while pilferage during shipment and handling has been reported by 104 of 153 companies surveyed by the New York State Waterfront Commission (*Crime and Its Impact*, 1967:49). The Interstate Commerce Commission reported that motor carriers in 1973 estimated the loss due to theft and related offenses at over $16.5 million, with an additional $141 million due to cargo "loss" or damage. While the specific amounts of these and other areas of employee theft are not presently known, there is evidence to indicate that the losses are phenomenally high.

White collar crime presents a substantial problem not only to business in particular, but to society in general, especially through the indirect costs that are passed on to the consumer. The most insidious forms of this offense, including political kickbacks, bribes, conflicts of interest, illegal political contributions, and similar crimes, can have even more decided and long-lasting effects upon the social health of society. The Watergate conspiracy and its related criminal involvements exemplified the degree to which white collar crime could enter the political arena. Yet, at the same time, it also tended to expand general public understanding about the degree to which such offenses permeate the nation's overall social existence.

Organized Crime

A great deal of literature and documentation has been generated in the area of organized crime, particularly on the organization that has been widely called the Mafia, La Cosa Nostra, the Syndicate, the Underworld, or, on a local level, as the "mob" or the "rackets." Since the Kefauver senatorial committee first recognized the Mafia as a nationwide crime enterprise in 1951, the FBI has been applying specific attention to unearthing the scope and participants of this organization. The late director of the FBI, J. Edgar Hoover, described organized crime and its enterprises before a House of

Representatives Appropriations Subcommittee in 1966 (President's Crime Commission, *Challenge of Crime in a Free Society*, 1967:192) and stated:

> La Cosa Nostra is a criminal fraternity whose membership is Italian either by birth or national origin, and it has been found to control major racket activities in many of our larger metropolitan areas, often working in concert with criminals representing other ethnic backgrounds. It operates on a nationwide basis, with international implications, and until recent years it carried on its activities with almost complete secrecy. It functions as a criminal cartel, adhering to its own body of "law" and "justice" and, in so doing, thwarts and usurps the authority of legally constituted judicial bodies. . .

While inroads recently have been made against organized crime, it exists today as a large and rich enterprise. In the preceding chapter, for example, the 1973 proceeds of organized crime were estimated at $37 billion, which makes it the largest industry in the country.

It is believed the organization and operation of La Cosa Nostra centers around a few dozen core units or "families" with constituent memberships that operate the various street-level enterprises, as illustrated in Figure 5.1. Families are structured in a way similar to conventional corporations, with lines of authority and communications and division of labor and responsibilities. In addition, the family is both a government and a business enterprise in that it enacts controls over the lives, activities, and allegiances of its members in order to make profits. The various families at the same time are ruled by a joint body or the "commission" which is comprised of a number of the largest and strongest of the families. The commission acts as the supreme decision-making authority between families establishing the rights and privileges of each in organizational and jurisdictional matters. The TV series "The Untouchables" and movies such as "The Godfather" depicted these operations.

Organized crime's largest sources of income are derived from gambling on horse races and other sporting events, the numbers lottery, and, some officials believe, from casinos where gambling has been legalized. In cities where organized crime is well established, few gambling operations are independent from that of the syndicates. In such cases, hierarchies of communications and interactions are so concealed that tracing the chain of command is extremely difficult, even at the lowest levels.

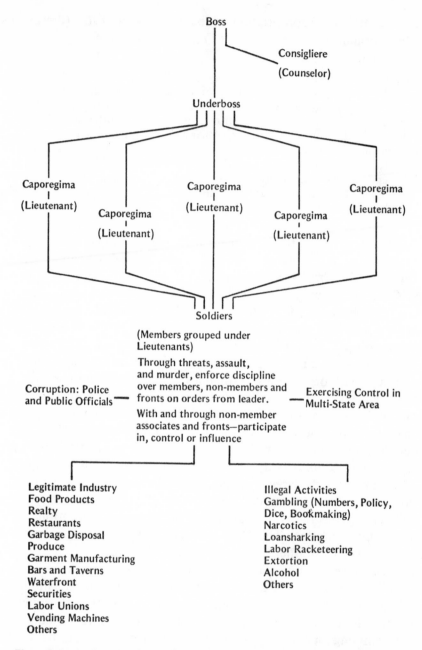

Figure 5-1. An Organized Crime Family.
Source: President's Commission on Law Enforcement and Administration of Justice. *The Challenge of Crime in a Free Society*. Washington, D.C.: U.S. Government Printing Office, 1967, p. 196.

Despite the vast amount that has been written on the subject, there is no way to determine the exact proceeds from gambling and other organized crime activities. The President's Crime Commission placed the figure at about $6 billion to $7 billion annually. The profits from the various gambling activities were calculated by the Commission (*Challenge of Crime*, 1967:189) to fall in the following general distribution pattern:

(a) Bookmakers (including horse racing, elections, fights, etc.); $10 billion turnover, $3 billion-plus profit.

(b) Numbers, lotteries, punchboards: $5 billion turnover, $1.5 billion-plus profit.

(c) Illegal dice games: $3.5 billion turnover, $1 billion-plus profit.

(d) Illegal professional card games: $1 billion turnover, $300 million-plus profit.

(e) Illegal coin machines (all types): $500 million turnover, $150 million-plus profit.

Narcotic sales also produce a large volume of proceeds for the syndicate. This business, as other enterprises, is organized around a number of distribution levels or hierarchies and with connections on an international scale involving importing, wholesale, and retail operations. The magnitude and operating expenses involved in international transactions of this type tend to eliminate (or incorporate) the small-scale dealer in favor of the syndicate. Retailing of narcotics, on the other hand, can more frequently be handled by the small-scale peddler, which reduces the high degree of risk in such distribution for the "kingpins."

Loan shark activities are a major source of revenue for organized crime and considered second only to gambling operations by the President's Crime Commission. Loan sharking involves the lending of money at usurious rates to individuals, many of whom are low- and moderate-income blue collar workers. The loan shark, who generally is employed as part of an organized crime network, may frequently operate at a specific industrial or manufacturing facility where he can make regular contacts with his "victims." In this way, the shark can also observe the habits and financial needs of his targets and encourage their involvement in other areas of organized crime activity such as gambling or narcotics. Lending of money to his victims, in this way, forms an on-going cycle and ensures the loan shark's continued business and profits.

One's ability to collect payments and installments, often at rates as high as 150 percent a week, depends a great deal on the fear that is generated during these transactions. Default or failure to pay in a prescribed manner can frequently result in the most brutal of treatment, and victims infrequently report such assaults to the police.

Other activities of organized crime also include the infiltration of legitimate business enterprises. Investments in legitimate or quasi-legitimate businesses form another means of expanding the economic hold and profitability of organized crime, serve as good "fronts" of respectability for syndicate personnel, and as a means of "laundering" illicit money. One study of the involvement of 200 individuals from crime "families" established connections with over 400 major businesses of various types (Bers, 1970).

While the diversity of their business involvements is substantial, Bers suggests there is a marked preference for such enterprises as food, apparel, trucking, warehousing, eating and drinking establishments, and the amusement and recreational industry. Additionally, investments in legitimate businesses may not be directly related to a criminal enterprise but may involve the use of such methods as intimidation and coercion (including extortion and blackmail), union and labor control, and the corruption of political officials. In a sense, these efforts can be viewed as facilitators for the expansion of illegitimate as well as legitimate profit-making enterprises. Control of political power and other sources of authority appear to be essential elements in organized crime.

While illustrations and case examples of organized crime activities abound, there is no way to measure accurately its integration into and impact upon society. According to Bers (1970:13), the register of full members of organized crime families includes at least 5,000 individuals, with another estimated 50,000 "associates" engaged in illegal pursuits. The increased use of organized crime "strike forces" in major cities has had some impact on the volume of convictions over the past 10 years, yet there is no way of knowing what proportion of organized criminals this represents.

Professional Criminal

The classification of "professional criminal" is an attempt to differentiate between the various levels of involvement, commitment, and skills of offenders in criminal activities. Walter Reckless (1967) developed a system which stratifies offenders into three criminal career patterns rather than placing all criminality into and along the same continuum of crime. A brief digression to consider this system here will help to illustrate the concept of the professional criminal, although it is not our intent to reconsider classification systems as such.

Reckless maintained that criminality can be classified in terms of the offender's relative acceptance and adherence to criminal values and ways. At one level, the *ordinary criminal* is most typically the property offender who is reflected in official statistics (UCR) due to his vulnerability to apprehension. In general, this individual is the least sophisticated or "polished" in his activities and reflects the orientations and value systems of the lower socio-economic classes. The *professional criminal*, at a second level of criminal careers, in a sense is an ordinary criminal who has become a master technician at his criminal trade. The professional, however, is more often from a higher socio-economic level, utilizes a more polished and intellectual approach to crime, and typically reaps higher returns with less risk. The third level of criminal career in Reckless's system is that of *organized crime*. As we have seen, this career pattern demands a total life commitment from its principal members, who operate in a highly structured bureaucracy.

While this classification system is useful for descriptive purposes, it suffers as do other systems from a lack of precise differentiation, particularly between ordinary and professional career patterns. Yet, it is the case that the professional criminal has a different conception of himself as compared to the amateur who lacks a similar level of both skills and contacts. Rather than dealing part-time or only occasionally in crime, the professional is a full-time practitioner and crime specialist. The professional may also be segregated according to his level of expertise, with the more experienced and skilled applying time in selective and well planned activities rather than in more recurrent and less frequently prosperous endeavors.

The most successful professional frequently operates in groups combining skill areas with other professionals to meet the demands of particular crimes. These associations are neither "gangs" in the street sense of the word nor in the organized crime sense. Rather, they are generally organized only by necessity and exist primarily on a temporary (*ad hoc*) basis depending upon their immediate needs and the skill requirements of the "job."

The professional can be involved in any number of different

types of common thievery but, by and large, he tends to be associated with the more intellectual yet stealthy types who commit such crimes as hotel theft; confidence games; passing illegal checks, money orders or other papers; extortion, blackmail, and counterfeiting. Contacts with "legitimate" society in the course of criminal activity also differentiate the professional from the ordinary criminal. The *fence*, for example, is the source for the sale of stolen property. He is generally utilized by the professional who prefers not to risk retailing his own goods even though the fence generally demands a high percentage return for his efforts. The fence is also uniquely qualified to distribute or otherwise "unload" stolen merchandise, particularly in large quantities, which places him in an essential relationship to the professional criminal.

While the fence is necessary for the distribution of goods, the *fix* is invaluable in that it ensures that the professional criminal will have the necessary leverage with law enforcement agencies to avoid arrest and prosecution. The fix may involve direct dealings between the official and the professional criminal or it may involve another individual with added contacts who acts as a go-between to make necessary bribes and agreements.

The professional criminal undoubtedly accounts for a large volume of property crime, particularly where considerable amounts of money and property are involved. Because of his skill and strategic contacts, he is least frequently the offender who becomes a part of official crime statistics. For this reason, principally, it is difficult to establish the number of criminals who may fall into this offender classification.

Career Criminal

One should not confuse the professional criminal with what has been conveniently referred to as the "career" or habitual criminal. The career criminal is principally an administrative designation rather than one which serves to segregate offenders through a typological system.

Law enforcement, particularly federal agencies, has come to use this term in order to designate the large group of offenders who are repeatedly arrested or who form the bulk of the *recidivist* population. From the perspective of Reckless's typological system (1967), these individuals are most commonly ordinary criminals who lack the cunning, skill, connections, or other means to avoid detection and prosecution. Like those who make up the bulk of prison/jail inmates (and related official statistics), they are overly represented by the poor and ethnic minorities in society.

A majority of known criminal offenses in this country is committed by recidivists, or those with a history of previous arrests and convictions. Indeed, the arrest of one individual frequently clears several other offenses, for they are often committed by the same person. The point when one can be referred to as a career criminal is, of course, relatively arbitrary, for it seems to involve not only repeat offenses, but a mental attitude on the part of the offender to pursue crime on a full-time basis. It is as though it were an occupation.

Yet, federal programs have been established for purposes of identifying and tracking the career criminal, and ensuring swift prosecution. The Justice Department's Law Enforcement Assistance Administration, for example, has recently sponsored a $3 million program to accomplish this end in several target cities. The LEAA program provides for "case review units" within a police department for the purpose of identifying individuals with several recent offenses. A "Major-Violation Bureau" operating out of the prosecutor's office then presses for speedy trials and "stiff" sentences. In large measure, these tactics are meant to screen the career criminal from other offenders rather than allow him the advantage of being handled as a routine offender. Speedy trials help to ensure the availability of witnesses and the credibility of testimony, and, in the case of the career criminal, alleviate the possibility of "plea bargaining."

In 1974, Attorney General Saxbe placed a great deal of the burden of crime on the one-half million criminals he believed to be in this category. He emphasized that for this type of offender, attempts at "rehabilitation are a myth." Whether or not this is in fact the case, there is little doubt that a substantial portion of criminal offenses are attributable to this type of habitual offender.

The Political Offender

Political crime may be the oldest kind of crime, for in its basic form it is represented by extremist reactions to what are perceived as illegal practices, immoral demands, and unfair restrictions by the state on the citizenry (Schafer, 1974). In times of relative social tranquility, political crime is not highly noticeable. But during periods of rapid social change and turmoil, the classification of political criminal is brought into greater relief.

In this country, the classic example of politically based crime may be the actions of some of our Founding Fathers in their rejection of King George III's English rule. More recently, "extremist" reactions and particularly student leftist movements against the Vietnam war have been equated with political crime. While the substantive points of these two examples vary widely, they both share a rejection of the established legal order and political rule.

In order to understand political crime it is necessary to recognize that political power, which represents the dominant interests in society, and the legal order that it creates, are neither alike throughout the world nor permanent over time. Political systems vary as widely as those in China and the United States and can change as rapidly as that of South Vietnam in the 1975 Communist takeover. What may be considered criminal in one culture or at one time may not be considered as such in another culture or at a different period in the same culture. George Washington was officially a traitor under the established British rule of the period, but once the Revolution was successful, a label of "hero" was more appropriate.

As well, the political value systems of a country cannot possibly represent *all* of the interest groups or values within the country, but must represent a *choice* between the values and needs of differing groups of people. In the final analysis, the dominant interest group is most frequently represented in the political and legal order. One may construe this to mean that all crime is political in that it rejects established authority. While this is true, for purposes of classifying an act as political crime, one's political *motivation* must be considered. Certainly, the ordinary sneak thief rarely has any conscious concern for the political implications of his behavior, whereas a conspiring traitor does, of course.

One approach by which political crime can be structured has been suggested by Moran (1973), who segregates political crime into three separate categories. In *totally political crime*, the political reasons for the offense predominate, such as in cases of treason, espionage, and sabotage. These acts are in direct confrontation to the power of the state and represent attempts to overthrow or protect national interests.

Politically relevant crime is not directly political in nature, although it may have immediate political consequences for the state. Movements for the removal from legal control of the so-called victimless crimes such as abortion, homosexuality, drug use, prostitution, and gambling, are of such a character. Although the commission of any of these acts may not be considered as political in nature, the general anti-establishment force which they present on a collective basis has political consequences.

Finally, *politically conditioned crime* incorporates acts that are either direct or indirect challenges to the distribution of power in society. For example, the social disorder of the 1960s gave rise to a number of activist groups, many of which widened their attacks on administrative war policy to include the entire scope of socio-economic arrangements in this country. Left-wing student groups, such as SDS and SNCC, gave rise to other groups such as the Black Panthers and the Black African Republicanists. In many instances, crimes committed under the real or imagined guise of social oppression are of a political nature.

In any event, political crime is a collective or individual attempt to challenge or otherwise alter the politically established order. Aside from movements among many minority, disadvantaged, and disenfranchised groups, the nature of political crimes has taken numerous forms. The February, 1974, kidnapping of Patricia Hearst by the anti-capitalist Symbionese Liberation Army, for example, apparently combined a number of independent although ill-defined motives, all of which were of a political nature. Moreover, crimes of terror, such as kidnappings and extortion, which frequently involve political or self-styled political motives, increased between 1971 and 1973 by 164 percent and 35 percent respectively, according to the FBI Uniform Crime Reports (1974). Bombings at the same time, however, decreased by 65 percent.

Nevertheless, whether or not these and other acts are politically motivated depends to a large degree upon the offender's belief systems. As we have noted, since all crime could potentially involve political motivation, the actual level of this type of crime relies primarily on the way in which one applies definitions, regardless of how arbitrary they may be.

Other Offender Categories

In the foregoing sections of this chapter we have devoted attention to several of the broad and general classifications of crime. In a similar fashion, the following sections will highlight several of the more specific offender categories since they are commonly isolated for judicial or administrative purposes.

One reason for special treatment of these offender categories involves the view, according to some, that they cannot or should not be dealt with in the criminal justice system at all. Such categories as the sexual psychopath, chronic alcoholic, and narcotic addict, they argue, go beyond the practical and legal purview of the criminal justice system. And so, it is held, these offenders would be better served through use of quasi-judicial means, including a medical or treatment model.

A body of literature has developed around the civil commitment of these types of offenders under special statutes. It is, of course, not within the scope or intent of this text to provide a review of the various arguments that have been presented in the context of each of these offense classifications. It may be sufficient at this point merely to note that these statutes have been generally criticized, first for their failure to provide offenders with due process considerations, and second for their failure either to protect the public in a more substantial way or to aid the offender toward rehabilitation. [The interested reader may wish to explore these areas further by referring to such works as that of Hickey and Rubin (1971) and Kittrie (1971).]

Sexual Psychopath

The term "psychopathy" is an ill-defined concept even among psychiatrists who typically use it in broad and widely divergent ways. The "sexual psychopath" is just as cumbersome a term with regard to its usage. Moreover, the public's concern over sexual deviation in general and the sex offender in particular has led to the frequent misuse of this designation by both lay and professional persons.

There is legislation in each state dealing with specifically prohibited sexual acts. In addition, some of the states invoke special commitment procedures for offenders—frequently designated as sexual psychopaths—who are considered to be particularly dangerous to society. These commitment procedures, as in insanity cases, carry with them confinement for indefinite periods of time or until a "cure" is effected. Obviously, such indeterminate sentences can and often do result in extensive periods of confinement.

One of the major problems, of course, is the inability to segregate and label accurately the "dangerous" sexual offender from among the numerous other sexual offenders. The many misconceptions which traditionally have surrounded the sexual offender have done little to aid in the legal and medical identification and handling of these individuals. Kittrie (1971:194) identifies four principal *misconceptions*:

> 1. Sex offenders comprise a separate and homogeneous group of criminals.
> 2. Sex offenders regularly progress from minor offenses such as exhibitionism to major offenses such as forcible rape.
> 3. The sex offender is more dangerous than other types of criminals.
> 4. A higher degree of recidivism exists among sex offenders than among other criminals.

Sex offenders do not constitute a homogeneous group, but are part of a much broader range within the general public who engage in so-called "abnormal" or deviant sexual activities. The classification of sexual psychopathy fails in this respect to distinguish adequately between that which might be considered immoral and that which is, or *may become*, criminal.

Progression from minor to major types of sex crimes is not verified either by psychiatrists or by examination of crime statistics (Korn and McCorkle, 1965:163). Moreover, the sexual offender is not characterized by a high rate of recidivism according to several studies that have been conducted in this area.* Finally, the typical characterization of the sexual offender as an "oversexed fiend" appears to be faulty, for most, except the forcible rapist, tend to be unaggressive and relatively timid persons.

In order to get at the heart of the problem, some organizations, including the National Council on Crime and Delinquency, have advocated that sentencing of sex offenders be based on the degree of dangerousness rather than lodged in a statute which is based on ill-defined psycho-therapeutic concepts. Massachusetts and Illinois are among those states which now utilize a "Sexually Dangerous Person" statute which has limited the scope of sexual offenses. While problems still exist in the application and availability of

---

*See, for example, studies cited by Hickey and Rubin (1971:7), particularly that of Louise Viets Frisbie, "Treated Sex Offenders Who Reverted to Sexually Deviant Behavior." *Federal Probation*, 29 (965)2:59–57. See also Chapter 16, "Parole," in this text.

effective treatment resources, this represents some improvement in the approach to the problem.

Drug Offender

According to the FBI's Uniform Crime Reports (1974), arrests for narcotic law violations between 1960 and 1973 increased 774 percent for adults and 4,673 percent for juveniles. These figures tend to confirm the general public's belief that narcotics and dangerous drug abuse has become more visible and serious in our society. While we refer generally to the "drug offender" in this section, the term tends to be used in identifying users of both "narcotics" and "dangerous drugs." Therefore, a brief description of these terms and the types of drugs which they utilize appears appropriate at this time.

A *narcotic* is a generic term that applies to various classes of drugs which have been grouped together for legal control. Opium and its derivatives (particularly morphine) are relaxants and pain relievers which have significant medical applications. However, heroin (known as "horse" or "smack") is a morphine derivative which has become the primary source of addiction in the United States. The influence of organized crime in maintaining the flow of this drug into the country is substantial. Cocaine is a narcotic and a potent stimulant. Because it does not lead to physical addiction, it is not as associated with criminal activities as is heroin. Therefore, the drug does not present a major law enforcement problem as does heroin, even though its use appears to be on the increase. Marijuana, which is also a narcotic under most state statutes, is the most common among the illicit drugs. Cultivated principally both in Mexico and locally in the United States, marijuana, and to a lesser extent hashish, is available widely on the streets.

Dangerous drugs are non-narcotics that include those drugs with stimulant, depressant, or hallucinogenic effects. Stimulants of widest use are the amphetamines, which are available under a variety of names. Depressants, typically barbiturates, are also available under numerous labels and nicknames. As in the case of stimulants, one can develop a tolerance for many of these drugs which are believed to have harmful effects. Finally, hallucinogens, such as LSD and PCP, are also considered to be in the dangerous drug category.

Law enforcement's concern over drug use has revolved around a number of issues, including the widespread belief that drugs are physically harmful to the user, "immoral," increase the proceeds of organized crime, and frequently force the user into patterns of crime to finance illicit use. Use of the law to reduce or control the supposed "danger" involved in narcotics abuse has been attacked by many. They claim law enforcement not only fails to control the problem, but that the approach is also overly moralistic (Kittrie, 1971:223). Some also argue that heavy penalties for users of narcotics and "dangerous" drugs have encouraged underworld activities and the need for users to pursue illegal means to meet the high costs which are demanded. While much of this is undoubtedly true, legal restrictions remain and narcotics addiction exists as a major national problem. The actual scope of the problem, of course, is vague due to lack of accurate data.

Marijuana use was explored in a 1972 survey by the Gallup organization and the results are presented in Table 5.1. As one would expect, the greatest reported use is among youth and young adults. Additional survey data for these populations in college are presented in Tables 5.2 and 5.3. The reduction in criminal penalties for marijuana use from felony to misdemeanor charges, as well as the increasing decriminalization of the offense in several states, reflects a liberalization of public attitudes in this area, if not an altered pattern of public consumption, especially in the white middle class.

Even with respect to more serious drug offenses, such as the use of narcotics, there is growing belief that both use and trafficking have increased. Yet the degree of that increase and the overall levels of current usage and addiction are unclear, irrespective of the fact that arrests for these offenses significantly have increased.

Arrest statistics, in any event, principally involve charges of possession rather than sale or distribution. As a result, the magnitude of the illicit drug trafficking industry is also subject to a good deal of speculation. Nonetheless, what is commonly recognized is that international drug trade is indeed "big business." For example, *Forbes* (1970) referred to this illicit drug market as an industry which does an estimated $3 billion in the U.S. alone, amounting to a major growth industry of 10 percent or more yearly. It is also an industry where one does not have to spend any money for product advertising, where $350 worth of raw material can be worth $500,000 at the retail level, and where profit margins range from 15 to 1,000

TABLE 5.1. General Population Reporting They Have Ever Tried Marijuana, by Demographic Characteristics, 1972 (In percent)

NOTE: These results are based on a sample survey conducted by the Gallup organization's American Institute of Public Opinion. The study was designed to be representative of American adults (18 and older) and includes results from approximately 3,347 interviewees.

Question: "Have you, yourself, ever happened to try marijuana?"

	Yes	No
National	11	89
Sex:		
Male	16	84
Female	7	93
Race:		
White	10	90
Nonwhite	18	82
Education:		
College	20	80
High school	10	90
Grade school	5	95
Occupation:		
Professional and business	15	85
White collar	10	90
Farmer	1	99
Manual	12	88
Age:		
18 to 20 years	31	69
21 to 29 years	29	71
30 to 49 years	7	93
50 and over	2	98
Religion:		
Protestant	7	93
Catholic	13	87
Politics:		
Republican	7	93
Democrat	9	91
Independent	16	84
Region:		
East	13	87
Midwest	10	90
South	7	93
West	18	82
Income:		
$15,000 and over	12	88
$10,000 to $14,999	10	90
$7,000 to $9,999	13	87
$5,000 to $6,999	11	89
$3,000 to $4,999	14	86
Under $3,000	8	92

TABLE 5.1 Continued

	Yes	*No*
Community size:		
1,000,000 and over	20	80
500,000 to 999,999	15	85
50,000 to 499,999	13	87
2,500 to 49,999	10	90
Under 2,500, rural	3	97

Source: American Institute of Public Opinion, Study No. 846, as quoted by Hindelang et al., Sourcebook of Criminal Justice Statistics, 1972, U.S. Dept. of Justice, LEAA, 1973:165.

percent. In discussing heroin use specifically, *Forbes* (1970:19) describes it as being a complex and sophisticated business enterprise which is well-organized:

> One thing few law abiding citizens understand is that a criminal enterprise obeys the same economic laws as any other business, including the law of supply and demand. Like any legitimate industry the heroin industry has its bankers, its exporters and importers, its manufacturers, jobbers, retailers, salesmen. Like legitimate businessmen moreover, the merchants of heroin strive constantly to diversify, and with a good deal of success. Heroin has financed many other enterprises.

For the addict, the problems of financing a habit frequently result in law violations. The President's Advisory Commission on Criminal Justice Standards and Goals (*Police*, 1973:247) noted that of nearly 20,000 persons arraigned on felony warrants in Detroit Recorder's Court in 1970, about 36 percent admitted that they were involved in some form of narcotics and drug abuse. Shoplifting, which is considered to be a primary means for obtaining funds by addicts, has increased substantially over the past years. Yet as the Commission adds (1973:247), "the primary relationship between other criminal acts and narcotics and drug abuse violations is not known, but it has been established that the relationship is a factor in the total crime problem, from traffic violations to homicide."

The Public Inebriate

The public inebriate has presented a major challenge to law enforcement agencies for years, not because of the severity of the offense

TABLE 5.2. College Students Reporting Having Used Marijuana In Last Thirty Days, by Demographic Characteristics, 1970 and 1971
(In percent)

	1971	1970
All students	30	28
Sex:		
Male	36	31
Female	23	23
Class in school:		
Freshman	26	24
Sophomore	33	32
Junior	33	27
Senior	34	30
Graduate	29	31
Age:		
18 years and under	25	22
19 years	30	32
20 to 21 years	39	29
22 years and older	24	24
Type of college:		
Public	24	26
Private	35	32
Denominational	26	26
Area of study:		
Humanities	35	31
Math, science, and engineering	24	25
Social science	34	36
Business	25	24
Education	28	15
Father's education:		
Grade school	20	14
High school	24	25
Some college	35	28
College graduate	37	36

Source: American Institute of Public Opinion. Special Drug Studies, 1970 and 1971, as quoted by Hindelang et al, Sourcebook of Criminal Justice Statistics, 1972, U.S. Dept. of Justice, LEAA, 1973:168.

itself, but because of the sheer magnitude of the problem. For this reason, public drunkenness has been a primary target for diversionary programs, which primarily are systems designed to utilize community mental health agencies or hospitals for treatment as an alternative to arrest and incarceration.

According to the St. Louis Detoxification Center's project report (1974:i) alcoholism is the nation's third largest public health

TABLE 5.3. College Students Reporting Having Used Marijuana In Last Twelve Months, by Demographic Characteristics, 1970 and 1971
(In percent)

	1971	1970
All students	41	39
Sex:		
Male	47	44
Female	32	33
Class in school:		
Freshman	36	35
Sophomore	45	43
Junior	42	44
Senior	45	40
Graduate	39	43
Age:		
18 years and under	35	32
19 years	39	46
20 to 21 years	50	42
22 years and older	37	36
Type of college:		
Public	39	39
Private	48	44
Denominational	34	32
Area of study:		
Humanities	47	44
Math, science, and engineering	32	38
Social science	46	52
Business	37	35
Education	36	23
Father's education:		
Grade school	36	23
High school	34	36
Some college	45	41
College graduate	46	50

Source: American Institute of Public Opinion. Special Drug Studies, 1970 and 1971, as quoted by Hindelang et al, Sourcebook of Criminal Justice Statistics, 1972, U.S. Dept. of Justice, LEAA, 1973:168.

problem; it is estimated there are 6.5 million people in the United States with serious alcohol problems. Of that number, 1.5 million are thought to be chronic addictive alcoholics, with other Americans addicting at the rate of 200,000 per year. These individuals are found in all segments of society, in all classes, and at all occupational levels. The "skid row bum" or public inebriate constitutes an estimated 8 percent of the chronic, addictive alcoholic population.

From a law enforcement perspective, the volume of arrests for public drunkenness highlights the significance of the problem. Traditionally, arrests for public drunkenness have exceeded any other single category of offense. In 1973 (UCR, 1974), for example, arrests of this type exceeded the combined total of all arrests for major property and violent crimes, for a total of 1,599,000 individual arrests.

This volume is still evident in spite of a marked 31 percent reduction in arrests for this offense between 1960 and 1973 (UCR, 1974). The reduction is in large measure due to increased use of diversionary programs in lieu of arrest, corresponding de-emphasis of arrests for this offense by police departments, and changes in the legal status of the offense in many states from that of a criminal violation to that of a civil violation. Over the same period, however, arrests for persons under 18 years of age increased 88 percent. Along with drug abuse, alcohol use among youths apparently is increasing significantly.

Weis (1974:73) puts the burden of this alcohol-abuse law enforcement in clearer perspective when he cites what appears to be a typical example of its ramifications:

> In Erie, Pennsylvania, a mid-sized community of 134,000 people, an average of 144 arrests were made monthly in 1969, over 30% of all arrests. In that city, the police chief estimated that every drunkenness arrest required one hour of patrol car and wagon pickup time. Since there were two men assigned to each patrol car and one man to the wagon, the total task of arresting one man for public drunkenness called for the services of three policemen for three hours, or a total of 432 hours monthly, 5,184 hours annually. Erie police officials estimated that 35–40% of police time was devoted to the resolution of problems dealing with public inebriates.

At the same time, this arrangement does not meet the physical, legal, or social well-being of the inebriate or the community in which he lives. The totality of effects involved in such traditional forms of handling are well summarized by Plaut (1967:110–111):

> The traditional handling by the police, the court, and jail systems of the very large number of persons found drunk on the streets is inhuman as well as ineffective. There is general agreement that the current "revolving door" system of repeating arrests and jailings does not alter the drinking behavior of any significant number of problem drinkers, and thus is not effective either as a deterrent or treatment. Many questions have been and

are being raised about the constitutionality of treating such persons as criminals. If a man's drunkenness is part of his illness—and thus a non-voluntary act—he should be treated as a sick person and not as a criminal. Clearly it is not a crime to suffer from alcoholism, a characteristic of which is the inability to control one's drinking; thus it seems bizarre, inappropriate, and unconstitutional to punish an individual for being intoxicated.

In addition, the present handling of public drunkenness offenders is often demoralizing to the police, judicial, and jail personnel. It is an immense economic drain—in terms of men, time and space—on these agencies. Furthermore, it seriously undermines the professional character of the work of policemen, judges, district attorneys, and others, and often makes a mockery of the American judicial system. In most courts the average time spent by the judge in the "trial" and sentencing of each public drunkenness offender probably is less than three minutes. This system of handling defendants undoubtedly violates the traditional American conception of the "due process of law."

In a thorough discussion of this subject, the report adds (1967:111):

There is an immediate need to find substitutes for the current legal handling of public drunkenness. Police, judges, and prison officials generally do not view public drunkenness offenders as criminals, but they are trapped in the present system by the absence of any alternatives. Since the public wants intoxicated persons removed from the streets, other means of accomplishing this are needed.

The use of diversionary programs has relieved many of the law enforcement problems associated with this offense. Yet, the mere availability of these programs does not ensure their effective use or substantial "cure" rates. As well, where alcoholism and drunkenness are associated with a crime, diversionary programs generally are not utilized.

Available evidence indicates that crime and alcohol use are often related. A large number of studies reviewed by Frank *et al.*, (1973:2) led them to conclude that as many as 50 percent of all murders *could* involve alcohol use. Similar associations were found in the areas of aggravated assault and robbery within the literature review by the same authors. When one takes into consideration the costs and impact of alcohol-related traffic accidents, the total impact of excessive alcohol use in American society is staggering.

Victimless Crime

"Victimless crime" is a frequently employed term which is used in relation to a number of offenses, including prostitution, homosexuality, gambling, drug use, and public intoxication. The term has been used in attempts to characterize these offenses as essentially harmless, or as issues of morality and personal choice, rather than proper areas for legal sanctioning.

It is not within the scope or intent of this text to give complete treatment to the various arguments on this subject. The question of personal and social harm that may flow from these acts as well as the relationship of morality and the law are intricate and involved subjects. It can be stated fairly, however, that the criminal justice community is beginning to address these questions from functional and operational perspectives. For a number of years, and particularly since publication of the President's Crime Commission reports in 1967, authorities have recognized the practical limitations within their agencies, as well as the overall criminal justice system, in their attempts to control and rehabilitate such persons who have been arrested and convicted. Resources are limited and must be utilized in the most prudent and practical of ways, which, according to some (Schur, 1965), means that victimless crimes should no longer be proscribed.

Major crime is, of course, the most significant of the system's priorities and increasingly has become pressing due to public and political clamor over rising crime rates. The criminal justice community, in order to apply itself in the most propitious manner to these ends, has sought alternative approaches for the control and treatment of many of the victimless crimes. Diversionary programs of a number of types have been developed, which are designed to utilize other community agencies and resources for the handling of these offenders. Diversion of the public inebriate, for example, has already been cited in this capacity. The use of methadone and other medical programs for treatment of the narcotic addict is also rather widely employed, although its impact on the addiction problem and its "success" have been questioned lately.

Many of these offenses increasingly are being de-emphasized, particularly with respect to law enforcement policies. The legalization of gambling in the form of lotteries and off-track betting, the reduction of criminal penalties for marijuana use, as well as its decriminalization in some states, as examples, have been both a cause and a result of these changing policies in the law enforcement and general communities. In addition, the influence of several movements which have developed to reduce the stigma and increase the rights of persons engaged in such practices as homosexuality, prostitution, and drug usage is being felt increasingly.

With these and related factors involved, criminal justice agencies have begun to shift much of the responsibility for control and treatment of these offenders back into the community. While not all of the procedural implications of these moves have been resolved, such as those in the area of civil commitments, the basic prudence of alternative handling of these offender categories, according to many, is beginning to be recognized.

References

Bers, Melvin K.
　　1970　　The Penetration of Legitimate Business by Organized Crime—An Analysis. Washington, D.C.: LEAA, U.S. Government Printing Office.
Federal Bureau of Investigation
　　1974　　Crime in the United States—Uniform Crime Reports—1973. Washington, D.C.: U.S. Government Printing Office.
Forbes
　　1970　　"There Are People Who Say: 'Well, Business Is Business.' " 105 (April 1):19.
Frank, Collin H., W.C. Mooney, Jr., and G.C. Pavloff (eds.)
　　1973　　Proceedings of the Seminar on Alcoholism Detection, Treatment and Rehabilitation within the Criminal Justice System. Washington, D.C.: U.S. Government Printing Office.
Hickey, William L. and Sol Rubin
　　1971　　Civil Commitment of Special Categories of Offenders. Washington, D.C.: National Institute of Mental Health, U.S. Government Printing Office.
Kittrie, Nicholas N.
　　1971　　The Right to be Different. Baltimore, Maryland: The Johns Hopkins Press.
Korn, Richard R. and Lloyd W. McCorkle
　　1965　　Criminology and Penology. New York: Holt, Rinehart and Winston.
Moran, Richard
　　1973　　"A Political Perspective on Crime." South Hadley, Massachusetts:

Department of Sociology and Anthropology, Mt. Holyoke College. (Mimeo.)

National Advisory Commission on Criminal Justice Standards and Goals
1973   Police. Washington, D.C.: U.S. Government Printing Office.

NBC-TV
1975   "White Collar Rip-Off." Telecast June 1, 1975.

Plaut, Thomas F.A.
1967   "Alcohol Problems: A Report to the Nation." New York: Oxford University Press, Cooperative Commission on the Study of Alcoholism: 110-111 (as cited by Weiss, 1974:5).

President's Commission on Law Enforcement and Administration of Justice
1967   Task Force Report: Crime and Its Impact—An Assessment. Washington, D.C.: U.S. Government Printing Office.

1967   The Challenge of Crime in a Free Society. Washington, D.C.: U.S. Government Printing Office.

Reckless, Walter C.
1967   The Crime Problem. 4th ed. New York: Appleton-Century-Crofts.

Reiss, Albert J., Jr.
1967   "Studies in Crime and Law Enforcement in Major Metropolitan Areas." Field Surveys III, President's Commission on Law Enforcement and Administration of Justice, Vol. I. Washington, D.C.: U.S. Government Printing Office.

Ross, Irwin
1961   "Thievery in the Plant." Fortune (October). (As cited in Task Force Report: Crime and Its Impact—An Assessment. 1967:49).

St. Louis Metropolitan Police Department
1974   The St. Louis Detoxification and Diagnostic Evaluation Center—Final Evaluation Report. Washington, D.C.: LEAA, U.S. Government Printing Office.

Schafer, Stephen
1974   The Political Criminal: The Problem of Morality and Crime. New York: The Free Press.

Schur, Edwin M.
1965   Crimes Without Victims: Deviant Behavior and Public Policy. Englewood, Cliffs, New Jersey: Prentice-Hall.

Smith, Richard A.
1969   "The Incredible Electrical Conspiracy." In Donald Cressey and David Ward (eds.), Delinquency, Crime, and Social Process. New York: Harper and Row: 884-912.

Sutherland, Edwin H.
1940   "White Collar Criminality." American Sociological Review 5 (February): 1-12.

Weis, Charles W.
1974   Diversion of the Public Inebriate from the Criminal Justice System. Washington, D.C.: LEAA, U.S. Government Printing Office.

CHAPTER 6

CAUSATiON OVERViEW

Concern For Cause

Philosophers and theologians have a long history of attempting to explain man's behavior. Criminologists, influenced by this concern, have sought to understand the differences between criminals and noncriminals. Since the explanation of criminal behavior has so many important consequences, a great deal of effort has gone into this task. It is believed that if we understand the reasons why some people commit criminal acts and why others do not, it will be possible to design and implement preventive, realistic treatment, and control strategies. Over the years, there have been many "theories of causation" (etiology). However, not one single theory nor any combination of theories satisfactorily answers the question of why some people engage in criminal behavior.

The early students of crime had a relatively easy time trying to explain deviant behavior. Man was thought to be possessed by evil influences. Therefore, the best way to control and deter such behavior was through ostracism, death, banishment, and, on occasion, through repentance. Later, when Classical criminology was developing, it was thought that man had "free will." That is, man consciously behaved in ways that would bring him pleasure and avoid pain. The notion of "possession" seemed dead. Through the influence of Darwin and concern for scientific procedure, and as the Positive tradition in criminology developed, the concept of free will was laid aside and the notion of "determinism" gained a foothold. Deterministic philosophy holds that man is a "victim" of the pulls, pushes, and tugs of life and, as a consequence, is not truly a master of his own destiny. Hence, sociological, constitutional, political, psychological, and economic forces were thought to have considerable influence on man's behavior. Man behaves, then, as a result of all of these forces and criminologists seek explanations of criminal behavior in terms of the way a criminal responds to these various and mitigating forces in his life.

Webster (1951:132) defines cause as "That which occasions an end result." In other words, causation is anything which effects or produces a result in something else. It does not mean that if a particular causal factor is absent, the end result will not occur. It does mean that if a particular force or factor is present, the end result of something else is inevitable. A may cause B to occur, however it is also possible that C or D (and even C *and* D) may produce the same result. As an example, if I were to hit someone, I would *cause* a bruise to occur. The bruise in this instance would not have occurred unless I did the hitting (A causes B to happen). However, it is also possible for someone to obtain a bruise by falling, being hit by someone else, or bumping into something. Therefore, in the latter examples, C, D, or even E did the causing. When we see someone with a bruise, then, we cannot be certain whether A, C, D, E, or X was the causal factor. Investigation and analysis, however, may give us the answer if we proceed on a scientific basis to uncover the "truth."

Sometimes, as a result of scientific inquiry, we think we have some answers to causation, but we are fooled by the "facts." In other words, what appears to be causation is nothing more than a *relationship* or *correlation*. That is, a factor may be influencing the result or may be associated with the result, but it does not actually *cause* the result: A does not cause B, it is only related to it. In a classic study done on the frequency of rape in a large Midwestern city, researchers found that whenever a large amount of ice cream was consumed by the public, there was a high incidence of rape. Thus eating ice cream (A) appeared to "cause" rape (B). It would appear to anyone with common sense that eating ice cream could not conceivably cause rape. And further analysis showed that A did not cause B to occur, but they both occurred when another factor, C, happened. In this example, the consumption of ice cream and the incidence of rape were indeed *related* or correlated, but one did not cause the other to happen. As a matter of fact, C, the weather conditions, wound up being the culprit or a causal factor of A and B. That is, as the temperature and humidity increased, there was a significant increase in the amount of ice cream consumption *and* the incidence of rape: A did not cause B to occur. An increase in C results in an increase of A and B, but intervening forces may also affect the outcome. When researchers talk about "relationship" then, they are referring to the "association" of one factor to another, not necessarily in terms of causation. In our example, ice cream consumption and incidence of rape are *related* because of a third factor, but one did not cause the other to occur.

Does a "Broken Home" Cause Delinquency?

One of the problems we have in studying criminal causation is that too many researchers express causal theories which are in reality only descriptions of relationships or correlations. For example, it is commonly believed that a "broken home" causes delinquency. As a matter of fact, we do not know this for certain—in terms of a theory of causation. If it were *truth* and indeed a real cause, we would not be at a loss to explain why so many youngsters who come from broken homes do not engage in delinquent behavior. What we may have here is not a question of "Does A cause B?" but a question of whether or not other forces or factors are influencing delinquent behavior—that is, are C, D, E, and X operating to produce this result?

If we investigate the many factors and forces associated with the notion of broken homes causing delinquency, we may be able to illustrate the point about the complexity of causation and its implications. In law enforcement training programs, as well as in university courses on delinquency, the notion that a broken home causes delinquency is sometimes taught. When the policeman observes two youngsters breaking windows, for example, he is likely to intervene and talk to them. If the first youngster appears apologetic and tells the policeman that he is likely to be in trouble with both his parents as a result of the incident, it is possible the policeman will let him go with a "warning." If the other youngster does not appear to be remorseful and indicates that he comes from a broken home, it is possible that the officer will make a referral to the juvenile court. In this example, the policeman, believing that a broken home causes delinquency, makes the referral in order to "help" the youngster obtain the kind of supervision needed to thwart further delinquent behavior. The behaviors of the two youngsters were exactly the same; only the behavior or reaction of the policeman differed—and that was based on his notion about cause.

When researchers review court records in an effort to explain delinquent behavior, they become struck with the *fact* that a disproportionate number of youngsters do indeed come from broken homes. Therefore, they publish their results which suggest that broken homes do indeed cause delinquency. But obviously, this is not *truth*. All they may say is that among those youngsters who wind up in court, more of them than not come from broken homes. Causation has not been proved. What has been demonstrated is that there is a *relationship* between broken homes and delinquent behavior, but *only* among those youngsters who actually are referred to the court. Whether or not coming from broken homes causes delinquency can only be tested when we look at youths who are not referred to the court *as well as* those who are referred, when they all have engaged in exactly the same kind of delinquent behavior.

The criminologist attempts to explain criminal behavior by studying its causes. That is, he is interested in the differences between criminals and noncriminals. As Sutherland and Cressey (1974: 73) indicate:

> The problem in criminology is to explain the criminality of behavior, not behavior, as such. . . . Criminal behavior is human behavior, has much in common with noncriminal behavior, and must be explained within the same general framework used to explain other human behavior. However, an explanation of criminal behavior should be a specific part of a general theory of behavior. Its specific task should be to differentiate criminal from noncriminal behavior. Many things which are necessary for behavior are not for that reason important to the criminality of behavior. Respiration, for instance, is necessary for any behavior, but the respiratory process cannot be used in an explanation of criminal behavior, for it does not differentiate criminal behavior from noncriminal behavior.

Levels and Types of Causal Explanations

One of the problems we have in studying causation is identifying and understanding various levels or stages of causation. That is, the *chronology* of events may help us to understand various stages or levels of activities that lead to certain kinds of behavior. The order in which events or factors occur is significant: what is the sequence of relevant factors which leads to the final happening or event? In the Sutherland and Cressey example above, respiration occurs, but it is not seen as relevant to explaining the difference between criminal and noncriminal behavior. In the example of the "broken home," its influence on delinquency causation may become confusing because we cannot be sure whether the absence of a parent, the influence of other relatives' behavior on the child as a reaction to the absence, or the reaction of the child to the absence of the parent is the factor which most nearly influences or causes delinquent behavior. Perhaps all of the factors have some influence, but, if so, in which *order* do they occur that finally results in a given youngster committing a given delinquent act? Furthermore, what kind of precipitating factor or factors actually *cause* the specific delinquent act? That is, what starts the causal chain, what factor follows, etc.? It may turn out, in this example, that the reaction by the relatives to the absence of a parent has little or nothing to do with the causation of delinquent behavior on the part of the youth. But, then again, it may be the precipitating cause.

Scientific explanations of criminal behavior have tended to fall into two basic categories. The first, known generally as "mechanistic" or "situational," is concerned with understanding the forces or processes at work at the moment the crime is occurring. The second is concerned with the processes that were operating during the earlier history of the offender and is generally called "historical" or "genetic." Mechanistic types of explanations are those generally used by physical scientists, but not always favored by social or behavioral scientists. This model requires studying the most immediate and precipitating factors causing the delinquent act. It does not always answer the question of what factors or forces helped to lead to the immediate situation. Sutherland and Cressey (1974:74) comment:

> ... criminological explanations of the mechanistic type have thus far been notably unsuccessful, perhaps largely because they have been formulated

in connection with the attempt to isolate personal and social pathologies among criminals. Work from this point of view has, at least, resulted in the conclusion that the immediate determinants of criminal behavior lie in the person-situation complex.

That is, working with scientific procedure, Sutherland and Cressey are suggesting that a combination of both models may be helpful in understanding delinquent behavior. An understanding of background as well as situation, they believe, would help to unravel the mysteries of criminal causation.

Scientific Procedure

Some people have said that human behavior is so complex it cannot be studied as scientifically as the physical sciences. But, as Sellin has pointed out (1938:12–13), while this position may have important considerations, ". . . they do not permit us to assume that social facts cannot be studied scientifically and laws of social life gradually established. They merely recognize that the social scientist has great hazards to overcome." Applying scientific procedure to the study of criminal causation merely means that rigor is needed before anyone dare claim that A causes B. It means that one must be accurate, sure, and complete in much the same way that a laboratory technician operates in seeking causes of disease.

When an attempt is made to study deviant or criminal behavior from a scientific point of view, it is important to describe the processes associated with the behavior. This is true whether the orientation is mechanistic or historical. Understanding in their simplest form the various possible cause and effect relationships associated with the processes is the scientific procedure. Such understanding is the main purpose of science. Generalizations about these cause and effect relationships are generally stated as *probabilities*. That is, it is *probable* that certain things are related to other things (A is related to B), and that if one thing (A) is changed, it will probably cause something else (B) to occur.

Anyone engaging in scientific procedure, in zoology as well as human relations laboratories, tries to put some order (cause and effect relationships and/or probabilities) into a series of ideas, facts, or pieces of information. In order to understand what is happening, the scientist tries to develop *types* or *categories* or *typologies*. This is what the zoologist does when he classifies animals into various species. All animals belonging to the same type possess similar characteristics: they may look alike, act alike, and certainly can be identified according to the type to which they belong. In the scientific study of criminals, the task is not so easy. Attempts have been made to type offenders and offenses in order to better understand what characteristics may be held in common, but without too much success. As simple as this fact may sound, what we have discovered is that not all criminals possess the same characteristics; they do not necessarily look alike; they do not always behave alike; they do not come from the same kinds of background; nor do they have the same kinds of criminal careers. The result is that although we can study criminal behavior from a scientific point of view, we have thus far not been able to differentiate criminals from noncriminals insofar as causation is concerned. All we basically know is that the criminal, at least, has been caught and adjudicated, while the noncriminal has never been caught—even though he *may* have engaged in the same kinds of criminal behavior.

Clinard (1963:32) comments on the use of scientific procedure with regard to the study of deviance and points out that

> The social scientist, as contrasted with those who make unscientific claims about human behavior, is willing to do three things. First, he is willing to subject his hypotheses to tests. Second, he avoids making generalizations which are not based on empirical studies. Third, he will state his confidence in a proposition according to the degree to which it has been verified by a test using experimental or empirical data.

In summary, Clinard suggests that one who wants to use scientific procedure must be willing to deal openly by stating what it is he hopes to find, test the findings, and develop a procedure which a neutral observer could replicate if he chose to. Incidentally, it is when another experimenter, following identical procedures but at a different time and place, comes up with similar findings that we begin to uncover "fact" and "truth." It is when repeated experiments produce the same response time after time after time—without any deviation whatever—that we are able to declare a "law" or a "universal truth."

Steps in Scientific Procedure

Generally, the steps in scientific procedure are the same regardless of what is being studied. The criminologist, who wants to be scientific in understanding causation, must follow the same steps as those followed by the physicist. The procedure is as follows:

1. Become aware of some kind of problem which can be researched.
2. Develop a preliminary hypothesis. (This, in effect, is answering a question which is being raised in step 1.)
3. Design a procedure to collect real data or information about the problem.
4. Observe and collect the data or information about the problem.
5. Classify and analyze the data and information obtained in step 4.
6. Arrive at cautious conclusions from the findings and make generalizations that are extremely careful not to go beyond the findings. (This answers the question of whether the hypothesis is confirmed or not confirmed.)
7. Replicate the study and compare the results with studies using a similar procedure—at different times and places.

A review of the steps indicates that scientific procedure begins with the development of a *hypothesis*. This is nothing more than a statement (a hunch) suggesting that a relationship appears to exist between two or more "things" (variables). An example of a hypothesis is "broken homes cause delinquency." To test this hypothesis, the criminologist would first have to define very precisely such terms as broken homes and delinquency. But he probably would also have to re-write the statement or hypothesis in a form which is testable and subject to precise measurement. In this case, we might have to state the hypothesis in the following form: "A significantly greater proportion of youths who come from homes in which one parent is absent commit delinquent acts and are adjudicated as such than youths who come from homes where both parents are present."

The researcher will then have to develop a procedure to obtain real data about youth who come from both kinds of homes. After he obtains *appropriate* and *relevant* data, he proceeds with analyses of the data in order to reach a conclusion about the hypothesis. Of course, the well-qualified researcher knows what procedures to follow—including statistical—that will produce the most "honest" data from which he can reach the most "honest" conclusions. Unlike the physical or applied scientist who can develop and analyze "hard" data from laboratory experiments, the social scientist generally must develop other techniques for obtaining data. In criminology, as in other sciences, the researcher frequently obtains data and information from a representative sample, simply because it is not possible to examine everyone. It would not be possible to gather data or information from every youngster who comes from a "broken home" and from intact homes. The task for the researcher is to gather data on a *sample* basis—a sample which *truly* represents both groups. The analysis of the data obtained from both groups then permits the researcher to make comparisons. Comparisons then lead to conclusions, which, in turn, permit the researcher to answer the original questions contained in the hypothesis. In the final analysis, the researcher can answer the question of whether or not his hypothesis is confirmed. Through the use of statistics, he can also determine how accurate his answers are, or, in statistical language, the level of *significance* of his findings.

In our example, the hypothesis would be confirmed or *verified* if the data reveal a relationship between "broken homes" and delinquency. That is, if a higher rate of delinquency (actual and adjudicated behavior) is found among youngsters from broken homes than among those who come from intact families, the researcher can state that a definite *relationship* or *correlation* exists. He may not yet state that A causes B—only that A is related to B. He cannot state that there is causation because he does not yet know enough information. For example, while the two factors may be related, he does not know which factor comes first: does delinquency occur first, followed by a break-up in the family, or the other way around? To determine the answer to that question requires additional research. He does not know what other factors may be influencing the results: are X, Y, and Z factors also involved? Additionally, the researcher has to be cautious in making his generalizations too broad. It will not be until other researchers come up with the same findings in similar research, at different times and places, that the meaning of the results can be understood.

It is frequently said that scientific discovery is *cumulative*. That is, each piece of research builds upon the findings of prior research. The findings or results of one study frequently help another researcher to build his hypotheses, and so on over the years. As results are published, researchers can study findings and develop other kinds of relevant research. Over the years, knowledge accumulates. From this knowledge, hopefully, additional understanding is gained. Curiosity helps, and when it is satisfied according to scientific procedure we are in a better position to apply knowledge. When we have a better understanding of the causation of criminality, we will be in a better position to deal adequately with such issues as treatment, prevention, and control. Put another way, it is the opposite of what Disraeli once said: the practical man is one who practices the errors of his forefathers. That is, we must learn from past experiences and avoid repeating our errors.

Early Causation Research

An understanding of causation in criminology demands that attention be paid to the development of *theory*. As Bloch and Geis (1962: 78) comment:

> One of the reasons that authentic and sound scientific theory has been slow to develop in the field of criminology is that it has not been firmly rooted within the context of general theories concerning human nature and human behavior. A sound theory which purports to give an adequate explanation of a restricted form of behavior, whether in the field of physics or in the field of criminology, must push its roots into broader principles of which the given application provides a special kind of operation.

However, the use of theory as the underpinning for scientific research into the causes of crime did not develop until criminologists became interested in the general areas of psychology, sociology, psychiatry, and biology. Researchers in these fields, like the philosophers, tried to understand the form of human behavior called criminality. Research in the areas of physiognomy (the study of features) and phrenology (cranial structure) preceded true scientific research by trying to relate the appearance and structure of the face and the cranial structure of criminals to their delinquent behavior. These "pseudosciences" were widely accepted until the middle of the 19th century. One of their problems was in distinguishing between criminals and noncriminals—a problem still faced by researchers today. This was and remains so because, as many people indicate, a principal difference between the two is that the former have been caught and the latter have not. As much contemporary research reveals, many people who have never been apprehended as offenders admit to having committed delinquent acts. Therefore, the distinction between a criminal and a noncriminal may be more artificial than real. The only real difference may indeed lie in the fact that some persons have been caught and others have not. Also, what constituted a crime at one time in our history may no longer be a crime at another time. Therefore, who is a criminal may be determined not so much by behavior as by a label affixed to some people who have been caught and dealt with by the legal authorities.

But, it is highly probable that the research of these early "pseudoscientists," along with Darwin, had a profound influence on the Italian criminologist, Cesare Lombroso (1835-1904). Lombroso began to look at causation of criminality and he was the first to develop a "scientific" basis for describing some persons as "born criminals." In effect, through scientific procedure, he began to examine man as a product of genetic forces, some of which "caused" some persons to be criminals. Before Lombroso, however, the French psychiatrist Phillipe Pinel (1745-1826) developed his conception of mental illness as a degeneration in the mental faculties. As Elliott (1952:384-385) indicates, Pinel's theory was carried further through Benedict A. Morel (1809-1872). Morel believed that mental degeneration was hereditary and along with other psychiatrists of the 19th century did much to perpetuate the notion that heredity was a major factor in criminality.

Henry Maudsley (1835-1918), a British psychiatrist, diagnosed the criminal as "morally insane" and also believed strongly that criminality was inherited. In an interesting book, *Responsibility in Mental Disease*, Maudsley (1878:28-29) had this to say:

> The few and imperfect investigations of the personal and family histories of criminals which have yet been made are sufficient to excite some serious reflections. One fact which is brought strongly out by these inquiries is that crime is often hereditary; that just as a man may inherit the stamp of the bodily features and characters of his parents, so he may also inherit the impress of their evil passions and propensities; of the true thief as of the true poet it may be indeed said that he is born, not made.

As Positive criminology gained momentum, writers began to express the opinion that factors other than heredity had an influence on criminal behavior. Guerry (1802-1866) investigated the relationship between ecology (where a criminal lived) and crime. Quetelet (1796-1874) held that age, sex, and climate were interrelated and affected crime rates. Marx and Engels in the mid-1850s developed their theory of socialism and maintained that all crime was the effect of the capitalist system. The relationship between economics and crime was further discussed in the writings of William Bonger, a Dutch sociologist. His book, *Criminality and Economic Conditions*, published in 1905 in Amsterdam, rejected psychological and biological conceptions of criminality. He used extensive statistics to show that crime was more closely related to the economic status of the individual offender and to economic conditions in general.

One of the early sociological studies on the causes of crime in the United States was published in 1893 by Charles R. Henderson and was called *An Introduction to the Defective, Dependent and Delinquent Classes*. Later, in his 1914 *The Causes and Cure of Crime*, he discussed an early multiple-cause theory by suggesting that both personality and environmental factors were related in the development of criminal behaviors. However, he believed that social factors were the most important causes of crime, for they were the factors which society could most hopefully expect to control or eliminate.

As a result of the extensive research into the causes of crime by the turn of the century, particularly in the social and behavioral sciences, a special conference was convened on the subject. Called the National Conference on Criminal Law and Criminology, it was held at Northwestern University in Evanston, Illinois in 1909, in celebration of its School of Law's 50th anniversary. According to Elliott (1952:386), the 150 delegates represented medicine, psychology, sociology, and penology, as well as persons actively engaged in juvenile court work and legal aid societies, judges of criminal courts, leading lawyers, and representatives of state attorneys' offices. Elliott indicates that as a result of this conference, universities became interested in the study of criminology as a discipline and began to sponsor significant research into the causes, control, and prevention of crime and delinquency.

In 1932, Jerome Michael and Mortimer J. Adler published a critique of existing criminological research, called *Crime, Law and Social Science*. They stated that all of the causation research conducted and reported thus far on the subject was practically worthless. They further suggested that as a result of poor research procedures, no precise theory of crime causation could be developed from the published materials. They argued that criminality had to be a *result* of other significant factors than those reported and its extent would be influenced by the nature of these other factors, whatever they might be. They also stated that most of the research attempted to develop causal theories when the researchers should have been content to explain mere relationships of factors. They demanded that criminological research in the future be more mathematically oriented, for that, according to them, was the only true science available to the social scientist. Elliott writes (1952:389) that Michael and Adler had much to contribute to the development of rigorous thinking in the field of criminology, but she rejects the need for a commitment to mathematics:

> ...no research in crime can reasonably expect to measure criminality as an entity by means of a precise mathematical formula. Any such attempt is doomed at the outset, because human behavior (whether criminal or law abiding) cannot be resolved into a measurable entity or a mathematical formula by any known psychological or sociological device. Behavior, we have reason to believe, is always a function of many variables within the personality of the individual, his group relationships, and the stimuli within the community and the general cultural milieu.

Contemporary research criminologists might argue that both positions represent an extreme and that a compromise would be more helpful in developing an understanding of just how research into the causation of criminality ought to proceed. In other words, while all research should not be discarded because it does not produce mathematically perfect explanations, attention to mathematics and sound statistical techniques is useful. Additionally, many researchers would be better able to develop sound generalizations from their research if they paid more attention to scientific procedure. While early researchers can be excused for their lack of scientific rigor, contemporary researchers have cumulative knowledge which should be applied in their work.

Unitary and Multiple Factor Theories

Early writers in the field of criminal causation looked to single or unitary factors for explanation, such as Lombroso's "born criminal." These simple unitary explanations for crime included all the attempts to explain criminality for all classes of people and offenses. They included single personality characteristics that were the result of heredity, physical handicaps, or defective physical structure, low mentality, or emotional frustration. These writers also looked for such unitary factors (even though complex in themselves) as environment, including broken homes, immoral parents, bad neighborhood, poor housing, lack of recreational facilities, inadequate schooling, no employment, poverty, the capitalistic system, improper socializing experiences, and lack of religion.

Modern criminologists are almost thoroughly convinced that unitary or single factor explanations are without foundation and must be totally rejected. For one reason, research has demonstrated that not one of the theories can account for all criminality. Further, no single theory explains why some people, for example, become criminals who are from "bad neighborhoods" and why others become law abiding citizens. Single theories do not demonstrate the order in which factors influence behavior and certainly do not account for any precipitating or immediate factor which literally "pushes" someone into criminal behavior. How does a "bad neighborhood" or "lack of recreational facilities" *cause* someone to steal a car or embezzle bank funds? Those who reject single theory explanations recognize that if there is a "straw that breaks a camel's back," there are other forces, factors, pushes, and pulls in the offender's background that must also be considered. Unitary explanations of crime—which is itself a complex of many behaviors and labels—do not help us to understand how the same factor alone could possibly *explain* why one person engages in murder, another steals, and a third commits rape.

Multiple factor theorists argue that there is no one single factor which can possibly explain all crime and all criminality. Rather, they believe that there is a combination of interrelated factors which contribute to crime and delinquency. These factors, they add, may be different for different people and at different times. A combination of a broken home, poverty, lack of educational opportunities, and political disorganization in the community may all contribute to the criminality of one person. For another, a different combination of factors may contribute.

When early multiple factor theorists looked to their "model" for unraveling the mysteries of crime causation, they were not too dissimilar from the single theory exponents. That is, they believed that it was possible to uncover an interacting group of factors which could explain criminality, even though such a collection of factors was different for different people. Today, those who engage in multiple factor research are not as committed to causation as they are to relationships of factors. That is, most researchers are content to show how one factor may be related to another, but they do not make sweeping generalizations about causation.

Multiple factor researchers generally study causation from particular points of view or disciplines, including sociology, psychology, economics, jurisprudence, and political science. As they strive for a scientific understanding of human behavior in general and criminality in particular, they have a difficult task. On the one hand, it is important to combine what is unique as well as similar in order to describe such uniformities and similarities. On the other hand, it is dangerous to go too far in making generalizations when such similarities are slight or when the evidence is inadequate. Researchers proceed on the basis of what others have reported; this is the notion of cumulative knowledge. However, we cannot expect anyone in criminology to have more knowledge or greater understanding than his or her contemporaries. Few people have such insight that the finding of *truth* becomes inevitable. Researchers are products of their own times and must rely on the knowledge which is available to them. Many centuries ago, it would have been unheard of to assume that the world was not flat. Even if someone had had the insight and engaged in research based on that "fact," his findings would have been disregarded by others. Today, we are not so quick to disregard the research findings of those who appear to be out of the mainstream of scientific inquiry, but we demand, at least, sound scientific procedure, honest reporting of findings, and rigor in research methodology.

Cause Re-examined

When we engage in study of criminal causation, we are forced to recognize that causation is neither a simple matter nor easily defined. However, cause, as Tappan (1960:71) states:

> ...means simply a more or less direct and meaningful relationship in which one factor or event tends sensibly to produce another. Cause as an abstract concept does not imply any specific degree or kind of relationship but only a power of one variable to produce the particular consequence

involved. Hence a cause may be very slight or very important in its effect . . . (and) the cause that is very important in one case or context may be very slight in another. Causes operate not in isolation but in related interplay, so that a factor has no constant significance in different cases. The influence, for example, of the broken home . . . may have very different significance in varied contexts because such . . . (influence is) associated with diverse other variables that both take meaning from and give meaning to the particular case involved.

Criminogenesis is the word often used today to describe the study of causation of criminality. Although it is researched from particular points of view or by persons in varying areas of study, a "multiple disciplinary orientation" seems to be popular today. It is not uncommon to find a sociologist, psychologist, social worker, lawyer, and psychiatrist working together as a team on a particular project analyzing causal behavior. This, in effect, is a recognition of the complexity of the interrelationships of the many forces and factors which might have influence in terms of criminogenesis. This is true in terms of developing an understanding of causation in general or causation insofar as a particular person is concerned. It marks a clear and distinct break with earlier researchers who devoted all of their energies to finding "the answer" for all of criminal causation.

In the chapter that follows, some detailed consideration will be given to theories and findings related to criminal and delinquent behavior. Early and contemporary theories will be discussed as they may be classified into three basic categories: physical, psychological, and social. While such categories may be convenient for the student, it should be pointed out that where human behavior is concerned, such separations or categorizations may be artificial and misleading. As Tappan indicates (1960:81):

Mind and personality are inextricably linked with heredity and constitution. Response to the social-cultural environment is related both directly and indirectly to the mind and the body. It is true . . . that man does not live in a vacuum. It is equally true, however, as the physical and behavioral sciences make fully clear, that the individual's biochemical and psychological composition determines the meaning of environmental forces.

Kluckhohn and Murray (1953:65) put it another way:

There is the organism moving through a field which is structured both by culture and by the physical and social world in a relatively uniform manner, but which is subject to endless variation within the general patterning due to the organism's constitutionally-determined peculiarities of reaction and to the occurrence of special situations.

One final note is indicated with regard to the following chapter on criminal causation. Vold (1958:4–8) states that two different but general kinds of views of criminality have been advanced over the years: the "demonological" and the "naturalistic." Demonological views entertain the belief in "other world" powers of spirits as being at the root of criminality. Naturalistic theories look for events and characteristics from that which can be observed directly in the physical or material world as the active agents producing crime.

Demonological concepts will be summarized even though they are entirely discredited today. The selected theories which will be presented in the chapter that follows primarily will be those based in naturalistic beliefs. These are the only ones which have any link to contemporary social and behavioral sciences and the only ones being actively researched today. No effort has been made to discuss all of the theories which have developed over the years. Those which have had some significant impact, however, are described and, for the most part, in relatively brief terms.

References

Bloch, Herbert A. and Gilbert Geis
    1962   Man, Crime, and Society: The Forms of Criminal Behavior. New York: Random House.
Clinard, Marshall B.
    1963   Sociology of Deviant Behavior, Rev. ed. New York: Holt, Rinehart and Winston.
Elliott, Mabel A.
    1952   Crime in Modern Society. New York: Harper and Brothers.
Kluckhohn, Clyde and Henry A. Murray
    1953   "Personality Formation: The Determinants." In C. Kluckhohn, H.A. Murray, and D.M. Schneider, Personality in Nature, Society, and Culture. 2nd ed. New York: Knopf: 53–72.
Maudsley, Henry
    1878   Responsibility in Mental Disease. New York: D. Appleton.

Merriam-Webster
   1951   Webster's New Collegiate Dictionary. 2nd ed. Springfield: G. and
           C. Merriam Co.
Michael, Jerome and Mortimer J. Adler
   1932   Crime, Law and Social Science. New York: Bureau of Social
           Hygiene.
Sellin, Thorsten
   1938   Culture Conflict and Crime. New York: Social Science Research
           Council.
Sutherland, Edwin H. and Donald R. Cressey
   1974   Criminology. 9th ed. Philadelphia: J.B. Lippincott Co.
Tappan, Paul W.
   1960   Crime, Justice and Correction. New York: McGraw-Hill.
Vold, George B.
   1958   Theoretical Criminology. New York: Oxford University Press.

CHAPTER 7

CAUSAL THEORIES

In the preceding chapter, we touched on some causal explanations for criminal behavior. The focus of this chapter will be to summarize some of these explanations in greater detail as they were developed chronologically. We will examine the Preclassical, Classical, Neoclassical, and Positive notions of criminology and how these various orientations produced theories of causation. We will first present the basic philosophies of these orientations in terms of their beliefs about man and his behavior and then how these beliefs became associated with theories of causation and methods of crime control.

Preclassical Criminology

One of the earliest explanations for criminal behavior was borne out of the strong religious beliefs of pre-feudal Europe. Man at that time believed that an infinite spirit could be pleasant, kind, and a benefactor to man if the gods were pleased, or harsh, tormenting, and ruthless if the gods were angered. Angry spirits were thought to mete out punishments including plagues, pestilence, and famine to those who did not believe or who engaged in behavior against the will of the gods. These beliefs, which lasted almost up to the 18th century, were not so much theories about crime as they were methods of punishment.

Life during these times was very complicated in that man not only had to please the gods, he also had to ward off the "evil spirits" who were known to be the cause of his discomfort. Barnes and Teeters (1951:121) point out that at this time, "Crime was the result of succumbing to the temptations of the evil spirits." In order to determine guilt or innocence for persons who yielded to those evil influences, ritual trial procedures were developed, i.e., "trial by battle, trial by ordeal . . . testimony under oath," etc. (Vold 1958:6). Once guilt was determined, punishment usually took the form of execution, banishment, and, occasionally, repentance. The emphasis of the administrators of justice at this time was to err on the side of caution "in protecting the community and in placating the gods." Medieval justice placed the burden of proof on the accused; it was he who had to "bear the law." He was guilty unless he could prove his innocence, which was almost impossible to do.

Evidence of this school of thought can still be found in certain religious and social institutions as well as codified law. As recent news articles attest, some churches maintain the "rite of exorcism" for possessed members. Accounts of hexing by the Pennsylvania Dutch are legion in folklore, and today hex signs on buildings are readily visible indicators of this magical form of protection. Besides the infamous Inquisition, a notable example of how these beliefs were practiced occurred during the trials of the Salem, Massachusetts witches. Many young women in 17th century Salem were tried according to the existing laws for deliberately casting spells and using demonic devices against others. Their punishments tended to be death, although some were banished.

Clearly in the above, the decision of guilt or innocence, and discretion in punishment which was traditionally harsh, lay in individual interpretations by judicial authorities.

Since theorists and philosophers of the period were oblivious to scientific procedure, the "spirits" and "demons" themselves were not explainable, nor were they understood. As a consequence, they served as convenient rationalizations for everything that was difficult to understand, especially those who were deviant and particularly criminals.

The Judeo-Christian tradition introduced the concept of an omniscient, omnipresent, all-powerful God, which took hold in beliefs and practices throughout much of the world. Those who were followers believed the stories of the Old Testament and credited this God with the creation of the world, regarding Him as One who was able to tumble the walls of Jericho and to arrange the miracle of the Egyptian exodus. In all of this, there was no explanation other than an all-powerful God who could do anything He wanted to do.

During the Middle Ages in Europe, these beliefs, along with the concept of demonology, were fused into the political and social organization of the Church. The Inquisition became the symbol of the resulting theocracy, which justified witch hunting, cruel punishments, and suspension of state intervention in criminal justice proceedings. Crime and criminal behavior became the work of the Devil and those who were possessed could be dealt with in no other way than harshly and punitively, lest others be inflicted as though they were contagious.

Classical Criminology

As various governments became established and developed legal codes, especially in Europe, judicial authority became more and more arbitrary. Individual rights were nonexistent as the sovereignty of rulers and the aristocracy of the Church were almost totally absolute. Classical criminology represents that period of time, beginning just prior to the French Revolution in the 18th century, when a number of persons began to revolt against the many abuses of the legal codes.

Laws were ill-defined in matters relating to religious beliefs and how people ought to behave as citizens of the state. Those who ruled used these laws to convict and punish people for virtually any actions which went against the desires and wishes of those who were the most powerful. Those who served as the police were especially harsh, punitive, and repressive. They had virtual authority to arrest anyone and almost for any reason. They not only tried to repress crime, they were concerned with the political opinions and moral behaviors of the citizens. Spies operated regularly. The police arrested, judged, and punished their "victims." They also made extensive use of *lettres de cachet*, which meant that a person could be arrested by the police and then detained for an indefinite period of time on unspecified charges.

When those who were arrested finally were brought to trial, there was little justice. No person had the right to counsel, witnesses were questioned in secret, and the nature of the charge was seldom revealed. Torture was often used to extract confessions and, as we will discuss in the chapter on punishment, once the defendant confessed, the punishment often resulted in death. However, those who were of the noble class often escaped degrading punishments, while those who were of the servant class received the harshest punishments.

But it was also during the 18th century that "humanistic" thinking about people and their relationships to the state and society began to evolve. Philosophers began to write about reason, freedom, equality, and fraternity of mankind. The French and American Revolutions made extensive use of these ideas and the period became known as the Age of Enlightenment. The writings of Descartes, Voltaire, Montesquieu, and Diderot began to have impact on the practice of criminal law in Europe as they complained about injustice and judicial improprieties.

These writers appeared to be greatly optimistic about man's ability to reason and live freely. Rousseau, for example, believed that reason and common sense could be powerful tools to use against repression and corruption. They criticized the abuses of power which were flagrant and the use of superstition and demonism to legitimatize cruelty. They became known as the "social contract" writers. These "rebels" began to put forth a theory about the rights of man, his relationship to established authority, and the relationship between the two. Their starting point was an attempt to discover the "natural laws of the universe" and the application of reason to the study of human behavior. It was argued further that individual freedom was the most precious of all goods and that every man had the right to pursue freedom, provided he did not infringe upon the rights—and freedom—of others.

As these writers focused on the criminal law of the day, they criticized the severity with which justice was administered. Montesquieu and Voltaire, for example, believed that all citizens should be equal before the law and that the laws of the state should protect the individual. Picking up on these concepts of social justice, Cesare Bonesana, Marchese de Beccaria (1738-1794) and Jeremy Bentham (1748-1832) became very instrumental in reforming the legal systems in Europe, especially France and Italy.

Beccaria believed that the source of law was the legislature and not the judges (Beccaria, 1809:11). He believed in the principle of *free will*. This belief held that man, having full will to seek pleasure and avoid pain, would be motivated to avoid criminal behavior if he knew precisely what behaviors would not be tolerated by the state and what precisely he would receive in the way of punishments should those laws be violated. Translated into the French Code of 1791, the judge, as the lawful instrument of the legal system, would be responsible only for deciding the accused's guilt or innocence and then applying the specified punishments upon conviction. As a revolt against the caprices and whims of the Preclassical period, according to Gillin (1945:229), the judge would not be able to exercise any discretion, nor would he be able to consider any extenuating or mitigating circumstances of the violation in the case before him.

Beccaria was interested in crime control and believed that if the laws and punishments were precise, man would be deterred from violating them. He believed in the presumption of innocence, rather than guilt, which was summarized in the slogan that "it is better that ten guilty men escape than that one innocent man should suffer." However, because every person was responsible for his own behavior, it was believed he should also be held accountable for his misbehavior, especially his criminal acts.

Many European states revised their criminal codes as a result of the influence of these Classical writers. The French Code of 1791 and the Bavarian Code of 1813 were perhaps among the most significant. While the administration of justice became more manageable, there were also many difficulties in the application of criminal codes. Vold (1958:24) summarizes some of the problems:

> a. The complete ignoring of individual differences and the significance of particular situations. This was the ideal, probably never a reality but, obviously a point of controversy.
> b. The fact that it attempted to treat first offenders and repeaters exactly alike on the basis of the criminal act committed, not on the basis of what kind of individuals they might happen to be.
> c. The fact that minors, idiots, insane, and other incompetents were treated as though competent—on the basis of the act committed not

the personality of the offenders in determining guilt and the punishment that should be imposed.

Classical concepts, which waned as Positive criminology gained a foothold, have begun to receive attention in contemporary criminal justice. The notions that "the punishment should fit the crime," judges should not have so much discretion in sentencing, and "swift and sure punishment" have become popular once again. And, as criminal codes are being revised in the United States, these ideas are again being considered for implementation.

Neoclassical Criminology

Several writers during this period began to question some of the lack of discretion associated with Classical concepts. Although they did not disagree with the basic idea of free will, they did assert that not everyone should be held accountable for criminal behavior. As a consequence, they began to demand certain code revisions to take into consideration specific exceptions which, in effect, amounted to some attention to individual differences. Taft and England (1964:62) suggest that there were three basic exceptions:

   a. Children under age 7.
   b. Feebleminded persons.
   c. Extenuating circumstances.

These exceptions did imply that children under age 7, the feebleminded, and a few others did not have the free will to act responsibly. This absence of free will mitigated some of the guilt and hence some of the punishment for crimes. It is here that we also find premeditation introduced (under c above) as a measure of freedom of will (Vold 1958:25). Many of these Neoclassical revisions can be identified as having roots in biological and behavioral science disciplines which were gaining popularity at the time. They also resulted in the establishment of tests for criminal responsibility, such as the M'Naghten Rules, which, in effect (Caldwell, 1966:360), became ways of excusing some and protecting others from a harsh system of legal procedures. These Neoclassical concepts served, in part, as the basis for the development of Positive criminological concepts and remain as part of our contemporary system of criminal justice.

Positive Criminology

The Positive school was also called the "Italian school" because of the influence of three noted Italian scholars: Cesare Lombroso (1835-1904), Enrico Ferri (1856-1928), and Raffaele Garofalo (1852-1934). These writers all shared a common interest in the physical sciences, especially biology, and sought to apply physical science logic to the study of the criminal. Mannheim (1960:366-367) credits this Positive tradition in criminology with (1) the application of scientific methodology to the study of the criminal and (2) the substitution of a natural definition of crime for the legal definition. He states further (1960:366):

> The Classical School defined crime in legal terms; the Positive School rejected the legal definition of crime. The Classical School focused attention on crime as a legal entity; the Positive School focused attention on the act as a psychological entity. The Classical School emphasized free will; the Positive School emphasized determinism. The Classical School theorized that punishment had a deterrent effect, the Positive School said that punishment should be replaced by a scientific treatment of criminals calculated to protect society.

In the above we still see the emphasis on protection of society—or the control of crime—as the desired outcome, but the means to that end reflect the new Positivist *determinism*. This concept stated that man was not as free as the Classicists maintained. Instead, man was viewed as being controlled by his own mental and physical processes and by cultural processes which acted on him and determined his behavior. These were "pushes and pulls" or forces over which he had little or no control.

Chronologically, the Positive school of thought began in the 1800s with Cesare Lombroso, who, being heavily influenced by Darwinian evolution theory, looked at man primarily as a biological animal. As such, man was subject to genetic or hereditary forces and his behavior was a consequence of such forces. Based on such notions, Lombroso believed that the inferior criminal population was at a lower rung on the evolutionary ladder than noncriminals. He called criminals "atavistic throwbacks"—primitive humans. This belief led Lombroso to make extensive physiological comparisons of the cadavers of a number of violent criminals against prehistoric human body artifacts (Taft and England, 1964:64). Using very elementary scientific procedures, he found what he believed to be a physiological link between the criminal and prehistoric man. These findings, combined with the influence of the then blossoming fields of social causation, led him to propose the following classification scheme for criminal populations (Vold, 1958:30):

1. *BORN CRIMINALS.* Genetic throwbacks, identifiable by physical characteristics (one-third of offender population).
2. *INSANE CRIMINALS.* Mentally incompetent, alcoholics, imbeciles, and epileptics.
3. *CRIMINALOIDS.* Those not genetically inferior but who occasionally engage in vicious criminal behavior.

Lombroso's research activities, based on a denial of the free will principle, were to gain favor in the ensuing years and have served as the basis for most crime control procedures in contemporary society.

Enrico Ferri, one of Lombroso's pupils, added social, economic, and political determining forces to Lombroso's biological determinants. As Vold (1958:33) explains:

His original thesis was that crime is caused by a great number of factors, classified as (1) physical (race, climate, geographic location, seasonal effects, temperature etc.); (2) anthropological (age, sex, organic and psychological conditions etc.); and (3) social (density of population, customs, religion, organization of government economic and industrial conditions etc.).

Ferri's rationale for the control of crime was the removal of the above conditions (determining forces) which would then make crime less likely to occur (Taft and England, 1964:65). As a socialist, Ferri believed that the state should accept responsibility for reducing criminal activity and thus for reducing the effect the above factors had in the lives of the citizens of Italy. In fact, it can readily be seen how the political realities of a socialist state would easily allow for the implementation of so direct a mechanism for citizen control (Vold, 1958:35). Both Ferri and Lombroso provided theoretical principles based on a belief that man possessed a minimal amount of free will, but behaved instead because of various determining forces.

The third Positivist, Raffaele Garofalo, adds an interesting dimension to the works of Lombroso and Ferri. He expressed the belief that *knowledge* of right and wrong is bred into the human race by evolutionary processes (Garofalo: 1914:7–9). He said that everyone in society has the same frame of reference except the criminal, who is deficient in his ability to judge right from wrong. This lack of ability in the criminal then forces or determines him to violate two basic beliefs upon which society is based, including:

PROBITY—(virtue) which explains offenses against property, and
PITY—(compassion) which explains offenses against persons.

The claims of the Positivists were summarily refuted by Charles Goring (1919:iii-xvi, 9–33, 269–75) who comprehensively examined several thousand criminals and noncriminals in England. He found no indication that there were physical typologies which distinguished criminals from the noncriminal population and therefore no evidence for a genetically produced criminal type, as Lombroso originally maintained.

The Positivists, even though they believed that the criminal was such because of hereditary factors and that criminal behavior came about in ways beyond the control of individual violators, nonetheless also believed that criminals were a danger to society and needed to be controlled. Notwithstanding this belief, the criminal was still considered legally and socially responsible for his conduct. However, it meant that society should *reform* a convict rather than merely *punish* him for his criminal misconduct. The Positivists believed that they could control crime if they identified the needs of the individual offender and treated him accordingly. They proposed doing this on the scientific basis of observing criminals and determining appropriate means of treatment. They wanted to be humane and fair, but they were also concerned with protecting society from those who could not—or were unable—to control their own criminal behavior. They eventually believed that replacing the concept of guilt with that of dangerousness and rehabilitation could be applied not only to those who had already committed crimes, but also to those whose predetermined dangerousness was likely to continue.

It is the Positive tradition which remains with us today. Although the early works have been criticized for their lack of scientific rigor and for an overwhelming commitment to biological or hereditary forces, the traditions of examining forces which contribute to criminal behavior and for looking more at the criminal than the crime continue today. We will examine other theories of crime causation, which are all "naturalistic" or Positivistic in orientation, as well as some of the major criticisms leveled against them.

Other Biological Theories of Causation

Franz Joseph Gall (1758–1828) sought to base a biological type of theory on the thesis that the shape of a criminal's head is different from that of a noncriminal. He reasoned that since the mental facilities of the criminal mind were different from the noncriminal, the shape of the brain housing would be different. His efforts at proving his theory of "craniology" or "reading the bumps" was extended by Spurzheim (1776–1832) and finally labelled "phrenology" by Thomas Forster in 1815.

However, early proponents of the Lombroso tradition, not to be discounted, proposed numerous other physiological indicators of crime. Earnest Hooten believed that criminals and noncriminals differed in a number of physiological characteristics. He took body measurements of bathers on a Massachusetts beach, members of a military outfit, and firemen in Nashville, Tennessee. He concluded that the criminals were indeed biologically inferior to these law abiding persons and thus criminals, as a type, could be expected to succumb to the complex of environmental, biological, and social forces. He argued further that criminality could be reduced by the removal—or regeneration—of the criminal population (Hooten, 1939).

Hooten's research provoked considerable reaction and criticism. There was obvious bias in his sampling procedure: firemen and military men are probably more physically fit than inmates of a prison who are idle and have to eat food high in starch content. Hooten also was unable to substantiate many of his claims for genetic transmission of inferior traits. This left little doubt that his contributions to criminological science were of little if any real value toward understanding criminal causation.

William Sheldon and his associates at Harvard University sought to relate personality to body type only one year after Hooten's study was published. They developed three basic body types, which were considered to be associated with temperaments (Sheldon: 1940:236):

1. *Endomorphic-Viscerotonic:* a person having a soft round smooth body; generally favoring luxurious surroundings.
2. *Mesomorphic-Somatotonic:* a person having a large well-muscled body; generally active, assertive, and dynamic.
3. *Ectomorphic-Cerebrotonic:* a person having a delicate fragile body; generally characterized by allergies, chronic fatigue, sensitivity to noise and distractions, and seeking solitude.

Sheldon's view of body-personality interaction met with little support in criminological circles. In fact, many have argued that Sheldon never proved conclusively that such a direct correlation between body type and personality characteristics existed. The mode of attack on his work centered around the lack of substantiation of cross-cultural similarities of physical characteristics with personality. There was also some question in the minds of some theorists that this approach was a dangerous one in that the only remedies to a truly biologically determined criminal type might be biological eradication of these individuals from the gene pool of the human species (Barnes and Teeters, 1951:148).

Another biologically oriented theory centered on the notion that endocrine gland dysfunction could cause emotional instability leading to criminal behavior (Schlapp and Smith: 1928). While most theorists today agree that treatment of glandular problems can clear up *some* behavior problems, there is little evidence to prove that there is any more of a causal relationship between glandular dysfunctions in criminal populations than in the general population.

The Gluecks (1951 and 1956) attempted to integrate Sheldon's body typing theory with a "multifactoral social approach." They saw the delinquent (1956:249) as an impulsive individual who had a great deal of conflict with both parents, but generally with his father, and one who caused trouble at school. They related these social characteristics to the body type of the delinquent and concluded that a delinquent type of body makes a person more prone to fall into socially unacceptable behavior. Their findings have met with a great deal of controversy among other criminologists. The debate centers around two questions: (1) Do most or all delinquents have the delinquent body type? (The Gluecks' research indicates only a 60 percent chance of this.) (2) Is body typology the best way to explain delinquent behavior? Many researchers concluded, and it is almost totally believed today, that body type is not the primary causal agent of delinquent behavior nor the most efficient way of studying delinquent behavior.

Another biological theory is expressed in the current interest in XYY chromosome structure. Scientists, in locating this "supermale" chromosomal anomaly, have related it to criminality, since this factor has been found on occasion in the criminal population—at least in those who are incarcerated. In actuality, the incarcerated population has been the handiest to study, and this is the group upon which most early studies were conducted. Responding to the results of these early and some recent research studies, we note that a recent conference of scientists and criminologists concluded (Shah, 1970:5):

> The demonstration of the XYY karyotype in an individual does not, in our opinion, in our present state of knowledge, permit any definite conclusions to be drawn about the presence of mental disease or defect (including criminality) in that individual. A great deal of further scientific evidence is needed.

Further (1970:33), the conference report states:

> ... lacking rigorous ... studies in the general population, definite causal links between the XYY chromosome complement and deviant, criminal or violent behavior cannot be established ... Further, it seems unlikely that such variable and socially defined and determined problems as delinquency and crime, are primarily and directly linked with possession of an extra Y chromosome.

In general, there has been no definitive evidence substantiating a relationship between any biological factors and crime causation. The technical weakness of most research in this area apparently lies in appropriate sampling and statistical procedures, which, if they were more scientifically rigorous, *might* show a direct link between a biological factor and specific criminal behavior. This concept, however, continues to be researched—and by qualified scientists.

Psychoanalytic and Psychological Approaches

As the earlier discussion indicates, much controversy has arisen over the relationship between the behavior of the criminal and his biological and mental processes. The view that all criminal mentality rests on the question of sanity versus insanity resulted in mixed reactions from early researchers. Many researchers chose either a plan of trying to prove all criminals to be insane or of relating certain offenses with insanity. Once insanity or mental incompetence had been established, they believed, perhaps in the form of "feeblemindedness" or mental illness, treatment could be prescribed. For some treaters, the only answer was incarceration forever in a facility in order to control the criminal behavior of the individual. For others, it involved massive doses of psychiatric and psychological analysis. Whatever the treatment plan, the end result was determined by the efficiency of the treatment in its protection of society and its success in rehabilitating the criminal.

The roots of this rehabilitative approach began in the work of Lombroso, Garofalo, Ferri, and others who saw a biological cause of criminal behavior. Upon this groundwork, the works of Freud, Adler, Jung and other psychoanalysts took hold as providing some programs of treatment for particular criminological disorders. Basically, the thesis of these psychoanalytic writers was that within each person there is an internal mental struggle. Psychopathology occurred when the results of this struggle were unacceptable to the mind. These elements were then submerged in the *unconscious* portion of the mind to be held there by a mental censor. These repressed elements continued to try to be expressed and surfaced in the *conscious* mind. They sometimes did so in a disguised form (symbolic behavior) or in dreams while the individual slept. This internal struggle could result in criminal behavior, under certain conditions.

The expression of the conflict, these writers argued further, could result in the release of pent-up guilt and repression. This could take the form of criminal behavior as a way of allowing the criminal to punish himself in order to remove guilt. In effect, the criminal unconsciously wishes to be caught so that he can be punished and released from his guilt feelings. This interesting notion has been followed in the writings of Adler, Rank, and others who emphasize one aspect or another of this intra-psychic conflict. They have contributed a large volume of case research to explain step by step how this process takes place in the psyche.

Vold (1958:125) criticizes this psychoanalytic approach as a method for studying crime in that the data upon which the clinical diagnosis and treatment strategies are based are out of reach of objective measuring devices. He writes:

> A methodology (as in psychoanalysis) under which only the patient knows the "facts" of the case, and only the analyst understands the meaning of these "facts" as revealed to him by the patient, does not lend itself to external, third person, impersonal verification or to generalization beyond the limits of any particular case.

There seems to be an endless number of other explanations for the development of criminal mentality, perhaps as many explanations as there are criminals. However, there is continuing belief that the psychoanalytic model is valuable for explaining criminal behavior. It remains in vogue with many contemporary criminal justice treatment practitioners—witness the number of employed psychoanalytically oriented clinicians in courts and corrections—notwithstanding the failure of the psychoanalytic model to "rehabilitate" offenders (see Chapter 11).

The psychological approach had its origins in the rehabilitative concerns for the "feebleminded" or mentally deficient. Early psychological thought was aimed at relating mental aberrations to crime and thereby providing a solution to the problem of crime control and retraining the mentally deficient to be productive citizens. Early studies indicated that there might be a link between mental deficiency and criminal behavior (see, e.g., Goring, 1919:269–75). Albert Morel and Henry Maudsley both viewed the problem of criminal behavior directly as one of degeneracy. Moreover, with the development of intelligence tests, these investigators finally had a measuring tool to assess this alleged cause of crime.

Henry H. Goddard, Director of the New Jersey Training School for the Feebleminded at Vineland, was especially interested in the role of feeblemindedness in the causation of crime. After extensive tests, he concluded that feeblemindedness was responsible for a large portion of criminal behavior (Goddard, 1920:73). This view spread in the United States, but was challenged by many American psychologists. Goddard subsequently altered his thinking and admitted that anyone, not only the feebleminded, could be a potential delinquent (Elliott, 1952:327).

Following in Goddard's footsteps, users of intelligence tests to equate criminal activity with low I.Q. ratings believed they found some evidence to substantiate their claims. However, most of these attempts have since been labelled failures. To date, there is no valid or reliable proof of any relationship between feeblemindedness and any criminal population. In fact, Barnes and Schalloo (1940:688, 689) indicate that since we are only treating criminals who have been caught, the unapprehended "criminal class as a whole is more intelligent than the mass of our citizenry." Schuessler and Cressey (1950: 476–84) report on a survey of 113 studies of objective personality tests applied to delinquent and nondelinquent populations. They conclude that "as often as not the evidence favored the view that the personality traits are distributed in the criminal population in about the same way as in the general population." It should be noted here that the use of personality tests to diagnose illness is not being debunked, but that personality tests *per se* cannot be used to identify criminal types any more than any other kinds of tests.

Nevertheless, two additional studies regarding the use of personality tests for examining the differences between the personality make-up of criminals and noncriminals are worth mentioning. In research conducted by the Gluecks (Glueck: 1951), comparisons were drawn in a very carefully controlled study of 500 delinquent boys with 500 nondelinquent boys. These individuals were carefully matched for age, general intelligence, national origins, and residence in underprivileged neighborhoods. The Rorschach Ink Blot Test also was utilized, supplemented by psychiatric interviews. The similarities and differences as to the extent and nature of mental pathology indicated that the nondelinquent and delinquent groups were similar in terms of certain traits. These traits included feelings of insecurity, feelings of not being wanted or loved, and markedly good contacts with others. The Gluecks summarize the differences they found as well (Glueck, 1951:75):

> A meaningful pattern does tend to emerge from the interweaving of separately-spun strands: on the whole, delinquents are more extroverted, vivacious, impulsive, and less self-controlled than the non-delinquent. They are more hostile, resentful, defiant, suspicious, and destructive. They are less fearful of failure or defeat than the non-delinquent. They are less concerned about meeting conventional expectations, and are more ambivalent toward or less submissive to authority. They are, as a group, more socially assertive. To a greater extent than the control groups, they express feelings of not being recognized or appreciated.

Another study used the Minnesota Multiphasic Personality Inventory (MMPI) to differentiate the delinquent from the nondelinquent (Monachesi, 1948:487–500). Monachesi found that the differences between delinquents and nondelinquents on this personality scale are very small when measured at the mean level. His early work as a contribution to the field of behavioral psychology has been viewed as valuable, however it leaves us without an adequate explanation of any predictable behavior based on the findings of the MMPI.

The above psychiatric and psychological approaches both emphasize the role of the *abnormal personality* in delinquent or criminal behavior. There is some evidence that the criminal mentality, as with the mentality of individuals in all of society, may be at times somewhat abnormal. However, there is yet to be proved a causal relationship between the "abnormal personality" and the criminal act. Nonetheless, the influence of this basic approach in contemporary criminal justice remains a primary focus in crime control programming. The heavy reliance in corrections upon psychologists and psychiatrists for the development of treatment strategies indicates that psychology is a principal foundation for rehabilitative measures. While this is a fact, placing emphasis solely on psychological problems traditionally forces us to view criminality as an individualistic phenomenon. However, the influence of social groups upon the behavior of the individual, the role definition which that person finds in such groups, in conjunction with the psychological and psychiatric impressions, may lead to more understanding about causation of crime and delinquency. Yet, this remains unproved conjecture.

Sociological Approaches

Early students of criminal causation attempted to isolate biological, physiological, and social forces which produced criminal behavior. Studies in Europe in the 19th century were aimed at gathering and analyzing statistical data on crime rates and relating the findings to social conditions. A.M. Guerry first attempted to relate geographical dispersions of criminal behavior to the quality of social interaction. Gabriel Tarde advanced the theory that people learn criminal behavior by imitating criminals in their environment. Emile Durkheim stated that societies are naturally evolving and must possess some degree of freedom to evolve and that some persons, as a result, will abuse this freedom and become criminals (Barnes and Shalloo, 1940: 704). William A. Bonger, a Dutch criminologist, studied the writings of Karl Marx and, utilizing Marx's philosophy, traced the causes of crime to the capitalist economic system. Bonger said that man's behavior in such a system is *determined* by his environment and thus man does not possess free will. Bonger's work stimulated a great deal of activity among psychologists who tried to balance his concepts of "social determinism."

This early work in studying social forces tipped the scale of interest away from the biological approach. The problem, however, which modern students find with the above research work, is that of basic methodological weaknesses and some unsupported conclusions.

Studies of criminal activity, particularly in the United States, began to take on an *ecological* focus in the 1940s. The ecological approach studied crime in terms of the location of the criminal act in a given geographical area. Or, as Morris (1958:1) writes:

> Human or social ecology is concerned with the relationships which exist between people who share a common habitat or local territory and which are distinctly related to the character of the territory itself; it is a study of social structures in relation to the local environment.

The best known urban ecological survey was done by Clifford Shaw in Chicago. Shaw found that the delinquency rate varied inversely with distance from Chicago's Loop (downtown) district; that is, the further away you went from the Loop, the lower the rates of delinquency. He found this area physically deteriorated, with a high percentage of absentee landlords, large numbers of recent immigrants, and an absence of active social agencies (Shaw and McKay, 1931). His principal finding was that as industry moved into a residential area, the neighborhood became less and less an agent of social regulation. This idea is still considered actively by modern researchers, although Shaw's conclusions have been criticized on methodological grounds and because he over-generalized his findings. However, ecological studies have provided us with valuable data regarding the distribution of crime in urban, rural, and even national areas.

Thorsten Sellin, in *Culture Conflict and Crime* (1938:21-41), defined the causes of criminal behavior to be the result of conflict with social conduct norms. He stated that certain persons in a society lacked the "personality elements" which would allow them to accept the norms of the society. It, therefore, was the task of criminologists to isolate and define these "personality elements" for research purposes. This task, however, remained a difficult one, in that the elements which allowed for violation of the social norms were difficult if not impossible to identify and measure.

Robert Merton, in "Social Structure and Anomie" (1938), saw the primary causal force in crime as a tension between culturally defined goals, individual interests, and the way in which the social structure provided acceptable means for individuals to achieve these goals. In order for a person in society to achieve his goals, he had to participate in the society and be given the opportunity to achieve. Criminal behavior, according to Merton, occurred when opportunities to achieve were not open to all, which would result in illegitimate behavior on the part of some to reach goals. Crime and other forms of social deviation, therefore, interacted with societal norms. This produces "anomie" or a breakdown in the social structure. Merton argued that his theory accounted for certain kinds of crimes and delinquency, but he did not predict which individuals who did not have access to their goal objects would commit crimes.

Following this vein of thought, Albert Cohen (1955:25–157) maintained that there was a "nonutilitarian" subculture of delinquent juveniles who committed crimes as a reaction against their traditionally lower-class status. He reasoned that middle-class values were incorporated into the social structure, and lower-class individuals were denied opportunity to achieve these culturally defined goals. Lower-class individuals lacked the opportunity or access to tools which would allow them to compete successfully in society (success being defined in terms of the middle-class value system).

Sutherland argued that in order to study criminality in any organized way, the focus should be on the analysis of "systematic criminal behavior." In this way, we might understand criminal causation in light of all of the forces impinging on the criminal. Vold (1958:192) states that this has become one of the most respected of all sociological theories of crime causation. Originally developed by the late Edwin H. Sutherland, it was first published in 1939 and is commonly referred to as the "differential association" theory of criminality. Vold goes on to state (1958:192):

> (The theory) . . . is not especially unique or new . . . but it attempts a logical, systematic formulation of the chain of interrelations that makes crime reasonable and understandable as normal, learned behavior without having to resort to assumptions of biological or psychological deviance. It is peculiarly a "sociological theory" in that it centers attention on social relations—the frequency, intensity, and meaningfulness of association—rather than on the individual's qualities or traits, or on the characteristics of the external world of concrete and visible events.

In the 9th edition of Sutherland's text, *Criminology* (Sutherland and Cressey, 1974:75–77), the following nine propositions (which were modified last in 1947) describe Sutherland's concept of differential association. The description is quoted in considerable length since many sociologists subscribe to many parts of the concept.

1. *Criminal behavior is learned.* Negatively, this means that criminal behavior is not inherited, as such; also, the person who is not already trained in crime does not invent criminal behavior, just as a person does not make mechanical inventions unless he has had training in mechanics.

2. *Criminal behavior is learned in interaction with other persons in a process of communication.* This communication is verbal in many repects but includes also "the communication of gestures."

3. *The principal part of the learning of criminal behavior occurs within intimate personal groups.* Negatively, this means that the impersonal agencies of communication, such as movies and newspapers, play a relatively unimportant part in the genesis of criminal behavior.

4. *When criminal behavior is learned, the learning includes (a) techniques of committing the crime, which are sometimes very complicated, sometimes very simple; (b) the specific direction of motives, drives, rationalizations, and attitudes.*

5. *The specific direction of motives and drives is learned from definitions of the legal codes as favorable or unfavorable.* In some societies an individual is surrounded by persons who invariably define the legal codes as rules to be observed, while in others he is surrounded by persons whose definitions are favorable to the violation of the legal codes. In our American society these definitions are almost always mixed, with the consequence that we have culture conflict in relation to the legal codes.

6. *A person becomes delinquent because of an excess of definitions favorable to violation of law over definitions unfavorable to violation of law.* This is the principle of differential association. It refers to both criminal and anticriminal associations and has to do with counteracting forces. When persons become criminal, they do so because of contacts with criminal patterns and also because of isolation from anticriminal patterns. Any person inevitably assimilates the surrounding culture unless other patterns are in conflict; a southerner does not pronouce *r* because other southerners do not pronounce *r*. Negatively, this proposition of differential association means that associations which are neutral so far as crime is concerned have little or no effect on the genesis of criminal behavior. Much of the experience of a person is neutral in this sense, e.g., learning to brush one's teeth. This behavior has no negative or positive effect on criminal behavior except as it may be related to associations which are concerned with the legal codes. This neutral behavior is important especially as an occupier of the time of a child so that he is not in contact with criminal behavior during the time he is so engaged in the neutral behavior.

7. *Differential associations may vary in frequency, duration, priority, and intensity.* This means that associations with criminal behavior and also associations with anticriminal behavior vary in those respects. "Frequency" and "duration" as modalities of associations are obvious and need no explanation. "Priority" is assumed to be important in the sense that

lawful behavior developed in early childhood may persist throughout life, and also that delinquent behavior developed in early childhood may persist throughout life. This tendency, however has not been adequately demonstrated, and priority seems to be important principally through its selective influence. "Intensity" is not precisely defined, but it has to do with such things as the prestige of the source of a criminal or anticriminal pattern and with emotional reactions related to the associations. In a precise description of the criminal behavior of a person, these modalities would be rated in quantitative form and a mathematical ratio be reached. A formula in this sense has not been developed, and the development of such a formula would be extremely difficult.

8. *The process of learning criminal behavior by association with criminal and anticriminal patterns involves all of the mechanisms that are involved in any other learning.* Negatively, this means that the learning of criminal behavior is not restricted to the process of imitation. A person who is seduced, for instance, learns criminal behavior by association, but this process would not ordinarily be described as imitation.

9. *While criminal behavior is an expression of general needs and values, it is not explained by those general needs and values, since noncriminal behavior is an expression of the same needs and values.* Thieves generally steal in order to secure money, but likewise honest laborers work in order to secure money. The attempts by many scholars to explain criminal behavior by general drives and values, such as the happiness principle, striving for social status, the money motive, or frustration, have been, and must continue to be, futile, since they explain lawful behavior as completely as they explain criminal behavior. They are similar to respiration, which is necessary for any behavior, but which does not differentiate criminal from noncriminal behavior.

It is not necessary, at this level of explanation, to explain why a person has the associations he has; this certainly involves a complex of many things. In an area where the delinquency rate is high, a boy who is sociable, gregarious, active, and athletic is very likely to come in contact with the other boys in the neighborhood, learn delinquent behavior patterns from them, and become a criminal; in the same neighborhood the psychopathic boy who is isolated, introverted, and inert may remain at home, not become acquainted with the other boys in the neighborhood, and not become delinquent. In another situation, the sociable, athletic, aggressive boy may become a member of a scout troop and not become involved in delinquent behavior. The person's associations are determined in a general context of social organization. A child is ordinarily reared in a family; the place of residence of the family is determined largely by family income; and the delinquency rate is in many respects related to the rental value of the houses. Many other aspects of social organization affect the kinds of associations a person has.

The preceding explanation of criminal behavior purports to explain the criminal and noncriminal behavior of individual persons. As indicated earlier, it is possible to state sociological theories of criminal behavior which explain the criminality of a community, nation, or other group. The problem, when thus stated, is to account for variations in crime rates and involves a comparison of the crime rates of various groups or the crime rates of a particular group at different times. The explanation of a crime rate must be consistent with the explanation of the criminal behavior of the person, since the crime rate is a summary statement of the number of persons in the group who commit crimes and the frequency with which they commit crimes. One of the best explanations of crime rates from this point of view is that a high crime rate is due to social disorganization. The term *social disorganization* is not entirely satisfactory, and it seems preferable to substitute for it the term *differential social organization*. The postulate on which this theory is based, regardless of the name, is that crime is rooted in the social organization and is an expression of that social organization. A group may be organized for criminal behavior or organized against criminal behavior. Most communities are organized for both criminal and anticriminal behavior, and, in that sense the crime rate is an expression of the differential group organization. Differential group organization as an explanation of variations in crime rates is consistent with the differential association theory of the processes by which persons become criminals.

We can see in Sutherland's reasoning similar elements contained in the works of Cohen and Merton above. Sutherland's study of delinquent boys somewhat supports his nine statements, however there have been consistent attacks on this theory for its almost exclusive emphasis on environmental determinants of behavior. The criticisms are summarized by Caldwell (1965:218-219) as follows:

1. *The theory cannot be proved or disproved on the basis of scientific evidence.* Sutherland was not always clear in explaining whether he meant differential association to mean association with behavior patterns or association with criminals.

2. *The theory falls into the error of reductionism.* Sutherland did not address any of the variables in the complex of criminal behavior other than association.

3. *The theory's largely a speculative construct whose meaning is obscured by a vague terminology.* Sutherland's definitions of the behavior he examined were imprecise.

4. *The theory has produced a cult which interprets and reinterprets the theory of Sutherland to fend off attacks of critics.* The continual redefinition of the theory leaves it open to too many scientifically unfounded interpretations.

5. *The theory reflects the influence of the culture to which it is functionally related.* Sutherland may only be reacting to the importance for him of environmental determinants.

Sutherland's emphasis on social disorganization as a causal explanation of crime and delinquency has prompted some to attempt to develop positive (rather than negative) associations for offenders and potential offenders. A notable example has been the recent efforts to provide community-based programs for adults and juveniles so that they might learn socially acceptable forms of behavior from peers, who, apparently at least, attempt to behave according to minimal societal demands (see, e.g., Warren, 1970).

Cloward and Ohlin, in *Delinquency and Opportunity* (1961: 145–186), have merged Merton's notion of striving for achievable social goals and Sutherland's differential association theory into a "differential opportunity theory." This, according to them, results in three classes of subcultures in society: the *criminal*, the *conflict*, and the *retreatist*. Each subculture depends on the kinds of support systems that exist for the maintenance of the subcultures; i.e., if there is no support for criminal activity in the social system, a criminal subculture will not develop. The *criminal subculture* will develop where there are criminal role models available to emulate and where there exist some illegal means for achieving success. The *conflict subculture* exists where the route to attainment of economic and status goals is frustrated and results in conflict among members of the local society. The *retreatist subculture* is typified by drug usage and other social retreatist mechanisms which are used to escape the belief that neither legitimate nor illegitimate means of success can be found by members within the social groups. Critics of this explanation of social deviance find too much emphasis on status-awareness of the youth they describe and too little emphasis on other factors such as the family influence, ethnic background, and race (Caldwell, 1965:194).

In an effort to explain delinquent gang involvement, Walter Miller studied street corner gang society. He found, from an extensive survey of delinquent behavior, that (1958:17):

> ...the dominant component of the motivation of "delinquent" behavior engaged in by members of lower class corner groups involves a positive effort to achieve states, conditions or qualities valued within the actor's most significant cultural milieu.

He believed that delinquent expressions take the form of toughness, trouble, smartness, excitement, fate, and autonomy. These concerns are expressions of "maleness" by boys brought up in essentially female-based households. Miller is cautious in his theory, believing that these concerns explain only street corner gang delinquency and cannot explain all forms of delinquency. Bordua (1961:127–131) criticizes these findings, in part by stating that Miller over-emphasized lower-class cultural features in this form of delinquency and without enough corroborating data; that he derived causal explanations from the observation of behavior and then used them to explain the behavior. Miller's research findings are but one part of an extensive literature in this area of gang delinquency and the relationship of lower-class individuals to street corner society.

The various research reports and theories described above apparently prompted Reckless (1962) to argue that a general theory of delinquency causation is unrealistic since any one makes too many general statements about too many segments of society. Notwithstanding this complaint, he proposes a theory of "containment" which does not require the concept of any single or multiple cause. He theorizes (1962:131–134) that there is an *external containing social structure* which restricts individual activity and an *internal containing buffer system* which "protects people against deviation of the social and legal norms." He cites the family as an example of modern agents of external containment and the clan, neighborhood, village, caste, tribe, etc., as earlier sociological containment agents, all of which act as external buffers for the individual. Internal containment depends on an individual's concept of self and his personal strengths which allow him to bounce off other social forces which push or pull on him. He describes the existence of crime as due to weak external or internal buffers, which allow a person to be drawn or pushed into violating social norms since he has no need or mechanism for combating these forces. Critics of Reckless argue that he has not specified the environmental determinants accurately enough to predict criminal or norm-abiding behavior and thus, as a causal theory, there is much left to be desired.

David Matza (1964) theorizes that children "drift" into delinquent modes of behavior, not by an actual environmental push or pull, but through a "neutralization" of social norms. He believes that if an adolescent can say "Those laws don't belong to me," he has neutralized the effect the legal system has on guiding his behavior. The adolescent is then more likely to develop or seek out others having his same value system. But what exactly pushes or pulls one person into drift and into delinquent behavior, and another not, has not been satisfactorily defined, according to the critics of this theory.

The Future of Causal Explanations

Vold (1958:305) asserts that crime is such a varied phenomenon and theories of causation so varied themselves, that no real explanation for *all* crime and delinquency is possible. Furthermore, he states:

> Even as there is no generally satisfactory or completely adequate theory of human behavior in general, so there is no entirely adequate or generally accepted theory of criminal behavior.

Almost all students in the field of criminology agree that it is highly unlikely that any single theory of crime causation will ever satisfactorily explain the many varieties of behaviors that we label criminal or delinquent. Even though psychologists, psychiatrists, economists, lawyers, and sociologists continue to test theories and beliefs about causation, no single discipline nor any combination of interests is likely to produce the "final" answer. What is likely to occur, however, is a breaking out of kinds or types of criminality that may be explainable.

Vold (1958:314–315) summarizes the potential for criminological causal theory:

> It is not to be expected that criminological theory will develop wholly adequate and acceptable explanations of criminal behavior until the whole group of "the behavioral sciences" reaches a corresponding adequacy of theoretical explanation of human behavior in general. The criminal will continue to be a human being, and his behavior will be only in degree and in special ways different from that of the non-criminal. Hence, criminological theory and human behavior theory in general may be expected to make relatively parallel developments.

References

Barnes, Harry and J.P. Shalloo
  1940   Modern Theories of Criminology and Penology. New York: Appleton-Century-Crofts.

Barnes, Harry and Negley Teeters
1951   New Horizons in Criminology. 2nd ed. Englewood Cliffs, New Jersey: Prentice-Hall.

Beccaria, Cesare
1809   Essays on Crimes and Punishment. New York: Stephen Gould.

Bordua, David J.
1961   "Delinquent Subcultures: Sociological Interpretations of Gang Delinquency." Annals of the American Academy of Political and Social Science 338 (November):119-136.

Caldwell, Robert G.
1965   Criminology. 2nd ed. New York: Ronald Press.

Cloward, Richard A. and Lloyd E. Ohlin
1960   Delinquency and Opportunity: A Theory of Delinquent Gangs. Glencoe, Ill.: The Free Press.

Cohen, Albert K.
1955   Delinquent Boys. Glencoe, Ill.: The Free Press.

Elliott, Mabel A.
1952   Crime in Modern Society. New York: Harper and Row.

Garofalo, Raffaele
1914   Criminology. Boston: Little, Brown and Co.

Gillin, John
1945   Criminology and Penology. New York: Appleton-Century-Crofts.

Glueck, Sheldon and Eleanor
1951   Unraveling Juvenile Delinquency. Cambridge, Mass.: Harvard University Press.

1956   Physique and Delinquency. New York: Harper and Brothers.

Goddard, Henry H.
1920   Human Efficiency and Levels of Intelligence. Princeton, New Jersey: Princeton University Press.

Goring, Charles
1919   The English Convict. London: His Majesty's Stationery Office.

Hooten, Earnest
1939   Crime and the Man. Cambridge, Mass.: Harvard University Press.

Mannheim, Hermann
1960   Pioneers in Criminology. Chicago: Quadrangle Books.

Matza, David
1964   Delinquency and Drift. New York: John Wiley and Sons.

Merton, Robert K.
1938   "Social Structure and Anomie." American Sociological Review (October) 3:672-682.

Miller, Walter B.
1958   "Lower Class Culture as a Generating Milieu of Gang Delinquency." Journal of Social Issues 14:5-19.

Monachesi, E.D.
1948   "Some Personality Characteristics of Delinquents and Non-

Delinquents." Journal of Criminal Law and Criminology 38 (January/February):487-500.

Morris, Terence
1958   The Criminal Area. London: Routledge and Kegan Paul.

Reckless, Walter
1962   "A Non-Causal Explanation: Containment Theory." Excerpta Criminologica (March/April):131-134.

Schlapp, Max G. and Edward H. Smith
1928   The New Criminology. New York: Liveright.

Schuessler, Karl and Donald R. Cressey
1950   "Personality Characteristics of Criminals." American Journal of Sociology 55 (March):476-484.

Sellin, Thorsten
1938   Culture Conflict and Crime. New York: Social Science Research Bulletin 41.

Shah, Saleem A.
1970   Report on the XYY Chromosomal Abnormality. Rockville, Maryland: National Institute of Mental Health.

Shaw, Clifford and Henry McKay
1931   Social Factors in Juvenile Delinquency. Report on Causes of Crime, Vol. II. Wickersham Commission. Washington, D.C.: U.S. Government Printing Office.

Sheldon, William et al.
1940   Varieties of Human Physique. New York: Harper and Row.

Sutherland, Edwin H. and Donald R. Cressey
1974   Criminology. 9th ed. Philadelphia: J.B. Lippincott Co.

Taft, Donald and Ralph England
1964   Criminology. New York: Macmillan and Co.

Tarde, Gabriel
1912   Penal Philosophy. Boston: Little, Brown and Co.

Vold, George
1958   Theoretical Criminology. New York: Oxford University Press.

Warren, Marguerite Q.
1970   Correctional Treatment in Community Settings. Rockville, Maryland: National Institute of Mental Health.

CHAPTER 8

CRIMINAL JUSTICE OVERVIEW

The Criminal Justice Nonsystem

Most authors in the field of criminal justice administration appear to accept, without discussion, the "fact" that a criminal justice system does exist in the United States today. Either it has not been a matter of speculation or it has not been an issue with which they want to get involved. Writers go about their business of discussing specific problems and issues, each imploring, from the world of academics or practice, that his or her pet idea, formulation, or theory be accepted, or suggesting that others' ideas be rejected. These writings, in part, have contributed incrementally to the body of criminal justice knowledge, but they have not substantially, individually, or collectively, answered the question of whether or not a true system actually exists.

The President's Commission on Law Enforcement and Administration of Justice accepted the "fact" that criminal justice administration in the United States has been operating as a system, even though the Commission enumerates in elegant and considerable detail difficulties, problems, and issues associated with the concept. The Commission stated, for example, "Any analysis of the criminal justice *system* is hampered by a lack of appropriate data" (emphasis added) (1967:263).

The Commission's final report, *Challenge of Crime in a Free Society* (1967:261), also states: "The criminal justice *system* is an enormous complex of operations. Subjecting such a *system* to scientific investigation normally involves making changes in its operations in order to observe the effects directly" (emphases added).

The National Advisory Commission on Criminal Justice Standards and Goals continues to accept the "fact" of the existence of a system, even titling one of its volumes *Criminal Justice System*. This Commission's summary report, *A National Strategy to Reduce Crime* (1973:41), discusses numerous issues and problems associated with the system, including the nature and quality of manpower training, and concludes: "'Fragmented,' 'divided,' 'splintered,' and 'decentralized' are the adjectives most commonly used to describe the American *system* of criminal justice. . . . Words such as fragmented and divided, however, refer not only to demarcations in authority, but to differences in states of mind, and not only to physical distances, but to distances in philosophy and outlook" (emphasis added). As the last statement suggests, the Standards Commission and the President's Crime Commission decry the failure of the "system" to develop a philosophy of operations or a commonly accepted statement of goals and objectives.

Some authors in recent years have begun to challenge the system notion. They write from both theoretical as well as practical points of view that a "system" of criminal justice administration does not exist in the United States at this time. Bilek (1973:85–87) comments that a system does not exist and suggests that such a state of affairs has implications for criminal justice administration's apparent ". . . ineffective and inefficient operation (which) exacerbates the problem of high crime urban areas . . ."

Sigurdson *et al.* (1971) report that the failure to have a system results in impediments to effective planning. The American Bar Association (1972:1), which has recently taken an active role in studying and changing the administration of criminal justice services, refers to the "nonsystem" of criminal justice as it is practiced in the United States today.

One of the most comprehensive statements challenging the idea of a criminal justice "system" appears in *Law and Order Reconsidered*, a staff report to the National Commission on the Causes and Prevention of Violence (The Eisenhower Commission). In a paper presented to the Commission, Professor Daniel J. Freed (1969:366) writes:

> It is commonly assumed that ... three components—law enforcement (police, sheriffs, marshals), the judicial process (judges, prosecutors, defense lawyers) and corrections (prison officials, probation and parole officers)—add up to a "system" of criminal justice. The system, however, is a myth.
>
> A system implies some unity of purpose and organized interrelationships among component parts. In the typical American city and state, and under federal jurisdiction as well, no such relationship exists. There is, instead, a reasonably well-defined criminal process, a continuum through which each offender may pass: from the hands of the police, to the jurisdiction of the courts, behind the walls of a prison, then back onto the street. The inefficiency, fallout, and failure of purpose during this process is notorious.

What is a System?

It would appear that these authors are correct in describing the array (or disarray) of criminal justice services in the United States today as not being a system, or for being, in actuality, a nonsystem. Buckley (1967:41), a well-known authority on systems theory and one who has written extensively on the subject, defines a "system." Although he does not address the problems of systems as they may be associated with the delivery of criminal justice services, his definition is most apt:

> ... (a) system ... may be described generally as a complex of elements or components directly or indirectly related in a causal network, such that each component is related to at least some others in a more or less stable way within any particular period of time.... The particular kinds of more or less stable interrelationships of components that become established at any time constitute the particular structure of the system at that time, thus achieving a kind of "whole" with some degree of continuity and boundary.

While there are considerable disagreements concerning models, theories, and concepts associated with the notion of "systems" (see, e.g., Boulding, 1956; von Bertalanffy, 1962; and Buckley, 1968), all seem to agree that a systemic approach to organizational study must address such issues as interrelationships and goals. Thus, as we examine the criminal justice system or nonsystem, these factors, at least, are of essential importance. Without an understanding of how individuals and organizations relate to and among each other and without an understanding of the significance of goals, we cannot possibly understand the administration of criminal justice and its myriad of problems, conflicts, issues, and services.

Discussion regarding the evolution of criminal justice services and whether the network of such services constitutes a system or non-system would be a mere academic exercise were it not for the serious implications such an issue has for practical operations and policy making. That is, it would constitute no more than an interesting theoretical discussion were it not for the fact that the so-called criminal justice system has failed to understand and control crime, in part, simply because it is just not a system. Were it a genuine system, we probably would be much further along in our efforts.

A value judgment is implied in the above assertion that the network of criminal justice services in the United States would indeed be better were it a system, or that more progress could be made toward crime control if we were able to bring these currently disjointed services into a genuine system. That such a state of affairs is or would be beneficial must be explored further.

The Dangers of a True System

For example, if it were possible to bring all services and programs together and achieve a commonly accepted statement of objectives—e.g., eradication of crime—then it is possible that the accepted and acceptable techniques for such eradication would become controlling. With control accepted as a viable means for bringing about crime reduction by law enforcement, courts, and corrections, it is entirely possible that society could become very repressive and suppressive of its citizens. This philosophy could lead to the rejection of all forms of deviance, including criminality, whether they be of a "political" nature or not.

Durkheim (1950) has commented on the need for a healthy society to have some crime if it is to change and prosper. He does not advocate the increase of crime, in a conventional sense, but he does indicate that a society free of crime is not only impossible, it is undesirable. In a unified, goal-directed system, where crime control becomes the primary objective, it is possible that means could supplant ends and the democratic form of government, as a consequence, would be diminished. In a unified system, where all components are so interrelated that conflict is minimal, it is also possible that the current checks and balances now available in the nonsystem, and which partially serve to protect clients, would also diminish, to the detriment of democracy in general and individual liberty in particular.

The creation of a system in criminal justice administration in the United States today will require the development and maintenance of a genuine dialogue among and between the potential component parts of the system. Thus, police will have to speak more often with judges, probation officials with prosecutors, and defense attorneys with victims. In addition, all units of the system will have to speak with the clients of the various services and the public and in ways which heretofore have not been seen as necessary. A genuine dialogue, of course, would in and of itself be beneficial, for all of these components have not truly communicated before.

The danger, however, is that the powerful within the potential system are more likely to have their operational philosophies and goals accepted, leaving the meek and less powerful (and those outside the system—i.e. the public) without adequate voice in their own affairs. The result of unification then would not be a genuine system; it is more likely to result in a totalitarian organizational state, with the clients and the victims, in all probability, continuing to be the least heard and the least important.

Although the above represents conditions which might result from systematizing the criminal justice network of services, no one can say for sure what would actually happen. But, if the above represents a reasonable point of view on what could occur, then it is also reasonable to conclude that a "system" of criminal justice administration in the United States should not be our goal. At least, it should not be our goal until and unless these issues are resolved.

If it is desirable to develop a true system of service from the currently disjointed network of criminal justice programs, then a concerted effort will have to be made by practitioners and theorists alike. Not only will disparate groups have to engage in meaningful dialogue, but responsible persons will have to take into consideration the development of a goal which will serve not only the best interests of society, but the clients and victims of the system as well. In short, if a system is ever achieved, its services must reflect adequately the needs of *all* segments of society.

A Process for Systematization

It is highly unlikely that a true system will evolve in criminal justice administration in the United States in the immediate future. This is so, in the author's opinion, because there are too many vested interests, differing philosophies on how best to control crime and criminals, petty jealousies among top-level administrators, an overall lack of commitment for the creation of such a system, a genuine lack of leadership in the field, and citizen uninvolvement.

Although such a system may never come to fruition, and even though it might not be desirable, it is still possible that benefits could accrue if there at least were some efforts at systematization. Through greater coordination and integration of efforts, it may be possible to come closer to a real system, provided that problems, issues, philosophies, and concerns are dealt with honestly, meaningfully, and appropriately.

As reasonable and responsible officials commit themselves to systematization efforts, it is also possible that more positive and constructive interrelationships among and between individual persons and their agencies would accrue, not only for their collective benefit, but also for the welfare of the clients and communities they are supposed to serve. If responsible officials truly work at systematization in this way, they will refute the notion, according to some, that there is little leadership in the field.

We are willing to conclude, therefore, that systematizing the network of criminal justice services, even though there are some inherent dangers, nonetheless and on balance, probably could lead to greater effectiveness (not just efficiency) of services, as well as more balanced concerns for the needs and welfare of all of the component parts (Cohn, 1974).

Intramural Conflicts

The Standards Commission, in its report, *Criminal Justice System* (1973:1), suggests that one of the principal barriers to systematization of the network of criminal justice agencies is that of "intramural conflicts among the various components . . . " These conflicts lie in the differing roles and goals of police, courts, and correctional agencies, even though all are supposed to be concerned with the "formal responsibility to control crime." The need for cooperation among agencies appears to be indisputable, but the ways in which they should be working together and developing consensual philosophies and goals are not always clear. The President's Crime Commission (*Task Force Report: Science and Technology*, 1967:53) puts it this way:

> Police, court and corrections officials all share the objective of reducing crime. But each uses different, sometimes conflicting, methods and so focuses frequently on inconsistent subobjectives. The police role, for example, is focused on deterrence. Most modern correctional thinking, on the other hand, focuses on rehabilitation and argues that placing the offender back into society under a supervised community treatment program provides the best chance for his rehabilitation as a law-abiding citizen. But community treatment may involve some loss of deterrent effect, and the ready arrest of marginal offenders, intended to heighten deterrence, may by affixing a criminal label complicate rehabilitation. The latent conflicts between the parts may not be apparent from the viewpoint of either subsystem, but there is an obvious need to balance and rationalize them so as to achieve optimum overall effectiveness.

Most agencies in the network of criminal justice services enunciate some kind of underlying philosophy or goal statement, but they may not be too clear, may be contradictory, are frequently developed without any consideration of their "ripple" effects on other agencies, and are not always understood by the line workers (Cohn, 1972). In law enforcement, for example, Manning (1971:159) states that police agencies work at contradictory objectives: ensuring public order *and* protecting individual rights. Balbus (1973:25), in discussing the courts, suggests that the primary interests are those of order, formal rationality, and organizational maintenance (survival). While he is primarily concerned with correctional treatment, Martinson (1966:279) comments that corrections " . . . implicitly contains a built-in program for reform with no maximum limit except the 'logical' one of the total reduction of recidivism."

Wolfgang (1972:15–16), after examining the lack of consensual goals and the impact such absence has on systematizing criminal justice, states that this condition has contributed to failure and unaccountability:

> This so-called system is not a corporate entity. Its only allegiance is to itself. It has no moral conscience, no need to report to its immediate neigh-

> bors, let alone external agents . . . All parts of the criminal justice system
> should be accountable to the public at large, to the victim, and to the of-
> fender. Moreover, each subpart of the system should be accountable to the
> immediately preceding subpart . . .
>
> What we are getting is excessive accounting within each subsystem to
> such an extent that the basic and original functions are dissipated.

In the final analysis, according to Langan and Anderson (1975:
2), programmatic success is almost impossible to determine, not only
for each agency with the subsystem, but for the system itself.

Processing Offenders

The President's Crime Commission (*Task Force Report: Science and
Technology*, 1967:56) states that the first step in developing a system model for criminal justice " . . . is to describe in detail the events
that occur as offenders are processed through the system." Such a
model is that proposed in Figure 8.1, which is described by the Commission as very simplified and which may differ in many respects
from the realities in many jurisdictions.

Throughout the various stages in processing an offender through
the system, it is possible for an accused person to be diverted, dismissed, acquitted, discharged, or otherwise released to the general
population. Based on 2,780,000 Index Crimes reported to the police
in 1965, as illustrated in Figure 8.2, we find that only 727,000 arrests
were made, for a total of 26 percent of reported crime. Only 160,000,
or 22 percent of those arrested, were sentenced, which amounts to
less than 6 percent of the crimes reported. This drop-out process is
known as the "funneling effect." (The figures approximate those for
1974.) As Newman (1975:104) suggests, "As a system criminal justice can best be seen by what it does, or fails to do, rather than how
it is put together."

Although there are numerous parts and subparts in the processing of offenders, once a law has been enacted making certain behavior a crime, and that behavior is either observed by or reported to the
police, there are four critical junctures or decision-making points
which follow: arrest, indictment, trial, and sentence. Some of the
critical decisions which are made, as subparts, involve diversion,
arraignment, pretrial motions and hearings, bail, release, and appeals.

At each of these critical junctures, significant decisions are made about and for the offender and it is possible that he can "funnel" out of the system at any time.

Arrest

After the police have investigated a reported crime and have determined that they have reason to believe that a specific person has indeed committed the offense, the police may seize that person, i.e., make an arrest. The arrest is unlawful if the police lack probable cause (reasonable grounds) to believe that an offense has been committed by the person arrested. As soon as a person is arrested, i.e., taken into physical custody, he is to be transported to a police station where he is *booked*; that is, the offense and the accused are registered, and often fingerprinted and photographed. In some jurisdictions, the police may make arrests for misdemeanors (as contrasted with felonies) if they lack a warrant if the crime is committed in the "presence" of the policeman. The police are required to make an arrest for misdemeanors or felonies when a *warrant* is issued by a judge. This occurs when a complainant identifies someone as having committed an offense. In some minor offense categories, especially traffic, the police may issue a *citation*, which is an order to the suspect to appear before a judge in a particular court at a specified time in the future.

The police exercise wide latitude in making arrests because they have considerable discretion (LaFave, 1965; Goldman, 1963; Davis, 1969). Once an arrest has been made, and prior to any in-custody interrogation, the police *must* inform a suspect of his right to remain silent, that any statement may be used against him in court, that he has the right to the presence of his attorney before and during interrogation, and that counsel will be appointed for him if he is indigent. This right to counsel came about as a result of a Supreme Court decision, *Miranda* v. *Arizona* (384 U.S. 436) in 1966. Newman (1975: 165) summarizes the basis for the ruling as follows:

> The *Miranda* case . . . (involved a confession) following interrogation by the police in the absence of defense counsel. The Supreme Court held such confessions to be improperly obtained not because of any specific "third-degree" tactics of the police, but because the entire aura and atmosphere of police interrogation without notification of rights and an offer of assistance of counsel tends to "subjugate the individual to the will of his examiner."

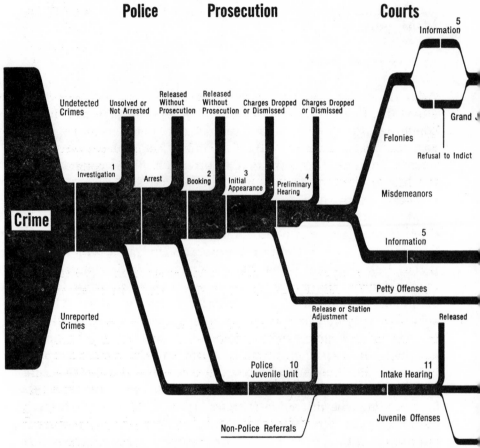

Police   Prosecution   Courts

This chart seeks to present a simple yet comprehensive view of the movement of cases through the criminal justice system. Procedures in individual jurisdictions may vary from the pattern shown here. The differing weights of line indicate the relative volumes of cases disposed of at various points in the system, but this is only suggestive since no nationwide data of this sort exist.

Figure 8-1. A General View of the Criminal Justice System. Source: President's Commission on Law Enforcement and Administration of Justice. *Task Force Report: Science and Technology*. Washington, D.C.: U.S. Government Printing Office, 1967, pp. 58-59.

1 May continue until trial.

2 Administrative record of arrest. First step at which temporary release on bail may be available.

3 Before magistrate, commissioner, or justice of peace. Formal notice of charge, advice of rights. Bail set. Summary trials for petty offenses usually conducted here without further processing.

4 Preliminary testing of evidence against defendant. Charge may be reduced. No separate preliminary hearing for misdemeanors in some systems.

5 Charge filed by prosecutor on basis of information submitted by police or citizens. Alternative to grand jury indictment; often used in felonies, almost always in misdemeanors.

6 Reviews whether Government evidence sufficient to justify trial. Some States have no grand jury system; others seldom use it.

Corrections

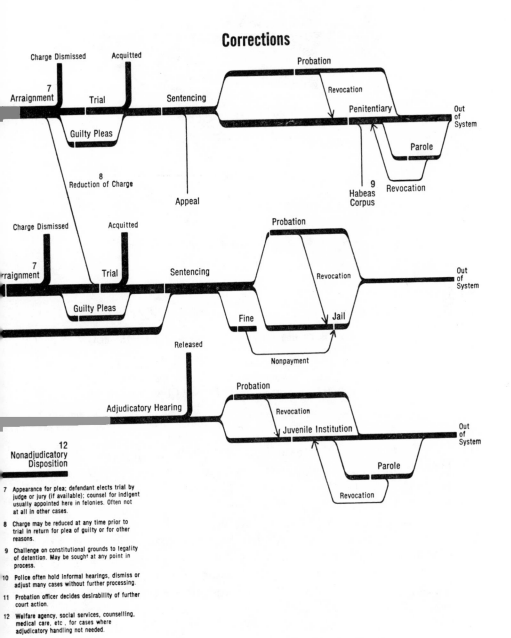

Charge Dismissed   Acquitted

Probation

7
Arraignment   Trial   Sentencing

Revocation

Penitentiary

Out
of
System

Guilty Pleas

Parole

8
Reduction of Charge

Appeal

9
Habeas
Corpus

Revocation

Charge Dismissed   Acquitted

Probation

7
rraignment   Trial   Sentencing

Revocation

Out
of
System

Guilty Pleas

Fine   Jail

Released

Nonpayment

Probation

Adjudicatory Hearing

Revocation

Juvenile Institution

Out
of
System

12
Nonadjudicatory
Disposition

Parole

Revocation

7 Appearance for plea; defendant elects trial by
   judge or jury (if available); counsel for indigent
   usually appointed here in felonies. Often not
   at all in other cases.

8 Charge may be reduced at any time prior to
   trial in return for plea of guilty or for other
   reasons.

9 Challenge on constitutional grounds to legality
   of detention. May be sought at any point in
   process.

10 Police often hold informal hearings, dismiss or
   adjust many cases without further processing.

11 Probation officer decides desirability of further
   court action.

12 Welfare agency, social services, counselling,
   medical care, etc , for cases where
   adjudicatory handling not needed.

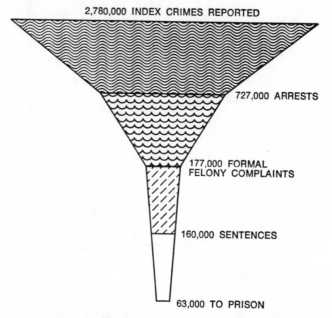

2,780,000 INDEX CRIMES REPORTED

727,000 ARRESTS

177,000 FORMAL
FELONY COMPLAINTS

160,000 SENTENCES

63,000 TO PRISON

Figure 8-2. Funneling Effect from Reported Crimes Through
Prison Sentence.
Source: President's Commission on Law Enforcement and Adminis-
tration of Justice. *Task Force Report: Science and Technology.*
Washington, D.C.: U.S. Government Printing Office, 1967, p. 61.

After a suspect is taken into custody, for a felony and for some
misdemeanors, he is fingerprinted and photographed. The fingerprints
are sent to the FBI for its files and to determine if the suspect is
wanted elsewhere for any other crimes.

After a suspect is arrested and booked, the law requires that he
be taken before a judicial authority for bail consideration. It is at this
time that a decision is reached whether or not the suspect is likely to
flee the jurisdiction or otherwise avoid appearance at future proceedings, in contrast to willingly returning to the court for future
proceedings. Reasonable bail may be set, or the suspect may be released on his own *recognizance*. That is, he promises to reappear at a
later date. This is known as ROR. For persons accused of some misdemeanors, especially traffic violations, a trial may be conducted or a
plea of guilty may be accepted at this initial appearance before a
judicial authority. For felons, only a bail determination hearing is

conducted at this time and a suspect is not required to enter a plea. The actual plea will be made at the time of *arraignment*.

The police then forward their evidence to the prosecuting attorney to determine if probable cause actually existed to arrest the suspect and to translate the facts of the case into proper statutory language. The prosecutor also makes a determination as to whether or not the evidence accumulated is sufficient to go to trial. If a decision is made to go to trial, the next step is to prepare formal charges.

Indictment

An *indictment* is the formal charge used to initiate prosecution, which comes about after the prosecutor presents evidence to a grand jury. Grand juries operate in secrecy with neither the suspect nor his counsel present. The prosecutor appears before the grand jury, presents his case, and asks for an indictment. If the grand jury believes that there is sufficient evidence to bring the suspect to trial for a specific offense, by a majority vote it will indict to the charge specified, to some other charge, or it has the right not to indict at all.

In states that have abolished grand juries and in many other states that have retained them, the prosecutor may bring formal charges against a suspect by issuing *an information*. Following his arrest, the accused is entitled to a *preliminary hearing*, which is a judicial examination into the existence of probable cause to believe that a crime has been committed. Here, in the presence of the defendant and his counsel, the prosecutor lays out at least some of his evidence, which details the probable cause for the belief that the particular defendant did indeed commit a specific crime. Witnesses may be presented and cross-examined. If the court rules that there is sufficient evidence that the suspect committed the offense, the way is cleared for further proceedings. If the court rules the evidence insufficient, the accused may be released or discharged. Contrary to popular beliefs, except for the insufficiency of evidence, few cases at this level in the legal procedures are actually thrown out of court for "technical reasons." For that matter, comparatively very few cases are overturned in appellate proceedings.

After an indictment or information has been issued against the accused, he is asked to plead to the charges at the arraignment. He may enter a plea of "not guilty" or "guilty." In many jurisdictions, he is also entitled to a plea of *nolo contendere*, which simply means that he is not contesting the prosecutor's charges contained in the bill of particulars. As Newman indicates (1975:108), the plea of *nolo contendere* "... has the same criminal effect as a plea of guilty, but unlike the latter, may not be used in any subsequent civil action as proof that the defendant committed the act."

A defendant may refuse to enter any plea, in which case a plea of not guilty is entered for him. Furthermore, a judge may refuse to accept a guilty plea, enter a plea of not guilty instead, and insist that the defendant go to trial. If a guilty plea is entered, there is no formal trial and the judge proceeds to sentence the defendant then, or at a later date if a presentence investigation by the probation department is requested or is required by law. A defendant may also petition the court to change his plea, especially if he had originally pleaded guilty and has decided that he wants a trial. He may also, at any time, enter a motion to change the plea from not guilty to guilty, especially in order to speed up the proceedings or to obtain leniency in sentencing. It is up to the court to accept or reject such motions for changes in the pleadings; denial of such a motion may be the basis for appeal.

Plea Bargaining

At any time during these proceedings, especially in felony cases, the defense counsel and the prosecutor may engage in the practice of *plea bargaining*. This involves a negotiation between the prosecutor and the defense over the charge and the pleading. It is common for defense counsel and the defendant to enter a plea of guilty in exchange for a reduction of the charges to an offense which carries a lesser penalty, or one which is more likely to result in probation rather than imprisonment for the defendant.

Some pleas that result from negotiation do not result in a change in the charge. Instead, for example, the prosecution may agree to recommend a specific sentence to the judge in exchange for a plea. Although this recommendation is not binding on the court, it is common for the judge to follow such recommendations. In these cases, the defendant is trading his right to trial for a promise from the prosecutor that he will attempt to influence the sentence.

The Standards Commission (*Courts*, 1973:43) points out that:

Under some circumstances, plea negotiation raises the danger that innocent persons will be convicted of criminal offenses. Underlying many plea negotiations is the understanding—or threat—that if the defendant goes to trial and is convicted he will be dealt with more harshly than would be the case had he pleaded guilty. An innocent defendant might be persuaded that the harsher sentence he must face if he is unable to prove his innocence at trial means that it is to his best interests to plead guilty despite his innocence. If these persons have a realistic chance of being acquitted at trial, a plea negotiation system that encourages them to forfeit their right to trial endangers their right to an accurate and fair determination of guilt or innocence . . . (as a result) the Commission believes that the manner in which plea negotiation is conducted in many jurisdictions creates a significant danger that (due process) . . . interests will be violated.

Despite the dangers inherent in plea bargaining practices, many experts believe that some kind of plea bargaining is inevitable and desirable and that efforts should be directed toward improving it rather than eliminating it. This is the position of both the President's Crime Commission and the American Bar Association (*Pleas of Guilty*, 1968). The Supreme Court has tended to approve plea bargaining, provided that the plea is intelligently and voluntarily made by the defendant (*Boykin* v. *Alabama*, 395 U.S. 238 [1969]; *McCarthy* v. *United States*, 394 U.S. 459 [1969]). In *Santobello* v. *New York* (404 U.S. 257 [1971]) the Supreme Court ruled that the negotiated plea, if entered upon a prosecutor's promise that the defendant will be given relief as a result of the plea of guilty, must be kept or the defendant is entitled to withdraw the plea of guilty. In the *Santobello* case, the Supreme Court also indicated that plea bargaining, if properly and constitutionally executed, can have important effects in reducing crowded court dockets and removing some of the risks and uncertainties for defense and prosecution that occur at actual trial.

Notwithstanding the above, the Standards Commission (*Courts*, 1973:46) recommends that by 1978 plea bargaining should be abolished completely.

Standard 3.1
Abolition of Plea Negotiation

As soon as possible, but in no event later than 1978, negotiations between prosecutors and defendants—either personally or through their attorneys—concerning concessions to be made in return for guilty pleas should be prohibited. In the event that the prosecution makes a recommendation as to sentence, it should not be affected by the willingness of the defendant to plead guilty to some or all of the offenses with which he is charged. A plea of guilty should not be considered by the court in determining the sentence to be imposed.

Until plea negotiations are eliminated as recommended in this standard, such negotiations and the entry of pleas pursuant to the resulting agreements should be permitted only under a procedure embodying the safeguards contained in the remaining standards in this chapter.

However, since the Commission also recognizes that the abolition of plea bargaining may take many years to effectuate, it recommends that seven other standards be accepted in the interim. These standards involve the following (*Courts*, 1973:50–65): (1) a record should be made of the plea and the agreement, (2) there should be uniformity in plea negotiation policies and practices, (3) there should be a time limit placed on the practice, (4) the accused should always be represented by counsel during negotiations, (5) the prosecutor should never coerce or induce the defendant to enter into plea bargaining, (6) the court should never enter into the negotiations, and (7) sentencing by the court should not in any way be influenced by the presence or absence of plea bargaining.

Trial

Along with plea bargaining, which can occur at any time up to and even during a trial itself, another condition which applies is the right of defense to enter *pretrial motions*. These deal with many legal and procedural issues, such as the validity of arrests, searches and seizures, the jurisdiction of the court to hear the case, and/or prejudicial pretrial publicity and the opportunity to obtain a fair trial. It is the latter situation which results in a request for a *change in venue*, which is merely a request to transfer the trial to another locality. In such motions, the defense may also ask the prosecution to reveal its evidence or the names of witnesses. The denial by the trial court of any of these motions may be the basis for an appeal.

For the defendant who enters a plea of not guilty, the next step in the process is that of the trial itself. In all felony cases, the defendant has the right to a trial by jury, which is available to misdemeanants usually only if the potential penalty exceeds six months. Although he has the right to trial by jury, the defendant may waive it and ask that the case be presented only before the judge.

Regardless of whether the trial proceeds before a judge alone or before a jury, the procedures which are to be followed tend to be very well defined in each jurisdiction. This has come about as a result of constitutional and statutory provisions, court rules, and appellate decisions. Guilt must always be established beyond a reasonable doubt and based on evidence which is properly and legally presented before the court. It is the responsibility of the prosecution to convince the court of the defendant's guilt; the defense need only deny the charges but he may rebut the evidence against him if he chooses. The defendant himself need not testify if he does not wish to.

The Standards Commission (*Courts*, 1973:103) expresses considerable concern over the usual delays in preparing for trial and actually conducting the trial. In fact, it recommends that the trial should be conducted within 46 days after the arrest of the suspect. (See Figure 8.3.)

The Standards Commission (*Courts*, 1973:103) suggests that considerable time could be saved during actual trials if the prosecution and defense engaged in less "oratory" and if the courts operated on a full-time basis and for full eight-hour working days.

Standard 4.15
Trial of Criminal Cases

In every court where trials of criminal cases are being conducted, daily sessions should commence promptly at 9 a.m. and continue until 5 p.m. unless business before the court is concluded at an earlier time and it is too late in the day to begin another trial. Jury selection in the next case should start as soon as the jury in the preceding case has retired to consider a verdict.

All criminal trials should conform to the following:

1. Opening statements to the jury by counsel should be limited to a clear, nonargumentative statement of the evidence to be presented to the jury.

2. Evidence admitted should be strictly limited to that which is directly relevant and material to the issues being litigated. Repetition should be avoided.

3. Summations or closing statements by counsel should be limited to the issues raised by evidence submitted during trial and should be subject to time limits established by the judge.

THE LITIGATED CASE: FROM ARREST TO TRIAL

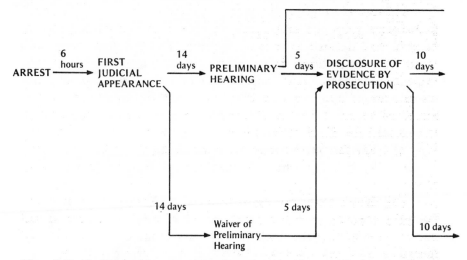

Figure 8-3. The Litigated Case: From Arrest to Trial.
Source: National Advisory Commission on Criminal Justice Standards and Goals. *Courts.*
Washington, D.C.: U.S. Government Printing Office, 1973, pp. xx–xxi.

4. Standardized instructions should be utilized in all criminal trials as far as is practicable. Requests by counsel for specific instructions should be made at, or before, commencement of the trial. Final assembling of instructions should be completed by support personnel under the court's direction prior to the completion of the presentation of the evidence.

The American Bar Association Project on Standards for Criminal Justice (1974:271–274) has also expressed considerable concern over trial procedures in the United States and recommends most strongly that there should be a "speedy trial" wherever possible. What the definition of a speedy trial is, however, remains open to debate. The Supreme Court has made several rulings on the subject in its attempt to interpret the Sixth Amendment right to speedy trial in federal courts and in 1967 it looked at the situation in the states (*Klopfer* v. *North Carolina*, 87 Sup. Ct. 988). However, as the ABA points out (1974:272):

Most states have enacted statutes setting forth the time within which a defendant must be tried following the date he was arrested, held to answer, committed, or indicted, and it is these statutes which have received prin-

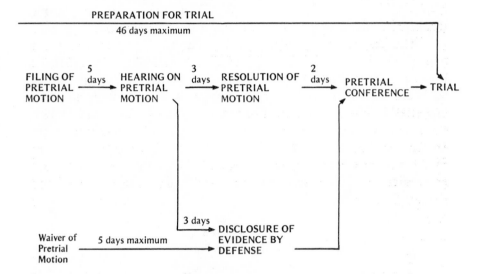

PREPARATION FOR TRIAL

46 days maximum

FILING OF PRETRIAL MOTION → 5 days → HEARING ON PRETRIAL MOTION → 3 days → RESOLUTION OF PRETRIAL MOTION → 2 days → PRETRIAL CONFERENCE → TRIAL

3 days → DISCLOSURE OF EVIDENCE BY DEFENSE

Waiver of Pretrial Motion — 5 days maximum →

cipal attention. If a statutory violation is found, there is seldom any inquiry into the alleged constitutional denial; and if the statute has not been violated, it is typically assumed that the constitution is satisfied. There exists considerable variety and uncertainty in these statutes on such matters as when the time begins running, what defendants are covered, and what the consequences of excessive delay are.

If the case is presented before a jury, when all evidence and testimony have been given, the jury will retire to meet in secrecy to determine the guilt or innocence of the accused. Most states require that guilt be determined by a unanimous verdict, but this may change as a result of the *Williams* v. *Florida* (399 U.S. 78, 100) decision of the Supreme Court in 1970, which said that states may allow other than unanimous verdicts in certain kinds of cases.

The selection and role of the jury also are issues under scrutiny. Some experts urge total abolition of the jury, but others think the process for jury selection can be improved. All adult citizens in a jurisdiction are subject to be called to serve as jurors, with the exception of such persons as convicted felons, the insane, and members of certain professions. Either the prosecution or the defense, however, may eliminate a potential juror if cause for such elimination can be established. This will happen if, for example, bias on the part of the

potential juror is discovered. Each side is also given the right to eliminate a specified number of jurors without having to give any reasons;
this is called the exercise of the *peremptory challenge.*

The Standards Commission has issued several recommendations,
one of which states that the size of the jury should be less than 12,
but more than 6 in all cases except those which can result in life
imprisonment. It argues that the 12-person jury requirement for criminal trials has been an accident of history. It cites (*Courts*, 1973:101)
the *Williams* decision, which states that the guiding principle should
be whether the group is "large enough to promote group deliberation,
free from outside attempts at intimidation, and to provide a fair
possibility for obtaining a representative cross-section of the community."

Standard 4.14

Jury Size and Composition

> Juries in criminal prosecutions for offenses not punishable by life
> imprisonment should be composed of less than 12 but of at least six
> persons. If a 12-member jury has been seated, a reduction in jury size
> during the course of a trail to not less than 10 members should be per-
> mitted where a jury member has died or is discharged for illness or other
> good cause. Corresponding decreases in size should be permitted in cases
> where there were less than 12 jurors initially, but no decrease should be
> permitted that will result in a jury of less than six persons.
>
> Persons 18 years of age and older should not be disqualified from jury
> service on the basis of age.

The question of whether or not any jury can be impartial and
render justice has been asked by numerous researchers in the field
of criminology. Defense counsel and prosecution alike have long
thought that certain kinds of individuals are "needed" on a jury if
the verdict is to be favorable to either side in the adversary proceedings. As a consequence, in some very notorious trials, large-scale
computer calculations have been developed in order to test what the
"ideal" composition of the jury should be; that is, ideal in terms of
which side you are on. Adler (1974:127–128) summarizes what we
know and the results of her own research on the subject:

> Many of our present (jury) selection systems introduce biases and raise
> questions about impartiality. Before we can decide on the importance of
> the issue it is crucial to approximate just how dependent a verdict is on the
> representativeness of the jury. Prior research has found that nationality,

race, and religion of jurors all play a crucial part in the rendering of a verdict. In the present research, it was found that socio-economic level
appears, however, to be the most important single extralegal factor associated with jury decisions. . . . The findings that discrepancy in occupational status between juror and defendant is related to trial outcome
provide evidence as to the critical importance of the jury selection process.

Sentencing

In *Sentencing Alternatives and Procedures* (1968:1), the American
Bar Association Project on Standards for Criminal Justice states:

> The consequences of a sentence are of the highest order. If too short or
> of the wrong type, it can deprive the law of its effectiveness and result in
> the premature release of a dangerous criminal. If too severe or improperly
> conceived, it can reinforce the criminal tendencies of the defendant and
> lead to a new offense by one who otherwise might not have offended so
> seriously again.

Sentencing is viewed as a very complex issue and one that involves not only the law, but judicial beliefs and temperaments as well.
It occurs after a conviction at a trial or the entry of a guilty plea.
Sentences are generally pronounced by the judge, but according to
Newman (1975:110–111), 12 states provide for jury sentencing in
noncapital cases, and in some jurisdictions, "Sentencing councils of
three or more judges may confer concerning sentencing alternatives."
Glaser *et al.* (1966:1) review the history of the criminal sentence and indicate that state legislatures began to restrict the discretion of judges in sentencing by specifying penalties for each offense.
As a consequence, many criminal codes provide for the minimum and
maximum penalties that may be imposed on a convicted offender,
but this, too, permits considerable discretion on the part of the sentencing authority. The court's discretion leads to *disparity* in sentencing simply because each judge makes his own determination as to
what penalty he will impose within the range of alternatives legally
allowed him. Glaser *et al.* (1966:3) state:

> It can be demonstrated statistically that judges within a single jurisdiction
> will vary markedly in the average sentence they impose, and in the type
> and severity of their sentences, even where cases are assigned in rotation,
> so they all receive a similar cross section. Sentencing disparity contributes
> to the maxim of criminal law practice, that the best way to serve a client
> who is criminal is to study the judges, not the law.

In most instances, there are several alternatives normally open to the court with regard to sentencing, including fine, order for restitution, probation, or institutional commitment. In some jurisdictions, it is possible to impose a *split sentence*. This means that the sentence may include both a period of incarceration and probation. A defendant may also receive combinations of the above sentences when he is convicted on several offenses at the same trial.

In Ohio, the judge has an opportunity to combine incarceration and probation, not in the usual sense of a split sentence, but as a result of a 1965 law popularly called *shock probation*. This law (Friday *et al.*, 1973:3) is a form of sentence which permits the judge to sentence a defendant to a specific period of incarceration in order to "'shock' and 'jolt' the individual into a realization of the realities of prison life . . ." The law is basically designed as a "treatment" tool and it makes any convicted felon eligible for early release ". . . provided he had not committed an act which would make him ineligible for probation in the State of Ohio" (Friday *et al.*, 1973:5).

Unlike the provisions of most split sentences, such as the federal model, shock probation is not part of the original sentence. According to the law, the offender is sentenced to a correctional facility and then he must file a petition to the court to suspend further execution of the sentence. This cannot be done any earlier than 30 days nor more than 60 days after the original sentence date. By law, the court must respond to the petition within 90 days of its receipt. The researchers of the law and its effects (Friday *et al.*, 1973:10) conclude that the data ". . . indicate that shock probation as a mechanism of crime control does hold some promise . . . (however,) success is concentrated . . . in the young . . . (and) the previously convicted, but not hard core, offender."

Ohio also has a new law commonly referred to as *shock parole*, by which a sentenced offender who already has been incarcerated can be released, not to probation status, but to parole status in a manner similar to that used for shock probation. In this instance, however, it is the paroling authority, not the judge, who makes the determination. Shock parole is the release of an inmate much earlier than he or she would have been released by normal parole release procedures. The effect is to mitigate the severity of the original sentence and provide an offender an opportunity to "adjust in the community," but it is too early to determine the actual success of this new law.

Where judges impose sentences as a result of mandatory requirements of the law, there tends to be less disparity, even though many
judges are ingenious in finding legal loopholes. For example, almost
all sentences can be judicially suspended. This means that even though
a sentence has been imposed, it will not be carried out. A judge may
even suspend part of the sentence and thereby reduce its severity.
But where the judge has the power to impose any sentence, within
minimum and maximum constraints, a great deal of disparity exists.
Sentencing decisions are usually viewed as not subject to judicial
review except for procedural irregularities during the sentencing.

In a paper examining judicial bias in sentencing and whether or
not the indeterminate sentence reduces such bias, Cargan and Coates
(1974:153) conclude that "... the indeterminate sentence, which
permits a judge the opportunity of committing an offender to the
supervision of a state authority and usually for imprisonment (in the
case of adult offenders) for an indefinite period, is not viewed by
many experts as being constitutionally sound. Even though a sentenced offender cannot do more time than the statutory maximum,
some have complained that it causes a great morale problem in the
prison since the offender does not know when he will be released. At
least with parole, he knows when he is eligible for consideration. In
the indeterminate sentence, eligibility for release is dependent upon
the decision-making of nonjudicial personnel, who supposedly make
scientifically and clinically valid judgments."

The indeterminate sentence is primarily used for delinquents
and youthful offenders. It is rarely used in sentencing adults simply
because most states have not enacted legislation authorizing its use.
While indeterminate commitment has been used with great frequency
in civil law to commit the mentally ill and retarded, in adult criminal
justice it tends to be used only for "defective" criminals and for
special offender categories, such as drug addicts and violent sex offenders. Although its use has been designed to protect the community, Tappan (1960:436) states: "... its primary aim is the care of
the defective and the cure, where possible, of those individuals whose
ills can be diagnosed with some precision." He goes on to state (1960:
436):

> These persons differ significantly from criminals, who display no specific
> pathology and for whom no effective clinical treatment techniques have
> been found ... (Because we lack) the knowledge, techniques and per-

sonnel to attempt this wholly clinical, positivistic approach to the criminal ... we have preferred the compromise of partially indefinite sentences in which minimum and maximum terms are fixed, with the time of release determined by a paroling authority.

Postconviction Remedies

Defendants generally may appeal their convictions to a higher court; usually such actions must be instituted within a specified period of time after conviction. For the most part, appellate courts will only review questions of law and then primarily on the issue of whether or not the trial judge himself made an error of law. These include an improper ruling by the judge with regard to the admission or exclusion of evidence, an error in the instructions to the jury, and an error related to the judge's judgment with regard to evidence or the verdict. An example of the latter error is when a judge allows the jury to decide a matter when no evidence has been submitted by the prosecution on that point. If such evidence is missing at the trial and the jury finds the defendant guilty, then the judge should not accept the verdict of the jury. If he does accept the verdict of the jury, then, as in the other situations of error, the conviction is subject to reversal on appeal.

The appellate process is time consuming and generally very expensive to bring to a conclusion. This is so if for no other reason than a case generally has to move through all of the state courts before it can reach the U.S. Supreme Court. However, before a case can move from state to federal review, state remedies must have been utilized. As we will discuss in the chapter on courts, it may be up to the appellate court to decide if it wants to hear the case. The review of the case in the appellate court does not include a new trial before it. The appellate court merely reviews transcripts, reads briefs submitted by both sides, and hears oral arguments if the court wishes to hear them.

In addition to concerns over law, appeals also deal with such issues as sentencing conditions, and they vary among the jurisdictions as to their nature and process. A defendant may challenge the fact that he is in custody or the conditions of custody that he finds himself in as a result of the conviction. As Newman (1975:228) points out, "Appeal of custody is commonly initiated by one of a variety of forms of the writ of *habeas corpus* (literally 'you have the body,' that is, the person in custody who must be presented to the court)." It is otherwise known as "The Great Writ" and it has been used with increasing frequency in attempts to secure the release of offenders already in custody or imprisoned.

Release

Most misdemeanants serve their full terms of imprisonment. This is so because their terms tend to be relatively short (generally less than one year) and because there generally is no paroling authority at the local level either to process their cases or provide supervision of them in the community. Felons, on the other hand, generally obtain their release from prison as a result of decisions made by a paroling authority. Some, however, actually finish their full terms and are released without any kind of supervision by agents of a criminal justice organization.

It is possible to "early discharge" or release probationers and parolees prior to the expiration of their specific sentences. This is not commonly arranged by their probation or parole officers because of the paperwork involved or because it is not traditionally done in their agencies. For those on probation, this must be approved by the sentencing judge; for those on parole, it must be ordered by the paroling authority.

As we discuss in the probation and parole chapters, some persons violate the condition of probation and parole or otherwise commit new offenses and are *technically violated*. If a probationer refuses to cooperate or fails to keep his appointments, as examples, the probation officer may bring him back to the court, detail the violations, and the judge may revoke the original sentence and commit him to a term of imprisonment, if he chooses. In the case of parolees, similar kinds of charges can be brought against them and the paroling authority has the power to revoke parole and send them back to prison to finish their original terms. Except for early discharge, probation, and parole, the only other way one is released from supervision is to complete the original term and thereby be eligible for complete discharge from sentence.

Records

Although almost all juvenile records are sealed and unavailable for public examination, this is not so for adults. Adult offenders, even though they have "done their time," remain subject to many stigmas and must carry the consequences of their criminal behavior with them for the rest of their lives. Especially for felons, these consequences can be severe, leaving them ineligible to vote, unable to obtain certain kinds of employment or licenses, or prohibited from working in certain professions. A lawyer, for example, if convicted of a felony, is likely to be barred from practicing law.

It is possible to have certain rights restored after a period of time subsequent to release from supervision, but this is a legally complicated process that frequently takes a great deal of time. If someone is officially *pardoned*, however, his guilt and conviction are removed from the books and all of his legal rights are thereby restored automatically. In some jurisdictions, the process of *expungement* is made available to ex-offenders. This is the legal way of destroying records concerning the conviction and may be accomplished by sealing the records so that there is theoretically no way of anyone obtaining information about the arrest, conviction, and sentence. Expungement appears to be increasing in popularity as a tool for removing criminal information from the books, especially for youthful offenders and those who have been "crime free" for a period of at least five years subsequent to their discharge from the last sentence. Both the President's Crime Commission (*Task Force Report: Corrections*, 1967:88–89) and the ABA Project on Standards for Criminal Justice state that there should be some process for softening the stigmatizing effects of having done time for those who successfully adjust in society. The ABA (Probation, 1970:54, 56), in fact, puts it this way:

> Every jurisdiction should have a method by which the collateral effects of a criminal record can be avoided or mitigated following the successful completion of a term . . . (under supervision).
> (We are) . . . not as concerned with the form which such statutes take as (we are) . . . concerned with the principle that flexibility should be built into the system and that effective ways should be devised to mitigate the scarlet letter effect of a conviction once the offender has satisfactorily adjusted.

References

Adler, Freda
  1974   "Empathy as a Factor in Determining Jury Verdicts." Criminology 12 (May) 1:127-128.
American Bar Association
  1968   Sentencing Alternatives and Procedures. Chicago: ABA Project on Standards for Criminal Justice.

  1968   Pleas of Guilty. New York: ABA Project on Standards for Criminal Justice.

  1970   Standards Relating to Probation. Chicago: ABA Project on Standards for Criminal Justice.

  1972   New Perspectives on Urban Crime. Washington, D.C.: ABA Special Committee on Crime Prevention and Control.

  1973   Quest for Justice: A Report of the Commission on a National Institute of Justice, Washington, D.C.: ABA.

  1974   Standards Relating to the Administration of Justice. Chicago: ABA Project on Standards for Criminal Justice.
Balbus, Isaac D.
  1973   The Dialectics of Legal Repression: Black Rebels before the American Criminal Courts. New York: Russell Sage.
Bilek, A.J.
  1973   "America's Criminal Justice System—A Diagnosis and Prognosis." In The Change Process in Criminal Justice. Washington, D.C.: LEAA:85-110.
Boulding, Kenneth
  1956   "General Systems Theory—The Skeleton of Science." Management Science 2:197-208.
Buckley, Walter
  1967   Sociology and Modern Systems Theory. Englewood Cliffs, New Jersey: Prentice-Hall.

  1968   (ed.) Modern Systems Research for the Behavioral Scientist: A Sourcebook. Chicago: Aldine Publishing Co.
Cargan, Leonard and Mary A. Coates
  1974   "The Indeterminate Sentence and Judicial Bias." Crime and Delinquency 20 (April) 2:144-156.
Cohn, Alvin W.
  1972   "Decision-Making in the Administration of Probation Services: A Descriptive Study of the Probation Manager." D. Crim. Dissertation. Berkeley, California: School of Criminology, University of California. (Mimeo).

  1974   "Training in the Criminal Justice Nonsystem." Federal Probation 38 (June) 2:32-37.

Davis, Kenneth C.
1969   Discretionary Justice. Baton Rouge: Louisiana State University Press.

Durkheim, Emile
1950   Rules of Sociological Method. 8th ed. Trans. by Sarah H. Solvay and John H. Mueller. Ed. by G.E.G. Catlin. Glencoe, Ill.: The Free Press.

Freed, Daniel J.
1969   "The Nonsystem of Criminal Justice." In J.S. Campbell, J.R. Sahid, and D.P. Stang (eds.). Law and Order Reconsidered: A Staff Report to the National Commission on the Causes and Prevention of Violence. Washington, D.C.: U.S. Government Printing Office: 265–284.

Friday, Paul C., D.M. Petersen, and H.E. Allen
1973   "Shock Probation: A New Approach to Crime Control." Georgia Journal of Corrections 1 (July):1–13.

Glaser, Daniel, F. Cohen, and V. O'Leary
1966   The Sentencing and Parole Process. Washington, D.C.: U.S. Government Printing Office.

Goldman, Nathan
1963   The Differential Selection of Juvenile Offenders for Court Appearance. New York: National Council on Crime and Delinquency.

LaFave, Wayne R.
1965   Arrest: The Decision to Take a Suspect into Custody. Boston: Little, Brown and Co.

Langan, Patrick A. and Etta A. Anderson
1975   "Problems of Administering Evaluative Research in Agencies of the Criminal Justice System." Paper prepared for the 1975 meeting of the American Sociological Association (mimeo).

Manning, Peter K.
1971   "The Police: Mandate, Strategies and Appearance." In J. Douglas (ed.) Crime and Justice in American Society. New York: Bobbs-Merrill: 149–193.

Martinson, Robert
1966   "The Age of Treatment: Some Implications of the Custody-Treatment Dimension." Issues in Criminology 2 (Fall):275–293.

National Advisory Commission on Criminal Justice Standards and Goals
1973   A National Strategy to Reduce Crime. Washington, D.C.: U.S. Government Printing Office.

Newman, Donald J.
1975   Introduction to Criminal Justice. Philadelphia: J.B. Lippincott Co.

President's Commission on Law Enforcement and Administration of Justice
1967   Challenge of Crime in a Free Society. Washington, D.C.: U.S. Government Printing Office.

1967   Task Force Report: Science and Technology. Washington, D.C.:
         U.S. Government Printing Office.

1967   Task Force Report: Corrections. Washington, D.C.: U.S. Govern-
         ment Printing Office.
Sigurdson, E., R.M. Carter, and A. McEachern
1971   "Methodological Impediments to Comprehensive Criminal Justice
         Planning." Criminology 9:246-267.
Tappan, Paul W.
1960   Crime, Justice and Correction. New York: McGraw-Hill.
von Bertalanffy, Ludwig
1962   "General Systems Theory—A Critical Review." General Systems
         7:1-20.
Wolfgang, Marvin E.
1972   "Making the Criminal Justice System Accountable." Crime and
         Delinquency 18 (January) 1:15-22.

CHAPTER 9

police

Historical Development

A number of years ago, a famous chief of police in Berkeley, California described the expectations the average person in the United States has of a policeman (Bain, 1939:5):

> The citizen expects police officers to have the wisdom of Solomon, the courage of David, the strength of Samson, the patience of Job, the leadership of Moses, the kindness of the Good Samaritan, the strategical training of Alexander, the faith of Daniel, the diplomacy of Lincoln, the tolerance of the Carpenter of Nazareth, and, finally, an intimate knowledge of every branch of the natural, biological, and social sciences. If he had all these, he might be a good policeman!

The consequences of the contemporary policeman's failure to demonstrate all of the above qualities has been discussed, analyzed, and researched over the years. However, we have arrived at no single consensus as to what constitutes a "good" policeman nor are we even sure what the function of modern policing should be. Except for some anarchists, we at least can be certain that almost all citizens want some kind of policing in their communities; the primary question is how that policing should be delivered to the communities being served.

Policing, as an executive branch of government service, is a relatively modern phenomenon. Although it has historical roots, the type of "law enforcement" that is practiced today throughout this country can be traced directly to the famous Metropolitan Police Act, which was passed in London in 1828. The first 1,000 metropolitan policemen were hired one year later. They had both day and night duty, were called "Peelers," "Lobsters," or "Bobbies," after Sir Robert Peel who had led the investigations concerning crime prevention in England, but they were not particularly well-liked as the program was developed.

The history of policing or law enforcement is not easily recounted. Although every society, civilized and primitive alike, has had its rules, regulations, norms, and traditions, it is not clear how all societies dealt with offenders and violators on an organized basis. For the most part, early history tells us that there were no police departments as we know them today. As a matter of fact, "policing" was a private matter. As we have previously discussed, it was the responsibility of individuals, clans, tribes, or families to right any wrongs committed against them. Rulers, kings, military officials, elders, magistrates, and judges were also concerned with violations of the "law," but for centuries no one was employed to enforce the law.

Except for the Laws of Hammurabi (2100 B.C.) which dealt with how people were to enforce their laws in Babylon and the Praefectura Urbis in Rome and Constantinople, we know very little about the development of law enforcement practices in the world until the 5th century A.D. It was about that time that Germanic tribes were invaded by the Romano-Celtic people of England. As the Anglo-Saxons developed communities called *tuns* (from which the word "town" is derived), a form of individual and group responsibility for policing began to evolve (Germann *et al.*, 1962:41).

In 785 A.D., the *Capitularies of Charlemagne* were issued in France, which organized the enforcement of the law through the feudal lord. France, at that time, was divided into geographical areas called *contes* (counties), supervised by an agent of the king known as a *conte* (count). Approximately 100 years later, the Marshals of France, who were responsible to the king for the maintenance of order and security in the country (Germann *et al.*, 1962:42), ". . . developed a body of armed men known as 'marechaussee,' whence come the gendarmerie which police France today."

Anglo-Saxon England gradually became more sophisticated and organized in terms of community development and citizen responsibility for obeying the laws. Trial by ordeal (survival tests), trial by combat, compurgation (taking serious oaths), branding, restitution, and involuntary servitude (slavery) became common characteristics of the "criminal justice system."

Based on the 7th century French system of *Frank-Pledge*—a method of establishing the responsibility of each man for his neighbor and of the group for each man—the English *borh* and *tithing system* was created. This was a program designed to establish a local system of justice and to protect each community from raiding tribes. A group of 10 families composed of freemen was called a *tithing*. A *tithingman* was elected by the group and it was his responsibility to "raise the hue and cry" and for delivering punishment to offenders. The *hue and cry* was the system by which all able-bodied men in the tithing joined together in the common chase for offenders. (It serves as the basis of what we currently call a citizen's arrest.) In the laws of Edgar (959–975 A.D.), according to Germann *et al.* (1962:43), the *tithingman* was called a peace official and probably served as the basis in Great Britain for police officials being known more as keepers of the peace than as law enforcement officials.

Every 10 tithings was referred to as a *hundred*, the leader of which was called a *reeve*. The person responsible for looking after the equipment, materials, and weapons of the hundred was known as a *high constable. Petty constables* were appointed for smaller units within the hundred, the towns, and parishes. As policing increased within the towns, the constable emerged as the principal peace officer. A group of hundreds formed a *shire*, which became the equivalent of a county and its chief was known as a *shire-reeve*, from which the word "sheriff" is derived. The shire-reeve became a very important official in England, for he was appointed by a nobleman or the king, who gave him powerful military and judicial responsibilities.

Germann *et al.* (1962:44) summarize the early English developments in peace keeping as follows:

This system came into existence between the seventh and ninth centuries. Alfred the Great, who made one nation of England in the latter part of the ninth century, found the system of great benefit in unifying the nation. Later, William the Conqueror refined the system to a great degree.

The system, however, had serious flaws. It was applicable to emergency situations, and worked well in an agrarian community where people were content to live in one place. When urban society began to develop, and people began to move about, the tithing system was difficult to keep intact. It also had a very serious defect in that it tended to encourage the concealment of crime and perjury in order that individual members of a tithing, or the tithing itself, might not have to make restitution for the acts of a tithing member.

Because of the disputes which began to arise between individuals and the inability of appointed officials to maintain the "king's peace," courts may have begun to develop. However, it is more likely that these courts developed to keep people from fighting with one another so that they could fight in the king's armies—rather than to settle disputes fairly and equitably (Korn and McCorkle, 1965).

Protection of Property

As societies and civilizations gained greater footholds in Europe, more and more people began to own possessions and property. Since it was believed that every freeman had the right to own such material goods and real estate, it became everyone's responsibility to protect what was personally owned and, concomitantly, theft came to be regarded as a serious offense. If someone did steal or commit any other offense, in England at least, it became appropriate to assume that it was everyone's responsibility to apprehend the wrongdoer. The development of official police organizations, then, was not seen as a necessary step in government for a long time, for it was thought that no one needed to be paid to do something that was already his duty to do without remuneration. Hall (1935:181) comments on this:

> Not only was it the right of all persons to apprehend offenders but there was a positive duty to drop all work when the hue and cry was raised, and to join immediately in the pursuit. To fail to do this or to withdraw from the pursuit too soon or without permission was tantamount to supporting the felon, and was punishable as a misdemeanor. . . . Universal police duty

was perhaps the most important manifestation of the conflict between offenders ... and society. ... This police duty, though it rested upon all freemen, was not discharged haphazardly. The ... tithingman, ... the sheriff and his staff, the constable, and later, with the development of towns, the local watchman could draft the laity into their *posse comitatus.* Long after frank-pledge ... hue and cry and its concomitant duties persisted. This communal obligation to repress crime was reflected in the financial liability of the hundred within which a crime was committed.

Policing began to increase as commerce, industry, and urbanization increased. Special protection was needed, therefore, because of the accumulation of wealth and property. Additionally, because more and more people left the agrarian way of life to become merchants and craftsmen, it was not as easy as it once was to drop one's work in order to join the hue and cry. Hall (1935:182) states that "Elected peace officers accordingly chose proxies to perform their duties in order that they might devote themselves to their businesses. The towns began to employ watchmen, though their efforts seem to have been generally ineffective."

At the instigation of Sir John Fielding, a police magistrate in London at the end of the 18th century, some property owners actually financed and organized the Bow Street Runners. These men chased thieves and other offenders and their success probably contributed greatly to the formation of the first modern police department in London in 1829.

Lay Police Organizations

The Bow Street Runners served as one example of lay organizations concerned with policing communities that were financed privately and especially for the protection of property and businesses. They probably had their origins in the *peace gilds* that were formed in London and in other communities as early as the 11th century. Based on the amount of property owned, members of the gilds contributed dues to form a common treasury. They enacted elaborate by-laws, ". . . providing for cooperation in the apprehension of criminals, particularly cattle thieves, and the payment of sums of money to reimburse members who sustained losses as a result of such thefts" (Hall, 1935:183).

Wherever there were concentrations of valuable property, these voluntary organizations developed so that by the year 1839 it was estimated that over 500 such organizations existed in England. They continued to form even after official police forces had been organized. They were composed either of a cross-section of the law-abiding community or of merchants or property owners who wanted special protection. But Hall (1935:184–5) states that a third type of lay organization engaged in police activities began to emerge:

> This was composed of a large number of self-nominated "thief-catchers" who appeared at the end of the seventeenth and the beginning of the eighteenth centuries. The immediate impetus given to this development was a statute passed in 1692 offering rewards for the apprehension of highwaymen and thieves. Not only were rewards offered, but "the gracious pardon of their Majesties" was also held out to any robbers who "afterwards discover two or more persons who already hath or hereafter shall commit any robbery, so as two or more of the persons discovered shall be convicted of such robbery." The reasons for enacting this and similar statutes and the results produced by them may well be imagined. There grew up a band of unscrupulous criminals who divided their activities between the commission of crimes and the turning-up of other offenders. ... In 1749 the discharge of many soldiers and sailors from service in the war added numerous recruits. Parliament increased the rewards for capture and conviction. The thief-taking business flourished—frequently at the expense of the heads of many innocent persons.

The English practice of using lay organizations for police activities was carried over to the United States, particularly in California after the Gold Rush in 1849. During 1848 and early 1849, it is reported that there were few crimes committed. This was so because most of the miners were industrious, there were enough claims for everyone, and there were ample supplies. In 1849, the numbers of claims and supplies diminished as newcomers, immigrants, criminals, and gamblers invaded the territory. Because of the increasing numbers of thefts, murders, and claim swindles, the small number of officials who did exist were totally unable to control the situation or provide order in the camps and communities. As a consequence, lay groups began to evolve, vigilante committees were formed, and people other than elected officials assumed law enforcement responsibilities. Although private policing such as vigilante groups are viewed as illegal, specialized privately financed policing flourishes in the United States today and employs even more persons than all government law enforcement agencies combined. (More will be discussed about private policing later.)

Early Policing in the United States

Almost all of the early Colonists came from England, so it was natural that they brought with them the English system of law enforcement. They settled in relatively small towns and villages. In the South, they tended to form rural-agricultural communities, while in the North, settlers depended more on commerce and business for their livelihoods. They utilized sheriffs and constables for police functions, most of whom were elected for short periods of time. As a consequence, these police officials tended to have very little authority and even less respect from the citizens.

In the larger communities, such as Boston, New York, and Philadelphia, *night watches* were formed. Germann *et al.* (1962:58-59) state:

> These early watchmen, like their counterparts in England at the time, were very lazy and inept. Minor offenders were sometimes *sentenced to serve on the watch* as punishment. Often called *leather heads*, the towns sometimes had to formalize even the most simple duties. New Haven, in 1722, had a regulation that "no watchman will have the liberty to sleep"; and a 1750 Boston rule stipulated that "watchmen will walk their rounds slowly and now and then stand and listen." These were not true police departments, but mostly volunteer groups, yet, up to 1800, these night patrols of "vigilantes" were the only law enforcement in the towns.

For the most part, the lack of pay for such watchmen resulted in poor services to the communities. In an attempt to rectify the situation, Philadelphia, in 1833, enacted an ordinance which provided for the hiring of 23 policemen to serve by day and 120 to serve at night. All were to be under the supervision of one captain appointed by the mayor. In 1848, Philadelphia abolished the night positions, but increased the day positions to 34 and reinstituted the separate night watch. By 1854, the position of captain was abolished and in its place a Marshal was to be elected for a two-year term. Later, the Marshal's position was changed to that of a chief of police, to be appointed by the mayor.

In 1845, New York City developed a similar plan by which the mayor was to appoint paid policemen. This plan was based upon enabling legislation passed by the state. It abolished the old night watch system and day and night watches were thus consolidated. The force was under the supervision of a superintendent, who was appointed by the mayor with the consent of the council. Chicago followed similarly in 1851, New Orleans and Cincinnati in 1852, Baltimore and Newark in 1857, and Providence in 1864.

Most communities, however, maintained the night watch system, even though they also had a paid day force. It was inevitable, therefore, that there would be much friction, and many citizens complained about the ineffectiveness of their police to maintain order and prevent crime. It was also a period in history known as the "Spoils Era," in which a widely accepted slogan was "to the victor go the spoils." Thus, politicians and political machines controlled not only the communities, but the governments and their employees as well. Those who were hired to be policemen were part of the political machine and frequently were appointed to their positions not because of expertise or commitment, but because of rewards for working hard for the politicians. Commenting on this spoils system, an officer in Boston wrote (Fosdick, 1921:69): "The Marshal seemed to think that things looked a bit squally, and under his direction we very quietly dabbled in a little politics at the election. Our choice was successful and we were in very good spirits at the close of the year, in anticipation of a longer job."

Modernization and Reform

In 1856, New York City police were required, by ordinance, to wear a standard uniform, an act which was disliked by most of the force. Each ward adopted its own uniform and continued to resist the 1855 law which stated that each policeman was to "wear a medal inside his clothes, suspended round his neck, both day and night when on duty, and shall expose the same when about restoring peace, or on making an arrest, or when performing any duty of that kind." Philadelphia police resisted having to show badges and it was not until 1860 that a standard uniform was adopted.

Sporadic efforts were attempted to reform, modernize, and remove from political control the supervision of police in the major cities. However, since it was the politician himself who had to vote for such changes and reforms, it was unlikely that he cared to change the system. The police forces themselves owed considerable allegiance to the politicians, hence little leadership and poor administration flourished, and the police remained as inefficient and as corrupt as ever.

Some efforts were made at modernization and at what today we would call professionalization. In 1871, for example, a number of police officials met in Philadelphia to develop a uniform crime reporting and recording system. The program was not particularly successful. In 1894, the International Association of Chiefs of Police renewed this interest in the compilation of criminal statistics. In 1929, a book published by the IACP (p. 2) entitled *Uniform Crime Reporting* states:

> It must be conceded that many police departments are not yet equipped to render complete and accurate accountings of offenses committed and persons charged with their commission. Their failure to develop sound record systems or to make local adaptations from systems operating elsewhere, arises partly from the confusion which has surrounded the subject, and partly from lack of any definable goal at which to aim.

In the 1870s and 1880s, there were efforts to increase the salaries of police as well as some of the fringe benefits they were receiving, particularly in the area of retirement. Because of the increase in a sense of personal security, police recruiting was made easier and more "qualified" candidates began to apply for positions, especially in the larger cities. Age, height, and weight requirements were established, but political influence in obtaining appointments had not particularly diminished. Trojanowicz and Dixon (1974:35) report that in the Lexow investigation of 1894 it was revealed that $300 was the going figure to receive an appointment to the force in New York City and that promotions required higher payments to political officials. Thus, as they conclude (1974:35), "From the rookie's first involvement with the department, he was made aware of the systematic impact of political influence and bribery."

When President Garfield was assassinated by a disappointed office-seeker in 1881, the move for removing patronage from government gained impetus by the passage of the Pendleton Act. The Act provided for the establishment of a federal civil service system. Its impact began to be felt throughout state and local governments as they too passed similar legislation. Civil service did not remove graft and corruption from policing, but it did tend to curb the worst forms of political influence that affected law enforcement in the United States. Government officials still retain considerable power over policing, especially since most police chiefs are appointed by elected officials. But the appointment of line officers is based much more on qualifications than on "who you know."

Frontier Law Enforcement

Modernization of law enforcement proceeded with considerable difficulty in the major cities in the United States in the last years of the 19th century. And as settlers moved to the West and pushed the frontier eventually to the Pacific Coast, changes in law enforcement proceeded even more slowly than in the East. Most communities had sheriffs, but the areas they had to cover were so large that any effective system of law enforcement was almost impossible to develop or implement. It was common for individuals to take the law into their own hands and for town councils to pass many more laws than were ever possible to enforce. Because of the difficulties in establishing communities and the violence of the times, vigilante groups—of an on-going and *ad hoc* nature—were established. Prejudice, discrimination, and hostility developed between numerous groups, the brunt of which tended to fall on ethnic minorities. Based on who the person was and his socio-economic class, unequal and selective enforcement of the laws became more common than the exception. Carleton (1967:4) describes this condition as follows:

> All over the United States during the 19th century offenses by whites against Indians and by whites against free Negroes were treated lightly, as were offenses by Indians against fellow Indians and by free Negroes against fellow free Negroes, but this leniency stopped short when the offense was committed by Indian, Negro, or immigrant against a native white American—foreigners traveling in the United States were also astonished at the wide tolerance the Americans had for financial frauds and swindles. The scramble to appropriate the country's resources, develop them, and get rich quick was taken for granted. Americans found numerous ways to defraud the Federal government of vast amounts of land under the preemption of the homestead laws. There were many real estate frauds among private individuals too. Land sharks frequently fleeced newcomers to a community. Sales of real estate in developments and towns which existed only on paper were commonplace.

Puritan influence also helped to pass laws of a moral or religious nature. The famous "Blue Laws" which legislated against commerce on the Sabbath, laws governing sexual behavior, and the manufacture and use of alcohol were examples of ordinances frequently passed by frontier towns and cities.

Vigilantism grew considerably in the absence of effective law enforcement. Brown (1969:140) maintains that even though most vigilantes knew that their behavior was illegal, they persisted according to a self-developed philosophy containing three major components: (1) self-preservation, (2) right of revolution, and (3) economic rationale. Since everyone had a right to protect himself from harm, since the country was a nation born out of the ideal of revolution, and since it was cheaper for "volunteers" to enforce the law, the vigilante movement prospered and was uncontrollable for many years. Trojanowicz and Dixon (1974:40–41) comment:

> The local law enforcement officer, who took his duties seriously and operated responsibly often found that his method of functioning conflicted with the mood of the community and the vigilante groups that had been established for extralegal purposes. This atmosphere encouraged the local law enforcement officer to be sensitive to the mob and enforce only those laws that met with community acceptance or act in a manner congruent with at least the most powerful forces of the community, which were often vigilante groups. . . .
>
> When municipal law enforcement was ineffective, vigilante activities often became a desired mode of adaption in the larger cities, as well as the rural communities. The principle was always the same, that is, acting in an illegal manner as a substitute for the regular judicial and law enforcement processes, acting illegally to expunge crime and avenge the offender.

Consequences of Urbanization

As communities became larger and more urbanized and as industrialization swept the nation, particularly in the East, law enforcement became even more difficult to manage. After the Civil War, for example, conflicts between classes, and between blacks and whites, continued to rage. Labor unions were attempting to gain a foothold and the difficulties between labor and management factions often erupted into violent struggles. Carleton (1967:7), in describing the late 1800s and early years of the 20th century, states:

> These were the decades which witnessed the terrorizing activities of the Molly Maguire miners in the early 1870s; the anarchist riot and bomb throwing at the Chicago Hay Market in 1886; the massacre at the Homestead Steel Mills in 1892; the riots and arsons of the Pullman strike in

1894; the virtual civil war (and a bloody one) raised in Colorado between the mine operators and the Western Federation of Miners from 1902 to 1904 and the scores of dynamitings from 1906 to 1911, including the blowing up of a Los Angeles Times Building charged to the Structural Iron Workers Union; plus many acts of violence and terror said to have been perpetrated by the industrial workers of the world.

The police were called in to quell riots and otherwise suppress violence. Thus, at the turn of the century, the policeman came to be viewed—especially by the workingman and union member—as an arm of the government, dispenser of justice, but primarily a "tool" of the rich and upper classes. Many of the working people were immigrants and members of ethnic minorities and the policeman, who regulated some of their activities, came to be viewed as an oppressor. Police were considered the "enemy" and they came under bitter attack from many community and humanitarian groups because of the violence they used in the performance of their duties.

As police departments grew in strength and responsibility, a number of efforts was directed at improving their efficiency and management. A popular development was that of creating police administrative boards. This was designed to remove what was considered by many to be the last vestiges of political control, especially by mayors or city councils. The boards were given responsibility to appoint police administrators, set policies, and otherwise manage police activities. In an assessment of this movement, the President's Crime Commission (Task Force: The Police, 1967:6) states: "Unfortunately, this attempt to cure political meddling was unsuccessful, perhaps because the judges, lawyers, and local businessmen who comprised the administrative boards were inexpert in dealing with the broad problems of the police." It was the same kind of criticism that was later to be used in overcoming the initiative of civilian review boards in the middle of the 20th century.

In another effort, at the end of the 19th century, state legislatures enacted laws that required police administrators to be appointed by governors. Smith (1960:105–106) asserts that this attempt at state control over policing had little success and even created problems that had not been anticipated:

> For one thing, the theory of state control . . . was not uniformly applied. It was primarily directed at the larger cities, by legislatures seeking to (perpetuate) rural domination in public affairs.

For some cities, however, governors continue to be the appointing authority of the chief of police—Baltimore still being an example— but, for the most part, chiefs today are appointed by local officials.

Previous to urbanization, it had generally been assumed that the only way to "train" a policeman was to place him on the streets and through experience and working with a veteran officer, he would learn what he had to do. Additionally, few jurisdictions were concerned with "due process" issues, so that complaints aired against the police in terms of their practices and policies generally fell on deaf ears. At the turn of the century, however, some police training schools began to emerge in the fastest growing and largest cities. Recruits were required to attend classes of instruction in order to upgrade their performance. The movement had only sporadic interest and it was not until after World War II that large police departments actually created academies for pre-service and in-service instructional purposes.

Interest in the improvement and reform of policing in the United States continued to receive attention by many persons, but it was not until 1929 when President Herbert Hoover appointed a commission known as the "National Commission on Law Observance and Enforcement" that federal attention was focused on the subject. Known popularly as the Wickersham Commission, it addressed itself to a comprehensive survey of crime at the national level and also analyzed the role and function of the American police. The Commission's work was supervised by August Vollmer and its primary treatise, entitled *Police Conditions in the United States*, was written by David G. Monroe and Earle W. Garrett. Published in 1931, the Wickersham Commission made the following recommendations (1931:140):

1. The corrupting influence of politics should be removed from the police organization.

2. The head of the department should be selected at large for competence, a leader, preferably a man of considerable police experience, and removable from office only after preferment of charges and a public hearing.

3. Patrolmen should be able to rate a 'B' on the Alpha test, be able-bodied and of good character, weigh 150 pounds, measure 5 feet 9 inches tall, and be between 21 and 31 years of age. These requirements may be disregarded by the chief for good and sufficient reasons.

4. Salaries should permit decent living standards, housing should be adequate, eight hours of work, one day off weekly, annual vacation,

fair sick leave with pay, just accident and death benefits when in performance of duty, reasonable pension provisions on an actuarial basis.

5. Adequate training for recruits, officers, and those already on the roll is imperative.

6. The communication system should provide for call boxes, telephones, recall system, and (in appropriate circumstances) teletype and radio.

7. Records should be complete, adequate, but as simple as possible. They should be used to secure administrative control of investigations and of department units in the interest of efficiency.

8. A crime-prevention unit should be established if circumstances warrant this action and qualified women police should be engaged to handle juvenile delinquents' and women's cases.

9. State police forces should be established in states where rural protection of this character is required.

10. State bureau of criminal investigation and information should be established in every State.

These recommendations, like the ones which were to be developed by the President's Crime Commission in 1967, generally were met with only moderate acceptance by the public and law enforcement communities. They read well, but they were not particularly well implemented. In 1973, the National Advisory Commission on Criminal Justice Standards and Goals was to repeat the need for changing and upgrading law enforcement in the United States. While the Law Enforcement Assistance Administration is encouraging the adoption of many of the standards and goals at the state and local levels of government, it is too early to determine what kinds or the extent to which change will occur.

State and Federal Law Enforcement Agencies

As metropolitan areas began to develop around the large cities in the country, sheriffs and constables began to realize that they were unable to cope with the mounting criminal population. Additionally, as each local jurisdiction developed its own police force, state authorities, especially governors, came to the realization that they had no control over law enforcement in their states. Furthermore, states watched the failure of local authorities to regulate vice, control labor violence, enforce laws in rural areas, and to patrol the growing number of roads and highways. States had developed national guards and militias, and while they were utilized on an emergency law enforcement basis, they were inadequate for the major tasks associated with effective policing.

There had been several attempts to form state-wide policing organizations, such as the Texas Rangers in 1835 and a force of state constables in 1865 in Massachusetts. But these outfits primarily were concerned either with cattle rustling, marauding Indians, or, as in Connecticut in 1902, with responsibility for curtailing vice. The Pennsylvania State Police was the first real state police to be developed, in 1905, prompted for the most part by the violence which erupted during the state-wide coal strikes. Most state police systems were developed after World War I and today all states have some form of state law enforcement agency. A few are restricted primarily to patrolling highways, but most others have wide latitude in providing law enforcement services to rural and suburban communities throughout their states. Very often, they provide services to local police departments, such as identification bureaus, crime laboratories, liquor control bureaus, and investigative services.

Federal law enforcement activities and services have been slow to develop primarily because of the resistance of local authorities to federal responsibility and control. No national police force has ever been established. In discussing this aspect of law enforcement in the United States, the late J. Edgar Hoover, former Director of the Federal Bureau of Investigation said (1954:40):

I am unalterably opposed to a national police force. I have consistently opposed any plan leading to a consolidation of police power, regardless of the source from which it originated. I shall continue to do so, for the following reasons, which, in the same words, I have set forth on many earlier occasions:

1. Centralization of police power represents a distinct danger to democratic self-government.

2. Proposals to centralize law enforcement tend to assume that either the state or federal government can and should do for each community what the people of that city or county will not do for themselves.

3. The authority of every peace officer in every community would be reduced, if not eventually broken, in favor of a dominating figure or group on the distant state or national level. It is conceivable that such an official or group might be given the power by law to influence or dictate the selection of officers, the circumstances of their employment, and the decision they make in arresting and prosecuting those who violate the law.

But, as federal government grew and programs and activities flourished in such areas as interstate commerce, coinage of money, postal services, etc., it became necessary to develop some kind of policing at the national level. Many of these federal agencies with investigative responsibilities, over the course of many years, began to take on significant aspects of law enforcement. As a consequence, as Smith (1960:169) points out, it ". . . is difficult to distinguish between agencies of a police character and those which, though they have their law enforcement aspects, are primarily concerned with intradepartmental inspections and investigations."

Among such federal agencies with relatively minor policing responsibilities are included the Public Health Service; several bureaus within the Department of Commerce, the Department of Interior, and the Department of Health, Education and Welfare; the Veterans' Administration; the Bureau of Indian Affairs; and several units within the Department of Agriculture. Also included is a number of independent agencies, such as the Federal Trade Commission, Securities and Exchange Commission, Federal Communications Commission, the Interstate Commerce Commission, and the Food and Drug Administration.

There are many federal police agencies of a civil character which also have enforcement responsibilities. The most famous, of course, is the Federal Bureau of Investigation. Others include the Internal Revenue Service, the Bureau of Customs, the Secret Service, the Executive Protection Service, the Bureau of Narcotics, the Inspection Service of the Post Office, and the Immigration Service. In addition to numerous other agencies and bureaus, every branch of the military services has its own law enforcement unit, including Military Police and Criminal Investigation Divisions.

Number of Police Agencies and Costs

There is no accurate information available concerning the exact numbers of federal, state, county, and local police agencies and their personnel in the United States. The President's Crime Commission report of 1967 estimates the number of agencies to be 40,000, including 50 at the federal level, 200 at the state level, and the remaining dispersed among the various counties, cities, towns, and villages in all 50 states. This, of course, excludes the 290,000 persons who are employed by approximately 4,000 establishments which provide security or law enforcement services in the private sector (Kakalik and Wildhorn, 1971:10).

Table 9.1 depicts the profile of governmental law enforcement agencies and the dollars spent according to 1966 data, while Table 9.2 summarizes the numbers and finances of public and private policing in the United States, according to 1969 data.

Insofar as public law enforcement is concerned, it is obvious that the bulk of all such services is administered at the local level of government. Furthermore, as the Advisory Commission on Intergovernmental Relations (1971:75–76) points out, most local police departments in the United States are very small, but most local police employees are concentrated in a few very large departments. Data of 1967 reveal that almost 90 percent of the units of general local governments have police forces of under 10 full-time equivalent policemen, representing slightly more than 9 percent of all employed (public) police. As Table 9.3 also reveals, only 1 percent of all local governments employed 100 or more policemen for a total of 60 percent of all such personnel employed on a full-time basis. Table 9.4 illustrates that even in metropolitan areas with populations of 1 million or more, no more than 93 (or 6.6 percent of all such metropolitan areas) employ 150 or more full-time policemen.

There are three major law enforcement officials who are elected in the United States: the county sheriff, who is generally the chief law enforcement officer within the county (distinct from a county chief of police who is appointed); the constable, who generally is the law enforcement officer entrusted with police duties for the local justices of the peace; and the county coroner, who has legal charge of all inquests regarding cases of suspicious deaths within the county. Sheriffs are elected in 47 states and are constitutionally established in 33 states. Constables are elected in 38 states and are constitutionally provided for in 12 states. Coroners are elected in 26 states and have constitutional status in 19. Table 9.5 describes the numbers and types of elected law enforcement officials by state, as of 1967.

As Table 9.2 indicates, considerable monies are spent each year on policing in the United States. According to Kakalik and Wildhorn (1971:10), in 1969 well over $7 billion was devoted to security services and equipment for 0.85 percent of the gross national product. "One in every 100 persons in the civilian labor force, or one in every 250 persons in the entire population, was employed in security work,

TABLE 9.1. A Profile of Federal, State, and Local Law Enforcement Agencies

	Agencies	Full-time personnel				Dollars spent					
	Number in 1954	Number in 1955	Number in 1965	Percent of total in 1965	Percent average annual increase 1955-65	Total in millions 1955	Total in millions 1965	Per capita expenditure 1955	Per capita expenditure 1965	Percent of dollars 1965	Percent average annual increase, 1955-65
Federal	50	22,000	23,000	6.2	0.5	129	220	$0.78	$1.26	8.5	7.7
State	200	22,000	40,000	10.8	8.2	139	315	.84	1.79	12.2	12.7
Local	39,750	229,000	308,000	83.0	3.4	1,091	2,051	6.60	11.25	79.3	8.8
Total	40,000	273,000	371,000	100.0	3.6	1,359	2,586	8.22	14.20	100.0	9.0
Percent increase			35.9				90.3		72.7		

Source: President's Commission on Law Enforcement and Administration of Justice, Task Force Report: Police, 1967:7.

and over $40 per capita was spent on security (public and private)." Table 9.6 shows that in relation to total criminal justice expenditures of public monies in fiscal year 1971–1972, law enforcement or police protection consumed almost 60 percent of the almost $12 billion spent totally for all services.

Police Operations

> The multitude of police forces in any State and the varying standards of organization and service have contributed immeasurably to the general low grade of police performance in this country. The independence which police forces display toward each other and the absence of any central force which requires either a uniform or a minimum standard of service leave the way open for the profitable operation of criminals in an area where protection is often ineffectual at the best, generally only partial, and too frequently wholly absent.

These are the words of the 1931 Wickersham Commission Report (1931:125), quoted 36 years later in the President's Crime Commission report on the police. While no responsible official is suggesting that there be established a national police force, most students of the field of local law enforcement maintain that a great deal of upgrading is necessary, greater standardization of services is required, and more consolidation of efforts is needed throughout the country. Fragmentation and fractionalization have worked against efficiency and effectiveness at all levels of police service.

Whether we describe a 10-person department or the huge operations of New York City, administrators suggest that there are today at least six primary functions of a police department. These include peace-keeping, prevention of crime and disorder, the apprehension of offenders, recovery of lost or stolen property, protection of life, person, and property, and the provision of social services to the community. Unlike the British model of policing, where the role of the policeman is viewed basically in terms of civil service, the American "cop" has tended to view his role as that of a law enforcement agent. As a consequence, most police activities, including training, have been geared to the apprehension process. The welfare or social service function, along with police community relations activities, have become relatively recent concerns, but probably reflect as much on the day-to-day activities of the average policeman in contemporary society as any other program or activity.

TABLE 9.2. Summary of Estimated Public and Private Security Forces and Expenditures in the United States in 1969 (N/A indicates data not available)

Type of Security Personnel or Organization	Numbers of People		Expenditures ($ millions)	
	Security Personnel	Total Employment	Payroll Expenditures	Total Expenditures or Revenues
Public Law Enforcement				
Local police (city, county, township)	324,000[a]	432,000[b]	3,040[c]	3,326[b]
Reserve local police	N/A	N/A	N/A	N/A
Special local law enforcement agencies	N/A	N/A	N/A	N/A
State police or highway patrol	39,000[a]	}54,000[b]	}455[c]	}621[b]
Special state law enforcement agencies	N/A			
Federal law enforcement agencies	N/A	36,000[b,d]	344[c]	492[b]
Total Public Law Enforcement	395,000[e]	523,000[c]	3,839[c]	4,430[b]
Public (Government) Guards				
(all governments)	120,000[e]	N/A	N/A	~1,000
Total Public Sector (police and guards)	515,000	N/A	N/A	~5,400
Private Sector Security				
In-house detectives and investigators	23,900[e]	N/A	N/A	N/A
In-house guards	198,500[e]	N/A	N/A	N/S
Subtotal in-house security	222,400[e]	N/A	N/A	~1,600[f]
Contract detectives	8,100[e]	N/A	N/A	N/A
Contract guards	59,400[e]	N/A	N/A	N/A
Subtotal contract guards and detectives	67,500[e]	~110,000[g]	435[h]	620[i]

Patrolmen in contract agencies	N/A (included in contract guards)	N/A (included in contract guards)	N/A	N/A (included in contract guards)
Armored-car services		10,000g	73h	128j
Central station alarm services		N/A (included in contract guards)	N/A	120k
Total Private Sector	289,900e	N/A	N/A	~2,500
Security Equipment	N/A	N/A	N/A	~800
Grand Total	804,000	N/A	N/A	~8,700

aSources: FBI, *1969 Uniform Crime Reports*, and telephone conversations with personnel at International Association of Chiefs of Police. Figures are for sworn officers. Local police total shown includes 287,000 sworn officers in cities and suburbs and 37,000 officers in county sheriff departments. State figures include state police and state highway patrol officers.

bSource: *Expenditure and Employment Data for the Criminal Justice System 1968-69*, LEAA, U.S. Department of Justice, December 1970. Expenditure data are for FY 1968-69, and employment data are for October 1969.

cSource: Bureau of the Census publications (*Census of Governments* for various years, *Public Employment in 1968*, and *Governmental Finances*).

dThe 36,000 federal law enforcement employees include all employees of only five agencies: FBI, Secret Service, Immigration and Naturalization Service, Bureau of Narcotics and Dangerous Drugs, and Bureau of Customs. But only a fraction of these employees are actually investigators or law enforcement officers with police powers. From Hearings of the Committee on Government Operations, *Unmet Training Needs of the Federal Investigator and the Consolidated Federal Law Enforcement Training Center*, House Report No. 91-1429, U.S. Government Printing Office, 1970, it is estimated that the federal government's investigative force exceeds 50,000 employees.

eSource: Bureau of Labor Statistics publications and unpublished data. Excludes part-time employees unless their primary occupation is security-related.

fThis estimate derives from two sources: Predicasts, Inc., and a Rand estimate, both of which are discussed in Chapter IV of R-870-DOJ.

gSources: *1967 Census of Business: County Business Patterns for 1968 and 1969*. Includes part-time employees. See footnote e above.

hAssuming payroll is 57 percent of revenues, as estimated in the *1967 Census of Business*.

iSource: *1967 Census of Business* data extrapolated to 1969, utilizing revenue growth ratios equal to those achieved by large contract detective agencies and protective service firms.

jSource: *1967 Census of Business* data extrapolated to 1969, using revenue growth rates equal to those achieved by large contract detective service firms.

kSource: Predicasts, Inc., Special Study 56, *Security Systems, 1970*.

Source: James S. Kakalik and Sorrell Wildhorn. Private Police in the United States: Findings and Recommendations. Vol. I. Washington, D.C.: LEAA: 1971:11.

TABLE 9.3. Size of Police Department by Unit of General Local Government, 1967

General Units of Government Having	Number of Governmental Units	Percent of Total	Number of Police Personnel	Percent of Total
0–4 full-time equivalent policemen	31,422	82.3	14,884	4.4
5–9 full-time equivalent policemen	2,504	6.6	16,579	4.9
10–24 full-time equivalent policemen	2,463	6.4	37,387	11.0
25–49 full-time equivalent policemen	942	2.5	31,752	9.4
50–99 full-time equivalent policemen	481	1.3	33,378	9.8
100–199 full-time equivalent policemen	203	.5	28,081	8.3
200–299 full-time equivalent policemen	71	.2	16,977	5.0
300+ full-time equivalent policemen	116	.3	160,302	47.2
Total	38,202	100.0	333,790	100.0

Source: U.S. Bureau of the Census. *Compendium of Public Employment.* 1967 Census of Governments, Vol. 3, No. 2, Table No. 29.

Source: Advisory Commission on Intergovernmental Relations. State-Local Relations in the Criminal Justice System. Washington, D.C. 1971:305.

TABLE 9.4. Police Force Organization in Selected Metropolitan Areas by Size of Metropolitan Area, 1967

Size Class of Metropolitan Area	Number of SMSA's	Number of Local Govts	Number of Organized Police Forces	Size of Police Force				
				1-10	11-20	21-50	51-150	150-
1,000,000+ Population	30	3,415	1,403 (100.0%)	352 (25.1)	351 (25.0)	391 (27.9)	216 (15.4)	93 (6.6)
500-999,999 Population	18	849	229 (100.0%)	66 (28.8)	56 (24.5)	50 (21.8)	26 (11.4)	31 (13.5)
250-499,999 Population	19	511	134 (100.0%)	46 (34.3)	24 (17.9)	25 (18.7)	18 (13.4)	21 (15.7)
50-249,999 Population	24	428	92 (100.0%)	21 (22.8)	20 (21.7)	23 (25.0)	22 (23.9)	6 (6.5)
Total Metropolitan	91	5,203	1,858 (100.0%)	485 (26.1)	451 (24.3)	489 (26.3)	282 (15.2)	151 (8.1)

Source: Advisory Commission of Intergovernmental Relations Compilation from the following sources: U.S. Bureau of the Census. *Employment of Major Local Governments*. 1967 Census of Governments, Vol. 3, No. 1; FBI, *Uniform Crime Reports–1967*, Tables 55–56; International City Management Association, *Municipal Year Book–1968*, Table 4.

Source: Advisory Commission on Intergovernmental Relations in the Criminal Justice System. Washington, D.C. 1971:305.

TABLE 9.5. Number of Authorized Independently Elected Law
Enforcement Officials, Per Jurisdiction (By State, 1967)*

State	No. of Sheriffs	No. of Constables	No. of Coroners	Other Elected Law Enforcement Officials
Alabama	1/County	1/Precinct	1/County[a]	
Alaska	No Elected Law Enforcement Officials in State			
Arizona	1/County	1/Precinct	None	
Arkansas	1/County	1/Township	1/County	Marshal/2d Class Cities
California	1/County	1–2/JP District	1/County[b]	3 Commissioners/Police Protection District
Colorado	1/County	None	1/County	
Connecticut	1/County	1–7/Township	None	
Delaware	1/County	None	1/County	
Florida	1/County[c]	1/JP District	None	1/Marshal/Municipality
Georgia	1/County	2/Militia District	1/County[d]	
Hawaii	No Elected Law Enforcement Officials in State			
Idaho	1/County	1/Precinct	1/County	
Illinois	1/County	None	1/County	
Indiana	1/County	1/Township	1/County	
Iowa	1/County	2/Township	None	
Kansas	1/County	1/Township	None	1 City Court Marshal/ 1st and 2d Class Cities
Kentucky	1/County	1/JP District	1/County	
Louisiana	1/County	3–6/JP Ward	1/County	
Maine	1/County	None	None	
Massachusetts	1/County	1+/Town	None	
Michigan	1/County	4/Township	2/County[e]	1 Constable per Ward/4th Class Cities
Minnesota	1/County	2/Township	2/County[f]	2 Constables/Village
Mississippi	1/County	5/Supervisory District	1/County	1 Marshal/Municipality
Missouri	1/County	1/Magistrate District	1/County	1 Marshal/10–30,000 municipality in Class I county 1 Marshal/Mayor-Council 3rd Class Cities 1 Marshal/4th Class Cities
Montana	1/County	2/Township	1/County	
Nebraska	1/County	1/Township	None	
Nevada	1/County	1/Township	None	
New Hampshire	1/County	1+/Town	None	
New Jersey	1/County	None	None	
New Mexico	1/County	1/Precinct	None	
New York	1/County[g]	None	1–4/County[h]	

*Maryland data not available

TABLE 9.5, continued

State	No. of Sheriffs	No. of Constables	No. of Coroners	Other Elected Law Enforcement Officials
North Carolina	1/County	1/Township	1/County	
North Dakota	1/County	2/Township	1/Counties under 8,000	
Ohio	1/County	None	1/County	
Oklahoma	1/County	1/JP District	None	
Oregon	1/County	1/Cities of 50,000+	None	1 Marshal/Municipality
Pennsylvania	1/County	1/District or Ward	1/County[j]	
Rhode Island	Apt. by Gov.	1/Town	None	
South Carolina	1/County	None	1/County[k]	
South Dakota	1/County	4/County	1/County	
Tennessee	1/County	2/Civil District	None	
Texas	1/County	4–8 Precinct	1/County[l]	1 Marshal/Cities, Towns, Village
Utah	1/County	1/Precinct	None	
Vermont	1/County	1/Town	None	
Virginia	1/County, City	None	None	1 Sargent/Town
Washington	1/County	1+/Precinct	1/County[m]	1/Township[n]
West Virginia	1/County	1+/Magisterial District	None	
Wisconsin	1/County	1–3/Township	1/County[o]	1 Constable/Village
Wyoming	1/County	1/JP District	1/County	

[a]Coroner appointed in Jefferson County.

[b]Coroner appointed in five counties.

[c]Sheriff appointed in Dade County.

[d]Coroner appointed in three counties.

[e]35 counties appoint coroners.

[f]Henepin County appoints coroner.

[g]Sheriff appointed in Nassau and New York City.

[h]17 counties appoint coroner.

[i]Sheriff appointed in Multnomah County.

[j]Coroner appointed in Philadelphia County.

[k]Coroner appointed in Greenville County.

[l]Coroner appointed in three counties.

[m]Coroners are district attorneys in counties of under 40,000.

[n]Only applies to Spokane and Whatcom Counties.

[o]Coroner appointed in Milwaukee County

Source: U.S. Bureau of the Census, *Popularly Elected Officials of State and Local Governments,* 1967 Census of Governments Vol. 6., No. 1., Table No. 15.

Source: Advisory Commission on Intergovernmental Relations. State-Local Relations in the Criminal Justice System. Washington, D.C. 1971:272-273.

TABLE 9.6. Percent Distribution of Expenditure for the Criminal Justice System, by Level of Government, Fiscal Year 1971–1972 (Dollar amounts in thousands)

Activity	Amount				Percent Distribution		
	All Governments	Federal Government	State Governments	Local Governments	Federal Government	State Governments	Local Governments
Total criminal justice system[1]	11 721 194	1 873 217	3 341 507	7 372 509	(x)	(x)	(x)
Direct expenditure	11 721 194	1 491 855	2 948 091	7 281 248	12.7	25.2	62.1
Intergovernmental expenditure	(1)	381 362	393 416	91 261	(x)	(x)	(x)
Police protection[1]	6 903 304	963 108	1 048 094	4 978 854	(x)	(x)	(x)
Direct expenditure	6 903 304	962 149	992 801	4 948 354	13.9	14.4	71.7
Intergovernmental expenditure	(1)	959	55 293	30 500	(x)	(x)	(x)
Judicial[1]	1 490 649	179 099	371 014	973 918	(x)	(x)	(x)
Direct expenditure	1 490 649	179 099	346 290	965 260	12.0	23.2	64.8
Intergovernmental expenditure	(1)	—	24 724	8 658	(x)	(x)	(x)
Legal services and prosecution[1]	580 381	107 071	127 879	350 150	(x)	(x)	(x)
Direct expenditure	580 381	107 071	124 959	348 351	18.5	21.5	60.0
Intergovernmental expenditure	(1)	—	2 920	1 799	(x)	(x)	(x)
Indigent defense[1]	167 630	80 237	25 571	63 573	(x)	(x)	(x)
Direct expenditure	167 630	80 237	23 963	63 430	47.9	14.3	37.8
Intergovernmental expenditure	(1)	—	1 608	143	(x)	(x)	(x)
Correction[1]	2 422 330	146 491	1 467 524	961 338	(x)	(x)	(x)
Direct expenditure	2 422 330	133 272	1 377 776	911 282	5.5	56.9	37.6
Intergovernmental expenditure	(1)	13 219	89 748	50 056	(x)	(x)	(x)
Other criminal justice[1]	156 900	397 211	301 425	44 676	(x)	(x)	(x)
Direct expenditure	156 900	30 027	82 302	44 571	19.1	52.5	28.4
Intergovernmental expenditure	(1)	367 184	219 123	105	(x)	(x)	(x)

— Represents zero or rounds to zero.

x Not applicable.

[1] The total line for each sector, and for the total criminal justice system, excludes duplicative intergovernmental expenditure amounts. This was done to avoid the artificial inflation which would result if an intergovernmental expenditure amount for one government is tabulated and then counted again when the recipient government(s) ultimately expend(s) that amount. The intergovernmental expenditure lines are not totaled for the same reason.

In a report prepared for the President's Crime Commission by Lohman and Misner (1966:38), which included a survey of the literature and commentaries on police management, the following functions were listed as being important activities for police:

1. Prevention and repression of crime.
2. Maintenance of the peace (domestic tranquility).
3. Protection of persons and property (security).
4. Enforcement of laws.
5. Detection of crime.
6. Recovery of lost and stolen property.
7. Apprehension of offenders.
8. Regulation of noncriminal conduct.
9. Protection of individual rights.
10. Control of traffic.
11. Miscellaneous public services.
12. Preparation of cases for presentation in court.

While James Q. Wilson (1968a:407–417) suggests that the importance of the order-keeping function has led to its classification as the primary objective of policing and to the law enforcement function as the second objective, at least one recent study indicates that peacekeeping and the delivery of social services have become serious additional police activities today. Webster (1973:1) states:

> As urban, industrial America undergoes rapid and unprecedented social change, unresolved problems create ever increasing pressures and familiar institutions change their purposes and meanings in the attempt to cope with change. This is also true of the police.

In order to determine the activities, functions, and roles of an urban police department, Webster conducted a statistical count ". . . of all the events to which policemen of the patrol division of a West Coast city were dispatched during a 54 week period" (1973:6). Table 9.7 helps to illustrate Webster's basic conclusions that the "typical" policeman (at least in this West Coast city) spends more time on administrative and social service activities than he does in enforcing the law. He summarizes his findings as follows (1973:6, 13):

> The data indicate that unnecessary and incorrect emphasis is being placed by the public, police administrators and the police themselves on the role of the patrolman as a crime fighter involved in dangerous daily activities

which require the use of force and violence. Instead, what the investigation shows is that crimes against persons . . . actually constitute less of the daily realities of police work and consume far less of the patrolman's actual energies than popular conception supposes. . . . We are left with the astonishing discovery that *less* than *one-third* of an urban patrolman's time is involved in dealing with personal or property crimes and *over half*— about *two-thirds*—of his time is spent in administrative or social service tasks.

In a review and study of New York City's police training academy (the country's largest), McManus *et al.* (1970 report similar findings in a monograph entitled "Police Training and Performance Study." The authors examined the role and function of the police in the 20th precinct in 1967–1968 and were able to isolate 45 specific kinds of incidents or police duties. Tables 9.8 and 9.9 depict the time spent on each activity, frequency of occurrence, and average time spent per incident.

Skelly (1969:115) also examined the activities of the police in the 20th precinct in New York City over a period of six months and concluded that 85 percent of a patrolman's time is spent on preventive patrol and 15 percent is devoted to answering calls for service. Furthermore, of the time devoted to service calls, 30 percent is associated with crime while 70 percent is noncriminal in nature. Wildhorn (1968:7) adds to this analysis with the finding that "Of the 'criminal' category, crimes against property consumed the most time while, in the 'noncriminal' category, aid to sick and injured consumed the most time." As Table 9.10 illustrates, the patrolman in

TABLE 9.7. Categories of Events, Frequency, and Consumed Time by Police in a West Coast City

Activities	Frequency	Consumed Time
Crimes Against Persons	2.82	2.96
Crimes Against Property	13.76	14.82
Traffic	7.16	9.20
On-View	19.68	9.10
Social Service	17.27	13.70
Administration	39.28	50.19
	100.00%	100.00%

Source: Webster, John A. The Realities of Police Work. Dubuque, Iowa: Kendall/ Hunt Publishing Co. 1973:13.

TABLE 9.8. Incidents in the 20th Precinct, New York City Police Department, ranked in order of total time spent per incident, 1967-1968

Incident Type	Number of Incidents	Total Time (in minutes)	Average Time (in minutes)
1. Sick	4,552	202,143	44.4
2. Other	5,629	162,310	28.8
3. Other misdemeanors	1,190	106,034	89.1
4. Dispute	3,582	106,016	29.6
5. Burglary	2,518	104,881	41.7
6. Unfounded	5,132	102,881	20.7
7. Dead on arrival	402	60,126	149.8
8. Injured	1,170	46,063	41.1
9. Intoxicated person	1,555	41,830	25.9
10. Disorderly groups	1,693	37,780	22.3
11. Robbery	512	33,476	65.4
12. Auto accident	547	32,943	60.2
13. Alarm of fire	1,013	30,483	30.0
14. Felonious assault	309	26,982	87.3
15. Auto accident–injury	286	25,334	88.6
16. Larceny from auto	514	17,579	34.2
17. Malicious mischief	435	16,261	37.4
18. Utility trouble	378	14,502	38.4
19. Narcotics	59	13,582	230.2
20. Auto larceny	104	12,556	120.7
21. Grand larceny	235	11,598	49.4
22. Other felonies	64	9,559	149.4
23. Motor vehicle recovered	73	7,221	98.8
24. Traffic violation	270	7,201	27.1
25. Vehicles mechanical trouble	201	7,201	35.8
26. Accidental alarm	264	6,873	26.0
27. Grand larceny–pocket-book snatch	130	6,366	48.9
28. Auto safety check	126	4,175	33.1
29. Prowler	121	3,549	29.3
30. Dangerous condition	81	3,510	43.0
31. Found persons	46	2,802	60.9
32. Auto accident–serious injury or death	13	2,587	199.0
33. Arrest–serving summons	81	2,480	30.6
34. False alarm of fire	86	1,865	21.7
35. Property recovered	35	1,848	52.8
36. Homicide	6	1,744	290.6
37. Rape	29	1,622	55.9
38. Weapons	9	1,298	144.2
39. Missing persons	24	1,096	45.7
40. Prostitution	7	1,090	155.7
41. Attempted suicide	13	1,056	81.2
42. Gambling	7	813	116.1
43. Traffic court warrants	40	713	17.8
44. Suicide	6	607	101.2
45. ABC violation	5	160	32.0

Source: McManus, George P. *et al.* Police Training and Performance Study. Washington, D.C.: LEAA. 1970:15.

TABLE 9.9. Incidents in the 20th Precinct, New York City Police Department, ranked in order of frequency of occurrence, 1967–1968

Incident Type	Number of Incidents	Total Time (in minutes)	Average Time (in minutes)
1. Other	5,629	162,310	28.8
2. Unfounded	5,132	102,881	20.0
3. Sick	4,552	202,143	44.4
4. Dispute	3,582	106,016	29.6
5. Burglary	2,518	104,881	41.7
6. Disorderly groups	1,693	37,780	22.3
7. Intoxicated person	1,555	41,830	25.9
8. Other misdemeanors	1,190	106,034	89.1
9. Injured	1,170	46,063	41.1
10. Alarm of fire	1,013	30,483	30.0
11. Auto accident	547	32,943	60.2
12. Larceny from auto	514	17,579	34.2
13. Robbery	512	33,476	65.4
14. Malicious mischief	435	16,261	37.4
15. Dead on arrival	402	60,216	149.8
16. Utility trouble	378	14,502	38.4
17. Felonious assault	309	26,982	87.3
18. Auto accident injury	286	25,334	88.6
19. Traffic violation	270	7,201	27.1
20. Accidental alarm	264	6,873	26.0
21. Grand larceny	235	11,598	49.4
22. Vehicle mechanical trouble	201	7,201	35.8
23. Grand larceny—pocket-book snatch	130	6,366	48.9
24. Auto safety check	126	4,175	33.1
25. Prowler	121	3,549	29.3
26. Auto larceny	104	12,556	120.7
27. False alarm of fire	86	1,865	21.7
28. Arrest—serving summons	81	2,480	30.6
29. Dangerous condition	81	3,510	43.0
30. Motor vehicle recovered	73	7,211	98.8
31. Other felonies	64	9,559	149.4
32. Narcotics	59	13,582	230.2
33. Found person	46	2,802	60.9
34. Traffic warrants	40	713	17.8
35. Property recovered	35	1,848	52.8
36. Rape	29	1,622	55.9
37. Missing persons	24	1,096	45.7
38. Auto accident—serious injury or death	13	2,587	199.0
39. Attempted suicide	13	1,056	81.2
40. Weapons	9	1,298	144.2
41. Prostitution	7	1,090	155.7
42. Gambling	7	813	116.1
43. Homicide	6	1,744	290.6
44. Suicide	6	607	101.2
45. ABC violation	5	160	32.0

Source: McManus, George P. *et al.* Police Training and Performance Study. Washington, D.C.: LEAA. 1970:15.

the 20th precinct spends approximately one-half of his time in work other than routine patrol and criminal investigation.

In *Varieties of Police Behavior*, Wilson studied the work of the uniformed officer in eight communities. In this book (1968b:17–18), he states: "The problem of order, more than the problem of law enforcement, is central to the patrolman's role . . . except with respect to traffic laws." Based on a sample of calls made during a one-week period, he reports that in one city, at least, the patrolmen responded to no more than 32 law enforcement calls, which constituted only 10.3 percent of the workload. Table 9.11 depicts the data.

Evaluation of Police Performance

Evaluation of police performance comes about in one indirect and two direct ways. Indirectly, what the citizenry thinks and believes of its police department is reflected by the nature, kind, and quality of complaints issued against individual policemen and the department itself. Additionally, what the mass media have to say editorially in part reflects the level of confidence the community has in its law enforcement agencies. In the "hot summers" of the 1960s, for example, complaints about police brutality skyrocketed as individuals and groups feeling oppressed by the police voiced their complaints.

A consequence of this kind of hostility spurred the development of police community relations units. Unfortunately, many departments were unable to distinguish between public relations programs and genuine police community relations activities and therefore did not deal with the actual complaints of brutality, racism, discretionary enforcement of the law, and police harassment. Some departments, however, looked at the relationship of their organizations to the communities they were supposed to be serving and began to recognize that police community relations had to be viewed as an "outcome" of service rather than treated as another "unit" within the organization, such as traffic, vice control, or juvenile services. Consequently, these departments began to listen to as well as speak with representatives of the community, and they responded to issues with changed policies and procedures. Even with such "progressive" attitudes on the part of the police, departments and police officials have fought hard to resist community control (Was-

TABLE 9.10. Job Assignments for Patrolmen in One Precinct, New York City, 1969

Job Category	Foot Patrol		Motorized Patrol	
	Hours	Percent	Hours	Percent
Patrol and observation	42	53	342	36
Public service	14	17	166	17
Investigations	3	4	118	12
Disputes	1	1	34	4
Assist other agencies	0	0	28	3
Miscellaneous services	0	0	90	9
Enforcement	1	1	32	3
Reporting	2	2	34	4
Community relations	4	5	10	1
Other	13	16	106	11
Total	80	100	960	100

Source: John F. Skelly, master's thesis, 1969.

kow, 1969) and have successfully avoided the growth of such vehicles as civilian review boards (Cohn and Viano, 1976).

As far as direct measures of evaluation of police performance are concerned, they involve (1) departmental and intradepartmental evaluation, and (2) judicial review of individual cases. As Weston and Wells (1972:54) point out, police managers generally tabulate individual officer performances, decisions, and activities. How successful individual policemen are in apprehending offenders, obtaining evidence, clearing cases, and submitting reports are the kinds of information occasionally utilized in evaluating the role and performance of the officer; they may also be used as bases for promotion. In most cases, however, such performance evaluation comes about on a day-to-day basis by the supervising officer and is not routinized in any scientific way. Some larger departments, of course, maintain research, planning, and personnel units and they may have more elaborate procedures for evaluating performance, but smaller departments obviously are unable to measure performance in any elaborate fashion.

On a departmental basis, funding sources—such as city councils and state legislatures—review program budgets and make evaluations regarding success or failure, but these efforts at program evaluation cannot be anything but general, indirect, and politically influenced. On the other hand, published reports regarding departmental efforts

TABLE 9.11. Citizens Complaint Calls, Syracuse, N.Y.,
Police Department, June 3-9, 1966

Type of Call	Number	Percent
Information gathering	69	22.1
Book and check	2	–
Get a report	67	–
Service	117	37.5
Accidents, illness, and ambulance calls	42	–
Animals	8	–
Assist a person	1	–
Drunk person	8	–
Escort vehicle	3	–
Fire, powerline or tree down	26	–
Lost or found person or property	23	–
Property damage	6	–
Order maintenance	94	30.1
Gang disturbance	50	–
Family trouble	23	–
Assault, fight	9	–
Investigation	8	–
Neighbor trouble	4	–
Law enforcement	32	10.3
Burglary in progress	9	–
Check a car	5	–
Open door, window	8	–
Prowler	6	–
Make an arrest	4	–
Totals	312	100.0

Source: Wilson, James Q. Varieties of Police Behavior. Cambridge, Mass.: Harvard University Press. 1968. Based on Table 1, p. 18.

reveal the extent to which a police department is able to accomplish a stated mission. For example, in a study of patrol efforts in Kansas City, the Police Foundation examined the extent to which different kinds of patrol procedures might have influence on the crime problem, including its incidence and the public's level of fear. Kelling *et al.* (1974:v) describe the basic project and its findings:

Three controlled levels of routine preventive patrol were used in the experimental areas. One area, termed "reactive," received no preventive patrol. Officers entered the area only in response to citizen calls for assistance. This in effect substantially reduced police visibility in that area. In the second area, called "proactive," police visibility was increased two to three times its usual level. In the third area, termed "control," the normal level of patrol was maintained. Analysis of the data gathered revealed that the three areas experienced no significant differences in the level of crime, citizens' attitudes toward police services, citizens' fear of crime, police response time, or citizens' satisfaction with police response time.

Although this kind of study points out many issues regarding the substance of police work, it also serves as a means for assessing the kinds of police services which are needed in any given community, as well as processes for determining the extent to which such services lend themselves to successful operations. The Kansas City experiment, like the works of Wilson and Webster, illustrates that traditional procedures of policing, such as patrol, no longer may be valid in contemporary urban society. With the findings, for example (Kelling, 1974:4), that 60 percent of a police officer's time is typically noncommitted (available for calls) and that the patrolman spends as much time on non-police-related activities as he does on police-related events, police administrators should reassess processes for performance evaluation in order to provide quantified measures which answer the question: "How successful are we?"

The National Commission on Productivity examined policing in the United States and concluded that it is indeed possible to measure police performance, both at the individual and departmental levels of service. The report, *Opportunities for Improving Productivity in Police Services* (1973), bemoans the lack of empirical data collected and analyzed by typical police departments in the United States and suggests many ways such organizations can collect "hard" data for performance assessment. The report (1973:11) points out that any kind of measurement has its limitations and cannot be substituted for "sound professional judgment," but adds that:

> The principal purpose of measurement is to provide sufficiently precise information to enable police managers to: (1) evaluate their department's performance; (2) identify and diagnose problem areas; and (3) design solutions.

Judicial review of individual cases is another direct means for evaluating police performance, especially at the patrolman level. It is when a case comes to court that the decisions and behaviors of the policeman are evaluated, especially in terms of due process. If the policeman is responsible for enforcing the law, he is also required to uphold the law. This means that he must make lawful searches and seizures, he must make legal arrests, and he must deal with an offender in such ways as to ensure the person's constitutional rights. Cases are thrown out of court when a policeman violates the rights of others, and decisions can be reversed, in appellate review, when additional constitutional issues are raised.

However, as the National Commission on Productivity observes, it is not "fair" to evaluate the performance of an individual officer in terms of a conviction rate, for there are many reasons (other than of a constitutional nature) why cases are thrown out of court or offenders are not tried on the arrested offense: the prosecutor may not decide to prosecute, there may be plea bargaining, the defendant may become a state witness in the case, witnesses may not wish to testify and a whole host of other reasons. Nonetheless, what happens in court in terms of individual—and departmental—results with regard to specific cases must be analyzed. But, performance primarily should be evaluated in terms of those issues and behaviors over which the police have control—such as arrests, searches, and seizures—and not only in terms of those issues and performances over which they have little control, such as what happens in the courtroom.

Standards and Goals

The National Advisory Commission on Criminal Justice Standards and Goals has issued a monumental report called *Police* (1973). This 668-page document contains many recommended standards and goals related to policing in the United States. The Law Enforcement Assistance Administration, a federal agency in the Department of Justice, has expressed a desire to obtain implementation of many of these standards and goals at the state level. As a consequence, almost every state has developed some kind of commission or task force to look at police procedures and practices, along with the activities of all other agencies involved in the network of criminal justice services. Each state is examining its criminal justice system and many are beginning to change criminal and penal codes as a consequence.

The Standards Commission devoted most of its attention in law enforcement to the problems of metropolitan and suburban police agencies; however, its report states that the intent of the work was to help all law enforcement agencies and (1973:3) ". . . the standards were designed to serve the needs of all agencies regardless of size or demography." With a basic concern of reducing crime, the task force on the police identified seven basic objectives which it believes will improve service and reduce crime. The seven basic objectives and the standards recommended for implementation are listed as follows (1973:5–6):

Objectives and Related Standards

1. Fully Develop the Offender-Apprehension Potential of the Criminal Justice System.
   Immediately develop and apply all available police agency, community, and other criminal justice element resources to apprehend criminal offenders. This may be implemented through the following standards:

Standard 1.1	Identification of Priorities
Standard 3.2	Neighboring Security Program
Standard 5.1	Providing 24-Hour Police Service
Standard 8.1	Minimum Response Time
Standard 8.3	Deployment of Patrol Officers
Standard 9.4	State Assistance
Standard 9.7	Criminal Investigation
Standard 12.2	Crime Laboratory
Standard 23.1	Rapid and Accurate Telephonic Communication with Public
Standard 23.2	Rapid Processing of Emergency Calls
Standard 23.3	Two-Way Radio Communications

2. Get the Police and the People Working Together as a Team.
   Immediately develop and apply community resources to the reduction of crime through formal crime prevention and police support programs. This may be implemented through the following standards:

Standard 1.1	Local Definition of Police Function
Standard 1.2	Accountability to the Public
Standard 1.4	Communication with the Public
Standard 1.6	Public Understanding of the Police Role
Standard 3.1	Developing Community Resources
Standard 3.2	Community Crime Prevention
Standard 16.4	Police-Public Workshops and Seminars
Standard 19.2	Responding to Personnel Complaints

3. Get the Criminal Justice System Working Together as a Team.
   Actively pursue criminal justice system coordination and effectiveness to serve society. This may be implemented through the following standards and recommendations:

Standard 4.1	Cooperation and Coordination

Standard 4.3 Improving Police Effectiveness in Criminal Justice Sytem
Standard 4.4 Diversion from Criminal Justice System
Standard 4.6 Criminal Case Followup
Recommendation 4.1 Alcohol and Drug Abuse Centers
Standard 5.2 Combined Police Services
Standard 12.4 The Detention System
Standard 23.1 Accepting Misdirected Telephone Calls for Emergency Service

4. Clearly Determine and Act on the Local Crime Problem.

Immediately identify specific local crime problems and set crime rate reduction goals. This may be implemented through the following standards:

Standard 1.1 Establishing and Revising Priorities
Standard 1.4 Communicating with the Public
Standard 3.1 Neighborhood Meetings to Identify Crime Problems
Standard 9.1 Analyzing Crime to Determine Specialization
Standard 9.11 Use of Intelligence Information

5. Make the Most of Human Resources.

Immediately develop and apply every human resource to stop crime and apprehend offenders. This can be implemented through the following standards:

Standard 10.1 Civilian Police Personnel
Standard 10.2 Selection and Assignment of Reserve Police Officers
Standard 13.1 Police Recruiting
Standard 14.1 Police Salaries
Standard 14.2 Position Classification Plan
Standard 15.1 Educational Standards for the Selection of Police
Standard 16.3 Preparatory Training
Standard 16.5 Inservice Training
Standard 17.1 Personnel Development for Promotion and Advancement

6. Make the Most of Technological Resources.

Immediately develop and apply every available technological resource to stop crime and apprehend offenders. This may be implemented through the following standards and recommendations:

Standard 23.1 Police Use of the Telephone System
Standard 23.2 Command and Control Operations
Standard 23.3 Radio Communications
Standard 24.3 Data Retrieval
Standard 24.4 Police Telecommunications
Recommendation 23.1 Digital Communications System
Recommendation 23.2 Standardized Radio Equipment
Recommendation 23.3 Frequency Congestion

7. Fully Develop the Police Response to Special Community Needs.

Immediately develop and apply all available resources to respond to community needs. This may be implemented through the following standards:

Standard 1.4   Communicating with the Public
Standard 1.5   Training in Community Culture
Standard 1.6   Participating in Youth Programs
Standard 13.3   Minority Recruiting
Standard 16.4   Interpersonal Communications Training
Standard 17.4   Lateral Entry

References

Advisory Commission on Intergovernmental Relations
    1971   State-Local Relations in the Criminal Justice System. Washington, D.C.: ACIR.

Bain, Read
    1939   As quoted in Tappan, Paul W. Crime, Justice and Correction. New York: McGraw-Hill. 1960:273.

Bittner, Egon
    1972   The Functions of Police in Modern Society. Rockville, Maryland: National Institute of Mental Health.

Brown, Richard M.
    1969   "The American Vigilante Tradition." In Violence in America: A Staff Report to the National Commission on the Causes and Prevention of Violence. Washington, D.C.: U.S. Government Printing Office.

Carleton, William
    1967   "Cultural Roots of American Law Enforcement." Current History (July).

Cohn, Alvin W. and E. Viano
    1976   Police-Community Relations (in press). Philadelphia: J.B. Lippincott Co.

Fosdick, Raymond B.
    1921   American Police Systems. New York: The Century Co.

Germann, A.C., F.D. Day, and R.R.J. Gallati
    1962   Introduction to Law Enforcement and Criminal Justice. Springfield: Charles C. Thomas.

Hall, Jerome
    1935   Theft, Law and Society. Boston: Little, Brown, and Co.

Hindelang, Michael J. et al.
    1973   Sourcebook of Criminal Justice Statistics: 1973. Washington, D.C.: LEAA.

Hoover, J. Edgar
    1954   "The Basis of Sound Law Enforcement." Annals of the American Academy of Political and Social Science 291 (January).

International Association of Chiefs of Police
  1929   Uniform Crime Reporting. New York: IACP.
Kakalik, James S. and S. Wildhorn
  1972   Private Police in the United States: Findings and Recommenda-
          tions. Vol. I. Washington, D.C.: LEAA.
Kelling, George L. *et al.*
  1974   The Kansas City Preventive Patrol Experiment: A Summary Re-
          port. Washington, D.C.: The Police Foundation.
Korn, Richard R. and L.W. McCorkle
  1965   Criminology and Penology. New York: Holt, Rinehart and
          Winston.
Lohman, Joseph D. and G. Misner
  1966   The Police and the Community—The Dynamics of Their Relation-
          ship in a Changing Society. Washington, D.C.: U.S. Government
          Printing Office.
McManus, George P. *et al.*
  1970   Police Training and Performance Study. Washington, D.C.: LEAA.
National Advisory Commission on Criminal Justice Standards and Goals
  1973   Police. Washington, D.C.: U.S. Government Printing Office.
President's Commission on Law Enforcement and Administration of Justice.
  1967   Task Force Report: The Police. Washington, D.C.: U.S. Govern-
          ment Printing Office.
Skelly, John F.
  1969   Portrait of a Precinct. New York: John Jay College of Criminal
          Justice. Master's Thesis (unpublished).
Smith, Bruce
  1960   Police Systems in the United States. 2nd rev. ed. New York:
          Harper & Row.
The National Commission on Productivity
  1973   Opportunities for Improving Productivity in Police Services.
          Washington, D.C.: NCP.
Trojanowicz, Robert C. and S.L. Dixon
  1974   Criminal Justice and the Community. Englewood Cliffs, New
          Jersey: Prentice-Hall.
U.S. Departments of Justice and Commerce
  1974   Expenditure and Employment Data for the Criminal Justice Sys-
          tem 1971-1972. Washington, D.C.: U.S. Government Printing
          Office.
Waskow, Arthur I.
  1969   "Community Control of the Police." Trans-Action (December):
          4-7.
Webster, John A.
  1973   The Realities of Police Work. Dubuque, Iowa: Kendall/Hunt Pub-
          lishing Co.
Weston, Paul B. and K.M. Wells
  1972   Law Enforcement and Criminal Justice: An Introduction. Pacific
          Palisades, Calif.: Goodyear Publishing.

Wickersham Commission
    1931   Police Conditions in the United States. The National Commission on Law Observance and Enforcement. Washington, D.C.: U.S. Government Printing Office.

Wildhorn, Sorrel
    1968   "Research on New York City's Police Problems." New York: Rand Corp. (Mimeo).

Wilson, James Q.
    1968a   "Dilemmas of Police Administration." Public Administration Review 28 (September–October):407–417.

    1968b   Varieties of Police Behavior. Cambridge, Mass.: Harvard University Press.

Wilson, O.W. and R.C. McLaren
    1972   Police Administration. 3rd ed. New York: McGraw-Hill.

CHAPTER 10

COURTS

Early History

It is not possible to trace with any degree of accuracy the development of courts or the exact process whereby criminal behavior came to be prosecuted by the state. Private prosecution was a typical medieval practice and one which probably had its roots in the concept of private vengeance. Disputes between individuals, clans, and families were not the business of the state. It has been assumed that the modern version of the court had its beginnings when rulers and kings, through their absolute power, began to enforce their laws and decrees through tribunals appointed for such purposes. As Korn and McCorkle (1965) point out, this probably came about not in an evolutionary manner, but as a number of isolated developments which occurred here and there according to needs, desires, and whims; probably rulers did not like the idea that potential soldiers were using their energies in private feuds rather than being available for the kingdom's armies. Some tie the growth of king's courts to a desire for revenue from fines.

Unlike most modern societies, the United States developed a dual system of courts—federal and state—both of which are complicated structures and operate side by side. The origins of both kinds of court systems lie in the practices and traditions of English common law. According to English common law, criminal prosecutions were initiated and conducted by a private prosecutor in the name of the king. The concept of a public prosecutor developed for some unknown reason in the Colonies, with the first law providing for such a government agent enacted in Connecticut in 1704. The practice became well established by the time of the American Revolution and it has remained a hallmark of the American system of criminal justice ever since.

The development of the public prosecutor in the United States may have been influenced by the French practice. According to Elliott (1952:514–515), public prosecution was established in France with the rise of democratic thought during the 17th century.

> Jefferson and other revolutionaries in America became protagonists for the public prosecutor and under their influence the French pattern of public initiation of trial proceedings was widely copied. Today the American official prosecutor for both federal and state courts combines the features of the British Attorney General and the French *avocat general et procureur du roi.*

The dual structure of courts in America developed when the federal court system was created in 1789 to operate alongside the existing state courts. Jacob (1965:131) maintains that the creation of the federal court system was one of the triumphs of the Federalists at the Constitutional Convention of 1787 and the first Congress in 1789 and that:

> Having a court system of its own, the new national government would not have to depend on the good will of state courts to effectuate its laws. The fact that the states retained their own courts, however, attested to their continued strength.

The relationship between the two sets of courts has always been a complex one, especially since the Constitution stipulates that state judges must swear allegiance to its provisions and obey them regardless of the laws or constitutions of their own states. In fact, the issue of jurisdiction was made clear by the Judiciary Act of 1789. This gave the United States Supreme Court authority to review state court decisions that had ruled against any claim based on the federal Constitution, federal statute, or treaty. In 1816, in a landmark case known as *Martin* v. *Hunter's Lessee,* the Supreme Court ruled that state courts were bound by Supreme Court rulings on these matters. This, in effect, meant that state courts were bound by federal interpretations of the constitutionality of state laws.

Jacob (1965:132) states that while such decisions appeared to make state courts subordinate to the federal judiciary, state courts nonetheless tended to retain most of their autonomy. This has been so, for the vast majority of cases—criminal and civil—decided by the state courts do not raise federal or constitutional issues or questions. Nagel (1962), in an analysis of state court decisions, suggests that the proof of this autonomy is found in the fact that state judges *infrequently* cite Supreme Court decisions in their own rulings.

Soon after the Constitution of the United States was adopted in 1789, provision was made for the appointment of United States district attorneys. Given the responsibility for looking after the interests of the federal government, these agents were also given the authority to initiate both civil and criminal proceedings. Although the country had an Attorney General in its first Cabinet, it was not until 1861 that the Attorney General supervised the district attorneys. It was not until 1870 that a Department of Justice was established and not until 1909 that total control over federal prosecutions was placed in the hands of the Department of Justice. Today, practice and policy are determined by the Department and the prosecutors are called U.S. Attorneys, all of whom are in appointive positions.

Over the years, conflicts developed between the state courts and the federal judiciary because of their overlapping jurisdiction. However, because of the decisions of the various federal courts and the expanding responsibilities given to the federal courts by the Congress, federal courts' jurisdiction became greatly broadened. Previously, issues centering around civil rights and due process were heard in the state courts, with the federal courts only hearing appeals. But with the expansion in the late 19th century of federal statutory law in such areas as interstate commerce, taxation, criminal law, and civil rights, "Each new statute provided federal courts with new sources of litigation" (Frankfurter and Landis, 1927:12-13). By the beginning of the 20th century, according to Jacob (1965:132–133), litigants increasingly had a choice between state and federal courts. Furthermore,

> Sometimes federal courts were chosen in order to escape disadvantageous state rules. . . . At other times, state courts were chosen . . . in order to take advantage of the more favorable attitudes of state judges. Over the long run, however, state courts gradually lost ground in the competition with federal courts. Cases involving important public policy tended to go to federal courts because they dealt with federal statutes or claims under the federal Constitution. Just as state government in general became less important to national policy-making, so state courts—to a somewhat lesser degree—lost their preeminent position in the judicial system.

Structure of U.S. Courts

The development, organization, and structure of the courts in the United States, especially at the state level, came about without any specific plan. Tappan (1960:357) describes them as ". . . an awkward and inefficient complex of tribunals that are difficult and uneconomical to administer." Although states differ widely in the structure and administration of their judicial systems, there are four general types of courts in each jurisdiction: (1) inferior or courts of limited jurisdiction, (2) courts of special jurisdiction, (3) courts of general trial jurisdiction, and (4) appellate or courts of last resort.

Inferior Courts

Inferior courts or courts of limited jurisdiction include municipal courts, police or magistrates' courts, justice-of-the-peace courts, and recorders' courts. They are local in nature and are found at the city, township, and county levels of government. They are generally not courts of record, which means that records of proceedings, except for the final dispositions, are not kept unless there is a special request to do so. They typically handle minor criminal cases, such as misdemeanors, and render final decisions, which, of course, are subject to appeal. In most jurisdictions, they hold preliminary hearings in felony cases and set bail where appropriate.

The civil jurisdiction of these courts is frequently set in terms of a maximum dollar figure—such as $1,000. The criminal jurisdiction may be set in terms of the maximum fine (frequently $1,000) or the maximum length of incarceration (usually no more than 12 months) to which a defendant may be sentenced. In most instances, jurisdiction is also determined in terms of geography, that is, the civil or criminal event which led to litigation must have happened within the precinct, town, county, or city in which the court is held.

Many of these courts have part-time judges who are ill-prepared and poorly trained to administer justice, especially justices-of-the-peace. These courts tend to be conducted in very informal and summary ways which has led some critics to describe their procedures as "bargain basement" justice. There have been many efforts to reform and reorganize these courts, but there has been tremendous resistance toward such efforts. As Robertson (1974:vii) indicates, "If these courts represent the law, and determine in some significant way its influence in our lives, then it is a national shame that the lower court conditions . . . have been tolerated for so long." He goes on to say (1974:xix):

> . . . lower courts are visible institutions that, for purposes of supervision and evaluation, function invisibly. Only when corruption is uncovered or the periodic study commission enters the scene do judicial actions receive public attention. Even then the scrutiny is likely to be short-lived and easily deflected to other issues before permanent reform occurs . . . In such a setting judicial style tends to emphasize outcome over process, leaving the judge free to draw on extralegal criteria in his determinations.

The judges who preside over these brief and very routinized criminal trials are appointed or elected officials and tend to reflect most carefully the values of the communities they serve. Since most communities and most citizens are antagonistic toward the petty offender, it is not uncommon, as Tannenbaum (1938:17) suggests in a section of his book called "The Dramatization of Evil," that the innocent are presumed to be guilty:

> The attitude of the community (toward offenders) hardens definitely into a demand for suppression. There is a gradual shift from the definition of the specific acts as evil to a definition of the individual as evil . . .

Courts of Special Jurisdiction

Courts of special jurisdiction are also inferior courts but are organized to handle specialized kinds of cases, such as juvenile, domestic rela tions, traffic offenses, probate of estates, or small claims. They generally are not courts of record, are frequently presided over by the same quality of judges sitting on the bench in inferior courts, and may subject defendants to the same kind of "bargain basement" justice as previously described. The exception in this case can be found in juvenile or family relations courts, where judges do tend to have more training and judicial experience than those found in municipal, traffic, or justice-of-the-peace courts.

The President's Crime Commission devotes considerable attention to the condition of the lower or inferior criminal courts in the United States. In its *Task Force Report: The Courts* (1967:29), the Commission states that as many as 90 percent of the country's criminal cases are heard in these courts and concludes that many of these defendants are routinely deprived of essential due process and justice. The Commission recommended a massive overhaul of the lower criminal courts and went on to suggest that one partial solution would be that of integrating them into the higher trial court system of each of the states. Six years later, the National Advisory Commission on Criminal Justice Standards and Goals (*Courts*, 1973:164) made the same recommendation.

The National Advisory Commission, however, was not oblivious to the reasons why reform of the lower courts has not been realized. Incumbent judges have an interest in their local courts and do not want to see them changed. Legislatures are reluctant to pass laws dealing with the court structure; appellate courts have been unwilling to change procedures that affect lower courts; bar association officers and lawyer-legislators frequently practice in these lower courts and may have a personal stake in keeping them as they are because they become the sources of their income; and the general public is generally unaware of inferior court procedures and problems—unless they become defendants or witnesses. In short, except for some organized groups, occasionally including some bar associations, there generally has been little or no concerted effort to bring about change in these courts.

If complete unification of the trial courts is politically unrealistic at the present time, the Standards Commission recommends (1973: 162) that at the very least states should abolish justice-of-the-peace and municipal courts in metropolitan areas and replace them with unified county or multi-county systems, to be staffed by full-time, competent judges. This would permit greater centralization of efforts, lend itself to greater accountability, and facilitate, through better managerial processes, greater judicial efficiency and effectiveness.

Courts of General Trial Jurisdiction

The courts in which various commissions have recommended the lower or inferior courts be integrated are those called courts of general trial jurisdiction. These also have various names, such as county courts, common pleas courts, circuit and district courts, quarter sessions courts, or superior courts. They usually operate at the county level of government, but may include several counties, especially if it is a circuit court. Like the subordinate inferior courts, these courts render final decisions which are subject to appeal to higher courts. They are more frequently courts of record, although they frequently also handle misdemeanors, which may be recorded only upon special request. These courts hear felony cases which come up for trial from preliminary hearings and serve as the appellate court for cases originally heard in the lower courts.

Judges presiding over felony cases in these courts have the power to sentence convicted offenders to prison sentences and fines. For the most part, judges of these courts are lawyers. This means that they have had legal training, but it does not indicate that all who preside are competent. Jury trials take place in these courts, although the preponderance of cases tried, both civil and criminal, tend to be heard by the judge alone. In civil matters, it also is common for the cases to be settled out of court; that is, they are settled prior to or during a trial, but before a finding is reached by the court.

There is considerable lack of uniformity of structure and organization of trial courts in the various states. Some are very fragmented and specialized with limited jurisdiction. According to the American Bar Association (1971:9–10), this fragmentation, especially in highly metropolitan areas ". . . may impede the realization of full judicial efficiency and contribute(s) in some measure to congestion and delay in the handling of certain categories of cases . . ."

Friesen *et al.* (1971:27–28) comment that where a forced and rigid specialization is imposed upon the structure of the courts by the distribution of jurisdiction to courts of different names, "effective operation of the courts is impaired. A court of special jurisdiction to deal with a particular area of the law is, by its nature, suspect. . . .

The definition of a court's authority based upon subject—matter classification is an example of historical restriction on effective court management. Its abandonment is warranted but difficult to accomplish."

Appellate Courts

Appellate, supreme, or courts of last resort hear cases primarily on appeal following trials held at lower level courts. In many jurisdictions, the presiding judge sits as the chief administrative officer for the entire judicial system in the state. In some states, these appellate courts are themselves tiered, which means that there are at least two layers: the court of last resort, which is usually the supreme court of the state, and intermediate appellate courts, which hear appeals prior to an appeal to the state supreme court. According to the American Bar Association (1971:8), 17 states had such an intermediate court system:

> In the federal judicial system, and in states where the volume of appellate business requires, the review of cases from the trial courts of general jurisdiction should be in intermediate appellate courts, where the final disposition of most of the reviewed cases would be had. The highest court in the system, then, would be limited in jurisdiction to certain cases . . . which would be appealable of right or to cases where it was necessary to resolve a conflict of decisions in the lower courts.

Although we are committed to the idea that "every man is entitled to his day in court," this means only that every person has a right to his day in trial court. Green (1965:15) points out that appeal has not been a matter of right ". . . but of grace which the legislature could grant or withhold, and this still remains the law in the absence of a specific right to appeal found in a constitution." Green (1965: 15) argues that while appeal is not a matter of right anymore, "The present trend is that in every case provision should be made for review of a judgment by a court other than the one which rendered it. There have been side-effects of this view that appeal is a matter of right." As a consequence, he maintains that the creation of intermediate appellate courts will relieve the burden of review by courts of last resort. This view is also being argued by Chief Justice Burger for the federal judiciary, who claims that the United States Supreme

Court is over-docketed and that another intermediate tier of appellate courts would relieve court congestion.

The state courts of last resort, usually called supreme courts, have as their primary function the review of actions of the lower courts. They most commonly receive cases by petitions from dissatisfied litigants on a case by case basis. A case may be presented to an appellate court by a writ of *certiorari*, which is a request for review, which the court may deny. In some cases the defendant has a right to appeal. Cases are not retried on their merits; instead, the court reviews the record of proceedings to determine whether or not the lower court committed any procedural errors or errors in the application of substantive law to the facts of the case. The court receives briefs from both sides and commonly hears oral arguments.

The appellate courts may also exercise superintending control over the lower courts through the extraordinary writs. Green (1965: 16) states:

> The principal ones are (1) *mandamus*, by which a lower court is ordered to do something, such as grant a change of venue or grant a jury trial; (2) *prohibition*, by which a lower court is forbidden to proceed in a case in which it does not have jurisdiction, or in which it is exceeding its jurisdiction; and (3) *habeas corpus*, by which a lower court is directed to justify its action in holding a person in custody alleged to be illegal.

Such control over the lower courts occurs generally when aggrieved parties petition the highest state court directly, often prior to the usual time for appellate review, especially if significant constitutional issues are being raised, if life or liberty is at stake, and/or if the saving of time is of the essence. The highest court may also control procedures in lower courts by the issuance of rules for the lower courts to follow in all cases.

Federal Courts

As is found in the states, the federal court system represents the third branch of government, the other two being the legislative and executive. While the federal criminal code contains almost 3,000 sections, there are far fewer criminal cases heard in the federal courts than are heard in the various state courts throughout the country.

The federal courts hear cases concerning criminal law violations, as well as civil matters, primarily in relationship to the code, but also cases which concern interstate matters. Thus, the theft of an automobile is normally a state offense, but the transportation of a stolen vehicle across state lines becomes a violation of the Dyer Act—a federal offense.

There are three kinds of general courts in the federal system: district courts, courts of appeal, and the Supreme Court. These are in addition to specialized courts, such as those for military, tax, and customs matters. The district courts are the lowest level courts and there are 91 of them throughout the country, excluding Guam, the Canal Zone, and the Virgin Islands. They are the trial courts which have jurisdiction over federal offenses. The 11 courts of appeals, commonly called circuit courts, are regionalized throughout the country and receive appeals from district courts and federal administrative agencies. The Supreme Court takes up questions of constitutionality and by and large decides for itself which issues it wishes to hear.

The Administrative Office Act of 1939 provided for judicial conferences in the several federal circuits once a year. These were to be advisory in nature. Along with the judicial councils, which were created for supervisory purposes, the Act placed the burden of supervising the lower courts in the hands of the judges sitting on the courts of appeal, thus relieving the Chief Justice of the United States Supreme Court of that responsibility. These judges were given a mandate by the statute "to make all necessary orders for the effective and expeditious administration of the business of the courts" within their circuits. The district judges were directed to comply with any orders developed.

According to the American Bar Association (1971:37), states have tended to create judicial councils, for administrative and supervisory purposes, rather than judicial conferences, which are primarily advisory in scope. Many states, however, have annual judicial meetings to exchange information and ideas and to review procedures.

Judges

Aristotle once said that members of the public look upon the judge as "living justice," that is, as one who personifies the legal order. Justice Cardozo wrote that "In the long run, there is no guarantee of justice except the personality of the judge." It is the *trial judge* in this country, whether elected or appointed, who handles the bulk of the criminal cases, and it is this officer who determines, in large measure, the quality of justice administered by our courts. Therefore, whether one is a justice-of-the-peace or an Associate Justice of the U.S. Supreme Court, there is a responsibility placed on his shoulders to be fair, honest, and committed to the concepts of justice. That all judges are not fair, honest, and just has received considerable attention in the literature and remains a concern which is not easily resolved.

Election by popular vote is the primary method of selection of judges in this country. In approximately 12 states, election has never been the prevailing method, although some of the judges are indeed elected. In those states where election is the model, the power to appoint to fill vacancies is also permitted, except in one state. Yet, as the American Bar Association (1971:44) points out, even in these states where election is the rule, most judges sitting on the various benches are initially appointed to those positions, primarily as a result of filling vacancies. Where there are elections, ballots are usually nonpartisan in nature, yet most of the candidates' party affiliations are known and their candidacies supported by the parties.

In non-elective states, appointments are usually made by an elected official, such as the governor. In a few states, they have been appointed by state legislatures. These methods were used during Colonial times and until the mid-19th century. In the 1830s, popular election for short terms became common. This was a reaction against a politically selected judiciary. As the ABA (1971:44–45) indicates:

> The harm in political selection of judges lies not in the fact that it tends to put politically oriented people in judicial office. Prior service in the legislature or other governmental posts can undoubtedly be valuable to a judge. It has been well said:
> "There is no harm in turning a politician into a judge. He may become a good judge. The curse of the elective system is that it turns every judge into a politician."

It was thought by many people that politics could be removed from judicial elections by having nonpartisan ballots. However, the experiences of the states using such a system appears to indicate that while some of the evils of partisan elections are removed, the elections remain highly political. This is so because selection appears to be related more to nonjudicial than judicial qualifications. It becomes more a matter of who can get on the ballot rather than who is the most qualified candidate.

Any kind of election of judges gives a heavy advantage to anyone who can finance a campaign to convince the public to vote for him or her. It becomes almost impossible for the voting public to evaluate competency. Thus, in partisan elections, the candidate with the greatest party support or the incumbent who is best known is most likely to win voter approval. Furthermore, it is common to have as few as 10 percent of the electors vote on the judicial ballot, making possible a selection of a judge by barely more than 5 percent of the voters.

The American Bar Association believes that judicial selection by appointment is the soundest means. While political influence cannot be discarded entirely, the ABA argues that in this method evaluation and comparison of possible candidates can be made by those who are more qualified to evaluate than the general voting public. The Merit Plan for judicial selection was developed over 50 years ago by Professor Albert M. Kales of Northwestern University. It has been described as a device for overcoming the defects of the politicality of both elections and appointments. But it also provides security of tenure for judges, preserves for the people an opportunity to vote on their judges, and affords a fairer measure of ensuring selection of competent persons. The Merit Plan was first sponsored by the American Judicature Society and then endorsed by the American Bar Association in 1937 in the following form (ABA, 1971:47):

> (a) The filling of vacancies [shall be] by appointment by the executive or other elective official or officials, but from a list named by another agency, composed in part of high judicial officers and in part of other citizens, selected for the purpose, who hold no other public office.

> (b) If further check upon appointment be desired, such check may be supplied by the requirement of confirmation by the State Senate or other legislative body of appointments made through the dual agency suggested.

> (c) The appointee after a period of service should be eligible for reappointment periodically thereafter, or periodically go before the people upon his record, with no opposing candidate, the people voting upon the question "Shall Judge Blank be retained in office?"

The best known example of the Merit Plan is the Missouri Non-partisan Court Plan, which was adopted in 1940 and, according to the ABA, not only remains popular with the electorate, but has resulted in a high quality judiciary. By 1970 (ABA, 1971:48), the number of states using all or part of the Plan for all or part of their judiciary had risen to 21, and approximately as many states were moving toward its adoption.

The National Advisory Commission on Criminal Justice Standards and Goals (*Courts*, 1973:147) has also recommended the adoption of the "Missouri Plan." The language of the Commission is as follows:

Standard 7.1
Judicial Selection

The selection of judges should be based on merit qualifications for judicial office. A selection process should aggressively seek out the best potential judicial candidates through the participation of the bench, the organized bar, law schools, and the lay public.

Judges should be selected by a judicial nominating commission. Representatives from the judiciary, the general public, and the legal profession should organize into a 7-member judicial nominating commission for the sole purpose of nominating a slate of qualified candidates eligible to fill judicial vacancies. The Governor should fill judicial vacancies from this list.

With the exception of the judicial member, the members of the commission should be selected by procedures designed to assure that they reflect the wishes of the groups they represent. The senior judge of the highest court, other than the chief justice, should represent the judiciary and serve as the commission's presiding officer. The Governor should appoint three public members, none of whom should be judges or lawyers. No more than two should be of the same political affiliation or be from the same geographic vicinity. Three members from the legal profession should be appointed or elected by the membership of the unified bar association or appointed by the Governor when no such organization exists. A lawyer member of the commission should not be eligible for consideration for judicial vacancies until the expiration of his term and those of the other two lawyer members and three lay members serving with him. Commission members representing the public and the legal profession should serve staggered terms of three years.

For the appointment procedure to function efficiently, the commission staff should maintain an updated list of qualified potential nominees from which the commission should select a minimum of three persons to fill a judicial vacancy on the court, unless the commission is convinced there are not three qualified nominees. This list should be sent to the Governor within 30 days of a judicial vacancy, and, if the Governor does not appoint a candidate within 30 days, the power of appointment should shift to the commission.

Number of Courts and Judges in the United States

A National Survey of Court Organization (1973) was conducted by the Bureau of the Census in late 1971 for the Law Enforcement Assistance Administration. This was done as a preliminary step to establishing some kind of national program of judicial statistics, which does not yet exist. The purpose of the survey was to document the existing organization of courts in the 50 states and the District of Columbia. Toward that end, the survey was primarily designed to identify state and local courts, their major subdivisions, and the location of court records.

Tables 10.1, 10.2, and 10.3 summarize the data available concerning the numbers of courts and judges in the state system, as of January 1, 1972.

The over 17,000 courts in the United States, excluding the federal system, employ over 23,000 judges. However, as the Tables reveal, approximately 96 percent of all judges throughout the states work in courts with maximums of three judges. Over 80 percent operate out of single judge courts. Almost 67 percent of all courts hear civil as well as criminal cases, as Table 10.1 shows, and approximately one-half of all courts are of limited or special jurisdiction.

TABLE 10.1. Number of Courts by Type of Legal Jurisdiction

	Type of Legal Jurisdiction			
Level of Court	Total	Civil	Criminal	Civil and Criminal
Total	17,057	1,665	3,736	11,656
Appellate	206	26	7	173
General	3,630	231	10	3,389
Limited and special	13,221	1,408	3,719	8,094

Source: National Survey of Court Organization. Washington, D.C.: LEAA. 1973:1.

The states with the largest numbers of courts include New York with 1,634, Texas with 1,421, and Georgia, Indiana, Kansas, New Jersey, and Pennsylvania, each of which has at least 600 courts.

As Table 10.4 indicates, the annual expenditure for the judiciary in this country, in 1972–1973, amounted to almost one and one-half billion dollars, the bulk of which was spent for the inferior courts.

Prosecution

The prosecutor is one of the most important persons in the cast of characters in the network of criminal justice agencies in the United States. It is his responsibility not only to determine initially whether there is sufficient evidence to bring an offender to trial, he also must recommend the release of people where the evidence is insufficient to go to trial. He, in consultation with the police, determines the actual charges and is usually the representative of the state who decides whether or not a compromise will be worked out in the charges. It is this act of "plea bargaining" which has caused a great deal of controversy, especially since it has been without outside control and without many legal safeguards. Plea bargaining is nothing more than an arrangement whereby an offender pleads guilty to a lesser offense (or to one or more of several charges) than that initially charged against him, and receives the lesser penalty for that reduced offense. It also means that no trial will be held—it remains only for the judge to pronounce sentence.

The criticism of "plea bargaining" is that it has contributed to lack of respect for due process, especially when offenders who might otherwise be innocent are coerced into "copping pleas." Its proponents argue that if all cases had to go to trial, court dockets would become so clogged that almost no one would receive any justice and what they would receive would occur many years after the initial arrest. (See Chapter 8 for more discussion on plea bargaining.)

The prosecutor, also called a district attorney, corporation counsel, solicitor, state's attorney, or county or city attorney, operates in every criminal court as the state's representative in the adversary proceedings. The language of the 1704 Connecticut statute depicts his original role, which is not altogether different from that of today (Germann *et al.*, 1962:182):

TABLE 10.2. Number of Courts, by Level of Jurisdiction, by State, January 1, 1972

State	Total Courts	Courts of Appellate Jurisdiction	Courts of General Jurisdiction	Courts of Limited and Special Jurisdiction
United States	17,057	206	3,630	13,221
Alabama	345	3	73	269
Alaska	71	1	4	66
Arizona	161	3	14	144
Arkansas	413	1	172	240
California	370	6	58	306
Colorado	220	2	63	155
Connecticut	171	1	12	158
Delaware	38	1	6	31
District of Columbia	2	1	1	–
Florida	546	5	67	474
Georgia	602	2	159	441
Hawaii	9	1	4	4
Idaho	45	1	44	–
Illinois	108	6	102	–
Indiana	652	2	129	521
Missouri	531	4	117	410
Montana	123	1	56	66
Nebraska	296	1	93	202
Nevada	76	1	17	58
New Hampshire	87	1	10	76
New Jersey	630	2	42	586
New Mexico	155	2	32	121
New York	1,634	8	119	1,507
North Carolina	202	2	100	100
North Dakota	212	1	53	158
Ohio	594	89	88	417
Oklahoma	251	5	77	169
Oregon	213	2	36	175
Pennsylvania	659	3	67	589
Rhode Island	56	1	4	51
South Carolina	531	1	46	484
South Dakota	150	1	64	85

Iowa	183	1	99	83
Kansas	615	1	105	509
Kentucky	594	1	120	473
Louisiana	551	5	65	481
Maine	64	1	16	47
Maryland	73	2	24	47
Massachusetts	106	1	14	91
Michigan	303	2	84	217
Minnesota	276	1	87	188
Mississippi	346	1	184	161

Tennessee	506	3	196	307
Texas	1,421	16	254	1,151
Utah	120	1	29	90
Vermont	48	1	14	33
Virginia	425	1	140	284
Washington	378	4	39	335
West Virginia	530	1	66	463
Wisconsin	276	1	142	133
Wyoming	89	1	23	65

– Represents zero or rounds to zero.
Source: National Survey of Court Organization. Washington, D.C.: LEAA. 1973:11.

TABLE 10.3. Number of Court Systems by Number of Authorized
Judgeship Positions

Level of Court System	Total Judgeship Positions	Number of Court Systems*					
			Number of Judgeship Positions				
		Total	1	2-3	4-6	7-10	Over 10
Total	23,073	14,745	11,720	2,429	326	121	149
Appellate	727	129	3	35	44	42	5
General	4,929	1,569	938	367	124	53	87
Limited and special	17,417	13,047	10,779	2,027	158	26	57

*As distinguished from individual courts.
Source: National Survey of Court Organization. Washington, D.C.: LEAA. 1973:6.

TABLE 10.4. Judicial Expenditures by State Government:
Fiscal Year 1972-1973 (Thousands of dollars)

State and Type of Government	Total	Direct Expenditure		
		Total	Direct Current	Capital Outlay
United States, Total	1,461,098	1,461,098	1,395,135	65,963
States	419,247	385,619	371,730	13,889
Local, Total	1,082,257	1,075,479	1,023,405	52,074
Counties	753,316	747,000	723,961	23,039
Municipalities	335,987	328,479	299,444	29,035

Source: Expenditure and Employment Data for the Criminal Justice System: 1972-1973. Washington, D.C.: LEAA. 1975:188.

... Henceforth there shall be in every countie a sober, discreet and religious person appointed by the countie courts to be atturney for the Queen to prosecute and implead in the laws all criminals and to doe all other things necessary or convenient as an atturney to suppresse vice and immoralitie ...

Almost all chief prosecutors are, within their jurisdictions, independent of each other and are relatively independent of state control or supervision. They are, for the most part, elected officials and therefore, like judges, frequently give the appearance of being more concerned about re-election than they are in ensuring the just administration of justice. Many are part-time officials who, as lawyers, are also engaged in private legal practice, which may produce conflicts of interest at times. The prosecutor's political concern for an image as a "tough prosecutor" is described aptly by Sutherland and Cressey (1974:421–422):

> The urban prosecutor must be careful not to antagonize any large organized group, and his record must show a large proportion of convictions in cases which go to trial.... They avoid trials unless they are confident of conviction, or unless the case is well publicized. Thus, the prosecutor's reaction to crime must be, and is, selectively punitive. If he is to continue in his position or advance to a higher political office, he must seek the severest punishments possible in some cases, but he must intentionally fail to prosecute other cases.

There are approximately 2,700 chief prosecutors in this country, but as Table 10.5 indicates, the total number of persons employed in the prosecutorial role is about 55,000, almost two-thirds of whom are working for local and county governments. Thus, while the top-level prosecutors are elected officials, like sheriffs, most of the staffs are composed of appointed persons, some of whom have poor credentials to serve in the positions they occupy. Some communities have large staffs of assistant prosecutors, as in Los Angeles County where in 1967 there were 216 assistant prosecutors, or in Chicago, where there were 153 (President's Crime Commission, *The Courts*, 1967: 73). However, the great majority of prosecutors work in small offices with no more than one or two assistants, all of whom may even be part-time officials.

The President's Crime Commission reports that a recent survey (conducted by the National District Attorneys Association) revealed that some prosecutors in 21 states indicated their annual salary was less than $4,000. Furthermore, they also reported that they have insufficient funds to operate their offices efficiently. It is this kind of system, reports the Commission, that is unable to attract highly skilled lawyers to serve as prosecutors and which encourages private practice, leading to the conflicts of interest previously mentioned. Excluding the federal government, slightly more than one-half billion dollars is spent annually on legal services for prosecution, almost 74 percent of which is expended at the local and county levels of government. Table 10.6 depicts the data.

The President's Crime Commission (*The Courts*, 1967:74) states that it is unlikely that the basic elective method of selecting prosecu-

TABLE 10.5. Percent Distribution of Employment and Payrolls for the Criminal Justice System, by Level of Government, October, 1973 (Dollar amounts in thousands)

Activity	All Governments	Federal Government	State Governments	Local Governments	Percent Distribution Federal Government	Percent Distribution State Governments	Percent Distribution Local Governments
Legal services and prosecution:							
Total employees	54,781	6,649	11,082	37,050	12.2	20.2	67.6
Full-time employees	43,067	6,333	9,905	26,829	14.7	23.0	62.3
Full-time equivalent employees	47,304	6,395	10,490	30,419	13.5	22.2	64.3
October payroll	50,978	9,022	11,648	30,308	17.7	22.8	59.5

Source: Expenditure and Employment Data for the Criminal Justice System: 1972–1973. Washington, D.C.: LEAA, 1973:17.

TABLE 10.6. Legal Services and Prosecution Expenditures by State and
Type of Government, Fiscal Year 1972–1973 (Thousands of dollars)

State and Type of Government	Total	Direct Expenditure		
		Total	Direct Current	Capital Outlay
United States, Total	540,316	540,316	535,134	5,182
States	145,805	143,417	141,101	2,316
Local, Total	398,783	396,899	394,033	2,866
Counties	230,066	227,860	225,862	1,997
Municipalities	169,386	169,039	168,171	868

Source: Expenditure and Employment Data for the Criminal Justice System: 1972–
1973. Washington, D.C.: LEAA. 1973:223.

tors will soon be changed, especially since elections for these kinds of
officials is ingrained in our political traditions. As a matter of fact,
according to the Commission, experience has also demonstrated that
some career elected prosecutors have proved to be dedicated, highly
competent, and very responsive to community needs and wishes.
However, the Commission argues in favor of reducing political pressures. This would include the removal of assistant appointments from
political patronage, the appointment of only qualified persons, encouraging career opportunities through high salary and promotion
opportunity, and by placing appointments under the sponsorship of
civil service regulations. Assistants should not be involved in political
activities on a mandatory basis, but should be free to campaign or
contribute if they freely choose to do so. Finally, the Commission
recommends extensive and intensive training to raise the competency
levels of those elected as well as appointed.

Since prosecutors spend a great deal of their time in investigating
criminal activities (some even have investigators attached to their
staffs) and expend considerable efforts in actually presenting cases
during trial, a great deal of justice is administered with and without
judicial supervision. As a consequence, both the President's Crime
Commission and the National Advisory Commission on Criminal
Justice Standards and Goals recommend that prosecution in every
state be coordinated and supervised by someone such as the state's
attorney general. This state official, it is argued, could provide
technical and statistical services, arrange for training, set standards
for the employment of assistants, and develop rules of general

applicability for the various kinds of discretionary decisions prosecutors make. Working closely with a judicial council, the Attorney General would also be in the position to prepare guidelines for prosecutors based on procedural laws or case decisions rendered by the highest courts of the state. Such coordination would also ensure a greater standardization of services throughout the state, thereby helping to achieve a minimum level of services and justice.

The National Advisory Commission on Criminal Justice Standards and Goals has promulgated nine distinct standards it recommends for implementation throughout the country. The Commission states (*Courts*, 1973:228):

> The standards . . . are designed to promote the development of professional prosecutors' offices that will have the personnel, resources, and direction to perform their duties effectively. The basic premise of these standards is that the office of the prosecutor should be on the same level of professionalism as private law firms of comparable size.

Four standards relating to personnel and the state-wide organization of prosecutors are presented below:

Standard 12.1
Professional Standards for the Chief Prosecuting Officer

The complexities and demands of the prosecution function require that the prosecutor be a full-time, skilled professional selected on the basis of demonstrated ability and high personal integrity. The prosecutor should be authorized to serve a minimum term of 4 years at an annual salary no less than that of the presiding judge of the trial court of general jurisdiction.

In order to meet these standards, the jurisdiction of every prosecutor's office should be designed so that population, caseload and other relevant factors warrant at least one full-time prosecutor.

Standard 12.2
Professional Standards for Assistant Prosecutors

The primary basis for the selection and retention of assistant prosecutors should be demonstrated legal ability. Care should be taken to recruit lawyers from all segments of the population. The prosecutor should undertake programs, such as legal internships for law students, designed to attract able young lawyers to careers in prosecution.

The position of assistant prosecutor should be a full-time occupation, and assistant prosecutors should be prohibited from engaging in outside law practice. The starting salaries for assistant prosecutors should be no less than those paid by private law firms in the jurisdiction, and the prosecutor should have the authority to increase periodically the salaries for assistant prosecutors to a level that will encourage the retention of able and experienced prosecutors, subject to approval of the legislature, city or county council as appropriate. For the first 5 years of service, salaries of assistant prosecutors should be comparable to those of attorney associates in local private law firms.

The caseload for each assistant prosecutor should be limited to permit the proper preparation of cases at every level of the criminal proceedings. Assistant prosecutors should be assigned cases sufficiently in advance of the court date in order to enable them to interview every prosecution witness, and to conduct supplemental investigations when necessary.

The trial division of each prosecutor's office should have at least two attorneys for each trial judge conducting felony trials on a full-time basis or the equivalent of such a judge. Each office also should have a sufficient number of attorneys to perform the other functions of the office.

Standard 12.3
Supporting Staff and Facilities

The office of the prosecutor should have a supporting staff comparable to that of similar-size private law firms. Prosecutors whose offices serve metropolitan jurisdictions should appoint an office manager with the responsibility for program planning and budget management, procurement of equipment and supplies, and selection and supervision of nonlegal personnel. Paraprofessionals should be utilized for law-related tasks that do not require prosecutorial experience and training. There should be adequate secretarial help for all staff attorneys. Special efforts should be made to recruit members of the supporting staff from all segments of the community served by the office.

The office of the prosecutor should have physical facilities comparable to those of similar-size private law firms. There should be at least one conference room and one lounge for staff attorneys, and a public waiting area separate from the offices of the staff.

The prosecutor and his staff should have immediate access to a library sufficiently extensive to fulfill the research needs of the office. Staff attorneys should be supplied with personal copies of books, such as the State criminal code, needed for their day-to-day duties.

The basic library available to a prosecutor's office should include the following: the annotated laws of the State, the State code of criminal procedure, the municipal code, the United States code annotated, the State appellate reports, the U.S. Supreme Court reports, Federal courts of appeals and district court reports, citators covering all reports and statutes in the library, digests for State and Federal cases, a legal reference work digesting State law, a legal reference work digesting law in general, a form book of approved jury charges, legal treatises on evidence and criminal law, criminal law and U.S. Supreme Court case reporters published weekly, looseleaf services related to criminal law, and if available, an index to the State appellate brief bank.

Standard 12.4
Statewide Organization of Prosecutors

In every State there should be a State-level entity that makes available to local prosecutors who request them the following:

1. Assistance in the development of innovative prosecution programs;
2. Support services, such as laboratory assistance; special counsel, investigators, accountants, and other experts; data-gathering services; appellate research services; and office management assistance.

This entity should provide for at least four meetings each year, at which prosecutors from throughout the State can engage in continuing education and exchange with other prosecutors. In administering its program, the entity should try to eliminate undesirable discrepancies in law enforcement policies.

In States where the local prosecutors are appointed by the State attorney general, the office of the attorney general may be the entity performing these functions. In other States, and where desirable in States in which local prosecutors are appointed by the State attorney general, an independent State agency should be created to perform these functions. The agency and its program should be funded by the State through the executive budget. It should have officers and a governing board elected by the membership; the attorney general of the State should be an ex officio member of the governing board. A full-time executive director should be provided to administer the agency and its program.

Defense Counsel

The role of defense counsel is often depicted in very romantic and colorful terms, especially when someone like Clarence Darrow is viewed as the prototype. For many years, however, counsel for the defense in criminal matters has been a role shunned by competent attorneys. Some people blame the legal profession itself for having neglected this kind of work and for even having put it down. Until recently law schools have failed to emphasize this branch of the practice of law, giving more status in their curricula to such fields as corporate and tax law.

With the advent of greater services to the indigent and a growing commitment to criminal law by young attorneys, criminal defense practice appears to be gaining more popularity. Leading bar groups, such as the American Law Institute, the American Bar Foundation, the National Defender Project, the National Conference of Commissioners on Uniform State Law, the Commission on Correctional Facilities and Services, and the Project on Standards for Criminal Justice, the latter two groups of the American Bar Association, have all helped to place greater emphasis on criminal defense. However, as the American Bar Association (1974:107) points out, ". . . a large obstacle to making criminal defense work more attractive as a career is the ambiguity of the defense lawyer's role, the uncertainty surrounding the standards of professional conduct applicable to its performance, and the public attitude toward lawyers who specialize in this field."

Due to the fact that our system of administration of justice is based on an adversary system, it is imperative that highly trained advocates for each side be available to the defendant as well as to the state. Even though our law recognizes the right of every offender to defend himself in court without the assistance of counsel if he so chooses, most observers of the criminal justice scene believe that justice tends to be undermined without professional advocacy. This is so because an accused person who is defending himself generally does not take full advantage of his legal rights.

The primary function of defense counsel is to act as champion for his client, ensuring that due process is adhered to, and to take those procedural steps and to recommend those courses of action which the client, were he an experienced advocate himself, would fairly and properly take for himself. Since most criminal clients are not perceived so positively by society (of which jurors are a part), it is up to the defense lawyer to counteract any hostility which may be present in order to assure his client a fair trial.

It is also the responsibility of defense counsel to protect the rights of his client at every step of the criminal justice process. In this regard, he often acts as an intermediary between opposing forces. If his client has violated the law, he works with the prosecution in plea bargaining to provide for his client "the best possible deal." The ABA (1974:110, 112) states:

> As intermediary, counsel expresses to the court objectively, in measured words and forceful tone, what a particular defendant may be incapable of expressing himself simply because he lacks the education and training. The defendant must not be judged on his own forensic skill or lack of it.

The defendant needs counsel not only to evaluate the risks and advantages of alternative courses of action, such as trial or plea, but also to provide a broad and comprehensive approach to his predicament which will take the most advantage of the protections and benefits which the law affords him.

Newman (1975:94–95) suggests that since the *Gideon* decision in 1963, the United States Supreme Court has significantly expanded the right of representation to a number of "critical stages" of the criminal justice process from in-custody interrogation by the police through appeal to various postconviction determinations. A major problem, however, is who shall pay for the lawyer's services. Newman goes on to indicate that provision for counsel falls into four major categories:

1) private counsel, whereby the defendant or petitioner hires with his own funds a practicing lawyer who is willing to take his case; 2) court assignment, a procedure by which the judge appoints lawyers randomly from bar lists or from a panel of attorneys who have expressed willingness to serve, or if possible, attorneys chosen by petitioners (but in each case in which petitioner's indigency is demonstrated, the attorney's fees are paid by the county or by other appropriate jurisdiction); 3) public defender, a system found in some jurisdictions in which a public defender's office is created and staffed much like the office of the prosecutor but with the mandate to defend indigents; and 4) legal aid services, involving a variety of programs, some subsidized by federal and state funds, others by local donations, whereby storefront law offices are set up and act very much like other Red Feather (i.e., "charitable") community resources for the poor, in this instance by providing both civil and criminal legal assitance.

The advantages and disadvantages of various assignment-of-counsel procedures to the indigent have been studied, but as Silverstein (1965:73) reports in an American Bar Foundation study, the results are inconclusive. Which way indigent defense will finally and conclusively go cannot be determined at this time, especially since we cannot be certain what the desires are of private counsel who are appointed to serve such clients. It is also a complicated issue in terms of the organization of services. For example, Newman (1975:96) states:

With the exception of public defender offices, the defense attorney function is not centered in a definable on-line agency of criminal justice. Defense attorneys are mainly entrepreneurs outside the organizational structure of the system and adversary to its processes. However, their presence throughout the process is now pervasive and their activities contribute directly and importantly to the shape and nature of criminal justice in our society.

The President's Crime Commission estimated that there were almost 348,000 felony defendants in state and federal criminal courts in 1965 and that a full-time lawyer, with adequate supportive and investigative back-up services, could handle approximately 150 to 200 felony defendants per year. This would mean that approximately 1,700 to 2,300 full-time defense lawyers would be needed each year. This, of course, is besides the numbers that would be needed for juveniles, misdemeanants, and traffic cases. The President's Crime Commission also stated that if between 8,300 and 12,500 defense lawyers are actually needed throughout the system and that if no more than half are paid by private funds, the necessary costs would fall somewhere between $84 million and $158 million per year.

These figures, however, are probably grossly inadequate for the late 1970s. According to the Law Enforcement Assistance Administration, the 1972-1973 data available on manpower and expenditures in the field of criminal justice reveal that the almost 6,000 employees in the field of indigent defense already cost all levels of government (including federal) almost $207 million dollars (LEAA, 1975:17). Thus, a picture emerges that indigent defense—counsel provided to the poor by government—is a costly enterprise and one that is likely to increase substantially in the years ahead. This excludes, of course, "volunteer" efforts (such as that provided by law students and neighborhood legal groups) and where private counsel is appointed by the court to represent the poor without fee.

The National Advisory Commission on Criminal Justice Standards and Goals (*Courts*, 1973) has promulgated 16 standards related to criminal defense, including two that indicate such services should be provided by government along with private counsel and organized at the state-wide level of government. Three of the standards are presented below:

Standard 13.1
Availability of Publicly Financed Representation in Criminal Cases

Public representation should be made available to eligible defendants (as defined in Standard 13.2) in all criminal cases at their request, or the request of someone acting for them, beginning at the time the individual either is arrested or is requested to participate in an investigation that has focused upon him as a likely suspect. The representation should continue during trial court proceedings and through the exhaustion of all avenues of relief from conviction.

Defendants should be discouraged from conducting their own defense in criminal prosecutions. No defendant should be permitted to defend himself if there is a basis for believing that:

1. The defendant will not be able to deal effectively with the legal or factual issues likely to be raised;

2. The defendant's self-representation is likely to impede the reasonably expeditious processing of the case; or

3. The defendant's conduct is likely to be disruptive of the trial process.

Standard 13.5
Method of Delivering Defense Services

Services of a full-time public defender organization, and a coordinated assigned counsel system involving substantial participation of the private bar, should be available in each jurisdiction to supply attorney services to indigents accused of crime. Cases should be divided between the public defender and assigned counsel in a manner that will encourage significant participation by the private bar in the criminal justice system.

Standard 13.9
Performance of Public Defender Function

Policy should be established for and supervision maintained over a defender office by the public defender. It should be the responsibility of the public defender to insure that the duties of the office are discharged with diligence and competence.

The public defender should seek to maintain his office and the performance of its function free from political pressures that may interfere with his ability to provide effective defense services. He should assume a role of leadership in the general community, interpreting his function to the public and seeking to hold and maintain their support of and respect for this function.

The relationship between the law enforcement component of the criminal justice system and the public defender should be characterized by professionalism, mutual respect, and integrity. It should not be characterized by demonstrations of negative personal feelings on one hand or excessive familiarity on the other. Specifically, the following guidelines should be followed:

1. The relations between public defender attorneys and prosecution attorneys should be on the same high level of professionalism that is expected between responsible members of the bar in other situations.

2. The public defender must negate the appearance of impropriety by avoiding excessive and unnecessary camaraderie in and around the courthouse and in his relations with law enforcement officials, remaining at all times aware of his image as seen by his client community.

3. The public defender should be prepared to take positive action, when invited to do so, to assist the police and other law enforcement components in understanding and developing their proper roles in the criminal justice system, and to assist them in developing their own professionalism. In the course of this educational process he should assist in resolving possible areas of misunderstanding.

4. He should maintain a close professional relationship with his fellow members of the legal community and organized bar, keeping in mind at all times that this group offers the most potential support for his office in the community and that, in the final analysis, he is one of them. Specifically:

a. He must be aware of their potential concern that he will preempt the field of criminal law, accepting as clients all accused persons without regard to their ability or willingness to retain private counsel. He must avoid both the appearance and fact of competing with the private bar.

b. He must, while in no way compromising his representation of his own clients, remain sensitive to the calendaring problems that beset civil cases as a result of criminal case overloads, and cooperate in resolving these.

c. He must maintain the bar's faith in the defender system by affording vigorous and effective representation to his own clients.

d. He must maintain dialogue between his office and the private bar, never forgetting that the bar more than any other group has the potential to assist in keeping his office free from the effects of political pressures and influences.

Court Management

In recent years considerable attention has been focused on the management or administration of the courts in this country. In the past, the presiding judge of each court traditionally was the chief executive or manager. However, as hospitals, public welfare agencies, and other "people-serving" organizations have learned, a professionally trained person in his or her appropriate discipline is not necessarily prepared to manage competently an organization. This is just as true in the courts as in every other field of endeavor. As a consequence, court administrators have begun to emerge as managers of the day-to-day affairs of the court.

In *Managing the Courts* (1971), Friesen *et al.* lay out the problems, policies, and practices associated with the notion of having a person other than a judge administer the courts. They maintain that the courts are manageable, but that only professional management can do the job effectively and efficiently. They state, for example (1971:125):

> The court executive is the principal source of support, advice, and information on management matters for the presiding judge and the entire court. The court, as his board of directors, gives him policy direction. The presiding judge, as the chairman of the board, is expected to support him in his coordination and control of all nonjudicial elements of the court operation.

In a report prepared for LEAA by Saari (1970:5), eight basic management functions of the court executive are listed. These include: (1) general, (2) personnel, (3) data processing, (4) financial, (5) calendar, (6) jury and witness, (7) space and equipment, and (8) public information and report.

Insofar as the future is concerned, Saari suggests that there are four considerations which need to be addressed. These include (1970: 25):

1. *Improve management*:
   Improved managerial capability must be developed in every court system to the greatest possible extent—and it should be started promptly. We should hasten the professionalization of the court executive.
2. *Exchange management ideas*:
   Judges and court executives from metropolitan, regional, state, and national judicial systems should exchange information and ideas about management practices regularly and frequently—at least monthly in some areas.
3. *Allocate more resources to management*:
   Increased expenditure of public funds and absorption of time on complex management problems must be encouraged in every court system by responsible budgetary and appropriating authorities inside and outside judicial systems.
4. *Change the court executive role*:
   There should be increased questioning about the concept of a sole "staff" or "advisory" characteristic of the court executive role, with more stress placed on a fuller concept of the court executive's entire capability and the increasing managerial responsibilities in the years ahead.

References

American Bar Association
    1971   The Improvement of the Administration of Justice. 5th ed. Chicago: ABA.

    1974   The Administration of Justice. ABA Standards. Chicago: ABA.

Elliott, Mabel A.
    1952   Crime in Modern Society. New York: Harper and Brothers.

Frankfurter, Felix and James M. Landis
    1927   The Business of the Supreme Court. New York: Macmillan.

Friesen, Ernest C., Jr., Edward C. Gallas, and Nesta M. Gallas.
    1971   Managing the Courts. Indianapolis: Bobbs-Merrill Co.

Germann, A.C., Frank D. Day, and Robert R.J. Gallati
    1962   Introduction to Law Enforcement and Criminal Justice. Springfield, Illinois: Charles C. Thomas.

Green, Milton D.
    1965   "The Business of the Trial Courts." In The Courts, the Public and the Law Explosion. Harry W. Jones, ed. Englewood Cliffs, New Jersey: Prentice-Hall: 7–28.

Jacob, Herbert
    1965   Justice in America. Boston: Little, Brown and Co.

Korn, Richard R. and Lloyd W. McCorkle
    1965   Criminology and Penology. New York: Holt, Rinehart and Winston.

Law Enforcement Assistance Administration
    1973   National Survey of Court Organization. Washington, D.C.: U.S. Government Printing Office.

    1975   Expenditure and Employment Data for the Criminal Justice System: 1972–1973. Washington, D.C.: U.S. Government Printing Office.

Nagel, Stuart
    1962   "Sociometric Relations among American Courts." Southwestern Social Science Quarterly 43:136–142.

National Advisory Commission on Criminal Justice Standards and Goals
    1973   Courts. Washington, D.C.: U.S. Government Printing Office.

Newman, Donald J.
    1975   Introduction to Criminal Justice. Philadelphia: J.B. Lippincott Co.

Robertson, John A.
    1974   Rough Justice: Perspectives on Lower Criminal Courts. Boston: Little, Brown and Co.

Saari, David J.
    1970   Modern Court Management: Trends in the Role of the Court Executive. Washington, D.C.: U.S. Government Printing Office.

Silverstein, Lee

1965   The Defense of the Poor in Criminal Cases in American State Courts. Chicago: American Bar Foundation.

Sutherland, Edwin H. and Donald R. Cressey

1974   Criminology. 9th ed. Philadelphia: J.B. Lippincott Co.

Tannenbaum, Frank

1938   Crime and the Community. New York: Columbia University Press.

Tappan, Paul W.

1960   Crime, Justice and Correction. New York: McGraw-Hill.

The President's Commission on Law Enforcement and Administration of Justice

1967   The Courts. Washington, D.C.: U.S. Government Printing Office.

CORRECTIONS OVERVIEW

Corrections Concerns

Man's concern for deviance and the correctional processes he has used to control those who violate the norms (laws) of society is long, complex, and constantly changing. Barnes and Teeters (1951: 342–343) believe that there has been an orderly process of evolution in correctional practices while Conrad (1965:17) suggests that "common sense" has helped corrections to reconcile conflicting correctional demands of "control and humanitarianism."

Korn and McCorkle (1959:368–370), on the other hand, maintain that what we have today has come about as a result of accident, power plays by rulers with vested interests, and meager attempts at innovation by correctional authorities. They further (1959:365) suggest that the decision about what to do with offenders in society historically has been based on one or more of a limited number of social objectives or purposes. These include retaliation, disablement, deterrence, protection of society, and reformation.

A number of authors, including Glaser (1964:203), Sutherland and Cressey (1970:325-29), and Schrag (1966) summarize the history of corrections by suggesting that there have been three basic stages, each characterized by a particular emphasis in the handling of offenders: first, revenge; second, restraint; and finally, reformation. Some authors now suggest that a fourth correctional emphasis is emerging—that of reintegration of the offender in the community.

Although Lovell and Nelson state (1969:27):

Each new emphasis (on the various goals of corrections) has been super-imposed upon the earlier ones so that the present network of goals and services is a potpourri in which all appear in various and often bewildering combinations in different correctional organizations and subsystems;

Timasheff concludes (1937:401):

The very possibility of overcoming the retributive structure of punishment (and correctional services) is doubtful . . . even the boldest reformers dare not break with tradition based on retaliation.

One might argue that Timasheff wrote almost four decades ago and that his view cannot be supported today, especially as a result of the so-called "successful" development of probation and parole services and the expanding nature of reintegration or community based programs throughout the United States in the 1970s.

Sutherland and Cressey (1970:356) are among the prominent exponents of this changing shift in correctional thinking. Taking a Positivistic point of view, they summarize the reasons for the shift from retribution to rehabilitation, which lays the groundwork for re-integration:

The official policy of individualized treatment for offenders developed out of the positive school's arguments against the practice of attempting to impose uniform punishments . . . It was, and is, argued that policies calling for uniform punishments are as obviously ineffective as would be a policy calling for uniform treatment of all medical patients, no matter what their ailments. This led some persons to advocate that the type of punishment be adapted to the individual offender; even today "individualization" is sometimes used to refer to a system for imposing punishments. However, as the treatment reaction has increased in popularity, "individualization" has come to designate a treatment process . . . involving expert diagnosis . . . and expert therapy . . .

As the above indicates, we have reached the stage in correctional practice in the United States whereby delinquents and criminals are perceived to be "sick" and in need of expert treatment and "cure." The rehabilitation model, based on Positive criminology concepts, assumes that crime and delinquency can be best understood in terms of the offender's behavior and the social situation. A number of other authors disagree with this perspective and raise questions about how deviance is defined and reacted to by the general community. Rubington and Weinberg (1968), Becker (1963), Cicourel (1968), and Goldman (1963), among others, write that deviance is "in the eye of the beholder" and that it is no more than a *social label* placed on those who act or appear to be different in society—especially delinquents and criminals. They argue that to completely understand why these persons behave as they do as well as understand social processes for control, it is also necessary to understand the process of "labelling."

This labelling approach requires that the study of offenders be structured not according to a *medical* model (diagnosis, prognosis, and treatment or cure). Instead, it requires a model which describes the *interaction* between the offender and the agents and agencies of social control who label him as deviant. It is a model which suggests that police, courts, and corrections frequently take too much for granted in assuming that deviance is merely a consequence of offender behavior or misbehavior. It is a model which questions how decisions are made in criminal justice administration and explores the extent to which "self-fulfilling prophecies" may occur as a result of official policies and practices. Further, it is a model which suggests that some offenders wind up in court primarily because of their race, age, sex, or other distinguishing characteristics, rather than only because of their deviant behavior. Who is arrested and who is merely admonished by the police when both kinds of persons commit the same offense is an example of the kind of situation interactionists or labelling theorists study (Rubington and Weinberg, 1968; Goldman, 1963; Piliavin and Briar, 1964).

Reform Movement

The reform movement reached its peak during the 18th century and is depicted as the Classical School of Criminology through the writings of such persons as Beccaria and Bentham. It gave way to the Positive School of Criminology during the latter part of the 19th century. (See Vold, 1958; Schafer, 1969; and Mannheim, 1965, for detailed discussions.) The transformation from theory to practice, however, probably began in the United States with the development of the first juvenile court in Chicago in 1899. It was here that the notion of rehabilitation was first implemented on a systematic basis, for delinquents were viewed as being "sick" and in need of treatment. As psychoanalytic theories gained in popularity (when Freud's writings began to influence American social planners), juvenile courts and the child guidance clinics frequently associated with them increased in numbers.

According to Platt, the "child savers" responsible for the development of the juvenile court movement were very much interested in the rehabilitation of the young. But, they also appeared to be concerned with the control of immigrants and the poor and thus strived, in the movement, to keep such "minorities" in their geographical and social places:

> The child savers viewed themselves as altruists and humanitarians dedicated to rescuing those who were less fortunately placed in the social order. Their concern for "purity," "salvation," "innocence," "corruption," and "protection" reflected a resolute belief in the righteousness of their mission (Platt, 1969:3).

These child savers were, in effect, the "moral entrepreneurs" (Becker, 1963:147–163)* of their era and persons whose beliefs still affect correctional activities today.

Due to the work of these concerned persons and moral entrepreneurs, the juvenile court system became firmly established on the basis of a *parens patriae* philosophy.

This notion held that the *state* had the right, if not the responsibility, to look after and care for its youth if the natural parents were unable or unwilling to do so. The program, according to Shireman (1962:vi) was designed to protect society through the process of rehabilitation:

---

*Becker defines "moral entrepreneur" as follows: "Rules are the products of someone's initiative and we can think of the people who exhibit such enterprise as *moral entrepreneurs*" (1963:147).

Social protection was to be achieved through the rehabilitation of the juvenile offender. Decisions in each case were to be made upon the basis of mature, clinical judgment. The age-old themes of vengeance, incapacitation, and deterrent punishment were to be replaced by humane understanding and compassion.

Cohen and Short (1966:84–85) in tracing the history of the juvenile court movement and the process of dealing with offenders—adult as well as juvenile—as "sick" persons, state:

> The manifest function (important or declared purpose) of the juvenile court . . . is usually phrased in the statutes in some such words as these: to secure for each child within its jurisdiction such care, custody, and treatment as should have been provided by the child's natural parents. It is not to punish but to "help children in trouble" to do what is in the best interest of the child and the state to "rehabilitate."

The attempt by most contemporary correctional workers to "cure" offenders has been approached with zeal and often with sophisticated programs in prisons, probation, parole, and other types of community based services. It has been geared to what Allen (1964:26) has called the "rehabilitative ideal":

> The rehabilitative ideal is itself a complex of ideas which, perhaps, defies an exact definition. The essential points, however, can be identified. It is assumed, first, that human behavior is the product of antecedent causes. These causes can be identified as part of the physical universe . . . Knowledge of the antecedents of human behavior makes possible an approach to the scientific control of human behavior. Finally . . . it is assumed that measures employed to treat the convicted offender should serve a therapeutic function; that such measures should be designed to effect changes in the behavior of the convicted person and in the interests of his own happiness, health, and satisfactions and in the interest of social defense.

Positivists, since Lombroso, who looked at causation from a constitutional or hereditary point of view, have attempted to control crime and delinquency by understanding the offender and the milieu in which he or she lives. It is the welfare of the offender and the ways in which he or she might be rehabilitated (or habilitated, according to some) that supposedly receive the primary attention. It is through this process, some say, that society will indeed be protected, as the rehabilitated offender will be able to be reintegrated back into society as a normal, constructive, and law-abiding citizen. It is questionable, however, that this "rehabilitative ideal" has ever been significantly implemented or, for that matter, that that truly is the primary goal of the correctional system.

As Cohn (1973) points out, this is not to say that correctional officials are "heinous" creatures who deliberately are against the rehabilitation of their clients (as some clients might indeed argue). But it may suggest that we do not yet have sufficient knowledge and/ or skills to successfully implement the "rehabilitative ideal." It may be that correctional officials know what they would *like* to do with and for convicted offenders, but they do not know precisely *how* to do it.

The objective of rehabilitation (and now of reintegration) is probably a very humanistic effort in correctional history. But it is possible that the so-called manifest (primary) function of change or cure of offenders has only been dealt with superficially, while the latent (hidden or secondary) function of custody and control of offenders—keeping them in their places—has really been the goal all along (Kassebaum, Ward, and Wilner, 1971). A more important question to ask might be: Does correctional rehabilitation work?

Seeking to determine the effectiveness of rehabilitation, Bailey (1966) evaluates 100 reports of correctional treatment programs (between 1940 and 1960) and concludes that the results are discouraging. Logan (1972) and Lipton *et al.* (1975) reach a similar conclusion based primarily on the inadequacy of research methodologies. Scarpitti and Stephenson (1968) evaluate probation as a treatment program and indicate that it does not work for seriously delinquent youths. Lohman, Wahl, and Carter (1965–1967), in the San Francisco Project, examine adult probation services; Murton (1969) reports on his attempts to bring about prison reform; Robison and Smith (1971) evaluate correctional programs in general; Lerman (1968) studies programs for institutionalized delinquents; Robison and Takagi (1968), Ward (1967), and Takagi (1967) independently examine parole systems. Lipton, Martinson, and Wilks (1975) evaluate 231 major rehabilitation research studies, covering the period 1945–1967, and published their conclusions in a book entitled, *The Effectiveness of Correctional Treatment.* Along with the aforementioned authors, the researchers report the devastating finding that *correctional rehabilitation does not work.*

The reports of Adams (1967), who evaluates the results of

small-caseload research projects, and Dash (1970), who studies the Offender Rehabilitation Project, offer some encouragement, but they are cautious nonetheless.

Rehabilitation vs. Custody

A number of authors, including Cressey (1965), Eaton (1962), McCleery (1969), Murton (1969), Nelson and Lovell (1970:68–69), and Piliavin and Vadum (1968:35–43) have recently suggested that the primary reason for the failure of correctional services in general and the prisons in particular to change or cure clients is the philosophical cleavage between those who favor rehabilitation and those who advocate custody or control. Those who want rehabilitation imply that they have the knowledge and skills to accomplish their goal but are interfered with by those who prefer punishment and control. Further, they decry the "meddling" of others and insist that, given ample resources and opportunity, they could improve the effectiveness of their treatment programs. They are not discouraged by the otherwise overwhelming evidence that rehabilitation has not worked to date.

Robison and Smith (1971:79–80) do not believe that such a cleavage exists:

> Punishment and treatment . . . are not opposites . . . In correctional practice, treatment and punishment generally coexist and cannot appropriately be viewed as mutually exclusive . . . The real choice in correction, then, is not between treatment on one hand and punishment on the other but between one treatment-punishment alternative and another . . . (But) *there is no evidence to support any program's claim of superior rehabilitative efficacy.*

Kassebaum, Ward, and Wilner (1971:vii) are not as confident that treatment programs and custodial concerns can or do co-exist:

> Our perspective is that departments of correction are bureaucratic organizations that are charged with a number of responsibilities by the larger community. The most important of these directions relate to the contention, held by some, that violators should be punished; the contention of many that lawbreakers should be rehabilitated while they are kept away from the rest of the community in correctional institutions. The reconciliation of these mandates is difficult in day-to-day prison

> operations (as well as in probation and parole services) . . . *We maintain that prisons and parole divisions operate first and foremost to achieve the goal of social control* (italics added). Peace and quiet are the first order of business in prison, and the detection of law violations or of signs of *impending* law violation is the first order of business of parole (and probation).

The authors go on to state their impression that some inmates of correctional institutions perceive treatment (especially the group counseling program they studied) not as rehabilitation at all but as a "new custodial device" (1971:2). Convicted offenders involved in programs of therapy, in prison, probation, parole, or other community based settings, are generally observed for changes which might occur in their attitudes or behavior. Those under such supervision who do not make sufficient "progress" or those who refuse to become involved in such treatment programs as may be prescribed for them stand little chance of being released from prison to parole (or to the "good" jobs inside the prison). Or, if under supervision in the community on probation or parole, they run the risk of being violated and returned to prison for their "lack of cooperation" or their "unwillingness to help themselves."

Technical violations for failure to cooperate are decreasing in numbers throughout the United States. Additionally there is probably somewhat less harassment of prisoners inside prisons today. Nonetheless, the rights of offenders *not* to participate in treatment programs are not respected by correctional authorities. It is as if correctional personnel hold the proverbial carrot in front of the offenders, promising them their freedom if they will only cooperate with the system and not "make any waves." The unwilling offender finds himself in "trouble" and his release from custody or supervision, more likely, will be delayed until he relents and cooperates with the treatment program which has been established for him by those "who know what is best for him." We will have more to say about treatment, services, and programs in correctional settings in forthcoming chapters.

Correctional Expertise

The attempt to determine "correctional effectiveness" is complicated because we are not sure exactly what the correctional worker is supposed to do. Among others, Nelson (1966:222) discusses the confusion concerning the correctional role and characterizes it as being:

> ... many things to many people. To some it is an area of professional practice; to others it is an academic discipline. To still others it is neither of these but merely an intersection of occupations which differ greatly in philosophy and technique.

Other writers, including Ohlin *et al.* (1956:211-225) and J. Hall *et al.*, also have deplored the dilemma of the correctional worker. The latter state (1966:493-494):

> Much more has been written about the offender and how he should be handled than about the correctional worker who must do the work or, for that matter, about the work itself. The upshot of this in the field of corrections is characterized by a "practice without theory" approach to its task; the only attention paid to the individual worker is in the form of prescribing the kind of person he *should be*, rather than a formulation of the task-relevant skills which should make him professionally unique ... Moreover, such an answer (to the question of who the correctional worker is) will not be forthcoming until the objectives of correctional agencies have been clarified to the point of allowing some measure of success or failure in the attainment of objectives.

In the face of these issues, it may be tempting to substitute high-sounding words for the realities faced in practice. Radzinowicz (1960:119-120) puts it this way:

> It is all very well for penal administrators, who can only use the resources society gives them, to adopt formulae such as *training for freedom,* or *turn them out of prison better men and women ... than they went in,* or *an offender is sent to prison as a punishment.* The hard figures combine with the studies of what actually goes on in the subcultures of prisons ... to cast a heavy cloud over claims such as these. They may provide a lofty charter, but they are far from expressing present penal realities.

Frank (1970:3) suggests that a basic problem is that "conflicting messages are carried by the word 'corrections.'" That is, the term is variously interpreted to include custody to protect the community, humane treatment, or rehabilitation of the offender. A number of writers believe that we are definitely in the stage of treatment or reintegration in correctional practice, and although we express commitment to the "rehabilitative ideal" (Allen, 1964; Cressey,

1968; and Bailey, 1966), Kassebaum *et al.* (1971) say it does not work, as we have previously discussed. Another (Sherwood, 1967: 42) puts it this way:

> There is also growing, if reluctant, agreement that corrections does not at the present time know how to go about successfully rehabilitating offenders. This general lack of knowledge exists even if in fact rehabilitation is actually taking place within one or more correctional systems. There are at least two basic reasons for this rather sad state of affairs: (1) no general, workable, agreed-upon definition of the meaning of rehabilitation has been developed; (2) with very few exceptions, procedures have not been built into correctional systems for finding out whether rehabilitation is taking place.

This "irrational equilibrium," as Conrad (1965:11) calls it, may now have become too delicately balanced to continue to be viable. And yet, of all the known alternatives for society's response to the lawbreaker, there is no substitute for corrections, regardless of its interpretation, either as a major objective in the administration of criminal justice or as a basic social policy for dealing with the offender.

Contradictory Assumptions

Frank (1970:3–4) states that there are two basic and contradictory assumptions concerning the belief that corrections is not achieving significant results. One assumption is related to existing knowledge:

> (a) that there is sufficient theoretical knowledge to explain the nature of delinquent and criminal behavior, and (b) that there is the scientific methodology to measure significantly the differential effectiveness of the various kinds of correctional programs.*

Frank (1970:4) adds that the second assumption involves expertness and competency:

> (a) that existing correctional programs are in themselves sound and sufficient but that the need is for additional manpower resources from the relevant professions and disciplines, and (b) that correctional practice can

---

*For discussions related to understanding the correctional mission and to the scientific process of measuring correctional achievements, see also Cohn (1970); Schrag (1961 and 1971); Hartung (1958); and Morris (1964).

better achieve its goals by defining its uniqueness and developing an expertness of its own.

Frank (1970:4) concludes that on the basis of these two assumptions, the most popular strategy has been to attribute the ineffectiveness of corrections

... to a quantitative lack of manpower rather than to any qualitative deficiency in theory or contemporary practice.

Although Frank's analysis appears to be incisive, we might add another *set of assumptions* upon which correctional programs and services are based: that there exists a correctional manager, who, trained and skilled in administration and competent to manage his organization, makes clear the goals which his workers are to implement, and ensures a level of accountability from his subordinates that makes sure workers provide adequate services to clients. That the correctional executive may *not* be the competent manager he is assumed to be is probably true (Cohn, 1972, 1973). Thus, lack of knowledge, lack of expertness, and lack of competent management all work against completely meaningful correctional programming at this time.

Cohn (1973) discusses the failure of correctional management in considerable detail, and it may be helpful to review several of his conclusions. He suggests that correctional managers strive more for security than innovative programs, are not supported by their own political superiors, adhere to the notion that offenders are "sick" and thus want to "treat" *every* offender when this is not necessary nor practical, are not trained in administration or management, are unable to set meaningful goals to which they can hold subordinates accountable, and are unable to turn to any "professional" organization for advice, counsel, standard settling, or set of ethics. A serious consequence, according to Cohn, is that correctional organizations tend to drift, provide less than adequate services to clients, and generally fail to protect communities.

Scope of Corrections

As incredible as it may seem, we do not know precisely how many offenders are involved in the correctional system in the United States.

We also do not know how much money—public and private—is being spent officially on offenders once they have been convicted and placed under correctional supervision. However, in a recent report (LEAA, 1974), the Law Enforcement Assistance Administration estimated that a total of $11.7 billion was spent by all levels of government on the entire criminal justice system during fiscal year 1971–1972. The study points out that local government units spend more than two-thirds of their money on police protection while state governments spend nearly 44 percent of their criminal justice funds on correctional activities, for a total of 2¼ billion dollars annually. The report states there are approximately 109,000 state employees in corrections, almost 46,000 persons employed by 312 of the largest county governments, and over 16,000 employed by 384 of the largest city governments, inclusive of all job categories.

Thus, a picture begins to emerge that corrections, as it is practiced in the United States today, is indeed a very large business. It is a business which concerns itself with the management of approximately 1½ million persons on a daily basis (Task Force Report: Corrections, 1967:1) in terms of government services. It is not known how many offenders are dealt with by private organizations, institutions, and/or self-help groups (Cohn, 1974).

According to the Task Force Report: Corrections of the 1967 President's Crime Commission, the American correctional system processes 2.5 million admissions in the course of a year in programs administered by federal, state, county, and municipal governments. The figures, however, exclude offenders temporarily incarcerated in police and sheriff "lock-ups," other detention facilities where offenders are held awaiting trial, or in institutions where offenders serve 30 days or less (misdemeanants). Table 11.1 depicts the numbers of adult and juvenile offenders under supervision by correctional authorities in 1965, the latest year for which we have any national figures; the approximate annual operating costs for the various services; and the numbers of correctional employees working with these offenders.

According to the National Advisory Commission on Criminal Justice Standards and Goals (NACCJSG: Corrections, 1973:2), corrections is defined as "the community's official reactions to the convicted offender, whether adult or juvenile." This simple definition suffers from a number of shortcomings, not the least of which

TABLE 11.1. Some Characteristics of Corrections in the United States, 1965

	Offenders		Operating Costs			Employees	
Type of Program	Average Daily Population	Percentage Distribution	Annual Operating Costs[1]	Percentage Distribution	Average Cost per Offender per Year[2]	Number	Percentage Distribution
Juvenile corrections:							
Institutions	62,773	4.9	$226,809,600	22.5	$3,613	31,687	26.2
Community	285,431	22.2	93,613,400	9.3	328	9,633	8.0
Subtotal	348,204	27.1	320,423,000	31.8		41,320	34.2
Adult felon corrections:							
Institutions	221,597	17.3	435,594,500	43.3	1,966	51,866	42.8
Community	369,897	28.9	73,251,900	7.3	198	6,352	5.2
Subtotal	591,494	46.2	508,846,400	50.6		58,218	48.0
Misdemeanant corrections:							
Institutions	141,303	11.0	147,794,200	14.7	1,046	19,195	15.8
Community	201,385	15.7	28,682,900	2.9	142	2,430	2.0
Subtotal	342,688	26.7	176,477,100	17.6		21,625	17.8
Total	1,282,386	100.0	1,005,746,500	100.0	0	121,163	100.0

[1] Rounded to the nearest $100.
[2] Rounded to the nearest dollar.
Source: Computed from the National Survey of Corrections and special tabulations provided by the Federal Bureau of Prisons and the Administrative Office of the U.S. Courts and as quoted in the President's Crime Commission, Task Force Report: Corrections, 1967.

is its lack of concern for a goal or mission statement. However, as the report (1973:3) goes on to state:

> The definition of corrections as the community's official reaction to convicted adult and juvenile offenders neither states nor implies what corrections should try to achieve. This is essential if realism is to replace rhetoric in the field. In particular, corrections is not defined here as being directed exclusively toward the rehabilitation (or habilitation, which is more often the case) of the convicted offender.... Corrections is limited to the convicted because there are other justifications for coercively intervening in their lives in addition to helping them. Clearly, the penal sanctions imposed on convicted offenders serve a multiplicity of purposes, of which rehabilitation is only one.

Standards, Goals, and Principles

In 1870, the forerunner of the American Correctional Association, the American Prison Association, met in Cincinnati and adopted a "Declaration of Principles." The principles, dealing with the kinds and qualities of services corrections should offer clients and communities, were revised in 1930, reformulated in more modern language in 1960, and then again in 1970—exactly 100 years after their adoption. In 1931, the Wickersham Commission studied the criminal justice system, and like the President's Crime Commission of 1967, many recommendations were made to upgrade the quality of correctional services in the United States. But, as the National Advisory Commission on Criminal Justice Standards and Goals points out, many of these worthwhile recommendations have not been enacted. One of the reasons for this is answered by the NACCJSG (Corrections, 1973:4–5):

> ...Principles and recommendations are neither self-fulfilling nor self-interpreting. Standards and goals may be much more precise, while retaining sufficient flexibility to allow agencies some freedom. When clearly formulated and precisely stated in measurable terms, they can serve as the basis for objective evaluation of programs as well as development of statutes and regulations relating to correctional services ... It prevents all of us from concluding that what we have is right simply because we have it. It reduces room for rationalization.

The various standards and goals which are promoted by the

National Advisory Commission, apparently, are being taken quite seriously by various governmental agencies. Through the Law Enforcement Assistance Administration, federal monies are being made available to all of the states to look into the entire system of criminal justice administration in their respective jurisdictions. The purpose is to enhance the delivery of all services, including those of a correctional nature. States are looking at their criminal codes, programs, and processes of social control and, perhaps, in the next decade, substantial improvements in corrections will be forthcoming.

As the President's Crime Commission states (Corrections, 1967: 13):

> The "new corrections" requires to achieve its goals several fundamental conditions: extended research and program evaluation; better decision-making; improved organization; and more and better qualified staff.

Corrections only deals with the convicted offender. Even though it is frequently involved in preventive and diversionary programs as well, correctional reform cannot possibly take place without understanding its relationship to needs and styles of punishment. Since sentencing generally is viewed as punishment, it is necessary to understand the various historical approaches to punishment, particularly how it has been handled in the United States. Therefore, the next few chapters will deal with the concept and practice of punishment, the juvenile justice system, and the adult correctional settings of probation, prisons, and parole.

References

Adams, Stuart
    1967   "Some Findings from Correctional Caseload Research." Federal Probation 31 (December): 48–57.
Allen, Francis A.
    1964   The Borderland of Criminal Justice. Chicago: The University of Chicago Press.
Bailey, Walter C.
    1966   "Correctional Outcome: An Evaluation of 100 Reports." Journal of Criminal Law, Criminology and Police Science 57:153–160.
Barnes, Harry E. and Negley K. Teeters
    1951   New Horizons in Criminology. 2nd ed. New York: Prentice-Hall.

Becker, Howard S.
    1963   The Outsiders: Studies in the Sociology of Deviance. New York: The Free Press.

Cicourel, Aaron V.
    1968   The Social Organization of Juvenile Justice. New York: John Wiley and Sons.

Cohen, Albert K. and James F. Short, Jr.
    1966   "Juvenile Delinquency." In Robert K. Merton and Robert A. Nisbet, eds. Contemporary Social Problems. 2nd ed. New York: Harcourt, Brace and World.

Cohn, Alvin W.
    1969   Problems, Thoughts, and Processes in Criminal Justice Administration. New York: National Council on Crime and Delinquency.

    1972   Decision-Making in the Administration of Probation Services: A Descriptive Study of the Probation Manager, D. Crim. Dissertation. Berkeley: University of California.

    1973   "The Failure of Correctional Management." Crime and Delinquency 19 (July) 3:323-331.

    1974   "Footnotes on the Future of Corrections." Paper delivered before the Ohio Correctional and Court Services annual meeting. (Mimeo).

Conrad, John
    1965   Crime and Its Correction. Berkeley: University of California Press.

Cressey, Donald R.
    1965   "Prison Organization." In James G. March, ed. Handbook of Organizations. Chicago: Rand McNally and Co.:1023-1070.

    1968   "Sources of Resistance to the Use of Offenders and Ex-Offenders in the Correctional Process." In Keith A. Stubblefield and Larry L. Dye, eds. Offenders as a Correctional Manpower Resource. Washington, D.C.: Joint Commission on Correctional Manpower and Training: 31-49.

Dash, Samuel (ed.)
    1970   Rehabilitative Planning Services for the Criminal Defense. Washington, D.C.: National Institute of Law Enforcement and Criminal Justice, Law Enforcement Assistance Administration.

Eaton, Joseph W.
    1962   Stone Walls Not A Prison Make. Springfield: Charles C. Thomas.

Frank, Benjamin (ed.)
    1970   "Basic Issues in Corrections." In Perspectives on Correctional Manpower and Training. (Staff Report). Washington, D.C.: Joint Commission on Correctional Manpower and Training.

Glaser, Daniel
    1964   "The Prospect for Corrections." Paper prepared for the Arden House Conference on Manpower Needs in Corrections. (Mimeo).

Goldman, Nathan
 1963 The Differential Selection of Juvenile Offenders for Court Appearance. New York: National Council on Crime and Delinquency.

Hall, Jay, M. Williams, and L. Tomaino
 1966 "The Challenge of Correctional Change: The Interface of Conformity and Commitment." Journal of Criminal Law, Criminology and Police Science 57:494–503.

Hartung, Frank E.
 1958 "A Critique of the Sociological Approach to Crime and Corrections." Law and Contemporary Problems 23:703–734.

Kassebaum, Gene, D.A. Ward, and D.M. Wilner
 1971 Prison Treatment and Parole Survival. New York: John Wiley and Sons.

Korn, Richard R. and Lloyd W. McCorkle
 1959 Criminology and Penology. New York: Holt, Rinehart and Winston.

Law Enforcement Assistance Administration
 1974 Expenditure and Employment Data for the Criminal Justice System: 1971–1972. U.S. Bureau of the Census and U.S. Department of Justice. Washington, D.C.: U.S. Government Printing Office.

Lerman, Paul
 1968 "Evaluative Studies of Institutions for Delinquents: Implications for Research and Social Policy." Social Work 13:55–64.

Lipton, Douglas, Robert Martinson, and Judith Wilks
 1975 The Effectiveness of Correctional Treatment: A Survey of Evaluation Studies. New York: Praeger.

Logan, Charles H.
 1972 "Evaluation Research in Crime and Delinquency: A Reappraisal." Journal of Criminal Law, Criminology and Police Science 63:378–87.

Lohman, Joseph D., A. Wahl, and R.M. Carter
 1965– The San Francisco Project. Research Reports 1–12. Berkeley:
 1967 School of Criminology, University of California.

Lovell, Catherine H. and Elmer K. Nelson, Jr.
 1969 "Correctional Management and the Changing Goals of Corrections." In Alvin W. Cohn, ed. Problems, Thoughts, and Processes in Criminal Justice Administration. New York: National Council on Crime and Delinquency.

Mannheim, Hermann
 1965 Comparative Criminology. Boston: Houghton Mifflin Co.

Morris, Norval
 1964 "Impediments to Penal Reform." University of Chicago Law Review 33:627–656.

Murton, Tom and Joe Hyams

1969   Accomplices to the Crime. New York: Grove Press.
National Advisory Commission on Criminal Justice Standards and Goals
1973   Corrections. Washington, D.C.: U.S. Government Printing Office.
Nelson, Elmer K., Jr.
1966   "Strategies for Action in Meeting Correctional Manpower and
          Program Needs." Crime and Delinquency 12:221-26.
Nelson, Elmer K., Jr. and Catherine H. Lovell
1970   Developing Correctional Administrators. Washington, D.C.:
          Joint Commission on Correctional Manpower and Training.
Ohlin, Lloyd E., Herman Piven, and D.M. Pappenfort
1956   "Major Dilemmas of the Social Worker in Probation and Parole."
          National Probation and Parole Association Journal 2:211-225.
Piliavin, Irving and Scott Briar
1964   "Police Encounters with Juveniles." American Journal of Sociol-
          ogy 69:206-214.
Piliavin, Irving and Arlene C. Vadum
1968   "Reducing Discrepancies in Professional and Custodial Perspec-
          tives." Journal of Research in Crime and Delinquency 5 (Janu-
          ary):35-43.
Platt, Anthony
1969   The Child Savers. Chicago: University of Chicago Press.
President's Commission on Law Enforcement and Administration of Justice
1967   Task Force Report: Corrections. Washington, D.C.: U.S. Govern-
          ment Printing Office.
Radzinowicz, Leon
1960   Ideology and Crime. New York: Columbia University Press.
Robison, James and Gerald Smith
1971   "The Effectiveness of Correctional Programs." Crime and Delin-
          quency 17 (January):67-80.
Robison, James and Paul Takagi
1968   Case Decisions in a State Parole System. Research Report No. 31.
          Sacramento: Department of Corrections, State of California.

1968   The Parole Violator as an Organizational Reject: Case Decisions
          in a State Parole System. Berkeley: School of Criminology,
          University of California. (Mimeo).
Rubington, Earl and Martin S. Weinberg
1968   Deviance: The Interactionist Perspective. 1st ed. New York: The
          Macmillan Co.
Scarpitti, Frank R. and Richard M. Stephenson
1968   "A Study of Probation Effectiveness." Journal of Criminal Law,
          Criminology and Police Science 59:361-69.
Schafer, Stephen
1969   Theories in Criminology. New York: Random House.
Schrag, Clarence
1961   "Some Foundation for a Theory of Corrections." In D.R. Cres-
          sey, ed. The Prison: Studies in Institutional Organization and
          Change. New York: Holt, Rinehart and Winston

1966   "Contemporary Corrections: An Analytic Model." Paper prepared for the President's Commission on Law Enforcement and Administration of Justice. Washington, D.C. (Mimeo).

1971   Crime and Justice: American Style. Rockville, Maryland: National Institute of Mental Health, Center for Studies of Crime and Delinquency.

Shireman, Charles R.
1962   "Foreward." In M.K. Rosenheim, ed. Justice for the Child. New York: The Free Press.

Sutherland, Edwin H. and Donald R. Cressey
1970   Criminology, 8th ed. Philadelphia: J.B. Lippincott Co.

Takagi, Paul
1967   Evaluation Systems and Adaptations in a Formal Organization. PhD Dissertation. Palo Alto: Department of Sociology, Stanford University.

Timasheff, N.F.
1937   "The Retributive Structure of Punishment." Journal of Criminal Law and Criminology 28 (September–October):392–406.

Vold, George B.
1958   Theoretical Criminology. New York: Oxford University Press.

Ward, David
1967   "Evaluation of Correctional Treatment: Some Implications of Negative Findings." Proceedings of the First National Symposium on Law Enforcement, Science and Technology. Washington, D.C.: Thompson Book Co.

punishment

Criminal Punishment Defined

The concept of punishment, similar to so many other issues related to criminology and the administration of justice, has a long, complicated, and not easily understood history. It certainly is a concept which arouses considerable passion, depending upon the position taken on the subject and the significance attached to its implementation. Punishment can be viewed as a very personal issue, not only by those on the receiving end, but by those who administer it. It is also a very complex issue, if for no other reason than there are many theories and concepts associated with it and because its purpose and function are subject to so many interpretations.

In reviewing the early history of criminal punishment a problem that immediately arises is where to begin. That is, when should we consider punishment as *criminal punishment*, distinct from other forms of punishment? Legal scholars, sociologists of law, and legal historians, among others, are divided over the appropriate starting point. Some urge that punishment is criminal punishment whenever laws are codified and the punishment can be linked to the violation of one or several of these laws. Thus, where there is written law, there is punishment for law violation (crime) and, hence, there is criminal punishment. Others, however, contend that this approach is not a sound one. They reason that simply because a primitive society was without written law is not justification to infer that such societies were lawless.

Legal writers following this second approach argue that a written code is not necessary for the enforcement of law because custom alone is sufficient for enforcement (Barnes, 1972:38). They also argue that violations of some conduct norms, although not codified, undoubtedly resulted in punishments that we would today label criminal punishments. There is yet a third major approach to the definitional problem. The viewpoint here is that the appropriate location of the starting point is with the emergence of the "state" as a politically organized society that systematically sanctions, regulates, and administers punishment. This is the viewpoint of many criminologists today and is seen in the definition of criminal punishment advanced by Packer (1968:21):

> (1) It must involve pain or other consequence normally considered unpleasant.
> (2) It must be for an offense against legal rules.
> (3) It must be imposed on an actual or supposed offender for his offense.
> (4) It must be intentionally administered by human beings other than the offender.
> (5) It must be imposed and administered by an authority constituted by a legal system against which the offense is committed.

To this list of criteria, Packer (1968:31) adds a sixth characteristic that considers the reasons for punishing the criminal:

> (6) It must be imposed for the dominant purpose of preventing offenses against legal rules or of exacting retribution from offenders, or both.

Packer's definition is quite adequate for viewing criminal punishment from the late Middle Ages to the present. If we were limited to that time period, we could celebrate the passing of the definitional point and move on. But primarily because primitive and ancient times were characterized by private revenge often unregulated by state law, only criteria (1) and (3) above appear wholly acceptable (although insufficient) for describing the earliest criminal punishment. Although some laws were codified by early rules as, for example, the Code of Hammurabi, the Ancient Laws of China, and early Roman Law, punishment followed the violations of norms that today would be considered legal. *Criminal punishment, then, is punishment involving pain or other consequences normally considered unpleasant and imposed by the state on an offender for violation of conduct norms (laws) that are today considered legal norms.* With this in mind, we can proceed to briefly describe criminal punishment during ancient times.

Ancient Criminal Punishments

There are numerous ways of describing the punitive sanction from its beginning, but a convenient way is to classify punishments along some criterion. We could, for example, group punishments and evaluate them according to the criterion of *certainty* of punishment. Thus, the degree of certainty of punishment for murder can be shown to be greater than the degree of certainty of punishment for theft. We could also group and evaluate punishments according to the criterion of *specificity*, or the degree to which suffering is limited to the individual offender. Other criteria for evaluation are *elasticity* (flexibility of the sanction gauged to the crime), *retribution* (the degree to which the offender can be provided compensation for unjust punishment), *severity, celerity* (how quickly the punishment is administered following the criminal act), and *subjective experience* (how painful the punishment is perceived by the offender).

Within a contemporary framework, it is appropriate to develop a classification according to the *value* affected by the punishment process. Thus, capital punishment is understood in its relation to the value of life; corporal punishment in its relation to bodily integrity; imprisonment, exile, and transportation of criminals out of the culture in relation to freedom of movement; economic penalties and restitution in their relation to the value of money; degradation penalties (resulting in humiliating the offender) in relation to the value of personal integrity; and the punishments of withdrawal of civil rights in relation to the value of citizenship.

From written records we read of the laws that governed early civilized man and of the criminal punishments that were meted out for violating laws. These records, from China, Egypt, Assyria, Babylon, Rome and elsewhere, serve as our sole source for understanding ancient criminal justice. One of the most widely known documents of ancient history, the Code of Hammurabi, describes the principle of justice announced by the King of Babylon (c. 2270 B.C.): the well known *lex talionis*, the "eye for an eye and tooth for a tooth" principle. In one sense we think of Hammurabi as one of the very first humanitarian legal reformers, since his principle of criminal justice reflects a restraint upon the avenging party to inflict no greater punishment than the harm that was done.

Hammurabi, like other early rulers, intervened only slightly in the control of crime. Crime control during Ancient Times was primarily a private matter between revenging parties. Consequently, the punishments that characterized this time period were capital and corporal in nature. As we have seen by the example of the Code of Hammurabi, there was an early attempt in regulating (in a restricted sense) these private feuds, and even up to the time of an early state-sanctioned criminal law system in England during the reign of Canute (1016 A.D.–1035 A.D.) there was sanctioning of private revenge (Kittrie, 1971:14). Moreover, state sanctioning of private feuds continued to as late as half a century after the Norman Conquest (1066 A.D.) by which the law of England still provided that (Kittrie, 1971:13):

> If anyone kill another in revenge ... let him not take any of the goods of the slain, neither his horse nor his helmet, nor his sword nor his money; but in the customary way let him lay out the body of the slain, his head to the west and feet to the east, upon his shield, if he has it ... Then let him go to the nearest vill and declare it to the first one he meets ... thus he may have proof and defend himself against the slain's kin and friends.

Not until the 15th century were private acts of vengeance such as cutting out the tongue of an enemy or putting out his eyes declared to be criminal acts in England.

The modes of punishment during Ancient Times varied along a continuum of severity. The ancient laws of China record beheading as the prescribed mode. Beheading was known in early Egypt and Assyria, but it is also recorded that offenders were sometimes ordered to kill themselves, usually by taking poison. This was also a practice in Ancient Greece and the punishment that ended the life of Socrates.

Other forms of the death penalty were hanging, throwing from a cliff, burning alive, stoning, burying alive, crucifying, and drowning. The Romans meted out an unusual death penalty for parricides (killing a parent). Offenders were placed in a sack which contained also a dog, a cock, a viper, and an ape and then thrown into the water (Laurence, 1960:3). Crucifixion was practiced by the Romans, Assyrians, Egyptians, Greeks and Persians. At the time of Jesus, crucifixion was considered by Romans as the most severe death and was reserved for slaves and other noncitizens. Anyone who had been sentenced to death even for the most heinous crime was executed in a manner other than crucifixion if he could prove his Roman citizenship (Laurence, 1960:221–222).

Corporal punishment, exile, and fines were administered during Ancient Times, but imprisonment was hardly known. In ancient Greece, Israel, and Rome, incarceration was limited to the temporary detention of offenders en route to trial. One writer (Kittrie, 1971: 17) suggests that personal freedom was apparently not sufficiently valuable to render its denial a punishment. However, it may be that imprisonment was simply not practical in the organization of early societies.

Criminal Punishment in England During the Middle Ages

The Middle Ages, along with the ancient times, practiced capital and corporal punishment, exile, transportation, economic and degradation penalties, and withdrawal of rights. It was during this time period that the administration and regulation of these punishments increasingly became a public or state function and less of a private matter. According to Quinney (1970:18) the modern concept of crime became firmly established with the reign of Henry II (1154–1189 A.D.). Henry worked vigorously to centralize government by removing authority from the local courts of the barons and the church. With a centralized government and control over its administration, Henry was able to insist that crime was a wrong against the state rather than against the church or even against the injured party. There was not, to be sure, a rapid transformation. The intervention of the state in the control of crime is clear under the 7th century law of King Ethelbert. The role of the state then was largely to act as a mediator between private parties in dispute. The English state attempted to regulate revenge by substituting a system of fines for corporal revenge and in the process soon discovered that crime control could be profitable. While the principal task of the courts was to fix the fine (and in the process extract a portion of the exchange), the enforcement of its payment was originally left to the victim, family, or clan. English law under Ethelbert, representing one of the earliest documents written in the English language, provided a list of fines victims might receive for a variety of crimes. According to Hibbert (1963:3-4):

> Every part of the body had its value, from fifty shillings for an eye or a foot to sixpence for a toe-nail. Injuries which interfered with a man's ability to work or fight were compensated at a higher rate than those which disfigured him. The loss of a thumb, for instance, was deemed to be worth twenty shillings and a disabled shoulder thirty shillings, but the loss of an ear was worth only twelve shillings and a front tooth six shillings. To break a man's thigh cost twelve shillings and to cut off his little finger eleven, but to lacerate his ear cost only six. To injure his power of speech cost the same as to break three of his ribs. To pierce his penis cost six shillings' compensation, but to break both collar bones cost twelve.

As we have said, change in the control of crime from a private to a state matter was gradual and, according to Bittner and Platt (1966: 88), the transformation was not complete until Henry VIII in the 16th century, who eliminated the last vestiges of locally authorized criminal jurisdiction. Thereafter the state's right to punish became absolute.

Laurence (1960:14) states that the penalty of death during this period of history began to be awarded a little less indiscriminately than before and was, to a large extent, reserved for legally recognized offenses. Compared to contemporary standards, however, the concepts of crime and criminal responsibility during the Middle Ages were vague and arbitrarily defined, reflecting the state of confusion and neglect of the criminal law during the period (Bittner and Platt, 1966:88). In fact, there are records of major protests in England over the state of justice administration. Hibbert (1963:18) notes that by the 15th century:

> ... the people's exasperation with private justice, with the partiality of the law, with those who so unfeelingly administered it and with those who so easily evaded it, had culminated in a revolt at least one of whose declared objects was the execution of all lawyers.

The partiality of the law was a major complaint of ordinary citizens throughout the Middle Ages and into Modern Times. The prejudices against the courts stemmed from many sources: the pervasiveness of bribery and corruption, special privileges granted to so many men, including the clergy and rich. An example of the partiality of medieval law is seen in the practice known as "benefit of clergy." Benefit of clergy meant originally that an ordained clerk charged with a felony had the right to be tried only in the ecclesiastical courts. It soon came to be accepted as a plea against capital punishment in any court and the benefit could be claimed not only by ordained clerks, but by anyone who could produce evidence of education. Usually his scholarship was tested by having him read a few lines of a prescribed text. Sometimes the offender could memorize the lines with the help of an accommodating jailer. In England, according to Laurence (1960:7), the examination consisted in the reading of a passage, usually the 51st Psalm, which was appropriately called the "neck verse." It was not until the early part of the 19th century in England that Robert Peel abolished this practice (Hibbert, 1963:66).

By the middle of the 10th century, punishments (following convictions) by mutilation or death were taking place of fines for a growing number of offenses. While trial by battle and private feuds were still to be observed in the 14th century, trial by ordeal had by then been abolished. Also the various courts, established over the centuries, by then were administering the law with some regard to the rules of evidence. They were also administering it with increasing severity and greater frequency. Not only were the Middle Ages accompanied by a substantial increase in the frequency of capital crimes, but the mode of inflicting the death penalty became more cruel. Torture, which had developed as a means for extracting confessions, often accompanied executions as well.

That human life was not highly valued is evidenced by the increased administration of the death penalty for very minor offenses. The mayor and the porter of the south gate of an English town during the reign of Edward I, for example, were both put to death because the gate of the town had not been closed to prevent the escape of a murderer. Up to the middle of the 16th century, many men were mutilated and some were hanged for little worse than idleness. It is said that during the 37 years of the reign of Henry VIII, 72,000 of his subjects were put to death, primarily by hanging. Although this figure is not certain, it is a fact that this

King made legal the horrible punishment of boiling to death (Hibbert, 1963:26). The first to suffer this fate was a cook, who in 1531 was accused of poisoning two people. The cook was publicly boiled to death in a cauldron suspended from an iron tripod over a fire. After two hours of agony, the man died.

Edward VI did not permit this form of the death penalty to be legal for long. In 1547, the law was repealed and an act was passed substituting hanging, except in the case of women who poisoned husband or child. In this instance, the woman was to be burned to death. Other forms of execution during the Middle Ages included drawing and quartering, breaking on the wheel, and sawing to pieces. Drawing and quartering was sometimes administered by hitching a horse to each leg and arm of the offender and then leading the four horses in opposite directions, thus pulling the victim to pieces. Under the penalty of breaking on the wheel, the prisoner's arms and legs were propped up on a wheel-like platform and were broken in several places with an iron bar. The mangled body was then turned rapidly until the victim eventually died. Sawing in pieces was also administered by English executioners. The victim was usually hanged by his feet and sawed in two vertically by two executioners.

The brutality sanctioned by English law was certainly no less than authorized by continental European law. Indeed, some historians conclude that criminal punishment on the continent was generally more severe than that in either England or in colonial United States. An example of European punishment is provided by the historical investigation into the origin of the Dracula myth. The investigator, Gabriel Ronay (1972), suggests that Bram Stoker, the author of *Dracula*, first published in 1897, created the vampire from historical accounts of a 15th century ruler of a principality which borders Transylvania. The cruel ruler was Vlad V (Dracula), whose passion for impaling on stakes anyone, including minor offenders and traitorous noblemen, had earned him the nickname of "The Impaler." Impaling on sharp wooden stakes was a particularly slow and painful form of execution and accounts cite instances in which Dracula was reported to have impaled over 500 men, women, and children at one time (Ronay, 1972:76). Another example of the severity of punishment on the continent is the case of the execution of an offender in France in 1757. In this year, a palpably insane man, Robert Francois Damiens, pricked King Louis XV with a penknife as the King was leaving the palace. For this alleged attempt on the life of the King, Damiens suffered a brutal death: his flesh was torn with red-hot pincers, the hand that carried the knife was burned off with lighted sulphur, his tongue was torn out at the root, and finally he was drawn and literally pulled in four pieces by horses (Kittrie, 1971:58).

The Middle Ages and the early centuries of Modern Times witnessed not only the increased use of capital punishment but of corporal punishments as well. The most widely employed form of corporal punishment was flogging, a measure that continued well into the 20th century. As late as 1920, the British Parliament legalized the use of the "cat-o-nine tails" in flogging those convicted of robbery (Barnes, 1972:57). Mutilation is a form of corporal punishment that was practiced in Ancient Times and was prevalent during the Middle Ages. The 1016 Laws of Canute, King of Denmark and of England, prescribed numerous forms of mutilation. Another form of corporal punishment, and a degradation penalty, branding, also dates as far back as late oriental and classical societies. The letters branded on the body of the English criminal usually bore at least a rough general resemblance to the nature of the crime committed. The murderer was branded with an "M"; idlers with an "S" (meaning slave); and fighters and brawlers with an "F" (Barnes, 1972:62). Hawthorne's famous *The Scarlet Letter* depicts the use of an "A" for adulteresses.

Criminal Punishment in England and the United States in Early Modern Times

England

In England, many of the punishment methods practiced during the Middle Ages continued into Early Modern Times. The number of offenses for which capital punishment was prescribed in England grew until it reached 350 in 1780, but it dropped to 17 by 1839. Hanging and burning alive were both practiced during Early Modern Times, but by the 19th century hanging became the sole method of capital punishment in England. In 1829, only 24 persons were hanged in London although in none of these cases had the offender committed murder (Laurence, 1960:14). As late as 1831, a boy of 9 years was publicly hanged, but in 1833 a boy of 9 who was sentenced to die for housebreaking was not hanged, partly because of public protest (Laurence, 1960:18).

It was the practice in England to make executions public until the 19th century when people became convinced that these displays did not deter others from crime. In 1807, two murderers were hanged before a crowd of 40,000 spectators (Hibbert, 1963:70). By the time the hanged men were cut down, nearly 100 dead and dying were found lying in the streets. In 1864, with the public hanging of one murderer, the London *Times* reported widespread robbery and violence among the spectators of that execution (Hibbert, 1963:71). Hibbert (1963:71) reports that in this same year an official committee recommended that executions should no longer be in public. The recommendation was based in part on a study of 167 people under sentence of death in a certain English town. The study found that 164 of the 167 people had witnessed a public execution and obviously had not been deterred from criminality. By 1868, public executions were abolished.

Another form of punishment widely practiced in England up to the middle of the 19th century was that of forced transportation out of the country. Between 1597, when the first law authorized transportation to English-owned colonies, and 1776, vast numbers of criminals and debtors were shipped to America (Barnes and Teeters, 1959:296). Estimates of how many were transported range from 50,000 to 100,000. By 1775, England was sending approximately 2,000 offenders to the English colonies each year. After the American War of Independence, England continued to deport criminals, but at a slower pace and to Australia and elsewhere rather than to the United States. Descriptions of this crime control measure are filled with examples of cruel and inhumane practices.

During Early Modern Times, England began to place criminals in prisons primarily as a means of short-term detention, but by the time of the death of the first prison reformer John Howard (1726–1790), prisons were constructed for the primary purpose of long-term confinement. Up to the time Howard brought to the attention of the world the sordid conditions of imprisonment practices, and for a time following his revelations, it was the practice to confine criminals in jails, prisons, and the hulks of English vessels. The early prisons and jails of England were horrible places where murderers, debtors, the young and the old, male and female alike, were confined in disease-ridden structures where they were poorly fed, if fed at all, often physically assaulted, or otherwise completely neglected. According to Howard, more people died of diseases contracted while imprisoned in 1773–1774 than were executed (Hibbert, 1963:135).

The effect of the publication in 1777 of Howard's *The State of the Prisons in England and Wales* was to eventually result in legislation in 1779 aimed at improving prison conditions. Howard lobbyed for the classification of prisoners according to their offense, separation of males and females, and of young and old, employment in useful labor, proper clothes and sanitation, adequate food and the appointment of inspectors to make sure improvements were carried out. Despite the 1779 legislation, prisons continued to be sordid places, for few of Howard's ideas were implemented. As late as 1823, some prisoners were still chained to the prison floor (Hibbert, 1963: 152) and as late as 1828, there were at least 4,000 convicts confined in British hulks (Barnes, 1972:117). It was not until the public became concerned over prison treatment in the first quarter of the 19th century, and not until the first Inspector of English Prisons, William Crawford, returned from a visit to the United States in 1836 with an enthusiastic report of the American experiment with prisons, that many of the reforms originally advocated by Howard were realized.

Between 1820 and 1861, the British criminal code was completely transformed. Legal reformers such as Jeremy Bentham (1748–1832) argued that punishments should be equated with the nature of the offense. Many of the cruel and unusual punishments were removed from the law codes during this period of legal overhaul.

United States

Toward the end of the Middle Ages, a new form of punishment, imprisonment, began to replace corporal punishment. The earliest facilities bearing some resemblance to what we today describe as prisons were the Bridwell House of Correction in London in 1553 for the temporary detention and reformation of the poor, the Rasp Huis built in Amsterdam in 1593 for women who were to be reformed by work and religious exercises, and the St. Michel prison for young offenders built by Pope Clement XI in 1703 (Kittrie, 1971:17). Barnes (1972:122) traces the origins of the modern prison to the 1703 Rome prison and to the prison in Belgium built in 1773. In both of these, prisoners were classified and segregated. Prisoners were made to labor and it was hoped that imprisonment would reform the criminal. The English prison reformer, John Howard, traveled to Rome and Belgium to inspect these facilities and reported on this humane method of handling criminals. Although Americans became aware of these early experiences with imprisonment through the writings of Howard, it is doubtful that these institutions greatly influenced the architects and penal reformers in the United States. Rather, prisons in this country represent an American innovation in penal reform. (For more details about imprisonment, see Chapter 15.)

Americans discovered the "cure" for crime not only in the building of prisons, but also in the overhaul of the law. Following the Revolutionary War, Americans were no longer forced to accept English law and, therefore, began an immediate program of legal reform along Enlightenment principles. By 1820, most of the states had changed their criminal codes. The death penalty was either abolished for all offenses except for first degree murder or strictly limited to a few very serious crimes. Corporal punishment was replaced by a system of fines, imprisonment, or probation, and degradation penalties were abolished.

Prior to the legal reforms, the methods of corporal and capital punishments were taken from the English. Hanging was the most popular mode of capital punishment. Burning of witches was also practiced at the end of the seventeenth century. Elsewhere among the Colonies, however, witchcraft was not viewed as a major problem. In the colony of Maryland, for example, only one "witch" was ever hanged (Semmes, 1970:19). In New York and Virginia, men were broken on the wheel for their crimes. The strict regulation of morals by law resulted in punishments meted out for fornication, adultery, swearing, drunkenness, blasphemy, gossiping, and for nagging of husbands. Semmes (1970:176–177) reports that for the offense of adultery and for telling some men that he was astonished that the world had been deluded by "a man and a pigeon" by which he referred to Jesus Christ and the Holy Ghost, one Maryland public official was removed from office and forbidden from holding any public office.

The idea that humiliation was an important element in the punishment process had been long recognized in colonial America. The stocks and the pillory, when not accompanied by other modes of punishment, were considered degradation penalties to bring humiliation and shame upon the offender. The stocks held the prisoner, sitting down, with his feet and hands fastened in a locked frame and the pillory held him, standing, with head and hands similarly locked in the frame. Sometimes the prisoner's ears were nailed to the beams of the pillory and when he was released he was made to loose his ears or have them cut off by the official in charge. Also, confinement by these devices was very frequently supplemented by making the person thus detained a convenient target for decayed vegetables, rotten eggs, and even stones. Occasionally unpopular persons placed in the stocks or the pillory were pelted to death.

The ducking stool was also a degradation penalty administered in colonial America. This was a device in which the victim was strapped to a chair, fastened to a long lever, and then dipped in the water by an operator who manipulated the affair from the banks of the stream or pond. Another degradation penalty commonly practiced in the Colonies was branding. In the East Jersey codes of 1668 and 1675 it was ordered, for example, that the first-time burglar be branded on the hand with a "T," a second-time burglar with a "B" on the forehead. Similarly, the adulteress of Vermont and other New England states was made to wear the symbolic scarlet letter "A" (Barnes and Teeters, 1959:292).

Criminal Punishment in the United States in the 20th Century

Bittner and Platt (1966:93) maintain that the decline in the severity of punishment was not a gradual development accompanying the growth of civilization, but a phenomenon associated peculiarly with the 19th and 20th centuries. We have reached a point in our history where corporal punishment, degradation penalties, and public executions are no longer sanctioned by law. We also live at a time when capital punishment has been rarely administered and is restricted to a small class of offenses. Federal courts, state courts, and military courts are authorized to order execution. The offenses for which each of these courts has ordered the death penalty from the period 1930–1970 are (U.S. Department of Justice, 1974):

(1) Federal courts: murder, rape, armed robbery (with homicide), kidnapping, sabotage, espionage.

(2) State courts: murder, rape, armed robbery, kidnapping, burglary, aggravated assault committed by prisoners under a life sentence.

(3) U.S. military courts (Army and Air Force): murder, rape, desertion.

Between 1930–1972 (U.S. Department of Justice, 1974:18), 3,859 civilians were executed, 3,826 by state authorities and 33 under federal jurisdiction. 86.4 percent were for murder, 11.8 percent were for rape, and 1.8 percent were for other offenses. 53.5 percent of those executed were Blacks, 45.4 percent were White, and 1.1 percent were of other races. Less than 1 percent were female. Also during this time period, the Army and the Air Force carried out 166 executions. The last execution in the United States was that of a convicted murderer who died by lethal gas on June 2, 1967 in Colorado after 3 years, 5 months, and 16 days under sentence of death, which is about the average waiting time (U.S. Department of Justice, 1971:2). The longest waiting period was that of a convicted murderer in Illinois who served 15 years, 3 months, and 16 days before he was put to death (U.S. Department of Justice, 1971:2).

The methods of carrying out the death penalty during the 1930–1972 period include electrocution (legal in 23 states), lethal gas (legal in 10 states), hanging (legal in 8 states), and the firing squad or hanging (the prisoner's choice in Utah). At the end of 1970, capital punishment was illegal in 9 states and had been almost totally abolished in 5 states (U.S. Department of Justice, 1971:2).

According to the U.S. Department of Justice (1974:1), the number of prisoners on death rows in United States prisons rose slightly between December 31, 1970 and December 31, 1971. This was a continuation of the annual upward trend that had been evident since at least the end of 1961. During the next 12 months, however, by the end of 1972, the prison population under sentence of death declined by 47 percent. The reversal of that trend and the unprecedented decline stemmed chiefly from widespread changes in the status of sentences following the U.S. Supreme Court finding in the case of *Furman* v. *Georgia* (June 29, 1972) that the death penalty, as imposed by the states up to that time, amounted to "cruel and unusual punishment" in violation of the Eighth Amendment to the U.S. Constitution.

Although the number of prisoners under sentence of death decreased from 620 at the end of 1971 to 330 at the end of 1972, the latter figure was larger than that for December 31 of any year before 1965. The relatively large number of prisoners on death row at the end of 1972 can be attributed to an accumulation of inmates under sentence of death resulting from the gradual decrease in executions, beginning early in the 1960s, and to their complete cessation after June 1967. Moreover, during the six-month interval between the *Furman* decision and the end of 1972, no state abolished the death penalty, and courts in some states continued to impose death sentences.

Most state legislatures in recent years have re-assessed their criminal codes with regard to the death penalty. Since this is an issue still under such consideration, it is not possible to determine with any accuracy how many states have abolished the penalty and how many are re-writing their criminal codes to conform to the impetus made by the *Furman* decision. It is likely, moreover, that another test case will soon reach the Supreme Court and that a definitive decision will be made once and for all regarding the constitutionality of the death sentence. Until that time, however, many states will continue to permit the pronouncement of the death sentence, but the United States is not likely to witness wholesale executions of those who have been detained on death rows for so many years.

Electrocution was first adopted in the State of New York and the first criminal to be electrocuted was a man named Kemmler who had killed his mistress (Laurence, 1960:63). He was condemned to death on June 24, 1889, but an appeal was immediately entered on the grounds that electrocution violated the Constitution's prohibition against cruel and unusual punishment. Thus, it was not until August 6, 1890 that Kemmler was electrocuted in Auburn Prison, after his appeal was denied. This first electrocution did not go well because the burning of Kemmler's flesh was evident, though there is little doubt that death was nevertheless instantaneous. A later execution (Laurence, 1960:65), on July 27, 1893, also did not go well. With the passing of the current, the electric chair broke and the prisoner fell semiconscious to the floor. He was removed from the execution site and given chloroform and "injections of morphia to keep him unconscious while the apparatus was being repaired." An hour later, when the current was restored, the execution was completed. Despite such terrible scenes when electrocution was first introduced, it is now a perfected method of execution, although there is still some question of whether it is completely painless.

Consensus is that execution by lethal gas produces the most painless death.

Criminal punishment during this century consists largely of a system of economic penalties (fines), imprisonment, probation, and parole. In addition, conviction for a felony offense is accompanied by the withdrawal of civil rights including the right to vote, otherwise known as "civil death."

Justifications For Punishment

Despite the obvious decline in the severity of punishment during this century, debates rage over the justifications for the penal sanction.

Packer (1968:36) discusses two historically developed justifications for criminal punishment: the nonutilitarian justification of *retribution* or revenge and the utilitarian justification of the *prevention* of crime. The justification for punishment according to the retributive view is the criminal act itself. This view holds that because man is responsible for his actions, he deserves to be punished if he violates the law. The rationale for punishment according to the utilitarian position differs from that of the nonutilitarian view in that punishment is justified only when punishment or the threat of punishment is theoretically or empirically linked to reduced future criminal behavior. When punishment is treated as a means to achieve a desired goal, a rational approach to crime control policies is described. It should be clear from this that evaluative research on the effectiveness of punishment makes sense only in the context of a utilitarian position. Nonutilitarian positions have nothing to do with the effectiveness of the criminal sanction.

General Punitive Prevention:
The Symbolic Effect of
Punishment

Within a utilitarian framework, two basic positions can be identified. The first position, the general punitive prevention viewpoint (also called general deterrence), holds that the threat of punishment and the spectacle of its actual infliction deters others who would otherwise commit crime. So long as people are made aware by threat that they can be punished for violating laws, they will be deterred. The highway driver who reads the sign "Speeders lose licenses" is presumably deterred from breaking the speeding law, or the person who reads in the newspaper of the murderer who is sentenced to prison for a life term is, likewise, presumably deterred from committing murder. General prevention (deterrence) operates according to the nature of the offense (Packer, 1968:48). The general public comes to realize that people who do certain things will be punished if they are caught, regardless of the personal characteristics of the offender. General prevention also operates on the principle that human beings can be used for the benefit of others—a principle that is morally debatable.

Though it is undoubtedly true that the threat of punishment acts as a general deterrent force for some, when and how this threat is effective is the problem with which crime control agencies must deal. Packer (1968:45) argues that the threat of punishment is most effective among that segment of the population that is least likely to break the law anyway. Consequently, the threat of punishment and the spectacle of the enforcement of the law serve primarily to *reinforce* their own value structure. Consistent with this view is the belief that punishment may stimulate habitual law-abiding conduct. Zimring (1971:34–48) discusses the relationship between personality type and the deterrent effect of the threat of punishment. Other issues involved in determining the deterrent effect are the type of criminal offenses threatened with punishment and public knowledge of punishments (Zimring 1971:49–65 and Andenaes, 1974:10–28), the risk of being punished, and the nature and magnitude of punishment (Andenaes, 1974:24).

Primarily because of the complexity of the problem of scientifically determining the effectiveness of the threat of punishment, we are still in the "pre-Lombrosian era" in this field according to Andenaes (1974:31). We do not know how effective general prevention is because we do not know the true extent of crime. We have no way of knowing the success of general prevention because there is no way of knowing how many crimes would have been committed if there had been no threat of punishment. At best, the studies and observations in this area provide some clues to the effectiveness of general prevention, but it cannot be denied that the conclusions drawn involve a great deal of guesswork.

One might wonder what the effect would be if the police force of a country were suddenly eliminated. Certainly the threat of punishment would be diminished by the reduction in probability of detection. Andenaes (1974:16–17) reports that just such an event occurred in Denmark in September, 1944, when the Germans arrested the entire police force. During the occupation, policing was done by an improvised and unarmed watch corps. It was found that for some offenses, particularly robbery and larceny, the crime rate rose dramatically. In all of 1939, only 10 cases of robbery were reported in Copenhagen, and in 1943 the rate rose to 10 a month— after the arresting of the police, the rate rose to over 100 a month and continued to rise.

Studies on the effectiveness of the death penalty in the United States have generally reported consistent results. These studies have been based on four different methods. The first method involves comparing the homicide rate in states which have abolished the death penalty with states which retain it. Sutherland and Cressey (1966:347) report that in general these comparisons show that the homicide rate in abolition states is only about one-third to one-half as high as it is in the other states. There is an obvious weakness in the method, however, because the death penalty is authorized in all the Southern states and Southern states have the highest homicide rates.

A second method which attempts to circumvent this methodological weakness is to divide the country into sections and compare the homicide rates of the states which have abolished the death penalty with those of the adjoining states which have retained it. The significant differences, as Sutherland and Cressey report (1966: 347) are not between the states that differ with respect to the death penalty, but between the different sections of the country. The implication is that the culture is more important than the presence or absence of the death penalty in determining homicide rates.

A third method for testing the deterrent effect of the death penalty is through comparison of crime rates just before and just after one or more executions has taken place. Does the fact that an execution has taken place affect the rate of homicides? Certainly the experiences in England with public executions during the 19th century, discussed earlier in this chapter, suggest that people are not deterred. More recent studies suggest the same. In one study of homicide rates 60 days prior to and 60 days subsequent to five executions in Philadelphia in the 1930s, no significant differences were found (Dunn, 1935). In another Philadelphia study of four highly publicized executions, Savitz (1958:338–341) found that the homicide rates eight weeks before the execution in areas where the criminals were known and where the crimes were committed were no different from the rates eight weeks after the execution.

Another method for studying the effect of the death penalty is by comparing the homicide rates in states before and after abolishing the death penalty. The general conclusions to these studies are, once again, that rates of homicides are unaffected by the presence or absence of capital punishment.

None of the research described above comes close to approximating classical experimental designs, and so long as criminologists are unable to control punishment policy for experimental purposes, deterrence research will remain subject to valid criticisms on methodological grounds. However, while most research suffers methodological deficiencies, not all deficiencies invalidate the research. Along the same lines, Zimring and Hawkins (1973:252), in their discussion of general deterrence research methodologies, make the point that a series of imperfect research studies can sometimes produce reliable conclusions because each different but imperfect method may remove an element of doubt left by its predecessor.

Special Punitive Prevention:
The Effect of Punishment
on the Offender

The second utilitarian justification for punishment, called here special punitive prevention (also called special deterrence), is that punishment prevents the commission of future crimes (recidivism) by punished offenders. It is held that the punished criminal will avoid future conduct that would lead to his punishment. Punishment, so the argument goes, teaches the criminal a lesson. But does it?

The strongest evidence that punishment deters criminality comes from observations on imprisonment. Those who justify incarceration on the grounds that society is protected so long as offenders are behind bars can find a great deal of evidence to support their view. Seldom are prisoners brought before our courts for having committed criminal offenses while incarcerated, primarily because they lack the means or opportunities to commit most types of crimes while in prison. At least, the short-term effectiveness of imprisonment can be justified on some theoretical and empirical grounds.

However, observations on the long-range effectiveness of imprisonment have by and large resulted in the opposite conclusion: that
there is little evidence that imprisonment deters criminality. Indeed,
many evaluative researchers have reached the conclusion that imprisonment actually accelerates criminal behavior.

Within the framework of special deterrence theory, it has become fashionable to justify punishment on the grounds that punishment may be used to prevent crime by rehabilitating the offender,
i.e., changing his personality by removing the sociopsychological
causes of his criminal conduct. It has also become fashionable to
reject the word "punishment" whenever we are talking about rehabilitation or reform treatment. Packer (1968:53–54) regards this
linguistic practice as misleading:

> However benevolent the purpose of reform, however better off we expect
> its object to be, there is no blinking the fact that what we do to the of-
> fender in the name of reform is being done to him for *our* sake, not for
> his. Rehabilitation may be the most humane goal of punishment, but it
> is a goal of *punishment* so long as its invocation depends upon finding
> that an offense has been committed, and so long as its object is to prevent
> the commission of offenses.

Packer is not saying here that punishment and treatment are the
same. Rather, he is reminding us that rehabilitation is a goal and
justification of punishment. While both rehabilitation and punishment are triggered by illegal conduct, the differences between the
two are (1) that punishment emphasizes the concern with the better-
ment of the offender; and (2) that punishment gives more emphasis
to the role of the offending conduct than does treatment. Justifications for imprisonment as punishment and for therapy as treatment
are both within the utilitarian framework, for they are concerned
with the offender primarily and only secondarily concerned with the
offense. Imprisonment is not justified when we ask the question,
"Will this person commit more crimes if he is set free?" and the
answer is "No." Only secondarily are we concerned with his offenses.
Similarly, treatment is not justified when we ask the question, "Is
the person amenable to treatment?" and the answer is "No." Again,
only secondarily are we concerned with the nature of the offense as
it may provide a clue to whether he is amenable. Punishment, it may
be concluded, may not involve treatment, whereas treatment always
involves punishment. Still, it is legitimate to say that some offenders

cease their criminal conduct because they have been punished whereas others are deterred because they have been treated. Do we know which has occurred? Thus far, the answer is "No."

It is interesting to note that the same objections that apply to punishment also apply to treatment. The argument that punishment is "immoral" applies to treatment when the questions are raised: "Does a man have the right to be 'bad'?" and "Is it perhaps immoral to manipulate a man's personality?" The other objection involves the effectiveness of what we do to offenders. We don't know how to effectively punish criminals, just as we are ignorant of how to rehabilitate them. Our ignorance of effective treatment is a conclusion drawn from the results of hundreds of evaluative research studies, as reported by Bailey (1971), Logan (1972), and Lipton, Martinson, and Wilks (1975). (See Chapter 11.) Logan (1972:381), in his review of 100 correctional evaluation studies, concluded, that:

> No research has been done to date that enables us to say that one treatment program is better than another or that enables us to examine a man and specify the treatment he needs. There is no evidence that probation is better than institutions, that institutions are better than escaping . . . So much of what is now being done about crime may be so wrong that the net effect of the actions is to increase rather than to decrease crime. Research could possibly shed some light, but none of the researchers to date answers these questions.

Thus, the utilitarian justifications for much of what we do to individual offenders, whether in the name of punishment or in the name of treatment, appears to receive little support from empirical research.

A Final Note

If the historical pattern of decline in the severity of criminal punishment continues, we should expect the future to bring with it the total abolition of the death penalty and less reliance on incarceration. Perhaps the future will also witness a major legal reform movement in which much of the conduct now sanctioned by criminal law will be decriminalized or at least depenalized. A reform movement might also result in a more just system of crime control. It is unrealistic to think, however, that any type of social reform can create a society free of crime and criminal punishment. Criminal punishment is, in the words of Packer (1968:62), "a necessary but lamentable form of social control." Given that we will always have to contend with this lamentable practice, it is unfortunate that more experimentation and research with our penal policies is either not permitted or is simply not done.

Perhaps Rothman's (1971:295) concluding comments to his historical study of the development of institutions (asylums) for incarcerating deviants and dependents aptly describes our current situation:

> ... The reformer's original doctrines were especially liable to abuse, their emphasis on authority, obedience, and regularity turning all too predictably into a mechanical application of discipline. And by incarcerating the deviant and dependent, and defending the step with hyperbolic rhetoric, they discouraged—really eliminated—the search for other solutions that might have been less susceptible to abuse.
>
> ... One cannot help but conclude this history with an acute nervousness about all social panaceas ...
>
> Still, there are alternative perspectives that can dispel some of the gloom. The history of the discovery of the asylum is not without a relevance that may be more liberating than stifling for us. We still live with many of these institutions, accepting their presence as inevitable. Despite a personal revulsion, we think of them as always having been with us, and therefore as always to be with us. We tend to forget that they were the invention of one generation to serve special needs, not the only possible reaction to social problems. In fact, since the Progressive era, we have been gradually escaping from institutional responses, and one can forsee the period when incarceration will be used still more rarely than it is today. In this sense the story of the origin of the asylum is liberating. We need not remain trapped in inherited answers. An awareness of the causes and implications of past choices should encourage us to a greater experimentation with our own solutions.

References

Andenaes, Johannes
    1974   Punishment and Deterrence. Ann Arbor: The University of Michigan Press.
Bailey, Waller C.
    1971   "An Evaluation of 100 Reports." In Leon Radzinowicz and Marvin Wolfgang, eds. Crime and Justice: Volume 3—The Criminal in Confinement. New York: Basic Books: 187-195.
Barnes, Harry E.

1972   The Story of Punishment. 2nd ed. rev. Montclair, New Jersey: Patterson Smith.

Barnes, Harry E. and Negley K. Teeters
1959   New Horizons in Criminology. 3rd ed. Englewood Cliffs, New Jersey: Prentice-Hall.

Bittner, Egon and Anthony M. Platt
1966   "The Meaning of Punishment." Issues in Criminology, 2 (Spring): 79-99.

Dunn, Robert H.
1935   "The Deterrent Effect of Capital Punishment." Friends' Social Service Series. Bulletin No. 29.

Hibbert, Christopher
1963   The Roots of Evil. Boston: Little, Brown and Co.

Kittrie, Nicholas N.
1971   The Right to Be Different. Baltimore: Penguin Books.

Laurence, John
1960   A History of Capital Punishment. New York: Citadel Press.

Lipton, Douglas, Robert Martinson, and Judith Wilks
1975   The Effectiveness of Correctional Treatment: A Survey of Treatment Evaluation Studies. New York: Praeger.

Logan, Charles H.
1972   "Evaluation Research in Crime and Delinquency: A Reappraisal." The Journal of Criminal Law, Criminology and Police Science. 63, No. 3:378-387.

Packer, Herbert L.
1968   The Limits of the Criminal Sanction. Palo Alto, California: Stanford University Press.

Quinney, Richard
1970   The Problem of Crime. New York: Dodd Mead & Co.

Ronay, Gabriel
1972   The Truth About Dracula. New York: Stein and Day.

Rothman, David J.
1971   The Discovery of the Asylum. Boston: Little, Brown and Co.

Savitz, Leonard, D.
1958   "A Study of Capital Punishment." Journal of Criminal Law, Criminology and Police Science 49:338-341.

Semmes, Raphael
1938   Crime and Punishment in Early Maryland. Montclair, New Jersey: Patterson Smith (Reprinted 1970).

Sutherland, Edwin H. and Donald R. Cressey
1966   Principles of Criminology. 7th ed. Philadelphia: J.B. Lippincott Co.

U.S. Department of Justice
1974   National Prisoner Statistics Bulletin: Capital Punishment. Washington, D.C.: Bureau of Prisons.

1971   National Prisoner Statistics, No. 46, Washington, D.C.: LEAA.

Zimring, Franklin E.
    1971   Perspectives on Deterrence. Rockville, Maryland: National Institute of Mental Health. Public Health Service Publication No. 2056.
Zimring, Franklin E. and Gordon J. Hawkins
    1973   Deterrence. Chicago: The University of Chicago Press.

CHAPTER **13**

juvENilE justicE

Historical Development

The system of juvenile justice in the United States is concerned not with one problem, but a host of many. While our society is concerned for the health and welfare of its youth, it is also concerned with protecting itself from those who would abuse their rights, privileges, and responsibilities. The process for dealing with juvenile deviants is not simply an issue of social control. It is also concerned with social policy, social action, and the traditions, folkways, and mores the society chooses to utilize in rearing its young. Solutions are difficult to arrive at and implement, but as Rubin (1970:1-2) states: "A rational, objective and scientific approach is necessary to the solution of this and the many other issues in the interest of sound social policy."

Tracing the development of services to juveniles in the United States within the last century is a complex task, for much of what we have done has been directed not only at delinquents, but at all youth as well. Nonetheless, as LaMar Empey (1973:13-14) points out, when we examine the current court-correctional system for juveniles, we can identify three principal forces or concepts which led to the removal of dependent, neglected, and delinquent children from the adult criminal justice process, to be substituted by a special system for them.

The first, known as *parens patriae*, is a concept which permits the state to intervene in the lives of all children, regardless of whether or not they are delinquent. The second is the development of the *juvenile court* itself, an effort designed by a group of social reformers known as "child savers" (Platt, 1969). The third principal force is the *psychological movement* which took hold at the turn of the 20th century and held that those who violated the law probably were acting-out unresolved conflicts and were in need of treatment.

As a consequence of these three historical developments, a series of practices and policies evolved, according to Empey (1973: 14), which emphasizes the following:

> (1) the right of the state to exercise wide jurisdiction over the lives of young people—the dependent, the neglected, and the "incorrigible"—as well as the law violator;
> (2) the use of the court to maintain the moral as well as the legal standards of the community; and
> (3) the implementation of treatment procedures designed to correct the emotional and social problems of children.

Definitions

The above suggests that the nature of services rendered to youth on behalf of society is complicated, especially since the scope of such services covers a wide range of behaviors including many which are not viewed as delinquent. Even a definition of delinquency is not easily accomplished, as was the case in our attempt to define crime and criminals. A direct, factual, and simple definition is possible, but the many inputs made by legal, clinical, administrative, judicial, and behavioral experts sometime lead only to greater confusion rather than clarity. Korn and McCorkle (1965:183) indicate that delinquency is viewed more broadly and vaguely than is the legal concept of crime, and for two reasons:

(1) it covers many behaviors that would not be considered criminal if committed by adults, and (2) the juridical definition of these behaviors (e.g., "incorrigibility") is frequently much more general than would be constitutionally tolerated in criminal statutes (for adults), which require precise descriptions of the activities as illegal.

Each jurisdiction has a juvenile code in the United States which defines in its statutes what is meant by delinquency, as well as the range of behaviors which are subject to juvenile court intervention. As a consequence, as Viano and Cohn (1975:166) illustrate, the court can label a youth as delinquent for committing a felonious act, such as murder, rape, or burglary; engaging in what would otherwise be called misdemeanors, such as shoplifting or simple assault; and/or acting in a way not consistent with societal norms, such as being incorrigible or beyond parental supervision. These latter behaviors, popularly called "status offenses," are currently under considerable scrutiny and there is a growing demand that they be removed from the jurisdiction of the juvenile courts. Some say these status offenses should be removed from the juvenile codes altogether, while others argue that the courts should retain jurisdiction but the services provided to youths with these kinds of problems should be placed in social service agencies. No consensus has been reached on this issue, and it will probably remain a serious concern for many years.

Since 1899, juvenile courts have been the official agencies of social control of delinquents, but they have also dealt with other matters, such as dependency and neglect. Children who come under the court's purview are either those whose behavior eventually can lead to adjudication as delinquent or those who have not committed adult-type offenses but are in need of supervision (based on the concept of *parens patriae*). This latter group includes those whose behavior falls into the category of status offenses, along with those who are labeled as minors in need of supervision (MINS) or persons in need of supervision (PINS). Sheridan (1967:27) comments on these categories, which helps us to further understand the complexities involved in defining delinquency:

With few exceptions, the same dispositions are permitted in the case of these children (MINS or PINS) that are authorized for youngsters who have committed acts that would be crimes if committed by an adult. In other words, children who have not indulged in criminal conduct find themselves thrown into the correctional system.

The Code of the State of Maryland illustrates contemporary attitudes toward dealing with children. In its latest Code, for example, nondelinquent children who are in need of supervision may not be committed to a juvenile training institution. However, the court still retains authority to institutionalize such a child if it believes confinement is in the child's best interests and welfare. Article 52A, Section 5, Paragraph (c) of the Maryland Annotated Code reads as follows:

> *Commitment of delinquent, mentally handicapped, dependent or neglected child or child in need of supervision* . . . Any juvenile court judge may commit: (1) any delinquent child that has been so adjudicated by said judge to the custody of the Secretary of Health and Mental Hygiene or to any public or private institution or agency other than the Department of Health and Mental Hygiene, or to the custody of a person selected by said judge; (2) any child in need of supervision that has been so adjudicated by said judge to the custody of the Secretary of Health and Mental Hygiene, or to any public or private institution or agency other than the Department of Health and Mental Hygiene or to the custody of a person selected by said judge; (3) any mentally handicapped child that has been so adjudicated by said judge to the custody of the Secretary of Health and Mental Hygiene; (4) any dependent child that has been so adjudicated by said judge to the local social services department, or to any other public or private agency which provides facilities for dependent children, or to the custody of a person selected by said judge; (5) any neglected child that has been so adjudicated by said judge to the local social services department or to any public or private agency that provides facilities or services for neglected children . . . Any child who has been determined in need of care or treatment within the provisions (of this Article) . . . shall remain under the continuing jurisdiction of the court in which his case was heard until that court finally determines jurisdiction.

Thus, every child in the state, depending on the label the court affixes, can be institutionalized for care and treatment, even though the child may not have committed an adult-proscribed deviant act. Maryland is rather unusual in that it provides to juveniles on a state-wide basis both probation and aftercare services, not in a youth commission or some similar agency, but in a Department of Health and Mental Hygiene. Nonetheless, the state defines the various categories of children who potentially come within the purview of its juvenile courts (Title 3, Subtitle 8, Sections 3–801–3–833, 1975 Cumulative Supplement):

(c) *"Child"* means a person under the age of 18 years.

(d) *"Child in need of assistance"* is a child who needs the assistance of the court because

(1) He is mentally handicapped or is not receiving ordinary and proper care and attention, and

(2) His parents, guardian, or custodian are unable or unwilling to give proper care and attention to the child and his problems provided, however, a child shall not be deemed to be in need of assistance for the sole reason he is being furnished nonmedical remedial care and treatment recognized by State law.

(e) *"Child in need of supervision"* is a child who needs guidance, treatment, or rehabilitation, because

(1) He is required by law to attend school and is habitually truant; or

(2) He is habitually disobedient, ungovernable, and beyond the control of the person having custody of him without substantial fault on the part of that person; or

(3) He deports himself so as to injure or endanger himself or others; or

(4) He has committed an offense applicable only to children.

(i) *"Delinquent Act"* means an act which would be a crime if committed by an adult.

(j) *"Delinquent child"* is a child who has committed a delinquent act and requires guidance, treatment, or rehabilitation.

Dependent children are described as those who have been deprived of adequate support, neglected children as those who require the aid of the court. However, all of these children, and delinquents as well, can be institutionalized or placed in facilities other than their homes by court action and according to rather vaguely defined statutes. Maryland may be unique, as indicated earlier, in that dependent and neglected children are institutionalized in facilities different from those to which delinquent children are committed. But children, nonetheless, can be taken away from their homes and families, and in almost every jurisdiction for indeterminate periods of time.

An examination of statutes and codes in other states related to the definitions of delinquency, dependency, and neglect suggests that the general terms of juvenile delinquency statutes permit courts to take hold in rather broadly and somewhat imprecisely defined circumstances of conduct, attitude, or social situation. Further, even though due process is supposedly assured to youngsters and their families, juvenile courts do in fact widely and increasingly exercise

their descretion to deal with cases deemed either presently delinquent or in danger of becoming so—cases involving dependent and
neglected children.

Noncriminal cases that frequently come to the attention of
other social agencies do not have attached the same kinds of stigmas
that are present in juvenile courts. Since agencies other than courts
(family service and private counseling groups) frequently deal with
youths who behave in deviant and disruptive but not necessarily
criminal ways, delinquency may have little specific behavior content,
either in law or in fact, other than the provision that acts that would
otherwise be crimes are defined for the juvenile as delinquency
(Shireman, 1962).

With the above in mind, we may now be able to proceed with
defining delinquency, however indefinitely and inconclusively.
Tappan (1949:30) offers the following:

> *The juvenile delinquent is a person who has been adjudicated as such by a
> court of proper jurisdiction* though he may be no different, up until the
> time of court contact and adjudication at any rate, from masses of children
> who are not delinquent. *Delinquency is any act, course of conduct, or
> situation which might be brought before a court and adjudicated* whether
> in fact it comes to be treated there or by some other resource or indeed
> remains untreated. It will be noted that under these definitions adjudicable
> conduct may be defined as delinquent in the abstract, but it cannot be
> measured as delinquency until a court has found the facts of delinquency
> to exist.

Tappan's definition, like his approach to the definitions of
crime and criminals, is somewhat legalistic in that he insists that no
delinquency exists unless and until a juvenile court says it exists. But
we know, and Tappan admits, that many delinquent acts do not
come to the attention of the court. Police constantly deal with
youthful deviancy. Just because the acts are not cleared or the persons are not referred to court does not mean that they have not
occurred. Only the official label is missing because the court cannot
possibly act unless and until someone brings an alleged delinquent
to the court's attention. Consequently, whatever the definitional
problems, we still have the reality of behavior that, although youth
committed, is nonetheless violative or against social norms as spelled
out in juvenile codes. Yet Tappan's definition is one which appears
reasonable.

Rates of Delinquency

The President's Crime Commission estimated in 1967 that 1 in every 9 children was referred to juvenile court for an act of delinquency before the 18th birthday—the usual cutoff age that separates juveniles from adults. According to the same source, the ratio for males was 1 in 6. The extent to which delinquency is on the rise is a debatable issue, for current arrest records only indicate that more delinquents are officially taken into custody than had been so in previous years. In question is whether law enforcement agencies are more diligent in arresting youthful offenders, police departments have more manpower and thus are better able to make arrests, or more delinquent acts are being reported to the police. The only certainty is that youths under the age of 18 are being arrested with greater frequency for serious as well as minor offenses than ever before.

From 1960 to 1965, according to the Crime Commission, arrests for serious crimes among youths under the age of 18 increased 47 percent, while the population increase for the same population was only 17 percent. According to the 1973 *Uniform Crime Reports* (FBI, 1973:30–31), 31 percent of all Crime Index offenses solved involved youths under the age of 18, while persons 10 to 17 years of age accounted for only 16 percent of the total United States population. In terms of arrests on a national basis, youths under the age of 15 made up 9 percent of all police arrests and those under the age of 18 accounted for 26 percent of all arrests. In the suburbs, those under 15 accounted for 12 percent of the arrests, while those under 18 represented 33 percent of the arrests. The FBI (1973:34) points out, however, that the increase in arrests among the youthful population is attributable in large measure to the violations of the Narcotic Drug Law. For example, 57 percent of the individuals arrested for violation of this Law in 1973 were persons under the age of 21, 26 percent of the marijuana arrests were persons under 18, and the number of drug arrests nationally was up 19 percent over 1972.

While the rate of increase in delinquency from 1960 to 1965 increased 47 percent, according to the FBI (1973:125), this rate may have slowed significantly, for as Table 13.1 reveals, the rate of increase from 1968 to 1973 was only 14.7 percent for those under the age of 18.

TABLE 13.1. Total Arrest Trends, 1968–1973
(3,256 agencies; 1973 estimated population 107,593,000)

	Number of Persons Arrested					
	Total All Ages			Under 18 Years of Age		
	1968	1973	Percent Change	1968	1973	Percent Change
Total	4,257,707	4,826,192	+13.4	1,103,340	1,265,959	+14.7

Source: Uniform Crime Reports. Washington, D.C.: FBI. 1973:125.

TABLE 13.2. Total Arrest Trends, 1960–1973
(2,378 agencies; 1973 estimated population 94,251,000)

	Number of Persons Arrested					
	Total All Ages			Under 18 Years of Age		
	1960	1973	Percent Change	1960	1973	Percent Change
Total	3,242,574	4,381,968	+35.1	466,174	1,138,046	+144.1

Source: Uniform Crime Reports. Washington, D.C.: FBI. 1973:124.

The picture, however, takes a dramatic turn when we examine the arrest trends over the period 1960 to 1973, for the FBI (1973: 124) reports that the increase in reported arrests jumped 144 percent, as Table 13.2 illustrates.

When we examine the nature of the offenses youths under age 18 commit, to account for the 31 percent of all clearances, we find that youth account for over one-third of all cleared property crimes, over 37 percent of all larceny-theft, and almost 37 percent of auto thefts, as Table 13.3 depicts. This population also accounts for slightly more than 12 percent of the violent crime, but no more than 5 to 6 percent of murder and manslaughter offenses.

Numerous agencies and resources, including the police, families, schools, churches, and welfare agencies refer youth to juvenile courts. Police unquestionably constitute the largest referral source and, compared to the juvenile court, dispose of more cases of alleged delinquency and deviant behavior than any other agency in the country. A comparison of dispositional patterns for handling juvenile offenders in 1966 and 1973 shows remarkable consistency, as

TABLE 13.3. Offenses Cleared, 1973, by Arrest of Persons Under 18 Years of Age
(Percent of total cleared; 1973 estimated population)

Population Group	Crime Index Total	Violent Crime	Property Crime	Criminal Homicide: Murder and Non-negligent Manslaughter	Criminal Homicide: Manslaughter by Negligence	Forcible Rape	Robbery	Aggravated Assault	Burglary—Breaking or Entering	Larceny-theft: Total	Larceny-theft: $50 and Over	Auto Theft
TOTAL CITIES												
4,729 cities; total population 115,413,000:												
Total clearances	1,251,451	281,299	970,152	9,859	3,033	17,543	79,884	174,013	294,307	571,043	150,668	104,802
Percent under 18	30.6	12.2	35.9	5.5	5.8	10.8	17.8	10.2	32.8	37.3	26.4	36.5

Source: Uniform Crime Reports. Washington, D.C.: FBI. 1973:112.

TABLE 13.4. Police Disposition of Juvenile Offenders Taken Into Custody, 1973 (1973 estimated population)

Population Group	Total	Handled Within Department and Released	Referred to Juvenile Court Jurisdiction	Referred to Welfare Agency	Referred to Other Police Agency	Referred to Criminal or Adult Court
TOTAL, ALL AGENCIES						
4,144 agencies; total population 100,816,000:						
Number	1,235,389	558,574	611,511	17,745	28,792	18,767
Percent	100.0	45.2	49.5	1.4	2.3	1.5

Source: Uniform Crime Reports. Washington, D.C.: FBI. 1973:119.

TABLE 13.5. Police Disposition of Juvenile Offenders Taken Into Custody, 1966 (1966 estimated population)

Population Group	Total	Handled Within Department and Released	Referred to Juvenile Court Jurisdiction	Referred to Welfare Agency	Referred to Other Police Agency	Referred to Criminal or Adult Court
TOTAL, ALL AGENCIES						
3,075 agencies; total population 95,623,000:						
Number	967,103	447,512	461,798	17,163	23,591	17,039
Percent	100.0	46.3	47.8	1.8	2.4	1.8

Source: Uniform Crime Reports. Washington, D.C.: FBI. 1966:105.

Tables 13.4 and 13.5 reveal. Although less than one-half of the total population of the United States is covered by the above data and therefore complete generalizations cannot be made, the data do suggest that reporting police departments dispose of almost 50 percent of all juvenile cases without making official referrals to the juvenile courts.

These data cover only *reported* official arrests; therefore, these baseline data do not reveal how many youths policemen stop, interrogate, interview, or otherwise deal with informally throughout the year. It seems reasonable to assume, however, that if reporting police agencies officially handled 1.2 million dispositions in 1973, they probably dealt unofficially with at least twice as many cases.

Dealing With Delinquents

For the most part, many of our approaches to dealing with delinquents have been based on theories of causation. Where poverty, lack of maternal affection, unavailability of jobs, or emotional problems have been viewed as root causes, programs have developed to counteract the problem both on the basis of prevention as well as treatment. This is not to say that all efforts to control or prevent delinquency have always been based on such a scientific procedure; it is only an attempt, admittedly an oversimplified one, to describe some of the motivations and intentions of persons who organize programs. This, in effect, is one of the primary reasons for the development of the juvenile court itself (Platt, 1969). The programs which are established tend to be based on the belief that the provision of essential services in specified areas of concern will have a direct impact on the delinquency problem.

That no single cause or combination of causes has been discovered has not deterred social planners from continuing in their attempts to prevent and control delinquency. Also, regardless of philosophy, juvenile courts and correctional agencies abound in almost every jurisdiction. Juveniles continue to commit offenses, both police and juvenile courts continue to deal with delinquents and MINS officially and unofficially, and all states have some kind of institutionalized services for the detection and treatment of the juvenile offender.

Yet, criminologists, social and behavioral scientists, and legal scholars, individually and collectively, agree that no perfect model is now known for effectively dealing with the delinquency problem. We do not know the causes of delinquency nor are we aware of the best processes to deal with it.

In a report, for example, on the nature and extent of crime and delinquency in the District of Columbia, researchers point out the high rate of recidivism among youthful offenders. They indicate, in fact, that almost 61 percent of those arrested had one or more prior referrals to the juvenile court. In discussing these data they add, "Although such statistics highlight only the failures of the system and none of the successes, they underscore the dimensions of the problem confronting this city" (*Report of the President's Commission on Crime in the District of Columbia*, 1966:656).

Numerous researchers have examined the *state of knowledge* about delinquency causation (see, e.g., Knight, 1972; Matza, 1964; Cicourel, 1968; Rubenfeld, 1965; and Sellin and Wolfgang, 1969). Others have examined *processes of delinquency prevention and treatment* (see, e.g., Schur, 1973; Lerman, 1970; and Cohn, 1973). Theorists are unable to agree on what causes delinquency, and practitioners similarly conclude that no known model is available for its effective prevention or control. In fact, those who have studied processes of delinquency prevention, control, and treatment have reached the almost inescapable conclusion that the criminal justice system has failed to even understand the problem. Lerman (1970: 326) discusses this issue and concludes with both a caveat and a warning:

> The consistent finding that treatment programs have not yet been proved to have an appreciable impact on failure rates should not be misinterpreted. For even though institutions for delinquents are probably not highly successful—regardless of treatment type—there is no reason to go back to harsher methods of child handling. It can be argued, rather, that even when boys are kept for only four months and treated with trust . . . there is no evidence that this "coddling" will yield greater failure rates . . . The need for a humanitarian approach needs to be divorced from any specific mode of treatment.

Schur (1973) is willing to go even further. He argues that the delinquency problem possibly may be reduced by taking two profound but unpopular steps. First, he argues that many offenses that bring juveniles to the official attention of the police and courts ought to be wiped off the books or decriminalized. For instance, he says that such status offenses as incorrigibility and truancy have no justification for being offenses. Second, he suggests that where "official" delinquency exists, agencies and agents of formal control ought not to intervene as often as they do, He believes that rates of "success" would be higher if more youths were left alone and allowed a greater opportunity to mature and grow up spontaneously. As the title of his book indicates, this is "radical non-intervention." Schur concludes (1973:171), "Our young people deserve something better than being 'processed.' Hopefully, we are beginning to realize this." In effect, Schur is asking that society tolerate more youthful misbehavior, increase its threshold for deviancy, and not be so quick to label as much behavior as delinquent. Whether or not society is prepared for such non-intervention is a matter that will have to be tested over the years. However, it is certainly unlikely that we will achieve such a level of non-intervention in the immediate future, except in the area of status offenses and, perhaps, in the area of minor drug abuse, such as marijuana.

Diversion

Short of the radical non-intervention that Schur proposes, one development which has been receiving increased attention is that of diversion from the juvenile justice system. Through this process, "someone" in official capacity makes a decision to refer a juvenile to an agency other than the court when misbehavior is detected. Diversion, of course, has been a popular activity of the police for many years, attested to by the high rates of youths handled informally and unofficially by individual policemen.

In recent years, a relatively new program development known as the Youth Service Bureau (YSB) has served as an official community resource for diverting youthful offenders. YSBs, which are increasing in number throughout the country, combine services and programs to deal with "troubled" youth and to prevent delinquency. In *The Challenge of Crime in a Free Society*, the summary report of the President's Crime Commission (1967:83), it was stated:

> Communities should establish neighborhood youth-serving agencies—Youth Service Bureaus—located if possible in comprehensive neighborhood community centers and receiving juveniles (delinquent and non-delinquent) referred by the police, the juvenile court, parents, schools, and other sources.

These agencies would act as central coordinators of all community services for young people and would also provide services lacking in the community or neighborhood, especially ones designed for less seriously delinquent juveniles.

Under the auspices of the National Council on Crime and Delinquency, the late Sherwood Norman (1972:3) assessed the state of affairs with regard to YSBs and in 1969 found that fewer than 12 agencies directly or indirectly were involved in delinquency prevention activities which:

(1) were strictly noncoercive, (2) were planned on a jurisdiction-wide basis, (3) were neighborhood-based, (4) received referrals from law enforcement agencies, schools, and other sources, and (5) coordinated appropriate resources on behalf of the child and followed through to see that he received the appropriate service. . . . Of course there were many prevention programs that met some of the above requirements but could not be considered Youth Service Bureaus in keeping with the total YSB concept formulated by the Crime Commission . . .

In his book, Norman (1972:173-174) developed a sample ordinance for the creation of a YSB, in which he indicates that it should be developed at a local level of government, have a citizens' board of directors, that the YSB should be noncoercive in nature, and that all records developed by the agency should be kept confidential:

SAMPLE ORDINANCE FOR THE JOINT SPONSORSHIP

OF A YOUTH SERVICE BUREAU

Ordinance Number _____

_____
(Name of City, Township, or Village)

It Is Ordained:

Section 1. There is hereby established a Youth Service Bureau (or program) in _____
                                              (Municipality)

in cooperation with _____
                                              (School District)

and _____
(County Juvenile or Family Court or other concerned agency)

Section 2. This ordinance embodies the _____ county Youth Services Plan. Its primary purpose is to prevent juvenile delinquency before it becomes serious enough for the official court. Its secondary purpose is to coordinate and strengthen existing services through the cooperative efforts of agencies, citizens, and the youth of the community.

Section 3. A General Citizens Committee or Board shall be established by the joint efforts of the local municipality, local school district, and the Juvenile (or Family) Court. This committee or board shall be nonprofit and nonpolitical; its membership shall represent the community and include youth and former offenders; members of the committee or board shall serve without compensation.

Section 4. The General Citizens Committee or Board shall not have any coercive authority. It shall develop its own bylaws and guidelines to carry out its responsibilities in relation to program, facilities and funds. Its services shall be voluntary and cooperative in relation to all concerned.

Section 5. Records and proceedings of the Committee shall be kept confidential and shall be highly guarded. When cases are closed, case files shall be destroyed within established procedures.

Section 6. Funds for staffing the Youth Services Bureau shall be the responsibility of the joint sponsorships.

Made And Passed by the _____ board of the
_____ this day of _____ 19

There is no accurate information available concerning the extent or nature of YSBs throughout the country, but impressionistic data suggest that they are increasing in numbers and programs. Spurred by financial assistance from LEAA, many appear to be formally or informally attached either to police departments or juvenile courts. At the very least, since they are diversionary in purpose, the YSBs work very closely with both police agencies and the juvenile court in the communities they serve.

In a monograph prepared for the National Assessment of Juvenile Corrections, entitled *Diversion from the Juvenile Justice System*, Cressey and McDermott (1973:vii) report that through direct observations and interviews in various communities, they were able to obtain information about practices, arrangements, and belief systems of personnel in various juvenile court *probation* departments "who are currently engaged in diverting youth either *from or within* that state's juvenile justice system." They go on to state (p. vii):

(The report) ... reveals the divergent conceptions of "diversion" and the dilemmas associated with differing objectives and modes of handling "predelinquents" and young offenders, short of full processing through the juvenile courts. The report raises fundamental questions about the actual outcomes for juveniles who are handled in these varying ways, about the interplay between juvenile justice personnel and community expectations and resources, and about the extent to which the values of humaneness and justice are served through these practices.

They conclude, however (1973:62):

If the policies and programs of diversion serve to pave the way for a better blend of juvenile justice theory and actual societal responses to the problems of youth, then they deserve to be lauded. If, however, diversion becomes merely a bureaucratic means of diverting attention from needed changes in the environment of youth, it will do great injustice. . . . But if other forms of true diversion receive adequate public and private support, they may ... serve as models for more effective and responsive youth service agencies.

An example of a program concerned with diversion as well as other kinds of youth services is the Philadelphia Neighborhood Youth Resources Center, which has been described by LEAA (1974) as "an exemplary project." The NYRC provides a broad spectrum of services, including crisis intervention, counseling, educational assistance, referrals to other agencies, and legal representation. It works with a target population of 4,000 youngsters, 13 hours a day, and is located in a high-crime, inner-city area. In 1973 (LEAA, 1974:3), it served 1,027 youths. Through direct assistance and diversionary programs, the NYRC, in a four-month study (1974:15), claims to have "significantly" lowered the felony and status offenses arrest categories among the target population. Other programs make similar claims and it appears that diversion of youthful offenders has come to mean keeping some youths away from the official juvenile justice system and, for others, reduced involvement.

The Juvenile Court

We have previously discussed (see Chapter 11) the development of the juvenile court movement in the United States; therefore, it is not necessary to review its history once again. However, one aspect of its development needs further attention and that is the two distinct approaches of dealing with delinquents which have influenced the main work of the court. According to Tappan (1960:4), these approaches have been classified as *legal* and *casework*.

In the legal approach to misconduct, the description of offenses and penalties in specific terms is customary in order to protect the citizen from unjust or arbitrary acts of the police or judicial authorities and, at the same time, to protect the community from dangerous persons. A legal approach in adult courts demands the following requirements (Tappan, 1960:4):

> ... (1) that a specific charge be alleged against the defendant, (2) it be defined in definite terms by law, (3) that the offense be proved rather conclusively, (4) that protection be given the accused during trial against conviction by false, misleading, prejudicial, irrelevant, or immaterial evidence.

Tappan (1960:5) then says that in a legalistic approach to dealing with delinquents:

> The full rigors of the criminal law are mitigated by reason of the offender's youth, but the judicial view would preserve in the hearings of children's courts a real test of the individual's status as a delinquent before applying to him the modern and individualized method of treatment. The child is not a delinquent unless the court has found him so.

In contrast to the formalism of the legal approach, the casework model presupposes that the delinquent is "sick or troubled" and in need of some kind of treatment. With this in mind, the juvenile court worker attempts to define the personal and situational problems that affect the juvenile, including his home, family, and community, and then proceeds to develop an individualized, nonmoralistic, and nonpunitive treatment plan. As a consequence, the worker frequently behaves in informal and sometimes extralegal ways in order to provide "what is best" for the child.

In describing the casework approach while tracing the history of the juvenile court movement and the process of dealing with offenders as sick or troubled persons, Cohen and Short (1966:84-85) assert:

> The manifest function of the juvenile court . . . is usually phrased in statutes in some such words as these: to secure for each child within its jurisdiction such care, custody, and treatment as should have been provided by the child's natural parents. It is not to punish but to "help children in trouble," to do what is in the best interest of the child and the state to "rehabilitate."

The nature of the casework approach was to avoid the stigmatizing effects of labeling a child as delinquent. Constitutional safeguards inherent in the criminal justice process, to which Tappan alluded earlier, particularly that of due process, were minimized. This was so since the only way an "unfortunate child" could receive expert attention, it was believed, was for court personnel to be free to seize every opportunity to do that which was "best for the child." Since normal rules of evidence were minimized, a child was always at the mercy of the court and those adults who made decisions about what was in his real best interests. We have come to learn, however, that such stigmatizing was never avoided and, in fact, the very process of judicial intervention was in and of itself stigmatizing—for dependent and neglected, as well as delinquent youth.

The *Gault* decision (*In re Gault*, May 15, 1967) drastically changed in theory and practice the idea that constitutional safeguards could be forever minimized or neglected in juvenile courts. In this historic Supreme Court decision, the justices stated that in many ways a juvenile court hearing is similar to a criminal proceeding, and as such a juvenile is entitled to due process of law. In the opinion, a 1953 observation of the late Arthur P. Vanderbilt (1967:61), Chief Justice of the New Jersey Supreme Court, was quoted:

> In their zeal to care for children neither juvenile judges nor welfare workers can be permitted to violate the Constitution, especially the constitutional provisions as to due process that are involved in moving a child from its home. The indispensable elements of due process are: first, a tribunal with jurisdiction; second, notice of a hearing to the proper parties; and, finally, a fair hearing. All three must be present if we are to treat the child as an individual human being and not to revert, in spite of good intentions, to the more primitive days when he was treated as a chattel.

The *Gault* decision, handed down in 1967, has had a dramatic impact on the nature of juvenile court structure and processes. In effect, it forced a blending of the casework and legal approaches to handling juveniles into a socio-legal approach in which the rights of the child and his needs are simultaneously considered.

The *Gault* decision did not remove the wide discretionary latitude of the juvenile court in adjudication and treatment processes. Almost every conceivable act, criminal and noncriminal, that a juvenile commits still falls within the purview of the court. It still permits intervention on the basis of rather vague measures of societal standards and norms. The impact of the decision is that it now assures each youngster greater fairness and due process at the hearings. Thus, a child whose behavior shows no specific and serious law violation can still be treated preventively if found to suffer from problems of a social or psychological nature. Courts continue to deal with dependent and neglected as well as delinquent children in administrative or legal fashion, even though some constraints on dispositional alternatives now exist. The *Gault* decision provided for juveniles the right to counsel, which has tended, in the final analysis, to remove from the juvenile court its tradition of complete informality, and to replace it with an adversary procedure, similar to that found in adult criminal courts. As the decision states (President's Crime Commission, 1967: 65–66):

> We conclude that the Due Process Clause of the Fourteenth Amendment requires that in respect of proceedings to determine delinquency which may result in commitment to an institution in which the juvenile's freedom is curtailed, the child and his parent must be notified of the child's right to be represented by counsel retained by them, or if they are unable to afford counsel, that counsel will be appointed to represent the child.

Juvenile Court Procedures

Although juvenile courts vary in terms of scope, services, structures, and procedures for processing delinquents, it may be a safe generalization that the following major decisions—or critical junctures— occur in each court: (1) intake or acceptance of referral, (2) whether or not to detain the youngster, (3) adjudication hearing, (4) dispositional hearing, and (5) closure of case, including that of violation.

At the referral level of decision-making, it is typical that an intake worker makes the decision whether or not the court has jurisdiction in the matter presented before the court by the referral source. At this time, the intake worker can decide if the case is to be handled on a formal or informal basis. Sometimes this decision must be approved by a magistrate, referee, or the judge. If the case is to be handled informally, the youngster and his or her family may be lectured, reprimanded, or otherwise referred for informal counseling to another agency. When possible, some cases can actually be diverted at this time, with a referral to a Youth Service Bureau, for example.

If the case is to be treated formally, a *petition* must be drawn up and it is at this time, as a result of the *Gault* decision, that counsel must be made available. Once a petition is drawn, the child is dealt with in formal ways and is on the way to adjudication and disposition. Sometimes a decision has to be made rather quickly if the child is to be placed in detention, and it is the intake worker, in many jurisdictions, who also makes this decision. For the most part, detention is arranged for those youths who either present a distinct danger to themselves or other persons, or for those youths who cannot remain in their own homes for some reason. When a parent makes a referral as a result of alleged incorrigibility or refusal to "obey" parents, intake workers may detain a child "in his best interests." In some courts, there must be a detention hearing and it is the judge who will decide if the child is to remain in detention and for how long a period of time.

After a petition is filed, it is common practice for a probation officer to conduct a social investigation of the youth, his or her family, and the conditions which prompted the delinquent behavior. This is very similar to a presentence investigation conducted for adult offenders and results in an official report which is presented to the judge who will use it as a basis for adjudicating the case and making a final disposition. It is not uncommon now for the presentation of the social history to be made after the adjudicatory hearing, which, in essence, is similar to an actual trial at which the offender's (the youth in this case) guilt or innocence is established. It is at the dispositional hearing where the judge determines what will happen to the child, which is similar to judicial sentencing of adults.

A number of dispositional alternatives is available to the court, depending on resources available in the community. If the child has committed a very serious crime, the court may also *certify* or *trans-*

fer the youth to a criminal court, where he will be tried as an adult. This does not occur with great frequency in most jurisdictions and generally occurs when the youth is older, is a chronic recidivist, and/or has committed such offenses as murder, forcible rape, or aggravated assault. In most cases, where jurisdiction over the youth is retained by the juvenile court, the judge may simply reprimand the child, place him or her on probation, commit to an institution, or otherwise make arrangements for the child to be placed in foster care, a group home of some kind, or a child-serving institution which may specialize in the "treatment" of specific kinds of youths, such as those who are handicapped, emotionally disturbed, or in need of special and remedial assistance. Every state has some kind of system for institutionalizing its committed youths, and these programs are usually administered by a state agency. Thus, when a juvenile court judge commits a child to a training school, for example, he generally is placing that child under the jurisdiction of the state, an agency of which then determines what shall happen next to the child. While some counties in the United States maintain their own institutions, such as Los Angeles, all states, including California, also have state-wide institutions for youths.

It is also the state which tends to supervise institutionally released youths in an aftercare program, which is similar to parole for adults. Thus, when a juvenile court commits a child to a state agency, in more cases than not it loses its jurisdiction over the child and the state assumes that responsibility until the child becomes of legal age—generally anywhere from 18 to 21. Aftercare services, however, are very similar to probation services, for the primary aim is to work with the child and the family, where possible, in order to help the child adjust to societal demands and otherwise prevent further delinquent acts, while still in the community.

The work of the juvenile court is often complicated by conflicting demands placed upon it by the community in which the court operates. While most people are willing to "give a kid a break," the increasing amount of delinquency, especially violent crime, has made many people much more concerned about delinquency prevention and the need to control those who repeatedly are referred to the court. In a paper prepared for the President's Crime Commission, Prof. Robert Vinter (1967:85) had this to say:

> Considerable evidence indicates widespread public expectations that juvenile courts should give special emphasis to maintenance of public

order. This concern receives very strong local support, and attempts to balance it against other aims often evoke indignant community protest. Futher, some among the general citizenry appear to have definite and ready-made notions of how public order can best be maintained: by prompt and strenuous action, by "setting examples," by strict application of punishments, and so forth. In contrast, the goals of justice and welfare are not so broadly defended, nor do they prescribe such clear-cut courses of action. As a consequence, these more precarious goals require special supports and protections. Since such protections are generally lacking for the juvenile court, a continuous drift toward emphasis on public order is to be expected.

Vinter (1967:87) concludes that because of the tremendous overload of cases in most juvenile courts, many of the youngsters are dealt with informally, referred to other agencies and organizations for services, or otherwise receive only cursory attention when many more efforts would be required to deal adequately with the problems being presented by the individual situation.

Costs

In a report presented at the Fourth National Symposium on Law Enforcement Science and Technology in May, 1972, Robert Gemignani, then Commissioner of the Youth Development and Delinquency Prevention Administration of the Department of Health, Education and Welfare, stated (1973:9–11) that it was impossible to determine with any degree of accuracy the precise costs for handling delinquency matters in the United States. However, it was estimated that the annual costs for each youth processed through the juvenile justice system in 1972 were as follows:

Referral and Intake	$100
Probation Service	500
Training Schools	5,700
Other Residential Commitments (foster care, group homes, halfway houses)	1,500

Gemignani (1973:10–13) also éstimated that by 1977 what

might cost as much as $1.2 billion for the juvenile justice system throughout the country could be reduced to less than $700 million, if at least 25 percent of all possible referred youth were instead diverted from the system. This means an actual diversion rate based on those who presently are actually being referred, not those who are now dealt with informally by the police and not being referred to the court anyway.

While most persons concerned with the system of juvenile justice believe that diversion of youngsters from the court is a responsible procedure and one which should be increased in scope and magnitude, Nejelski (1973:89) makes the following very reasonable point:

> Discretion can and should not be totally eliminated from decisions by police, intake officers, and other administrators in diversionary settings. A certain amount of discretion and flexibility is necessary in any administrative system. However, most attempts to divert increase the discretion available to system participants and increase the need of the judiciary or some other institution in our society, e.g. ombudsman or legislative oversight, to monitor the system on a permanent basis in order to review and control the exercise of discretion.

Juvenile Institutions

In 1971, LEAA completed a census of all public juvenile detention and correctional facilities. It was found that the 722 facilities were equally divided among state and local governments, and that on June 30, 1971 (the latest year for which data are available), these facilities held 57,239 persons: 44,140 males and 13,099 females. The report (LEAA, 1972) depicts six kinds of institutional settings, which together with their numbers are shown in Table 13.6.

The juvenile detention center is similar to the adult jail and is the most common type of residential facility, as the table reveals. Most centers are administered by a local rather than a state government, although the latter may have inspection and standard-setting responsibilities. Some may be administered on a regional basis, as in Virginia. Detention facilities are seen as temporary places for incarceration and tend to be physically restricting; that is, custody and security are generally provided. Shelters, on the other hand, while also temporary facilities, generally only provide brief care for young-

TABLE 13.6. Number of Juvenile Facilities, Number of Children Held on June 30, 1971, and Fiscal 1971 Average Daily Population by Type of Facility

Type of Facility	Number of Facilities	Number of Children Held on June 30, 1971		
		Total	Male	Female
All facilities in the U.S.	722	57,239	44,140	13,099
Detention centers	303	11,748	7,912	3,836
Shelters	18	363	237	126
Reception or diagnostic centers	17	2,486	1,988	498
Training schools	192	35,931	27,839	8,092
Ranches, forestry camps and farms	114	5,666	5,376	290
Halfway houses and group homes	78	1,045	788	257

Source: Children in Custody, Washington, D.C.: LEAA, 1972:1.

sters awaiting court disposition and are not generally so physically restricting. Shelters tend to provide more care for dependent and neglected youngsters than for delinquent youth, although in some jurisdictions there may be no more than slight differentiation among those confined. A shelter also tends to accept more referrals from parents or guardians when children have no other place to stay, while a detention center almost always deals with those who have been referred to the juvenile court. At the time of the census (LEAA, 1972:4), public shelters held less than one percent of all juveniles in public institutions.

Reception or diagnostic centers handle adjudicated delinquents almost exclusively, although some juvenile courts may commit a child to such a facility for a temporary time in order to obtain a diagnostic workup on the child. These institutions tend to be operated by state governments and number only 17 in the country. This number does not include special hospitals and diagnostic clinics which will also do workups upon special request of the juvenile court; it includes only those maintained by governments for handling official delinquents. Additionally, many correctional facilities also have diagnostic or classification units where new arrivals are screened for assignment to treatment and educational programs within the institution. These also sometimes service juvenile court referrals on a request basis.

The 306 training schools, ranches, forestry camps, and farms, are all facilities generally run by state governments (although some counties have some) and accept only those youngsters who have been adjudicated delinquent and committed. The training schools tend to be more security conscious than the other facilities and it is usually a training school to which a youngster is first sent, before being transferred to another less security conscious facility if it appears appropriate. Halfway houses and group homes have probably increased above the 78 figure by this time. Many are administered by probation departments and tend to be specialized institutions which are used for those youngsters needing special kinds of services and programs. These generally are much closer to the youngsters' homes and communities, so many of the youngsters attend regular schools or are employed, but live at the facility. The average length of stay for most youngsters who are committed to a facility is approximately eight months, but this will vary from state to state and also from time to time. If institutions are overcrowded, it is not unlikely that aftercare administrators will release them after shorter periods of stay. Many committed youths are released to an aftercare authority and generally for indeterminate periods of time.

Tables 13.7 and 13.8 depict the detention status of children in custody as well as their movements *into* the facilities, each according to their sex.

Table 13.9 depicts the movement of youngsters by sex *out* of the correctional facilities.

These 722 public juvenile facilities employed a total of 39,521 full-time workers in 1971, outnumbering part-time workers about 10 to 1. The report (LEAA, 1972:16) states that 70 percent of the staff was directly "engaged in treatment or educational activities," including psychiatrists, psychologists, social workers, teachers, aftercare workers, physicians, dentists, nurses, and vocational counselors. Table 13.10 illustrates the range of full-time staff services in the 722 facilities.

The various public and private institutions which abound in this country offer many services and programs for committed youngsters. However, it is not possible to evaluate their effectiveness, even though the nature of their services is spelled out, as Table 13.10 illustrates. Treatment programs, medical and academic services, and a

TABLE 13.7. Detention Status of Children in Juvenile Facilities by Type of Facility, June 30, 1971

All Types of Facilities	Total Population			Adjudicated Delinquents			Juveniles Held Pending Court Action			Dependent and Neglected Children			Juveniles Awaiting Transfer to Another Jurisdiction		
	Total	Male	Female	Total	Male	Female	Total	Male	Female	Total	Male	Female	Total	Male	Female
NUMBER															
All facilities	57,239	44,140	13,099	48,050	38,075	9,975	7,717	5,178	2,539	942	520	422	530	367	163
Detention centers	11,748	7,912	3,836	3,449	2,382	1,067	7,300	4,908	2,392	489	271	218	510	351	159
Shelters	363	237	126	36	23	13	164	106	58	153	101	52	10	7	3
Reception or diagnostic centers	2,486	1,988	498	2,462	1,973	489	4	3	1	18	11	7	2	1	1
Training schools	35,931	27,839	8,092	35,498	27,590	7,908	248	160	88	177	81	96	8	8	–
Ranches, forestry camps and farms	5,666	5,376	290	5,647	5,367	280	1	1	–	18	8	10	–	–	–
Halfway houses and group homes	1,045	788	257	958	740	218	–	–	–	87	48	39	–	–	–
PERCENT															
All facilities	100	77	23	83	66	17	14	9	4	2	1	1	1	1	*
Detention centers	100	67	33	29	20	9	62	42	20	4	2	2	4	3	1
Shelters	100	65	35	10	6	4	45	29	16	42	28	14	3	2	1
Reception or diagnostic centers	100	80	20	99	79	20	*	*	*	1	1	*	*	*	*
Training schools	100	78	22	99	77	22	1	*	*	*	*	*	*	*	–
Ranches, forestry camps and farms	100	95	5	100	95	5	*	*	–	*	*	*	–	–	–
Halfway houses and group homes	100	75	25	92	71	21	–	–	–	8	5	4	–	–	–

*0.5% or less. (Detail may not add to totals because of rounding.)
Source: Children in Custody. Washington, D.C.: LEAA. 1972:7.

TABLE 13.8 Movement Into Juvenile Correctional Facilities by Category of Admission, by Type of Facility, Fiscal Year 1971

Admissions	Total Admissions			Committed by Court				Returned from Aftercare/Parole		Transferred In		Other	
				First Commitments		Recommitments							
	Total	Male	Female	Male	Female	Male	Female	Male	Female	Male	Female	Male	Female
NUMBER													
All correctional facilities	85,080	69,029	16,051	41,460	10,410	6,075	490	10,869	2,837	6,871	1,131	3,754	1,183
Training schools	67,558	52,960	14,598	31,453	9,413	4,706	416	9,821	2,735	4,118	989	2,862	1,045
Ranches, forestry camps and farms	14,956	14,062	894	9,222	701	1,336	68	898	57	2,191	68	415	–
Halfway houses and group homes	2,566	2,007	559	785	296	33	6	150	45	562	74	477	138
PERCENT													
All correctional facilities	100	81	19	49	12	7	1	13	3	8	1	4	1
Training schools	100	78	22	47	14	7	1	14	4	6	2	4	2
Ranches, forestry camps and farms	100	94	6	62	5	9	*	6	*	15	*	3	–
Halfway houses and group homes	100	78	22	31	12	1	*	6	2	22	3	9	5

*0.5% or less. (Detail may not add to totals because of rounding.)
Source: Children in Custody. Washington, D.C.: LEAA. 1972:10.

TABLE 13.9. Movement Out of Juvenile Correctional Facilities by Category of Discharge, by Type of Facility, Fiscal Year 1971

Discharges	Total Discharges			Discharged Without Supervision		Placed in Aftercare/Parole		Transferred Out		Other	
	Total	Male	Female	Male	Female	Male	Female	Male	Female	Male	Female
NUMBER											
All correctional facilities	85,109	69,209	15,900	4,950	1,784	48,993	11,152	8,371	1,357	6,895	1,606
Training schools	68,749	54,164	14,585	4,269	1,695	37,825	10,164	6,415	1,258	5,655	1,468
Ranches, forestry camps and farms	14,141	13,343	798	558	37	9,994	614	1,684	73	1,107	74
Halfway houses and group homes	2,219	1,702	517	123	52	1,174	375	272	26	133	64
PERCENT											
All correctional facilities	100	81	19	6	2	58	13	10	2	8	2
Training schools	100	79	21	6	2	55	15	9	2	8	2
Ranches, forestry camps and farms	100	94	6	4	*	71	4	12	1	8	1
Halfway houses and group homes	100	77	23	6	2	53	17	12	1	6	3

*0.5% pr less. (Detail may not add to totals because of rounding.)
Source: Children in Custody. Washington, D.C.: LEAA. 1972:10.

TABLE 13.10. Number of Full-Time Staff and Ratio of Inmates to Full-Time Staff for General Categories of Personnel and Selected Treatment and Educational Positions in Juvenile Facilities by Type of Facility, June 30, 1971

| | | | | Full-time Personnel | | | | | | | | |
| | Total Full-time Personnel | Administrative Personnel | Treatment and Educational Personnel | Selected Treatment and Educational Personnel | | | | | | | Operational and Maintenance Personnel |
Type of Facility				Cottage Staff	Academic Teachers	Vocational Teachers	Social Workers	Recreational Workers	Psychologists	Psychiatrists	
NUMBER											
All types of facilities	39,521	4,441	28,165	16,583	3,475	984	1,471	544	268	29	6,915
Detention centers	9,229	1,047	6,994	4,518	662	76	148	125	51	2	1,188
Shelters	318	51	201	100	19	–	25	1	1	–	66
Reception or diagnostic centers	2,244	263	1,614	916	112	10	167	37	74	17	367
Training schools	24,037	2,515	16,751	9,845	2,345	828	966	353	135	10	4,771
Ranches, forestry camps and farms	3,125	473	2,201	940	305	70	140	21	6	–	451
Halfway houses and group homes	568	92	404	264	32	–	25	7	1	–	72
RATIO											
All types of facilities	1.4	2.9	2.0	3.4	16.5	58.2	38.9	105.2	213.6	1,973.8	8.3
Detention centers	1.3	1.2	1.7	2.6	17.8	154.6	79.4	94.0	230.4	5,874.0	9.9
Shelters	1.1	7.1	1.8	3.6	19.1	–	14.5	363.0	363.0	–	5.5
Reception or diagnostic centers	1.1	9.5	1.5	2.7	22.2	248.6	14.9	67.2	33.6	146.2	6.8
Training schools	1.5	14.3	2.1	3.6	15.3	43.4	37.2	101.8	266.2	3,593.1	7.5
Ranches, forestry camps and farms	1.8	12.0	2.6	6.0	18.6	80.9	40.5	269.8	944.3	–	12.6
Halfway houses and group homes	1.8	11.4	2.6	4.0	32.7	–	41.8	149.3	1,045.0	–	14.5

Source: Children in Custody. Washington, D.C.: LEAA. 1972:18.

myriad of other kinds of recreational, vocational, and religious activities are routinely offered, but not necessarily evaluated. Thus, it is not uncommon for an institution to develop these activities, but the extent to which they prevent or control delinquency cannot be determined. Nonetheless, we can assume, as a result of the recidivism rates of youngsters, that juvenile institutions, similar to those for adult offenders, do not materially reduce or control delinquency. It may be as a consequence of the above that the President's Crime Commission (1967) and other groups have recommended that these large institutions be abandoned and replaced with smaller facilities, such as group homes and halfway houses. This is precisely what Massachusetts has done, but it is too early to determine if this movement toward reintegration of youngsters into their own communities will turn the tide on delinquency (Coates, 1973).

In a study of six delinquent institutions, Street, Vinter, and Perrow (1966) assert that the belief systems of the administrators of these facilities mold the treatment programs in ways that make them different from institutions whose administrative leaders are not committed to treatment strategies. Notwithstanding the foregoing, Janowitz (1966:x) in his foreword to the book, states:

> The treatment type of institution must still be considered an experimental institution. It is an organization that can succeed on the basis of imaginative personal leadership, but it is one that has yet to solve its operational and administrative problems.

Street, Vinter, and Perrow (1966:279) respond to Janowitz' position in their conclusion and state:

> The goal of treatment becomes more pervasive throughout the corrections field but its implementation remains elusive . . . (in part due to the) piecemeal injection of counselling and other treatment programs into institutions that remain basically custodial.

Prevention

In a recent Youth Development and Delinquency Prevention Administration report (1972:1), it is stated:

> Currently it is a fact that our corrective efforts are insufficient for significantly preventing or controlling youthful deviance. The increased rates

speak for themselves as an indication of our inability to prevent. The high rates of recidivism, unfortunately true even of many sophisticated treatment efforts, speak to the failure of our control procedures.

One of our difficulties, as Bloch and Geis (1962:440) long ago pointed out, is that preventive programs which are designed to alleviate the problem must reach deeply into the American cultural system and into those facets of our life styles which precipitate and foster delinquency. As a consequence, when such radical changes are sought, they will be resisted and change will be slow to come about, if it can be arranged at all. Since we cannot be certain what exactly causes delinquency generally or such deviance specifically on the part of the individual, we will always have difficulty measuring the results of our work. Finally, as Bloch and Geis suggest (1962:441, 443):

> One of the ironic results of many of the specific efforts to cope with certain facets of delinquency, however, is that we can never be quite certain as to how effective our programs of deterrence have been even when rates appear to have been lowered.... (If we are not careful)...we will continue to delude ourselves with experiments in futility by pandering to the conspicuous displays of programs catering to public ignorance and political expedience.

References

Bloch, Herbert A. and Gilbert Geis
    1962   Man, Crime, and Society. New York: Random House.
Cicourel, Aaron V.
    1968   The Social Organization of Juvenile Justice. New York: John Wiley and Sons.
Coates, Robert D.
    1973   "From Institution Based Corrections to Community Based Corrections: Some Policy Questions Given the Massachusetts Reform Experience." Paper presented to the Maryland Department of Juvenile Services, Baltimore, Maryland. (Mimeo).
Cohen, Albert K. and James F. Short, Jr.
    1966   "Juvenile Delinquency." In R.K. Merton and R.A. Nisbet, eds. Contemporary Social Problems. 2nd ed. New York: Harcourt, Brace. 84-135.
Cohn, Alvin W.
    1973   "The Failure of Correctional Management." Crime and Delinquency 19 (July):323-31.
Cressey, Donald R. and Robert A. McDermott

1973   Diversion from the Juvenile Justice System. Ann Arbor, Michigan: National Assessment of Juvenile Corrections, University of Michigan.

Empey, LaMar T.
1973   "Juvenile Justice Reform: Diversion, Due Process, and Deinstitutionalization." In Lloyd E. Ohlin, ed. Prisoners in America. Englewood Cliffs, New Jersey: Prentice-Hall: 13-48.

Federal Bureau of Investigation
1973   Crime in the United States—Uniform Crime Reports. Washington, D.C.: U.S. Government Printing Office.

Gemignani, Robert J.
1973   "Diversion of Juvenile Offenders from the Juvenile Justice System." In New Approaches to Diversion and Treatment of Juvenile Offenders. Washington, D.C.: U.S. Government Printing Office: 8-38.

Janowitz, Morris
1966   "Foreword." In D. Street, R.D. Vinter, and C. Perrow. Organization for Treatment. New York: The Free Press: v-xiv.

Joint Commission on Correctional Manpower and Training
1969   A Time to Act: Final Report, Washington, D.C.: JCCMT.

Knight, D.
1972   Delinquency Causes and Remedies: The Working Assumptions of the California Youth Authority Staff. Sacramento: California Youth Authority.

Korn, Richard R. and Lloyd W. McCorkle
1965   Criminology and Penology. New York: Holt, Rinehart and Winston.
1972   Children in Custody. Washington, D.C.: U.S. Government Printing Office.

Law Enforcement Assistance Administration
1974   The Philadelphia Neighborhood Youth Resources Center: An Exemplary Project. Washington, D.C.: U.S. Government Printing Office.

Lerman, Paul
1970   Delinquency and Social Policy. New York: Praeger.

Matza, David
1964   Delinquency and Drift. New York: John Wiley and Sons.

Nejelski, Paul
1973   "Diversion of Juvenile Offenders in the Criminal Justice System." In New Approaches to Diversion and Treatment of Juvenile Offenders. Washington, D.C.: U.S. Government Printing Office: 83-92.

Norman, Sherwood
1972   The Youth Service Bureau: A Key to Delinquency Prevention. Paramus, New Jersey: National Council on Crime and Delinquency.

Platt, Anthony
1969   The Child Savers. Chicago: University of Chicago Press.

President's Commission on Law Enforcement and Administration of Justice
 1967   Challenge of Crime in a Free Society. Washington, D.C.: U.S. Government Printing Office.

        Task Force Report: Juvenile Delinquency and Youth Crime. Washington, D.C.: U.S. Government Printing Office.
Report of the President's Commission on Crime in the District of Columbia
 1966   Washington, D.C.: U.S. Government Printing Office.
Rubenfeld, Seymour
 1965   Family of Outcasts: A New Theory of Delinquency. New York: The Free Press.

Rubin, Sol
 1970   Crime and Juvenile Delinquency. 3rd ed. rev. Dobbs Ferry, New York: Oceana Publications.

Schur, Edwin
 1973   Radical Nonintervention: Rethinking the Delinquency Problem. Englewood Cliffs, New Jersey: Prentice-Hall.
Sellin, Thorsten and Marvin Wolfgang
 1969   Delinquency: Selected Studies. New York: John Wiley and Sons.
Sheridan, W.H.
 1967   "Juveniles Who Commit Non-Criminal Acts—Why Treat in a Correctional System?" Federal Probation 31 (March):26-30.
Shireman, C.R.
 1962   "Foreword." In Justice for the Child. M.K. Rosenheim, ed. New York: Free Press.
Street, David, R.D. Vinter, and C. Perrow
 1966   Organization for Treatment. New York: The Free Press.
Tappan, Paul W.
 1949   Juvenile Delinquency. New York: McGraw-Hill.
 1960   Crime, Justice and Correction. New York: McGraw-Hill.
Vanderbilt, Arthur P.
 1967   In Task Force Report: Juvenile Delinquency and Youth Crime. Washington, D.C.: President's Commission on Law Enforcement and Administration of Justice.
Viano, Emilio and Alvin W. Cohn
 1975   Social Problems and Criminal Justice. Chicago: Nelson-Hall Publishers.
Vinter, Robert D.
 1967   "The Juvenile Court as an Institution." In Task Force Report: Juvenile Delinquency and Youth Crime. Washington, D.C.: President's Commission on Law Enforcement and Administration of Justice: 84-90.
Youth Development and Delinquency Prevention Administration
 1972   Delinquency Prevention Through Youth Development. Washington, D.C.: U.S. Government Printing Office.

pROBATION

Historical Development

As man changed his notions about the nature of man, from that of the Classical point of view (where man was seen as an actor governed by free will and pleasure and pain principles) to that of the Positive tradition (where man was seen as one whose behavior is determined by many forces, frequently beyond his will), the ground was laid for the development of new ways to control crime and delinquency. The Classical criminologists sought to exercise such control by being concerned with the law and fixed kinds of punishments (especially to achieve deterrence). The Positivists, on the other hand, seek to control the lawbreaker by examining him, as a person, and those forces which may influence him to behave in deviant ways. In other words, early criminologists looked at the crime, while later (and many contemporary) criminologists look at the criminal.

As we trace the history of the ways in which society has sought to control the lawbreaker, various methods of punishment and control have been attempted. According to Sutherland and Cressey (1970:461), "probation is the suspension of a sentence during a period of liberty in the community conditional upon good behavior of the convicted offender." Tappan (1960:539) tends to agree, but elaborates slightly:

> Probation may be viewed both as a sentence of the court and as a correctional process. In the former sense, it combines the suspension of a punitive sanction against convicted offenders (ordinarily a prison or jail term) with orders for treatment under conditional liberty in the community. In the latter sense it includes the conduct of pre-sentence investigations as an aid to court dispositions and the personal supervision and guidance of selected offenders in accordance with the conditions that the court establishes.

The theory of probation developed from earlier practices in England and the United States, all of which were intended to lessen or otherwise mitigate the severities of the penal code. It is commonly believed that its origins come from English common law, where the courts, as early as the 14th century, were presumed to have the power to *suspend* sentence for specified purposes and periods. While it is unclear exactly which precedents permitted the introduction of the process that is now referred to as probation, there is some agreement that "Benefit of Clergy," "Judicial Reprieve," "Recognizance," "Bail," and "Filing of Cases" all made some contribution (Tappan, 1960:539–543; Dressler, 1959:6–11; Grinnell, 1941:15–34; United Nations, 1951:15–26; and Chute and Bell, 1956).

Probation in the United States

In the United States, criminologists tend to trace the development of probation to the work of John Augustus in Boston in 1841. In fact, it is believed that it was this bootmaker and philanthropist who was the first to use the term "probation" (Tappan, 1960:543). Dressler (1959:11–12) writes from an historical point of view and asserts:

> The social climate was right for the birth of probation in the nineteenth century (and in the United States). Thoughtful observers had become

convinced that prisons were not "teaching a lesson," penitentiaries were not making inmates penitent. It was also becoming clear that suspension of sentence without provision for supervision and guidance of the released person served little purpose. So it was that Matthew Davenport Hill, of Birmingham, England, pioneered in his country in 1841, the very year that John Augustus performed a like service in Boston for the United States.

Over the early years, those who provided probation services (all volunteers) developed a model that, superficially at least, included such activities as investigations, reports, home visits, and job placements (Tappan, 1960:544), although as England (1957:65) notes:

> Probation began not in a spirit prompted by a desire to apply to the offender the rehabilitative techniques based on scientific knowledge of human behavior, but rather in one reflecting a simple humanitarian wish to keep less serious and/or first offenders from undergoing the corrupting effects of jail terms.

In 1869, a state agency in Massachusetts was authorized by the legislature to accept the custody of juvenile offenders, with the right of placing them in private families. Although not officially a probation service, 23 percent of the juvenile offenders convicted in the courts of Boston in the year 1869–1870 were dealt with in this manner (Sutherland and Cressey, 1970:464).

But the first actual statutory provision for probation, which included provision for the hiring and payment of probation officers, was in Massachusetts in 1878. According to the statute, the mayor of Boston was authorized to appoint and pay a probation officer and authorized the municipal court to place offenders on probation. The legislature extended this power to all other mayors in the state in 1880, and in 1891 it "made mandatory the appointment of probation officers by lower court judges" (Sutherland and Cressey, 1970: 464). The first "State Commission on Probation" was established in Massachusetts in 1908 (Tappan, 1960:546).

According to Dressler (1959:20), Missouri enacted the next law, in 1897, with Vermont one year later;* and by 1900, Illinois, Minnesota, Rhode Island, and New Jersey had passed probation legisla-

---

*In Vermont, the bill was entitled: "An Act Relating to The Parole of Prisoners," which, according to Dressler (1959:20), indicates ". . . that the terms of probation and parole were used interchangeably . . . and (created) a confusion not yet dissipated."

tion. There were many variations in the early legislation or statutes: Illinois and Minnesota provided for juvenile probation only; Rhode Island excluded certain categories of offenders from probation consideration (which still occurs today in many jurisdictions); Vermont used the county plan of organization instead of state-wide services; while Rhode Island had a state-wide program and state-controlled administration.

Platt (1969) describes the history, philosophy and early development of the juvenile court movement, which was begun in 1899 in Chicago and which enhanced the development of adult probation services. Dressler (1959:20) comments that these first probation officers

> ... were not paid out of public funds, partly due to the dubious assumption that to offer salaries would attract individuals interested only in the compensation. Volunteers, it was felt, would be men and women of great heart, working for the sheer joy of serving mankind.

By 1945, all states had finally passed legislation authorizing juvenile probation (Dressler, 1959:20), but it was not until 1957 that provision for adult probation services had been provided by all of the states.

In a report prepared for the President's Commission on Law Enforcement and Administration of Justice, the National Council on Crime and Delinquency states (NCCD, 1967:160):

> Development of the legal basis for probation was accompanied by a definition of the duties and responsibilities of the probation officer, formulation of criteria for granting probation, provision for and definition of the presentence investigation, authorization of the imposition of probation conditions, and revocation, and refinement of policies, practices, and forms of administrative structure.

Professionalized Services

The early services of the unsalaried probation officers were seen as adequate, for not much was expected of them in terms of services. However, with the advent of psychoanalytic theories and the increasing activities of social welfare enthusiasts in the areas of crime and delinquency control, the growth of professionalized probation services, with trained officers, can be viewed as an inevitable development. By 1917, the founder of modern social work, Mary Richmond, published *Social Diagnosis*. In this text she devotes considerable attention to the role of the probation officer and the processes by which he was supposed to gather pertinent information about clients. Richmond points out the now obvious relationship between social casework and probation services, but also suggests that differences in settings have some bearing upon practice (Richmond, 1917:105):

> ...a probation officer is known to come from the court and to represent it, certain conditions, favorable and the reverse, are created by this fact; the officer has more authority but less freedom than a social worker who lacks the court background.

At least since 1898, when the Summer School of Philanthropic Workers was established in New York (replaced in 1908 by the New York School of Philanthropy), social casework has been identified with probation services, especially as the primary model by which, it has been thought, change could be brought about within the clients being served by the courts. This is still true today and, according to some, the consequences of providing casework services within the authoritarian setting of the court remains a significantly unresolved dilemma for practicing probation officers (Ohlin *et al.*, 1956). This is so because many social work theorists believe that successful casework can only occur when the client is motivated and seeks out such services, which presumably is not the case among involuntary court clients. Other social workers, however, maintain that if one is truly professional, it should be possible to "treat" the client anyway and bring about "successful" change.

The National Council on Crime and Delinquency (formerly the National Probation and Parole Association) has for many years promoted the notion that graduation from a school of social work (usually resulting in a master's degree in social work), with supervised experience in an ordinary social agency (such as a welfare, family service, or mental hygiene clinic), is the ideal preparation for work in corrections, especially in probation and parole (Chute and Bell, 1956:180). But due to such factors as prestige, status, salaries, and the authoritarian nature of the court setting, graduate social workers have been reluctant to seek such employment (Studt, 1954:21; Tappan, 1960:548; Epstein, 1970:87–92; and Wilensky and Lebeaux, 1965:Chapter XI).

Nonetheless, many probation (and parole) agencies throughout
the United States, such as those in California, Minnesota, New York,
and the Federal Service, stipulate that a master's degree in social
work is the *preferred* qualification for those seeking employment.
When those with master's degrees are unavailable, most agencies will
hire those who at least have bachelor's degrees. Sometimes they will
accept persons who have actual probation experience in lieu of
graduate education and training. We will discuss the actual roles and
responsibilities of the probation officer in a forthcoming section.

Probation Structures

Probation agencies are administered either by judges (courts) or by
administrators within some kind of department housed in the executive branch of government. Since probation developed as a service of
the courts, and in fact as a form of sentence, much of its control and
administration rests in the court structure. This is especially true
with regard to juveniles. As a consequence of agencies being housed
in courts, it is not uncommon to find that most probation officers,
according to statute, must be appointed by the court and, particularly, the judge. In the Federal Service, for example, probation officers
are, in reality, appointed by the various federal judges, but technically upon recommendation and approval by the Administrative Office
of the United States Courts—the administrative arm of the federal
judiciary. The same holds at the state level, for example in Massachusetts, where the Office of the Commissioner of Probation must technically approve the appointments made by the judges of the various
courts throughout the Commonwealth.

Sutherland and Cressey comment on this practice (1970:466):

> The stated objections (to the judge administering probation services) . . .
> are: *First*, the work of supervision is essentially administrative, not judi-
> cial . . . *Second*, the judge is not able to handle this administrative work
> efficiently . . . Consequently, there has been a trend toward the other
> method of appointment and supervision of probation officers.

While probation statutes usually define the limits of probation
practice and the administrative structure, they generally do not
specify the number of officers that may be appointed. According to
Rubin (1963:213), where the department is not within the judiciary,

the legislative appropriation governs the number of appointments. Where appointments are by the judiciary, they are rarely controlled by the probation statutes or appropriation acts. In other words, it is up to the judge to decide how many probation officers are needed to serve his or her court.

In 1956, Will C. Turndbladh, Director of the National Probation and Parole Association (now NCCD) stated (1956:306-07):

> I suggest that we think of the probation service not as a resource which the legislatures are being encouraged to expand as one of the many important public services. Rather, we have to think of the *right* of the court to probation service, and the *responsibility* of the legislature to guarantee its adequacy in the courts . . . Probation service—the keystone of the sentencing structure—is . . . an integral part of the court and the judicial process. The courts have a *right* to this service, a right no less substantial than their right to equipment and staff required for adjudication of guilt or innocence . . . The fact is that even now the statutes in some states declare that the judges may appoint probation staff as required by the work of the court. In these states the legislatures have *granted* to the judges the machinery for securing necessary funds for adequate probation staff. It is, then, clearly the judges' obligation and duty to demand the staff they need.

Sanfilippo and Wallach (1970:15), writing for the Joint Commission on Correctional Manpower and Training, discuss the difficulty in assessing both the structure and quality of probation services throughout the United States:

> The fact that probation services . . . are administered within widely divergent organizational arrangements by differing levels of government, further retards the realization of truly effective programs. The current state of probation . . . services across the country is such that it is impossible to obtain an accurate national picture.

Although all probation services are administered by a governmental agency (except in those relatively rare instances where only volunteers assist the court), it is not possible to determine the exact count of such programs at both the juvenile and adult levels. The nature and extent of such programs vary so widely that not even the special survey on correctional services, conducted by the National Council on Crime and Delinquency for the President's Crime Commission in 1967, is able to present a final and authoritative picture.

Probation is provided for juveniles as well as adults, for misdemeanants and felons, and occasionally is located in a court of domestic relations, where marital and other problems of family life are handled judicially. The programs may be at the state, county, municipal, or federal levels of government; may be part of a court, an independent administrative body, or located in such larger agencies as departments of corrections, mental health and hygiene, or in a social welfare program. Furthermore, there may be various combinations of services, such as a state-wide agency administering both probation and parole programs.

According to the President's Crime Commission (Task Force Report: Corrections, 1967:35–37), it is possible to identify 30 different organizational patterns of probation and parole services. While adult parole and juvenile aftercare (not usually called parole) services are usually administered by state-wide correctional agencies, the administration of adult and juvenile probation programs is generally found at the state and local levels (city and county). Table 14.1 summarizes the national picture of juvenile and adult probation services.

To further illustrate the variability in administrative structures, the Joint Commission on Correctional Manpower and Training conducted a national survey of all *state* probation and parole agencies in the United States. The Commission received responses from 94 agencies, which, it claims, represents nearly 85 percent of all such agencies. The kinds of organizational structures in which such services are provided are illustrated in Table 14.2.

The survey of corrections prepared by NCCD in 1967 reports that all counties in 48 of the states are covered by probation, and that of the 3,082 counties and districts* in the 50 states, 91 percent have some form of probation services. Adult probation is a county-operated system in 14 states, but it is a state-wide system operated by state agencies in 37 states (including 17 states in which there is some combination of county and state services). NCCD adds that of 14 states which have retained the county-organization structure, 9 are among the more densely populated states; 5 are in the Northeast, 3 are in the Midwest, and 6 are in the West (NCCD, 1967:164–165).

Thus, it is apparent that unlike many other types of governmental services, the administration of adult and juvenile probation programs varies widely in terms of structure and, in all likelihood, levels and qualities of services. According to the Joint Commission on Correctional Manpower and Training (Perspectives on Correctional Man-

---

*The total includes 5 "districts" in Alaska, 8 in Connecticut, 9 in Puerto Rico, and 5 in Rhode Island, all of which have districts instead of counties (NCCD, 1967:164).

TABLE 14.1. Administration of Juvenile and Adult Probation,
by Type of Agency, 50 States and Puerto Rico, 1965

	Number of Jurisdictions	
Type of Agency	Juvenile	Adult
State:		
Corrections	5	12
Other Agencies	11	25
Local:		
Courts	32	13
Other Agencies	3	1
Totals	51	51

Source: Task Force Report: Corrections, 1967:34.

TABLE 14.2. Organizational Structure of Probation and Parole
Services in 94 Agencies in United States, 1967-1968

Type of Agency	Number	Percent
State Corrections Agency	77	82
State Welfare Agency	8	9
State Corrections Department within a Welfare Department	6	6
State Department of Education	1	1
State Department of Health	1	1
State Department of Public Safety	1	1
Totals	94	100

Source: Perspectives on Correctional Manpower and Training, Washington, D.C.:
JCCMT. 1970:17.

power and Training, 1970:17), there are about 13,000 probation and
parole officers at state and local levels of government, providing services to more than 800,000 offenders on any given day, with 64 percent of all offenders on probation being handled by local (nonstate
or federal) probation agencies.

As a consequence, we can be certain of only three variables
which probably remain constant regardless of organizational structure or geographical location of the probation agency: (1) every
agency operates according to statutory authority; (2) every agency
services clients who are placed on probation by judicial action; and
(3) every chief administrative officer of a probation agency is answer-

TABLE 14.3. Administrative Patterns of 37 State Probation Agencies

Type	Number of States
Probation Combined with Parole Board, Commission, or Department (Independent of Corrections Department)	18
Division with Corrections Department	12
Probation Separate from Parole	
Commission	2
Board	1
Department	1
Bureau in a Department	1
Court Administrator	2
Total	37

Source: Correction in the United States. New York: NCCD. 1967:166.

able to some other superior, including judge, chief administrator, commissioner of a "super agency," or elected state or local official. Notwithstanding the above, every administrative official in probation is responsible for managing his or her organization, including the setting and implementation of goals, supervision of workers, upholding the law, and providing services and programs to clients and communities.

Use of Probation

Since the onset of probation in the United States, various jurisdictions not only authorized the use of probation, they frequently provided restrictions or exclusions as to who was—or is—eligible for probation. While it is not possible to summarize all such exclusions, for the most part they have been provided for in only the most serious of offenses, especially those for which life or capital punishment was provided. The American Bar Association Project on Standards for Criminal Justice (ABA, 1974:393) states:

> The legislature should authorize the sentencing court in every case to impose a sentence of probation. Exceptions to this principle are not favored and, if made, should be limited to the most serious offenses.

The report goes on to list five reasons why probation should be the desirable disposition in appropriate cases (ABA, 1974:394):

(i) it maximizes the liberty of the individual while at the same time vindicating the authority of the law and effectively protecting the public from further violations of the law;

(ii) it affirmatively promotes the rehabilitation of the offender by continuing normal community contacts;

(iii) it avoids the negative and frequently stultifying effects of confinement which often severely and unnecessarily complicate the reintegration of the offender into the community;

(iv) it greatly reduces the financial cost to the public treasury of an effective correctional system;

(v) it minimizes the impact of the conviction upon innocent dependents of the offender.

According to the President's Crime Commission (Task Force Report: Corrections, 1967:27), slightly more than one-half (or 53 percent) of the offenders sentenced to correctional treatment in 1965 were placed on probation. The Report also projected that by 1975, the percentage of offenders placed on probation would increase to 58 percent (a figure which is not possible to substantiate at this date). Table 14.4 summarizes the President's Crime Commission data.

The estimates for probation shown in Table 14.4 project a growth in the numbers of adults on probation almost 2½ times greater than the growth in institutional and parole populations. However, the statistics on the comparative use of probation are sparce and frequently incomplete and inaccurate. Hindelang *et al.* (1973:333), in compiling national criminal justice statistics for the Law Enforcement Assistance Administration, report only on federal data "... since no nationwide non-Federal data on probation are available."

As significant as the relative use of probation might be throughout the United States, the disparity in its use also is significant. Legislation always authorizes but does not mandate the use of probation as a sentence. That is, depending upon the nature of the case, personal belief systems of the judges, availability of community resources, and other such important factors, judges may use probation as an alternative to other sentences if they wish, but they do not have to if they do not so desire.

TABLE 14.4. Number of Offenders on Probation and on Parole
or in Institutions, 1965; Projections for 1975

Location of Offender	1965		1975	
	Number	Percent	Number	Percent
Probation	684,088	53	1,071,000	58
Parole or institution	598,298	47	770,000	42
Total	1,282,386	100	1,841,000	100

Sources: 1965 data from National Survey of Corrections and special tabulations provided by the Federal Bureau of Prisons and the Administrative Office of the U.S. Courts;
1975 projections by R. Christensen, of the President's Crime Commission's Task Force of
Science and Technology 1967.

California, which has been publishing data on the use of probation in all of its counties, provides us with information to illustrate the
use—and nonuse—of probation, and how its use has changed over the
years. Rubin (1973:248) points out that in 1956 the use of probation in California's superior courts ranged from 12.5 percent in one
county to 61.5 percent in two counties and that "Certain judges
used probation in even less than 12 percent of their cases, and others
used it much more than 61.5 percent." Further, he states, "The
contrast is between those judges who hardly use probation at all—in
effect they choose it only for defendants for whom no treatment
whatsoever is needed—and those who find that probation is a practical disposition for almost all defendants."

In 1972, the California Bureau of Criminal Statistics issued its
annual report on criminal justice statistics and revealed that between
the years 1968–1972, the range of use of probation state-wide for
adult offenders varied from a low of 33.4 percent (in 1968) to a high
of 38.8 percent (in 1971). In 1972, the overall percentage was 35.9
percent—a slight dip from the high of 1971 (1972:43). When the use
of probation is distinguished among non-drug felony offenses and
drug felony offenses, there is a dramatic difference. Non-drug felony
offenders receive probation 30.4 percent of the time, while the drug
users receive probation 47.1 percent of the time (1972:45). How
much this startling variation may be due to probation officer recommendation, judicial concerns for treatment of the drug offender in
the community, and the kinds of treatment resources which may be
available is not known.

The data may also be influenced by the fact that in California it is possible to sentence a defendant to jail *and* probation concurrently, a "split sentence." Non-drug offenders are sentenced to jail *and* probation at a rate of 35.7 percent, while drug offenders are sentenced to jail *and* probation at a rate of 34.7 percent (1972:45).

When we examine superior court decisions in 35 of the largest counties in California in 1967, we find a range of 77.0 percent as a high to a low of 37.0 percent insofar as the use of probation is concerned (California Bureau of Criminal Statistics, 1967:118–119). A further examination of the data reveals that the larger of the counties in California tend to use probation more often than the smaller counties. This may be due, according to Cohn (1970b), to a greater willingness on the part of the judges in the largest counties to use probation where community resources are indeed available, to the increased "professionalism" of probation staffs in such counties where the recommendation for probation is used more often, to a greater tolerance on the part of the largest communities to allow offenders to remain in their homes, or a combination of any of the above factors. In smaller communities, according to Cohn, it is more likely that judges and probation staff alike are more conservative in making recommendations and, thus, more offenders are sentenced to prison as a consequence.

As a result of research, however, we do know that judges tend to follow the recommendations made to the courts by their probation officers, which suggests that the final disposition of an offender is more in the hands of probation officers than in the hands of the judges who actually pronounce the sentences (Cohn, 1970a; Lohman *et al.*, 1965–1967; Robison, 1965 and 1969). Table 14.5 depicts the range of probation recommendations in California for 1967.

As a matter of fact, research suggests that judges follow probation officer recommendations in as many as 90 to 95 percent of the cases. Thus, probation, which used to be only tolerated by many judges, now has become an indispensable tool in sentencing in most courts in the country.

Duties of Probation Officers

The National Council on Crime and Delinquency has published the "Standard Probation and Parole Act" which sets out in *recom-*

TABLE 14.5. Commitments of Felony Defendants
by Counties in California, 1967

County	Total	Incarceration*		Probation	
		Rank	%	Rank	%
Alameda	1,446	29	25.0	6	68.3
Butte	143	6	49.0	34	37.7
Contra Costa	579	34	20.3	2	70.6
Fresno	586	18.5	34.1	18	53.3
Humboldt	127	3	52.8	35	37.0
Imperial	187	9	43.9	29	41.7
Kern	366	5	50.5	32	39.6
Kings	53	20.5	34.0	22	50.9
Los Angeles	17,270	25	27.2	15	59.3
Madera	62	4	51.6	30	40.3
Marin	171	16	35.0	12	63.2
Mendocino	131	7	46.6	20	51.9
Merced	162	14.5	37.0	23	50.0
Monterey	374	2	53.0	31	39.8
Napa	87	35	12.7	1	77.0
Orange	1,164	30	22.2	8	66.8
Riverside	798	17	34.5	24	49.7
Sacramento	970	12	42.5	26	44.7
San Bernardino	959	11	42.6	28	43.9
San Diego	1,986	28	25.1	7	67.2
San Francisco	1,722	32	21.2	5	68.8
San Joaquin	642	8	44.7	25	45.2
San Luis Obispo	116	24	30.2	11	63.8
San Mateo	510	31	21.4	4	69.8
Santa Barbara	337	10	43.6	27	44.2
Santa Clara	1,144	22	33.0	13	61.2
Santa Cruz	169	27	26.1	10	65.1
Shasta	160	1	53.2	33	38.1
Siskiyou	50	20.5	34.0	16	56.0
Solano	173	26	26.6	9	65.3
Sonoma	217	18.5	34.1	14	60.4
Stanislaus	426	13	39.2	19	52.6
Tulare	273	33	20.5	3	70.3
Ventura	372	23	31.2	21	51.1
Yolo	100	14.5	37.0	17	54.0

Source: Crime and Delinquency in California 1967. State of California, Department of Justice, Division of Law Enforcement, Bureau of Criminal Statistics. Sacramento: 1967: 118–119.

*Including both prison and jail commitments.

mended legal language provisions for the practice of probation. By and large, the probation officer, acting as an agent of the court, is responsible for two basic activities: (1) providing the court with information about the convicted offender which takes the form of a presentence report and is used by the court in order to determine the sentence (for juveniles it is frequently called a social history); and (2) supervising the offender sentenced to a term of probation. With regard to the presentence investigation, the "Act" recommends (1964:18):

> No defendant convicted of a crime the punishment for which may include imprisonment for more than one year shall be sentenced . . . before a written report of investigation by a probation officer is presented to and considered by the court. The court may, in its discretion, order a presentence investigation for a defendant convicted of any lesser crime or offense. Whenever an investigation is required, the probation officer shall promptly inquire into the circumstances of the offense; the attitude of the complainant or victim, and of the victim's immediate family, where possible, in cases of homicide; and the criminal record, social history, and present condition of the defendant.

In a discussion concerning the "Act," consideration was given to making a presentence investigation mandatory in every case. This was seen as an ideal not readily implemented in most courts due to the lack of staff and community resources. The American Bar Association Project on Standards for Criminal Justice (1974:395) states:

> All Courts trying Criminal cases should be supplied with the resources and supporting staff to permit a presentence investigation and a written report of its results in every case.
>
> The court should be explicitly authorized by statute to call for such an investigation and report in every case . . . and provide that such an investigation and report should be made in every case where incarceration for one year or more is a possible disposition, where the defendant is less than (21) years old, or where the defendant is a first offender, unless the court specifically orders to the contrary in a particular case.

The primary purpose of the presentence report is to provide the court with enough information that it can make a rational sentencing decision. The report is also used as a basis for making decisions about treatment strategies by a supervising probation officer, as a document which is forwarded to other community agencies when referrals are made (e.g., for marital counseling, academic or vocational assistance, etc.), as a source document for prison officials if the defendant is sentenced to an institution, and for guidance to a parole officer when the defendant is released from an institution and placed on parole status.

The content and scope of a presentence investigation varies among the many probation agencies throughout the United States. Each jurisdiction has its own traditions, needs, style, and format. It is a report, in effect, without any standardized or consensual agreement among probation or court officials on essential contents, format, or length. Generally, however, the report describes the offense for which the offender was convicted, his background and social history, relationships with significant persons in his life, and discusses the potential for change the offender may have if provided probation supervision while remaining in the community. In some jurisdictions, statutes and/or judicial tradition prohibit the probation officers from making actual recommendations to the court regarding disposition, do not allow discussion of the offense, and/or forbid a description of prior criminal convictions.

In some jurisdictions, the presentence report is made available to defense counsel, but this is generally not the case throughout the country at this time. As a matter of fact, making the report available is generally not approved of by probation officials who believe that defense counsel and defendants would not understand some of the materials contained therein. They also argue that revelation of such material upon which final recommendations are based might even jeopardize a future "therapeutic" relationship with the defendant. The American Bar Association, the National Council on Crime and Delinquency, and the National Advisory Commission on Criminal Justice Standards and Goals, however, all recommend that the report should be made available to defense counsel, except in very few extraordinary circumstances. At the present time, where statutes do not make provision for the sharing of the report, it is up to the judge's discretion as to who will be allowed to review the report.

Probation Conditions

Probation, as it has been generally defined, is a sentence imposed by the court which allows the convicted offender to remain in the community, but under the supervision of a probation officer and for a specified period of time. Once such sentence is imposed, it becomes the primary responsibility of the officer to supervise the *daily* activities of the probationer. This obviously is not possible, not only due to the high caseloads most probation officers have, but due to the impracticality of overseeing probationers' conduct over a 24-hour period. As a consequence, most probation agencies, through the sentencing court, impose "conditions" upon the probationer—what he or she may or may not do while under such supervision.

The ABA Standards Project (1974:398–399) spells out in great detail recommended standards pertaining to the imposition, implementation, nature, and determination of such conditions. While they are recommended standards, they are, for the most part, actually implemented in practice by many probation agencies in the United States, in one form or another:

> All conditions of probation should be prescribed by the sentencing court and presented to the probationer in writing. Their purpose and scope and the possible consequence of any violations should be explained to him by the sentencing court or at an early conference with a probation officer.
>
> Probation officers must have authority to implement judicially prescribed conditions; but the conditions should be sufficiently precise so that probation officers do not in fact establish them.
>
> The probationer should have the right to apply to the sentencing court for a clarification or change of conditions.
>
> It should be a condition of every sentence to probation that the probationer lead a law-abiding life during the period of his probation. No other conditions should be required by statute, but the sentencing court should be authorized to prescribe additional conditions to fit the circumstances of each case. Development of standard conditions as a guide to sentencing courts is appropriate so long as such conditions are not routinely imposed.
>
> Conditions imposed by the court should be designed to assist the probationer in leading a law-abiding life. They should be reasonably related to his rehabilitation and not unduly restrictive of his liberty or incompatible with his freedom of religion. They should not be so vague or ambiguous as to give no real guidance.
>
> Conditions may appropriately deal with matters such as the following:
>
> (i) cooperating with a program of supervision;
> (ii) meeting family responsibilities;
> (iii) maintaining steady employment or engaging or refraining from engaging in a specific employment or occupation;
> (iv) pursuring prescribed educational or vocational training;

(v) undergoing available medical or psychiatric treatment;

(vi) maintaining residence in a prescribed area or in a special facility established for or available to persons on probation;

(vii) refraining from consorting with certain types of people or frequenting certain types of places;

(viii) making restitution of the fruits of the crime or reparation for loss or damage caused thereby.

Conditions requiring payment of fines, restitution, reparation, or family support should not go beyond the probationer's ability to pay.

The performance bond now authorized in some jurisdictions should not be employed as a condition of probation.

Probationers should not be required to pay the costs of probation.

Conditions should be subject to modification or termination by the court. All changes in conditions should be presented to the probationer in the manner prescribed in . . . this Report. Where the proposed modifications would result in a form of confinement as a condition of continued probation, the probationer should be afforded . . . procedural rights . . .

According to Rubin (1973:237), probationary supervision should mean more than mere surveillance of the probationer; it should, in addition, provide sufficient service and assistance to the probationer through a helping relationship. Through observation and interviewing, the supervising officer should be able to help the probationer "change" or "overcome" his problems in such a way that he or she can become a productive, law-abiding citizen. As an agent of the court, the probation officer also has a responsibility to make the court aware of any violations by the probationer of the terms and conditions of probation which the court (or the probation officer) may have imposed upon the probationer. Where such violations may have occurred, it is the responsibility of the supervising officer to prepare a report for the court, detailing the exact nature of the violation(s), so that the judge may decide if the probation status is to be revoked.

Following due process considerations, if it is decided that the violation is serious enough to call for the court's attention, the probationer may be brought in by notice, arrest, or warrant, according to the circumstances and the requirements of given statutes (Rubin, 1973:239). Various appellate rulings now require that the court conduct a hearing on the alleged violation, that the hearing be preceded by notice of the charge, that the probationer have a right to be represented by counsel and to rebut the charges, and that the charges must be established by substantial evidence. However, since this is a hearing and not a trial, there is no right to a jury.

In past years, it was common practice for prosecutors, judges, and probation staffs to "engineer" revocations and cause probationers to be re-sentenced to a term in prison on relatively flimsy evidence. This occurred especially when the probationer was alleged to have committed a serious offense while under supervision, but the police and the prosecutor had insufficient evidence to bring about a conviction. If the probation officer wanted to be "cooperative," he found grounds for violation and persuaded the court to revoke probation. Today, such practices hardly occur, not only because of due process considerations, but because many probation agencies have established strict policies governing the conditions by which a probation officer may recommend violation. When probationers are accused of committing new offenses, it is generally the policy that such evidence must be presented at a trial and the probationer will be sentenced by the court if found guilty. For the most part, revocation is recommended only in cases where the probationer is totally uncooperative, has committed a series of minor offenses (misdemeanors), has absconded or run away, or has seriously violated the terms and conditions of probation.

Probation Officer Responsibilities

The role the probation officer assumes in the supervision of his or her clients depends, in part, upon the size and nature of the caseload being managed and upon the officer's personal belief system with regard to probation supervision. Probation officers are assigned cases for supervision typically in one of three ways: geographical distribution of offenders, i.e., according to districts or where the offender lives; type of offense or typology of offender, i.e., specialized caseloads for such types of offenses as sex, drugs, alcoholism, etc.; or numerically, i.e., each probation officer is assigned cases wherein balance of caseload size is the primary consideration.

The American Correctional Association suggests that whatever the basis for assignment, each probation officer is responsible for providing services to each client, while at the same time controls are provided. In the *Manual of Correctional Standards* (1966:107), the

ACA enunciates four guiding principles which should assist the probation officer in providing such services:

(1) Change comes from within a person; therefore, a probationer must be a participant in any treatment regimen designed to help him.

(2) The needs, problems, capacities, and limitations of the individual offender must be considered in planning a program with him.

(3) Legally binding conditions of probation are essential and to the best interest of the offender and to the community.

(4) The goal of supervision is to help the offender understand his own problems and enable him to deal adequately with them.

While the above principles tend to be somewhat simplistic, they do provide a framework within which probation supervision occurs. It should be noted, however, that since those principles were published in 1966, additional principles might be added, especially in view of recent developments. At least three come to mind:

(1) As an agent of the court, the supervising probation officer should at all times be aware of and adhere to standards of due process in dealing with probationers, guaranteeing to each client his or her constitutional rights; (2) although the probationer should participate in the development and implementation of treatment strategies, it should be the probationer's right to decline treatment if he or she so desires; and (3) the probation organization, through its officers, should provide in writing its own obligations, procedures, and policies governing probation service so that a probationer may have the right to redress any grievances he or she may have against the officer or the organization for any failure which may become known to the probationer and which affects his or her status.

Caseloads and Roles

Although the American Correctional Association has long suggested that probation caseloads should be of manageable size, this has not been the case in most probation jurisdictions. Since budgetary appropriations frequently lag behind operational requirements, it is usually the case that probation officers have much larger caseloads than they can manage from a practical point of view. The ACA (1966:109) argues that the workload standards be not more than 50 units. This is arrived at by the rating of 1 work unit for each probationer supervised by an officer and 1 work unit for each presentence investigation completed and written by the officer in a given month. Accordingly, a 50-unit workload may mean 50 cases of supervision, 10 presentence reports per month, or any combination thereof. Some experts in the field of probation suggest that the workload should be no more than 35 units, but others maintain that the size of the caseload has no relationship whatsoever to the quality of service and that, in fact, a probationer is just as likely to be "successful" in a 300-man caseload as in a caseload of only 15 (Lohman et al., 1965). Notwithstanding the above, the President's Crime Commission (Corrections, 1967) reports that 67 percent of the probation officers in a national sample each had over 100 persons under active supervision, while only 4 percent of those sampled had 40 or fewer persons in their caseloads.

One of the dilemmas in trying to determine the ideal caseload size results from research experiences which suggest that size of caseload is not related to success on probation, especially if success is defined to mean reduced recidivism. There have been numerous attempts to alter the size of the caseload, especially in creating small caseloads, but as we have discussed these attempts in Chapter 8, success has not been forthcoming, regardless of size.

Nevertheless, probation officers adopt various roles or strategies in dealing with clients. Ohlin, Piven, and Pappenfort (1956) suggest that even with sound casework principles borne in mind, probation (and parole) officers may adopt one of three basic styles: punitive, protective, or welfare. The *punitive* officer attempts to induce change in probationers through surveillance techniques in order to force adoption of middle-class standards and values. The *protective* officer wants to keep the offender from engaging in further criminal behavior and frequently threatens the probationer with revocation in order to assist him or her while at the same time trying to protect society. The *welfare* officer, on the other hand, desires to treat the offender and tries to assist him or her in making an improved adjustment in living standards and styles.

As part of a study evaluating the federal prison and parole systems, Pownall (1963) and Glaser (1964:429–442) discuss four basic styles of supervision, including welfare, passive, paternal, and punitive. These four styles are determined by the ways in which the officers accommodate themselves to two basic dimensions, control and assistance, which are the two most important variables of their job.

O'Leary and Duffee (1971) discuss correctional administrative or managerial styles, but since their work is based on philosophical beliefs of workers, the implications for probation supervision roles are unmistakable. They suggest that there are four basic organizational styles within corrections which reflect how workers attempt to bring about change in offenders. In one style, *rehabilitation*, workers and organizations believe that change will come about in offenders through clinical interventions, i.e., by treating the offender and helping him to change himself. *Reintegration*, as another style, holds that only through cooperative efforts by organization, worker, and client—working with the community—can meaningful and lasting change ever occur on the part of the offender. In the *reform* style, it is believed that change can come about only if the worker forces the offender to understand precisely what the community expects of him or her and induces such change without regard for the nature of the individual offender's needs. The *restraint* style suggests that change in offender behavior and attitudes is a matter for the offender to decide for himself or herself and that the worker, as an agent of the court, merely is available to remind the offender that he or she must do the changing without significant help.

Regardless of these research efforts, we find that probation and parole officers develop their own styles of dealing with those under supervision, and except for the constraints placed on them by their agencies, they supervise their caseloads in ways most comfortable to them.

Standards

The National Advisory Commission on Criminal Justice Standards and Goals (Corrections, 1973:333, 335, 337) has issued three standards concerned with probation services which are significant in terms of future developments. In the first, it recommends that services which are required to assist probationers should be developed and made available to probationers on a routine basis. In the second recommendation, the Commission suggests that probation services should be developed for misdemeanants, which does not occur with too much frequency in the United States today. The third deals with the development and training of probation manpower—a necessary program if probation services are to be effective and meaningful. The three sets of standards follow.

Standard 10.2
Services to Probationers

Each probation system should develop by 1975 a goal-oriented service delivery system that seeks to remove or reduce barriers confronting probationers. The needs of probationers should be identified, priorities established, and resources allocated based on established goals of the probation system. (See Standards 5.14 and 5.15 and the narrative of Chapter 16 for probation's services to the courts.)

1. Services provided directly should be limited to activities defined as belonging distinctly to probation. Other needed services should be procured from other agencies that have primary responsibility for them. It is essential that funds be provided for purchase of services.

2. The staff delivering services to probationers in urban areas should be separate and distinct from the staff delivering services to the courts, although they may be part of the same agency. The staff delivering services to probationers should be located in the communities where probationers live and in service centers with access to programs of allied human services.

3. The probation system should be organized to deliver to probationers a range of services by a range of staff. Various modules should be used for organizing staff and probationers into workloads or task groups, not caseloads. The modules should include staff teams related to groups of probationers and differentiated programs based on offender typologies.

4. The primary function of the probation officer should be that of community resource manager for probationers.

Standard 10.3
Misdemeanant Probation

Each State should develop additional probation manpower and resources to assure that the courts may use probation for persons convicted of misdemeanors in all cases for which this disposition may be appropriate. All standards of this report that apply to probation are intended to cover both misdemeanant and felony probation. Other than the possible length of probation terms, there should be no distinction between misdemeanant and felony probation as to organization, manpower or services.

Standard 10.4
Probation Manpower

Each State immediately should develop a comprehensive manpower development and training program to recruit, screen, utilize, train, educate, and evaluate a full range of probation personnel, including volunteers, women and ex-offenders. The program should range from entry level to top level positions and should include the following:

1. Provision should be made for effective utilization of a range of manpower on a full- or part-time basis by using a system approach to identify service objectives and by specifying job tasks and range of personnel necessary to meet the objectives. Jobs should be reexamined periodically to insure that organizational objectives are being met.

2. In addition to probation officers, there should be new career lines in probation, all built into career ladders.

3. Advancement (salary and status) should be along two tracks: service delivery and administration.

4. Educational qualification for probation officers should be graduation from an accredited 4-year college.

References

American Bar Association Project on Standards for Criminal Justice
    1974   Standards Relating to the Administration of Criminal Justice. Chicago: ABA.

American Correctional Association
    1966   Manual of Correctional Standards. 3rd ed. Washington, D.C.: ACA.

California Bureau of Criminal Statistics
    1967–   Crime and Delinquency in California. Sacramento: Department of
    1972   Justice.

Chute, Charles L. and Marjorie Bell
    1956   Crime, Courts and Probation. New York: The Macmillan Co.

Cohn, Alvin W.
    1970a   "We've Got the Whole Caseload in Our Hands." Popular Government 36 (May) 8:17–21.

    1970b   Decision-Making in the Administration of Probation Services. New York: National Council on Crime and Delinquency.

    1974   "Footnotes on the Future of Corrections." Keynote Address Presented at the Ohio Correctional and Court Services Annual Meeting, Cleveland, Ohio. (Mimeo).

Dressler, David
    1959   Practice and Theory of Probation and Parole. 2nd ed. New York: Columbia University Press.

England, Ralph W.
    1957   "What Is Responsible Satisfactory Probation and Post-Probation Outcome?" Journal of Criminal Law and Criminology 47:2–11.

Epstein, Irwin
    1970   "Professional Role Orientations and Conflict Strategies." Social Work 15 (October):87–92.

Glaser, Daniel
    1964   The Effectiveness of a Prison and Parole System. Indianapolis: Bobbs-Merrill.

Grinnell, Frank W.
1941   "The Common Law History of Probation." Journal of Criminal Law and Criminology 32 (May–June):15-34.
Hindelang, Michael J., C.S. Dunn, L.P. Sutton, and A.L. Aumick
1973   Sourcebook of Criminal Justice Statistics. Washington, D.C.: Law Enforcement Assistance Administration.
Joint Commission on Correctional Manpower and Training
1970   Perspectives on Correctional Manpower and Training. Washington, D.C.: JCCMT.
Lohman, Joseph D., A. Wahl, and R.M. Carter
1965-   The San Francisco Project. Research Reports 1-12. Berkeley:
1967   School of Criminology, University of California.
National Advisory Commission on Criminal Justice Standards and Goals
1973   Corrections. Washington, D.C.: U.S. Government Printing Office.
National Council on Crime and Delinquency
1964   Standard Probation and Parole Act. 1955 Revision. New York: NCCD.

1967   "Corrections in the United States." President's Commission on Law Enforcement and Administration of Justice. Crime and Delinquency 13 (January).
Ohlin, Lloyd E., Herman Piven, and Donald Pappenfort
1956   "Major Dilemmas of the Social Worker in Probation and Parole." National Probation and Parole Association Journal 2:211-225.
O'Leary, Vincent and David Duffee
1971   "Correctional Policy—A Classification of Goals Designed for Change." Crime and Delinquency 17 (October):373-386.
Platt, Anthony
1969   The Child Savers. Chicago: University of Chicago Press.
Pownall, George A.
1963   An Analysis of the Role of the Parole Supervision Officer. PhD Dissertation. Urbana: Department of Sociology, University of Illinois.
President's Commission on Law Enforcement and Administration of Justice
1967   Task Force Report: The Courts. Washington, D.C.: U.S. Government Printing Office.

1967   Task Force Report: Corrections. Washington, D.C.: U.S. Government Printing Office.

1967   Task Force Report: Science and Technology. Washington, D.C.: U.S. Government Printing Office.
Richmond, Mary E.
1917   Social Diagnosis. New York: Russell Sage Foundation.
Robison, James
1965   "Progress Notes: Toward the Proposed Study of Parole Operations." San Francisco Research Unit. (Mimeo).

1969   The California Prison, Parole and Probation System: A Special

Report to the Assembly. Technical Supplement No. 2. Sacramento: State of California.

Rubin, Sol
1963   The Law of Criminal Correction. 1st ed. St. Paul: West Publishing Co.

1973   The Law of Criminal Correction. 2nd ed. St. Paul: West Publishing Co.

Sanfilippo, Rudy and Jo Wallach (eds.)
1970   "Correctional Manpower in the Community." In Perspectives on Correctional Manpower and Training. Washington, D.C.: Joint Commission on Correctional Manpower and Training: 15-20.

Studt, Elliott
1954   "Casework in the Correctional Field." Federal Probation 17 (September):19-25.

Sutherland, Edwin H. and Donald R. Cressey
1970   Criminology. 8th ed. Philadelphia: J.B. Lippincott Co.

Tappan, Paul W.
1960   Crime, Justice and Correction. New York: McGraw-Hill.

Turndbladh, Will C.
1956   "Half Justice." National Probation and Parole Association Journal 2:306-307.

United Nations
1951   "The Legal Origins of Probation." In Probation and Related Measures. New York: Department of Social Affairs, United Nations. E/CN/.5/230:15-26.

Wilensky, Harold L. and Charles N. Lebeaux
1965   Industrial Society and Social Welfare. New York: The Free Press.

CHAPTER 15

pRiSONS

Early Philosophy

Much of the history of the American prison system is rooted in Anglo-Saxon society. Jail, which is the forerunner of the contemporary prison, has a long history, but, paradoxically, it is an institution about which we have scant knowledge. We do know, however, that its early origins centered around the need to protect communities from vagrants, beggars, the poor, and debtors, and, according to some, as places to obtain cheap labor, rather than as a place to "punish" deviants and other kinds of "wrongdoers." Jails were never places of comfort, and were used as houses of detention and safekeeping for those awaiting trial. Flynn (1973:49) states that the jail ". . . can be traced to the earliest forms of civilization, when it made its debut in the form of murky dungeons, abysmal pits, unscalable precipices, strong poles or trees, and suspended cages in which hapless prisoners were kept." Flynn also states (1973:49–50):

The American jail is a curious hybrid between the tenth century gaol with its principal function being to detain arrested offenders until they were tried, and the fifteenth and sixteenth century houses of correction with their special function being punishment of minor offenders, debtors, vagrants, and beggars. From its beginning, however, the jail, as to its function, was broadly conceived. It included punishment and coercion as well as custody. In fact, the earliest source of information on incarceration documents a punitive intent and traces that intent to the written laws promulgated by Alfred the Great (871-899 A.D.), the greatest figure in Anglo-Saxon history.

Rothman (1971:50-56) maintains that the use of jail for punishment was a later development in the American colonies, for the colonists tried to protect themselves from "deviants" through the use of fines, whippings, the stocks, and if offenders were truly incorrigible, hanging. Local jails were found throughout the colonies, but they had limited functions. Generally, they only held persons about to be tried, awaiting sentence or unable to discharge their debts. "They did not, however, except on rare occasions, confine convicted offenders as a means of correction" (Rothman, 1971:53). The colonists did not believe that confinement in a jail could or would "rehabilitate" an offender. They believed, in Calvinist tradition, that a man could not be reformed, that his basic nature included "natural depravity," and he was frequently influenced by the powers of the Devil. It was seen as far simpler and much more efficient to banish a person by sending him out of the town; only if no other alternative was available would they lock him up.

At about the time of the American Revolution, the nation's population had begun to increase significantly, especially in the cities. Between 1790 and 1830, according to Rothman (1971:57), the population of Massachusetts almost doubled; in Pennsylvania, it tripled; and in New York it increased five times. At the same time, manufacturing and mercantilism increased substantially. Progressive ideas began to challenge Calvinist doctrines, and Americans generally looked for growth and prosperity, as well as independence from an economic as well as political point of view. One consequence of these developments was that Americans began to question "inherited" practices from England and to devise new ones. "Inspired by the ideals of the Enlightenment, they considered older punishments to be barbaric and traditional assumptions on the origins of deviant behavior to be misdirected" (Rothman, 1971:58).

A number of writers, including Voltaire, Rousseau, and Montesquieu—all Frenchmen—had a profound effect on many other philosophers throughout the world in terms of their concepts of natural and equal rights. Challenging the Calvinist doctrine that man was basically a depraved creature and beyond redemption, Cesare Beccaria, in his famous *Essay on Crimes and Punishments*, first published in Italy in 1764, reasoned that punishment could be effective and just, but only if the penalties were *equally* administered to all. He also suggested that reform of the individual could occur if he were confined in a humane environment. In England, at the same time, Jeremy Bentham and John Howard ". . . extended the range of an indigenous humanitarian movement to include the welfare of jail inmates. Still an earlier stream of influence sprang from the Quakers, many of whom, from William Penn on, urged a more modest and charitable treatment of offenders" (McKelvey, 1972:1).

As the Classical period in criminology developed, Americans expected that a rational system of correction, which made punishment certain but humane, would discourage deviancy. This, of course, meant that the various states had to pass "proper" laws that would end the problem of crime. They felt that if the laws spelled out the *certainty* of punishment, *deterrence* would result. Korn and McCorkle (1965:410–411) comment that changes in practices for dealing with criminals in Europe were greatly affected by the American Revolution, which made transportation of convicted offenders to North America impractical. Further, "Not until great numbers of convicts, crowded into shore-side hulks during the long suspension of transportation, had begun to overflow their quarters did the State commence to interest itself seriously in prison construction."

John Howard toured the Continent and began to offer new ideas for penology, including the *maison de force* established in Ghent in 1773. This model, along with the one established by Pope Clement XI at Rome in 1704, provided for the separation of various classes of inmates and for the housing of inmates in individual cells. Each model also provided for the development of shops for the employment of the inmates at productive labor. Howard discovered similar provisions for inmates in some of the jails in Switzerland, Holland, Germany, and Milan, and his writings began to spur European governments to begin to revise their philosophies about penal affairs.

Birth of the Prison

Thus, at the beginning of the 19th century, two movements merged which helped to give birth to the belief in and construction of the prison as we know it today: law reform and an attack on "antiquated" methods of punishment. The movements merged, began to become synonymous, and each tended to reinforce developments in the other. Korn and McCorkle (1965:411) summarize the movement as follows:

> The reform of the criminal law, by reducing the number of capital crimes, restricting corporal punishment, and virtually abolishing mutilation, required a universal substitute. Imprisonment fulfilled this objective. At the same time, increasing concern for the welfare of prisoners, confined in hulks and noisome, overcrowded jails, sparked a demand for jail reform and new construction.

Rothman (1971:79) points out that the prison came about as a result of man's changing understanding of the nature of man and what eventually became the basis of the Positivist approach to understanding cause and control of criminality:

> Americans' understanding of the causes of deviant behavior led directly to the invention of the penitentiary as a solution. It was an ambitious program. Its design—external appearance, internal arrangement, and daily routine—attempted to eliminate the specific influences that were breeding crime in the community, and to demonstrate the fundamentals of proper social organization. Rather than stand as places of last resort, hidden and ignored, these institutions became the pride of the nation. A structure designed to join practicality to humanitarianism, reform the criminal, stabilize American society, and demonstrate how to improve the condition of mankind, deserved full publicity and close study.

Where Houses of Correction had existed in Europe, as Howard pointed out, the overcrowded conditions, mixing of kinds of offenders, and poor architectural design not only led to problems of discipline, but the conditions did not lend themselves to "correcting" or changing offenders. The earliest opportunity for a complete break with past programs and philosophies in America came shortly after the Revolution in the Quaker state of Pennsylvania. In 1682, almost 100 years before the innovation, William Penn urged the adoption of the "Great Law" by the Quaker Assembly. This law decreed that imprisonment should replace all other punishments for major crimes with the exception of murder, which was to remain capital. Although the Quakers provided workhouses with segregated quarters for male and female offenders, the program did not appear to last. At Penn's death in 1718, the Great Law was nullified, English criminal law was reintroduced, and the penal reforms were swept away. "Within a few years, conditions in the Pennsylvania workhouses had sunk to the level of the typical English county gaol" (Korn and McCorkle, 1965:412).

The Pennsylvania state legislature, by 1790, re-enacted the basics of the old Quaker charter and established a new jail on Walnut Street in Philadelphia. This new jail was to be operated according to an extension of Penn's original ideas.

All new prisoners were first quartered in solitary confinement, the more serious or dangerous offenders remaining isolated for the major part of their sentence. Minor offenders were permitted, after their initial period of isolation, to work together in silence during the day. The apparent success of the new system moved the Quakers to go further along the road toward complete isolation. In two new prisons—the Western Penitentiary, erected at Pittsburgh in 1818, and the Eastern Penitentiary, built at Cherry Hill in 1829—a completely solitary system prevailed. Each prisoner had his individual cell and exercise yard in which he lived and worked during the entire length of his sentence without once coming in contact with another inmate (Korn and McCorkle, 1965:412).

Pennsylvania System

This solitary system, which came to be known as the Pennsylvania System, generally was approved and copied by European criminologists working on penal reform in their own countries. In France, for example, the famous Penal Code of 1810 had not found great support by the liberal thinkers, especially since they believed it to be severe, repressive, and unresponsive to the criminal as a human being. In 1814, Louis XVIII signed an ordinance creating a pilot prison (*prison d'essai*) in Paris for youthful offenders, where the Pennsylvania System of treatment was to be applied and later extended to all prisons in the kingdom. Its purpose was to aim at the moral regeneration of the prisoner, but the program was never completed. In May, 1815, Napoleon returned from Elba and ". . . after the 'Hundred Days' the government was more occupied with settling its account with the rebels than with the reform of its prisons" (Sellin, 1964:xxxi).

Americans watched development of the Pennsylvania System and became divided over its utility. Only one other institution was built following the model and that was the New Jersey State Prison, in 1833. Charles Dickens wrote a detailed description of the possible consequences of isolation, from a psychological point of view, and added to the division of the country insofar as the best course of penal reform to follow.

Those who believed in the Pennsylvania System relied heavily on Quaker ideas and principles, including prayer, meditation, and hard work with regard to bringing about change in criminals. In Massachusetts, Louis Dwight, of the Boston Prison Discipline Society, objected to the Pennsylvania model and proposed that inmates be allowed to work together, but only on the basis of rigidly enforced silence. According to Holbrook, (1957:240–244), Dwight believed the new system ". . . would avoid the horrors of isolation without the risk of mutual contamination."

Auburn System

In Auburn, New York, in 1823, an institution was built in which these principles were to be put to work and, thus, the Auburn or Silent System became the new panacea for bringing about corrective reform of convicted offenders. According to Korn and McCorkle (1965: 413–414), the first warden at Auburn imposed a rigid system of discipline and repression in order to enforce the rule of silence. Inmates were forbidden to speak with one another, they were not permitted to look at each other face to face, and were not allowed to make any kind of a gesture which could be seen by another inmate.

> To ensure that the looks of prisoners would not meet, they were required to walk with downcast eyes, to remain in constant activity when outside of their cells, and, when traveling from location to location in groups, to march in a peculiarly shortened, heavy gait known as the *lock step*. Violation of any of these or a large number of other regulations could bring punishment by flogging.

In the following years, a great ideological battle ensued as to the rightness or wrongness of the two systems. It appears that the Auburn system had a larger following and when Beaumont and Tocqueville visited this country in 1831 in order to bring back ideas to France, they wrote about the two competing systems (1964:44–47):

The experiment made at Auburn ... (the fatal effects of isolation without labor) did not prevent Pennsylvania from continuing the trial of solitary confinement, and in the year 1827, the penitentiary of Pittsburgh began to receive prisoners. Each one was shut up, day and night, in a cell, in which no labor was allowed to him. This solitude, which in principle was to be absolute, was not such in fact. The construction of this penitentiary is so defective, that it is very easy to hear in one cell what is going on in another; so that each prisoner found in the communication ... an opportunity of inevitable corruption ... The bad success of this establishment proved nothing against the system which had called it into existence, because defects in the construction of the prison, rendered the execution of the system impossible. Nevertheless, the advocates of the theories in which it was founded, began to grow cool. This impression became still more general in Pennsylvania, when the melancholy effects caused by solitude without labor in the Auburn prison, became known, as well as the happy success of the new discipline, founded on isolation by night, with common labor during the day.

... In spite of the weight which Pennsylvania threw into the balance, in favor of absolute solitude with labor, the Auburn system, i.e. common labor during the day, with isolation during the night, continued to obtain a preference. Massachusetts, Tennessee, Maryland, Kentucky, Maine, and Vermont, have gradually adopted the Auburn plan, and have taken the Auburn prison as a model for those which they have caused to be erected.

Whatever the merits or demerits of the two plans, criminologists recognize the "correctional" nature of the programs over the penal. As states began to "classify" offenders and separate them into various kinds of institutions—however superficial such attempts at classification were, McKelvey (1972:13) maintains that "Here was recognized for the first time the existence of crimes for which society rather than the individual was responsible, and the corollary easily followed that society was obliged to train the neglected child and the unfortunate vagrant or drunkard for a more wholesome life." The advocates of the separate and congregate systems alike believed most strongly that institutionalization, with its isolation of inmates from conventional society and with its disciplined routine, would be able to overcome the corruptions within society which helped to produce the criminality. Since it was no longer believed that the convict was inherently depraved, it was thought that a comprehensively well-planned institutional program would inevitably lead to re-education and rehabilitation.

The penitentiary, free of corruptions and dedicated to the proper training of the inmate, would inculcate the discipline that negligent parents, evil companions, taverns, houses of prostitution, theaters, and gambling halls had destroyed. Just as the criminal's environment had led him into crime, the institutional environment would lead him out of it (Rothman, 1971: 82–83).

Through the establishment of such institutions, for adults as well as for children, we begin to see that in the 1830s the work of Beccaria began to take hold across distant shores, paving well the future work of Lombroso and the Positive tradition of criminology.

There is no doubt that it was the Auburn plan which finally took hold throughout the entire Northeast of the country and finally even in the West. But the problem of enforcement in the congregate system raised the question of whether obedience was worth any price. The result of the attempt to bring about obedience on the part of all inmates was to create repressive discipline for many years in American penal practices. This eventually led to another need for prison reform—to undo the repressive discipline that it had itself created. In New York's Sing-Sing prison in the 1830s, it is reported that officials were prepared to use every conceivable form of correction to develop and enforce order, which became more important than the rehabilitation the institution was supposed to create for the inmates. As a consequence, the whip was freely used once again and penal authorities defended its use.

In a most militant and military fashion, prison officials and prison reformers alike believed that it was imperative for inmates to learn how to obey authority—something which they had never learned in civilian life, or they would never have engaged in criminal behavior. The officials were not concerned, as Tocqueville and Beaumont pointed out, whether an inmate left prison an honest man, only that he contracted honest habits.

Types of Correctional Institutions

Prisons and correctional institutions are classified in a number of ways. For purposes of custody, the traditional classification includes maximum, medium, and minimum categories. According to Fox (1972:129), a maximum security institution for adult felons generally has walls, cell blocks with inside cell construction or back-to-back construction with each cell facing a wall, armed guard towers, wall towers, and similar security measures. A medium custody institution has at least a fence, but may have a wall, guard towers along the perimeter of the institution, but considerably less restriction of movement within the institution than in a maximum security facility. A minimum custody institution has the least amount of security and may not even have a fence around the facility. Inmates in this kind of institution require the least amount of supervision and generally enjoy the greatest amount of possible movement. Inmates are classified according to security risk, and where a correctional system has all three kinds of facilities, prisoners are sent to appropriate institutions when possible.

Correctional institutions are also classified according to whether the inmates have been convicted on misdemeanor or felony charges. In the case of the former, inmates are usually sent to a workhouse, jail, or detention facility and for periods of less than one year. Felons are always sent to a state (or federal) prison. The former institutions are usually administered by local authorities, while the latter by the state (or federal government). Classification also occurs for juveniles and adults, males and females, and for specialized function, such as for reception, diagnosis, classification, trade training, etc.

Jails

The President's Crime Commission (Task Force Report: Corrections, 1967:45–46) reports that there were 398 state facilities for adults in 1965 and 220 for juveniles, covering the range of types as previously discussed. Hindelang *et al.* (1973:108) report that according to the 1960 U.S. Census, there were 4,041 institutions, including those of a federal, state, and local nature. Either the U.S. Census was incomplete or there was a tremendous growth in the construction of local facilities in the next decade, for the National Jail Census of 1970 (1971: 1) reports the existence of 4,037 "local jails with 48-hour detention authority." Thus, how many correctional facilities exist in the United States today is not known precisely.

On March 15, 1970, perhaps as a typical day in corrections in the United States, these 4,037 local jails confined 160,863 inmates —an average of about 40 per facility. Among these inmates, 153,063 were adults; 7,800 juveniles; one in every 20 was a female; 83,079 (52 percent) were being held *prior* to trial and not yet convicted (two-thirds of whom were juveniles); five percent (8,688 adults) had been convicted but were being detained awaiting further legal action (such as sentencing or appeal); and only 43 percent (69,096) were serving sentences of varying lengths. See Table 15.1.

The 1970 National Jail Census (1971:1-2) also reports that the typical jail in the United States is poorly constructed, ill-equipped for rehabilitative programs, and generally is overcrowded and understaffed.

There are 3,319 jails in the United States which are either county level or located in municipalities of 25,000 or greater population. Eighty-six percent of these institutions provide no facilities for exercise or other recreation for their inmates. Nearly 90% have no educational facilities. Only half provide medical facilities; one in four has no visiting facility; and there are 47 institutions (about 1.4%) which are without an operating flush toilet. These 3,319 county and urban institutions contain nearly 100,000 cells. One in every four of these cells has been in use longer than 50 years, including more than 5,000 cells that are over 100 years old.

The nation's jails employed 28,911 full-time equivalent persons on March 15, 1970, for an average of about 5½ inmates per jail employee. The fiscal year 1969 operating costs amounted to $324 million, with planned construction expenditures for fiscal year 1970 anticipated at $171 million. The March 1970 payroll was $18 million for an average of $617 per full-time employee.

Conditions in local jails have not changed much over the last half century. As long ago as 1928 the noted German penologist, M. Liepmann (1928:231-232), after visiting a number of American jails, commented:

There are no words to describe the almost medieval conditions in (the county) jails. Usually no distinction is made between those who have been sentenced and those who are awaiting trial and who perhaps are innocent of any offense. There is no provision for giving the prisoners adequate work or exercise in the open air. In the matters of light and air, sanitary and hygienic conditions, the cells can without exaggeration be compared to stalls for animals, and at that to the neglected stalls that might have been found in country districts at least half a century ago. Furthermore, in many cities the jails are, as a regular thing, obliged to receive double and triple the number of inmates that they were built to accommodate.

... But on the whole, one must say that the jails are in striking contrast to the kind of institution that one has a right to expect of a civilized nation of the twentieth century, and that Americans especially, because of the important part that they have played in the past in the development of

TABLE 15.1. U.S. Jail Population, March, 1970

State	Number of Jails	Inmate Population	Inmates Not Convicted
U.S. total	4,037	160,863	83,079
Cities with population of 25,000 or more, and counties	3,319	156,816	80,764
Cities with population under 25,000	718	4,047	2,315
Alabama	107	3,018	1,597
Alaska	8	171	55
Arizona	39	2,142	887
Arkansas	110	1,224	707
California	166	27,672	12,730
Colorado	78	1,481	980
Connecticut*	–	–	–
Delaware*	–	–	–
District of Columbia	5	3,222	933
Florida	167	9,412	4,734
Georgia	240	6,726	2,752
Hawaii	4	97	61
Idaho	61	436	237
Illinois	108	5,324	3,508
Indiana	97	2,685	1,800
Iowa	93	691	369
Kansas	123	1,100	659
Kentucky	148	2,693	1,527
Louisiana	95	4,039	2,272
Maine	16	242	82
Maryland	23	2,758	1,976
Massachusetts	18	2,126	674
Michigan	92	5,789	2,716
Minnesota	77	1,476	487
Mississippi	98	1,636	865
Missouri	144	2,958	1,655
Montana	68	367	200
Nebraska	99	823	327
Nevada	23	755	472
New Hampshire	11	333	107
New Jersey	32	4,436	2,604
New Mexico	44	961	479
New York	75	17,399	8,707
N. Carolina	100	2,580	1,883
N. Dakota	50	158	94
Ohio	160	5,920	3,062
Oklahoma	112	2,214	1,175
Oregon	69	1,487	709
Pennsylvania	77	6,900	4,138

TABLE 15.1, continued

State	Number of Jails	Inmate Population	Inmates Not Convicted
Rhode Island*	–	–	–
S. Carolina	111	3,281	1,031
S. Dakota	60	307	175
Tennessee	116	3,622	1,773
Texas	325	10,720	7,654
Utah	34	522	326
Vermont	6	22	20
Virginia	96	3,416	1,540
Washington	83	2,277	1,113
W. Virginia	61	1,094	530
Wisconsin	75	1,978	618
Wyoming	33	173	79

*Jails are not locally administered but rather are operated by the state government.
Source: 1970 National Jail Census. LEAA:2.

an intelligent and social prison system, ought to bestir themselves with far more energy than they have thus far shown to abolish these unworthy conditions.

When Frank Tannenbaum wrote *Crime and the Community* (1938:320–321), he pointed out the deplorable conditions of the various local correctional institutions throughout the United States and strongly recommended that they be taken over administratively by the states. Four decades later, this recommendation has not been accomplished, even though many states have enacted legislation which requires the implementation of state standards of operations and routine inspections. The extent to which such standards and inspections have helped to raise the quality of the services being provided in such facilities is not really known, but it is doubtful that conditions are much better than those described by Liepmann.

Adult Correctional Institutions

The U.S. Department of Justice, through the National Prisoner Statistics program, has been collecting, analyzing, and publishing data about state and federal prisoners for a number of years. Like the *Uniform Crime Reports* published by the FBI, the reporting of these data is voluntary; thus, any published report is necessarily incomplete regarding the *total* prison situation. Nonetheless, as Table 15.2 indicates, in spite of the significant increase in overall population and the alleged dramatic increase in crime in the last several decades, the institutional population of adult felons in state and federal facilities throughout the United States increased approximately by only 17,000 persons from 1939 through 1970 (1970:2). According to the same source, among the 50 states, 25 of them reported decreases in inmate populations between the years 1950 and 1970. As Table 15.3 illustrates, some of the reductions were minimal. The table also reflects what may be varying penal philosophies among the states, for several, including California, Texas, Maryland, and Florida substantially have increased the number of institutional commitments. Between 1852, with the establishment of San Quentin, and 1965, California, as an example, established 12 major adult correctional facilities. According to the 1973 Directory of Correctional Institutions and Agencies published by the American Correctional Association, California reported a total "normal capacity" for these institutions of 24,187 inmates, with an "average" number of inmates at 19,311—suggesting "room" for almost 5,000 more commitments during the reporting year of 1972. As of December 31, 1970, California reported in the National Prisoner Statistics that there were 25,033 adult inmates confined in the state's correctional institutions (see Table 15.3).

Length of Stay

That there are varying philosophies about penal practices is illustrated in the President's Crime Commission's *Task Force Report: Corrections*. It reports (1967:178-179) that the length of stay of inmates in state correctional institutions varies according to the sentencing laws, the practices of the courts, its parole laws, and the practice of its releasing authority. A survey of such practices, however, reveals that the average length of stay in state correctional institutions ranges from less than 6 months in one state to as much as 5 years in several states. As Table 15.4 shows, in 12 states, the average is 18 months or less, while in 15 states, it is more than 30 months. Of course, many individual offenders may serve many more years than 5, but this, at least, is an average.

The average length of stay of inmates has many implications for institutional size, personnel requirements, program development, and

TABLE 15.2. Population of State and Federal Prisons at End of Year, United States, 1939–1970

Year	Number			Rate per 100,000 of the Estimated Civilian Population of the United States		
	All Institutions	Federal Institutions	State Institutions	All Institutions	Federal Institutions	State Institutions
1970	196,429	20,038	176,391[a]	96.7	9.8	86.8
1969	196,007	19,623	176,384[b]	97.6	9.7	87.8
1968	187,914	19,703	168,211[c]	94.3	9.9	84.3
1967	194,896	19,579	175,317	99.1	10.0	89.2
1966	199,654	19,245	180,409	102.7	9.9	92.8
1965	210,895	21,040	189,855	109.5	10.9	98.6
1964	214,336	21,709	192,627	112.6	11.4	101.2
1963	217,283	23,128	194,155	115.7	12.3	103.4
1962	218,830	23,944	194,886	118.3	12.9	105.3
1961	220,149	23,696	196,453	120.8	13.0	107.8
1960	212,953	23,218	189,735	118.6	12.9	105.7
1959	207,446	22,492	184,954	117.7	12.8	104.9
1958	205,493	21,549	183,944	118.8	12.5	106.3
1957	195,256	20,420	174,836	114.9	12.0	102.9
1956	189,421	20,134	169,287	113.5	12.1	101.4
1955	185,780	20,088	165,692	113.4	12.3	101.1
1954	182,848	20,003	162,845	113.8	12.4	101.3
1953	173,547	19,363	154,184	110.2	12.3	97.9
1952	168,200	18,014	150,186	108.8	11.6	97.1
1951	165,640	17,395	148,245	108.9	11.4	97.4
1950	166,123	17,134	148,989	110.3	11.4	98.9
1949	163,749	16,868	146,881	110.0	11.3	98.6

Year					
1948	155,977	16,328	139,649	106.6	11.2	95.4
1947	151,304	17,146	134,158	105.2	11.9	93.3
1946	140,079	17,622	122,457	99.7	12.5	87.2
1945	133,649	18,638	115,011	100.5	14.0	86.5
1944	132,456	18,139	114,317	104.2	14.3	89.9
1943	137,220	16,113	121,107	108.0	12.7	95.3
1942	150,384	16,623	133,761	116.4	12.9	103.5
1941	165,439	18,465	146,974	126.0	14.1	112.0
1940	173,706	19,260	154,446	132.0	14.6	117.3
1939	179,818	19,730	160,088	137.1	15.0	122.0

aFigure excludes Alaska, Arkansas, Rhode Island, Indiana Reformatory.

bFigure excludes Alaska, Arkansas, Rhode Island, Indiana Reformatory, and D.C. Women's Detention Center.

cFigure excludes Alaska, Arkansas, Delaware, North Carolina, and Rhode Island.

Source: U.S. Department of Justice. Federal Bureau of Prisons. "National Prisoner Statistics: Prisoners in State and Federal Institutions for Adult Felons, 1968, 1969, 1970":2.

TABLE 15.3. Population of State Prisons at End of Year, by State, 1950–1970

Number of Prisoners Confined, as of Dec. 31, 1970, by State

	1970	1969	1968	1967	1965	1960	1955	1950
California	25,033	27,535	28,435	27,741	26,325	21,660	15,230	11,056
New York	12,059	12,452	12,781	14,085	17,504	17,207	17,069	15,313
Texas	14,331	14,014	12,215	12,313	12,854	11,308	8,622	6,424
Ohio	9,185	9,567	10,189	10,323	11,374	11,111	10,483	9,128
Florida	9,187	8,512	7,946	7,261	6,995	7,084	4,830	3,973
Illinois	6,381	7,131	6,886	7,041	8,306	9,064	8,130	7,886
Michigan	9,079	8,049	7,743	7,037	7,342	9,550	9,547	8,591
Pennsylvania	6,289	5,780	5,519	5,674	7,116	7,802	7,342	7,432
North Carolina	5,969	5,856	NA	5,516	6,029	5,977	5,334	5,004
Georgia	5,113	5,085	5,175	5,300	5,966	6,985	5,701	4,545
Maryland	5,186	5,356	5,096	5,083	5,467	5,316	4,685	3,892
New Jersey	5,704	5,382	5,065	4,614	4,839	4,284	3,782	3,991
Louisiana	4,196	4,170	4,237	4,112	3,844	3,749	3,026	2,674
Virginia	4,648	4,407	4,126	4,033	4,533	5,775	4,869	4,439
Indiana	4,137	4,243	4,057	3,884	4,486	5,429	4,462	4,738
Alabama	3,790	4,140	4,017	3,881	4,377	5,369	5,222	4,454
Missouri	3,413	3,242	3,245	3,263	3,517	3,698	3,966	3,400
Tennessee	3,268	3,148	2,999	2,980	3,213	3,134	2,723	2,780
Kentucky	2,849	3,314	2,864	2,834	2,813	3,603	3,349	3,259
Oklahoma	3,640	3,230	2,893	2,756	2,829	2,679	2,600	2,401
Washington	2,864	2,765	2,599	2,738	3,202	2,455	2,443	2,290
Wisconsin	2,973	2,768	2,172	2,607	2,830	2,784	2,281	2,017
Colorado	2,066	2,107	2,338	2,514	2,766	2,078	1,800	1,490

State							
South Carolina	2,726	2,506	2,331	2,337	2,323	2,080	1,852	1,513
Kansas	1,902	1,980	2,185	2,289	2,791	2,313	1,974	1,959
Iowa	1,747	1,732	1,747	1,830	2,178	2,204	2,203	2,084
Massachusetts	2,053	1,966	1,912	1,824	1,929	1,920	1,995	2,375
Oregon	1,800	1,712	1,815	1,803	2,000	1,710	1,552	1,534
Mississippi	1,730	1,700	1,544	1,667	2,019	1,975	2,080	2,158
Minnesota	1,585	1,605	1,632	1,652	1,772	2,059	1,964	1,879
Arkansas	NA	NA	NA	1,651	1,970	2,016	1,751	1,541
Arizona	1,461	1,714	1,692	1,596	1,694	1,516	1,055	878
Connecticut	1,568	1,630	1,444	1,587	1,642	1,497	1,260	1,020
District of Columbia	1,423	1,504	1,466	1,268	1,604	1,958	1,943	1,478
West Virginia	938	1,001	1,124	1,208	1,477	2,407	2,269	2,904
Nebraska	1,001	937	950	971	1,151	1,269	1,080	1,147
New Mexico	742	857	850	892	1,002	1,243	724	705
Utah	491	488	640	651	701	553	554	562
Nevada	690	665	645	608	622	413	373	240
Maine	516	561	598	592	695	750	620	736
Montana	260	372	466	521	586	602	529	595
South Dakota	391	380	446	489	571	526	423	451
Idaho	411	348	328	391	481	549	520	514
Hawaii	228	256	296	364	463	558	NA	NA
Rhode Island	NA	NA	NA	350	310	255	305	284
Delaware	596	555	NA	308	315	226	172	158
Wyoming	231	246	257	254	336	338	287	368
New Hampshire	244	215	224	222	205	180	198	235
Vermont	162	170	226	220	263	269	285	259
North Dakota	147	161	156	182	208	248	228	235

Source: U.S. Department of Justice. Federal Bureau of Prisons. "National Prisoners Statistics: Prisoners in State and Federal Institutions for Adult Felons, 1968, 1969, 1970":10–11.

TABLE 15.4. Average Length of Stay in Adult Institutions, by Number of States

Average Length of Stay	Number of States	Average Length of Stay	Number of States
Less than 6 months	1	31 to 36 months	10
7 to 12 months	2	37 to 48 months	2
13 to 18 months	9	49 to 60 months	3
19 to 24 months	14	Unknown	3
25 to 30 months	8	Total	52

Source: Task Force Report: Corrections, 1967:179.

finances. The Crime Commission (*Corrections*, 1967:179) reports that one state, which sends its felons to federal institutions, spent only $379,000 in 1966, while another state spent $62 million, which does not include capital construction. "The cost of operating 358 state correctional institutions in the 52 jurisdictions totaled $384,980,648 in 1965 . . . (and) More than 46,000 employees guard, feed, and attempt to rehabilitate the 200,000 inmates."

Administrative Patterns

In the first third of this century, according to the President's Crime Commission, the prevailing administrative pattern for most state institutions for adult felons was one of independence. That is, each institution was independently run and administered, with the warden or superintendent reporting either directly to the Governor or to the Governor through a board. In 1945, among the 48 states, there were 8 states with such independently run institutions. By 1967, only 3 states retained this practice. In 1945, state boards with no other functions provided central administration for adult correctional institutions in 13 states. In 1967, the same situation prevailed, although many of them changed their name from prison board to department of corrections. In 1945, adult correctional institutions in 27 states were administered by an agency having additional functions. By 1967, this number increased to 34 states and Puerto Rico.

The National Advisory Commission on Criminal Justice Standards and Goals (Corrections, 1973:355–356) states that correctional practice in the United States seems to defy standardization, a comment previously made by the President's Crime Commission. It said, for example (1967:179) that "Standards call for the administration of state correctional institutions to be vested in a separate state department of correction or its equivalent . . . (but) Only 16 states partially meet this standard."

The National Advisory Commission in 1973 called for a halt in any new construction of major institutions for adult felons. It said (1973:357):

Each correctional agency administering State institutions for juvenile or adult offenders should adopt immediately a policy of not building new major institutions for juveniles under any circumstances, and not building new institutions for adults unless an analysis of the total criminal justice and adult corrections systems produces a clear finding that no alternative is possible. In the latter instance, the analysis should conform generally to the "total system planning" discussed in Chapter 9. If this effort proves conclusively that a new institution for adults is essential, these factors should characterize the planning and design process:

1. A collaborative planning effort should identify the purpose of the physical plant.

2. The size of the inmate population of the projected institution should be small enough to allow security without excessive regimentation, surveillance equipment, or repressive hardware.

3. The location of the institution should be selected on the basis of its proximity to:

a. The communities from which the inmates come.

b. Areas capable of providing or attracting adequate numbers of qualified line and professional staff members of racial and ethnic origin compatible with the inmate population, and capable of supporting lifestyles and community service requirements.

c. Areas that have community services and activities to support the correctional goal, including social services, schools, hospitals, universities, and employment opportunities.

d. The courts and auxiliary correctional agencies.

e. Public transportation.

4. The physical environment of a new institution should be designed with consideration to:

a. Provision of privacy and personal space.

b. Minimization of noise.

c. Reduction of sensory deprivation.

d. Encouragement of constructive inmate-staff relationships.

e. Provision of adequate utility services.

5. Provision also should be made for:

a. Dignified facilities for inmate visiting.

b. Individual and group counseling.

c. Education, vocational training, and workshops designed to accommodate small numbers of inmates and to facilitate supervision.

d. Recreation yards for each housing unit as well as larger recreational facilities accessible to the entire inmate population.

e. Medical and hospital facilities.

Halfway Houses and Group Homes

In view of the increasing costs to house an inmate in an institution, corrections has sought cheaper and more innovative ways to "rehabilitate" those under its supervision. Prerelease centers, group homes, and halfway houses in the last decade have sprung up as alternatives. These small, residential-type facilities have been developed to guide prisoners out of the institutions—or, for some, back in—as reintegration into the community is attempted. In other words, correctional authorities, long aware that many offenders need help and counselling without major institutionalization, have developed the very small institution. Here, an offender can receive services and participate in programs, based in the community, but without the pressures normally found in the large, congregate type of institution.

Initially, these programs were developed for offenders "halfway out" of institutions, as a means of easing the stresses "involved in transition from rigid control to freedom in the community . . . Recently the halfway house has come to be viewed as a potential alternative to institutionalization, and thus a program for those 'halfway in' between probation and institutional control" (*Corrections*, 1967:40). To the best of our knowledge, these small group homes have quadrupled since 1966 and now number at least 300 throughout the United States (Prestbo, 1972:1). There is considerable support for the halfway house movement, but there appear many unanswered questions concerning their extent, program, administration, and success. In a review of the literature on the subject, Cohn and Sullivan (1972) report:

> The reader of literature on the subject learns that most of the writings are unscientific reports on what people believe and think; there is a dearth of significant research that supports reliable and valid conclusions.

In an effort to provide direction to those administering group-home facilities, the Law Enforcement Assistance Administration supported a project sponsored by the International Halfway House Association to develop guidelines and standards. In the final report, the authors (McCartt and Mangogna, 1973:iii) state:

> Deliberate, systematic decisions have been made to change the course of corrections to community-based treatment, especially residential treatment. Consequently, the necessity of developing guidelines and standards for the establishment and operation of halfway houses has become increasingly evident. Agencies, both public and private, need some direction in order to chart the new course corrections is now taking.

While it may not be possible fully to evaluate the impact of the group home or halfway house at this time, Keller and Alper (1970: 173) in writing about the movement toward community based programs, state:

> Of all the fields of social endeavor which are starting now to feel the effect of the new winds which are blowing away old concepts and outmoded ways of treatment, only in the field of corrections has the fixed institution continued to be the major tool. Happily this bastion is finally being breached ... The correctional process is bound to profit from this new emphasis (of community-based treatment), and more than just incidentally, society at large may also benefit by reason of this re-examination and reorientation of its historic attitudes toward the offender.

Classification

We have previously discussed the historical development of correctional programs and various kinds of institutional settings to which adult offenders are committed. We have also suggested that offenders are classified according to various criteria—e.g., sex, dangerousness, and age, which often are the bases of the initial classification process. In states where the number of institutions is sufficient to present a choice, such as in California and the federal system, central reception institutions have been created to which all committed offenders are initially sent. These centers serve as diagnostic facilities where clinical staffs review case materials, examine the defendant, and attempt to reach a conclusion not only concerning the most appropriate institution to which the offender is to be sent, but the "treatment" program that is to be initiated to assist the offender to become "rehabilitated."

The correctional process generally includes organized procedures to integrate, coordinate, and otherwise provide a continuity of diagnosis, program planning, and treatment first in the institution and later in the community, while the offender is on parole. *Classification* is the term generally used to describe these organized procedures and is defined—in its ideal form—by the American Correctional Association (1966:351) as follows:

> Classification ... contributes to a smoothly, efficiently operated correctional program by pooling of all relevant information concerning the offender, by devising a program for the individual based on that information, and by keeping that program realistically in line with the individual's requirements. It furnishes an orderly method to the institution administrator by which the varied needs and requirements of each inmate may be followed through from commitment to discharge. Through its diagnostic and coordinating functions, classification not only contributes to the objective of rehabilitation, but also to custody, discipline, work assignments, officer and inmate morale and the effective use of training opportunities. Through the data it develops, it assists in long-range planning and development, both in the correctional system as a whole and in the individual situation.

The National Advisory Commission on Criminal Justice Standards and Goals (*Corrections*, 1973:197) points out the many inadequacies and operational problems of most classification procedures. It suggests that in more cases than not, state classification systems are designed more to control and manage inmates than they are designed to assist and develop individualized treatment programs. That is, institutional personnel can become more concerned with "running a smooth ship" and designing programs for staff convenience than in developing responsive and meaningful programs for offenders. Furthermore, since many correctional agencies have failed to spell out organizational goals (Cohn, 1973), a classification system could not possibly work until organizational goals are specified and in terms which are realistic and easily understood by staff and inmates. As the Advisory Commission points out (Corrections, 1973:200) even when goals are detailed, it is not uncommon to find that

> Discriminatory program decisions are made on the basis of ethnic background, offense pattern, and staff reactions to the offender's personality quirks. These discriminatory practices, planned or not, tend to be inimical to effective classification systems that would organize resources around

the offender's needs and not around the needs of the agency's administrative structure or its employees.

As a consequence of the above, along with many other considerations, the Advisory Commission (*Corrections*, 1973:210–211, 213) has recommended that the following two sets of standards be implemented by all state correctional systems:

Standard 6.1

Each correctional agency, whether community-based or institutional, should immediately reexamine its classification system and reorganize it along the following principles:

1. Recognizing that corrections is now characterized by a lack of knowledge and deficient resources, and that classification systems therefore are more useful for assessing risk and facilitating the efficient management of offenders than for diagnosis of causation and prescriptions for remedial treatment, classification should be designed to operate on a practicable level and for realistic purposes, guided by the principle that:

a. No offender should receive more surveillance or "help" than he requires: and

b. No offender should be kept in a more secure condition or status than his potential risk dictates.

2. The classification system should be developed under the management concepts discussed in Chapter 13 and issued in written form so that it can be made public and shared. It should specify:

a. The objectives of the system based on a hypothesis for the social reintegration of offenders, detailed methods for achieving the objectives, and a monitoring and evaluation mechanism to determine whether the objectives are being met.

b. The critical variables of the typology to be used.

c. Detailed indicators of the components of the classification categories.

d. The structure (committee, unit, team, etc.) and the procedures for balancing the decisions that must be made in relation to programming, custody, personal security, and resource allocation.

3. The system should provide full coverage of the offender population, clearly delineated categories, internally consistent groupings, simplicity, and a common language.

4. The system should be consistent with individual dignity and basic concepts of fairness (based on objective judgments rather than personal prejudices).

5. The system should provide for maximum involvement of the individual in determining the nature and direction of his own goals, and mechanisms for appealing administrative decisions affecting him.

6. The system should be adequately staffed, and the agency staff should be trained in its use.

7. The system should be sufficiently objective and quantifiable to facilitate research, demonstration, model building, intrasystem comparisons, and administrative decisionmaking.

8. The correctional agency should participate in or be receptive to cross-classification research toward the development of a classification system that can be used commonly by all correctional agencies.

and

Standard 6.2

Each correctional agency operating institutions for committed offenders, in connection with and in addition to implementation of Standard 6.1, should reexamine and reorganize its classification system immediately, as follows:

1. The use of reception-diagnostic centers should be discontinued.

2. Whether a reception unit or classification committee or team is utilized within the institution, the administration's classification issuance described in Standard 6.1 also should:

a. Describe the makeup of the unit, team, or committee, as well as its duties and responsibilities.

b. Define its responsibilities for custody, employment, and vocational assignments.

c. Indicate what phases of an inmate program may be changed without unit, team, or committee action.

d. Specify procedures relating to inmate transfer from one program to another.

e. Prescribe form and content of the classification interview.

f. Develop written policies regarding initial inmate classification and reclassification.

3. The purpose of initial classification should be:

a. To screen inmates for safe and appropriate placements and to determine whether these programs will accomplish the purposes for which inmates are placed in the correctional system, and

b. Through orientation to give new inmates an opportunity to learn of the programs available to them and of the performance expected to gain their release.

4. The purpose of reclassification should be the increasing involvement of offenders in community-based programs as set forth in Standard 7.4, Inmate Involvement in Community Programs.

5. Initial classification should not take longer than 1 week.

6. Reclassification should be undertaken at intervals not exceeding 6 weeks.

7. The isolation or quarantine period, if any, should be as brief as possible but no longer than 24 hours.

Prisoner Labor

Both the Pennsylvania and Auburn systems placed a premium on "hard labor" in the belief that through such work it would be possible to rehabilitate the offender. This work model became accepted as most important in every prison system in the United States, and some systems have even attempted to make themselves self-supporting economically as a result of very cheap prisoner labor. Fox (1972:141) reports that the New York prisons at Auburn and Sing-Sing were both paying for themselves financially as early as 1828, and other large industrial prisons were built in the Midwest and California with the expectation that they would pay for themselves and thereby not cost the taxpayer any additional monies.

The development of the industrial prison, or the leasing of prisoners to private industry or agriculture, continued well into the late 19th century. At that time, organized industry began to object to the "competition," the expansion of prison labor was curtailed, and restrictive legislation began to be enacted. Takagi (1974:82–84) comments that until 1890, the operation of prisons "was a highly profitable venture for the State and for private entrepreneurs who purchased or leased convict labor . . . Although the states continued to use convict labor . . . the prisons were never again able to show a profit . . . officials feared the adverse influence of idleness or aimless occupation as frankly 'disastrous' and calamitous."

The most serious federal legislation was the Hawes-Cooper Act of 1929, which divested prison-made goods of their interstate characteristics and which went into effect on January 1, 1934. Goods produced in prisons, then, could no longer be shipped across state lines. The Ashurst-Sumners Act of 1935 and the Act of October 14, 1940 further restricted interstate commerce of prison-made goods and many states passed legislation limiting the sale and use of prison-made products. According to Fox (1972:143) the result of the restriction on such manufacture and use of prison-made materials has produced a level of idleness in American prisons which has not yet been offset by any other kind of program, including those of an educational or academic nature.

At the present time, there are three systems of prisoner employment in use in most prison systems. Fox describes them as follows (1972:143):

> One is the public or state account system in which goods are produced in prison and sold on the open market. A second is the state use system in which goods are produced and used by other state agencies and offices or political subdivisions, frequently schools and jails. The third is the public works and ways system which provides labor for construction and maintenance of roads, parks, conservation projects, and other public facilities.

In addition to goods produced for sale or use by others, almost every prison utilizes inmate labor to farm, maintain, operate, or otherwise manage the daily activities of prisons. Since they are "total institutions" or communities, inmate labor usually provides all laundry, cleaning, cooking, and other vital services necessary to run and maintain the institution. Additionally, these programs are supposedly geared toward training and educating prisoners so that, upon release from the institution, the inmate will have obtained the necessary skills needed for reasonable employment. Most penologists agree, however, that such meaningful training has not occurred. A recent study of California prison industries found that the employment provided for inmates neither taught them useful skills nor was seen as much different from ordinary idleness (California Assembly, 1969:5).

Payment for work varies considerably between and among the federal and state correctional systems. In 1957, wages were paid to prisoners in 33 states, ranging from four cents to $1.30 per day (Sutherland and Cressey, 1974:564). The Federal Prison Industries, a governmental corporation which operates as the industrial division of the U.S. Bureau of Prisons, pays inmates according to the grade of work performed. In 1964, the average wage paid per month for those employed in manufacturing was about $40 (Bureau of Prisons, Annual Report, 1964).

According to the "Universal Declaration of Human Rights," adopted by the United Nations, it is stated that labor is the *right* of all prisoners. In commenting on this right, the former Chief of the Section of Social Defense in the United Nations (Lopez-Rey, 1958: 13) stated further that prison labor should not be considered treatment, that prisoners should receive the same rate of pay that their civilian counterparts would receive for the same work, and that prison labor should be part of labor in general.

With regard to prison labor and industries, the National Advisory Commission on Criminal Justice Standards and Goals (*Corrections*, 1973:387) recommends the following standard:

Standard 11.10

Each correctional agency and each institution operating industrial and labor programs should take steps immediately to reorganize their programs to support the reintegrative purpose of correctional institutions.

1. Prison industries should be diversified and job specifications defined to fit work assignments to offenders' needs as determined by release planning.

2. All work should form part of a designed training program with provisions for:

a. Involving the offender in the decision concerning his assignment.

b. Giving him the opportunity to achieve on a productive job to further his confidence in his ability to work.

c. Assisting him to learn and develop his skills in a number of job areas.

d. Instilling good working habits by providing incentives.

3. Joint bodies consisting of institution management, inmates, labor organizations, and industry should be responsible for planning and implementing a work program useful to the offender, efficient, and closely related to skills in demand outside the prison.

4. Training modules integrated into a total training plan for individual offenders should be provided. Such plans must be periodically monitored and flexible enough to provide for modification in line with individuals' needs.

5. Where job training needs cannot be met within the institution, placement in private industry on work-furlough programs should be implemented consistent with security needs.

6. Inmates should be compensated for all work performed that is of economic benefit to the correctional authority or another public or private entity. As a long-range objective to be implemented by 1978, such compensation should be at rates representing the prevailing wage for work of the same type in the vicinity of the correctional facility.

Prison Discipline

The maintenance of discipline in a penal institution requires staff and inmates alike to adhere to a set of orderly procedures. If these procedures are published, which they generally are, and handed to each inmate when he or she enters the institution, the inmate is expected to follow them or "suffer the consequences." In years past, there were few safeguards protecting the inmate from sadistic or capricious punishments. In fact, it was not uncommon that an inmate would be sent "to the hole" or otherwise deprived of the few privileges or liberty he might have felt he had inside the prison if he "crossed" a guard or other institutional worker. Today, the prisoner enjoys many more safeguards, but it is still maintained that correctional systems have far to go in the area of inmate protection from capricious discipline.

The American Correctional Association's *Manual of Correctional Standards* (1966:402–411) devotes considerable attention to the issue of prisoner discipline and suggests that there are seven essential elements:

1. Good morale. The only sound basis for good discipline is good morale. Conversely, proper discipline builds morale.

2. Custody and control. Custodial care is the supervision of inmates designed to prevent escapes or incidents. It does not mean that it is necessary that all prisoners be under close supervision at all times.

3. Contributing disciplines. The staff and all phases of the institutional program in their special ways contribute to the general discipline and morale of the institution.

4. Individualized discipline. Not only should discipline be consistent, reasonable, objective, firm and prompt, but it must be appropriately varied in terms of an understanding of the personalities of the inmates.

5. Preventive discipline. It is desirable to forestall punitive disciplinary practices with a workable program of preventive discipline.

6. Good communication. A good system of communication will replace mutual suspicion and other disturbed feelings between inmates and staff by greater mutual acceptance. It is particularly imperative to have good communication when instituting any change of program which affects masses of the inmate body.

7. Program and procedures for maintaining proper standards of institutional control. Since discipline in its broadest sense is one of the most important factors in institutional life, primary responsibility must rest with the senior officials who will develop good disciplinary practices and prevent undesirable disciplinary practices which are now considered archaic.

Discipline, with the immediate aim of good order and good conduct, looks beyond the limits of the inmate's term of confinement. It must seek to insure carry-over value by inculcating standards which the inmate will maintain after release. It must always be objective and must develop in the inmate personal responsibility to that social community to which he will return.

The nature of prison discipline and the procedures utilized to impose it are very sensitive issues both to inmates and correctional authorities. Nowhere else is the problem of "due process" more argued or contested. The problem of discipline is most important because its imposition on inmates frequently results in loss of "good time," time an inmate accumulates which, in effect, lessens the total amount of sentenced time which must be served in inmate status. The National Advisory Commission devotes considerable attention to the issues of "due process," "administrative justice," and "disciplinary procedures" (*Corrections*, 1973:555, 51–52):

Standard 16.2

Each State should enact by 1975 legislation patterned after the Model State Administrative Procedure Act, to regulate the administrative procedures of correctional agencies. Such legislation, as it applies to corrections, should:

1. Require the use of administrative rules and regulations and provide a formal procedure for their adoption or alteration which will include:
    a. Publication of proposed rules.
    b. An opportunity for interested and affected parties, including offenders, to submit data, views, or arguments orally or in writing on the proposed rules.
    c. Public filing of adopted rules.
2. Require in a contested case where the legal rights, duties, or privileges of a person are determined by an agency after a hearing, that the following procedures be implemented:
    a. The agency develop and publish standards and criteria for decisionmaking of a more specific nature than that provided by statute.
    b. The agency state in writing the reason for its action in a particular case.
    c. The hearings be open except to the extent that confidentiality is required.
    d. A system of recorded precedents be developed to supplement the standards and criteria.
3. Require judicial review for agency actions affecting the substantial rights of individuals, including offenders, such review to be limited to the following questions:
    a. Whether the agency action violated constitutional or statutory provisions.

   b. Whether the agency action was in excess of the statutory authority of the agency.

   c. Whether the agency action was made upon unlawful procedure.

   d. Whether the agency action was clearly erroneous in view of the reliable, probative, and substantial evidence on the record.

The above legislation should require the correctional agency to establish by agency rules procedures for:

   1. The review of grievances of offenders.

   2. The imposition of discipline on offenders.

   3. The change of an offender's status within correctional programs.

and

Standard 2.12

   Each correctional agency immediately should adopt, consistent with Standard 16.2, disciplinary procedures for each type of residential facility it operates and for the persons residing therein.

   Minor violations of rules of conduct are those punishable by no more than a reprimand, or loss of commissary, entertainment, or recreation privileges for not more than 24 hours. Rules governing minor violations should provide that:

   1. Staff may impose the prescribed sanctions after informing the offender of the nature of his misconduct and giving him the chance to explain or deny it.

   2. If a report of the violation is placed in the offender's file, the offender should be so notified.

   3. The offender should be provided with the opportunity to request a review by an impartial officer or board of the appropriateness of the staff action.

   4. Where the review indicates that the offender did not commit the violation or the staff's action was not appropriate, all reference to the incident should be removed from the offender's file.

   Major violations of rules of conduct are those punishable by sanctions more stringent than those for minor violations, including but not limited to, loss of good time, transfer to segregation or solitary confinement, transfer to a higher level of institutional custody or any other change in status which may tend to affect adversely an offender's time of release or discharge.

   Rules governing major violations should provide for the following pre-hearing procedures:

   1. Someone other than the reporting officer should conduct a complete investigation into the facts of the alleged misconduct to determine if

there is probable cause to believe the offender committed a violation. If probable cause exists, a hearing date should be set.

2. The offender should receive a copy of any disciplinary report or charges of the alleged violation and notice of the time and place of the hearing.

3. The offender, if he desires, should receive assistance in preparing for the hearing from a member of the correctional staff, another inmate, or other authorized person (including legal counsel if available).

4. No sanction for the alleged violation should be imposed until after the hearing except that the offender may be segregated from the rest of the population if the head of the institution finds that he constitutes a threat to other inmates, staff members, or himself.

Rules governing major violations should provide for a hearing on the alleged violation which should be conducted as follows:

1. The hearing should be held as quickly as possible, generally not more than 72 hours after the charges are made.

2. The hearing should be before an impartial officer or board.

3. The offender should be allowed to present evidence or witnesses on his behalf.

4. The offender may be allowed to confront and cross-examine the witnesses against him.

5. The offender should be allowed to select someone, including legal counsel, to assist him at the hearing.

6. The hearing officer or board should be required to find substantial evidence of guilt before imposing a sanction.

7. The hearing officer or board should be required to render its decision in writing setting forth its findings as to controverted facts, its conclusion, and the sanction imposed. If the decision finds that the offender did not commit the violation, all reference to the charge should be removed from the offender's file.

Rules governing major violations should provide for internal review of the hearing officer's or board's decision. Such review should be automatic. The reviewing authority should be authorized to accept the decision, order further proceedings, or reduce the sanction imposed.

Prison Social System

Erving Goffman (1961:xiii) defines a "total institution: as a place of residence and work where a large number of like-situated individuals, cut off from the wider society for an appreciable period of time, together lead an enclosed, formally administered round of life. Prisons serve as a clear example . . ." Considerable attention has been paid to this phenomenon, even though it may be argued by anyone who has studied prisons that, in many ways, they are anything but "closed." That is, as inmates can tell you, it is possible in most correctional facilities for an inmate to "purchase" almost anything he might desire—especially items which are considered "contraband," including drugs, alcohol, and other kinds of merchandise not normally available. This would suggest that the typical prison is really "open"—that is, one can purchase or otherwise obtain almost anything which is illicit or illegal.

But, the literature on the "total institution" concept generally discusses such issues as the prison culture, inmate-staff relationships, the inmate social system, the prison community, or the inmate subculture. (See for example, Cloward *et al.*, 1960; Cressey, 1966; Sykes, 1966; Carter, Glaser, and Wilkins, 1972; and Sutherland and Cressey, 1974). In effect, as Irwin (1970:67) suggests, ". . . studies of prison behavior (attempt to explain) . . . the convict social organization by posing the hypothetical question—how do convicts adapt to prison? It . . . (is) felt that this . . . (is) a relevant question because the prison is a situation of deprivation and degradation, and, therefore, presents extraordinary adaptive problems." These adaptations, according to Irwin, are based on the theoretical question every convict asks himself: "How shall I do my time?" Traditionally, the convict does it alone (by withdrawal or isolation) or collectively (with others as a group in opposition to the prison administration).

Whether or not an inmate chooses to do time alone or with others, it is commonly believed (Sykes, 1966:84–108) that everyone in prison begins to use special language or "argot"; ". . . different experiences mean a different language and the result—in prison, at least—is argot." Further (1966:84):

> The society of captives exhibits a number of distinctive tags for the distinctive social roles played by its members in response to the particular problems of imprisonment.

Sykes studied the New Jersey State Prison and devotes considerable attention in his book, *The Society of Captives*, to the various argot roles, including the following: Rats, Center Men, Squealer, Gorilla, Merchant, Pedlar, Fish, Wolves, Punks, Fags, Ball Buster, Real Men, Toughs, and Hipsters. Sykes (1966:107) maintains that as inmates work and speak together,

... the greater the extent of "cohesive" responses—the greater the degree to which the society of captives moves in the direction of inmate solidarity—the greater is the likelihood that the pains of imprisonment will be rendered less severe for the inmate population as a whole.

As a consequence of this inmate culture, the total organization of the prison, including the administration, recognizes the fact that there are certain "codes" to be followed. These are rules which govern staff-inmate contacts and behavioral expectations between and among inmates. They are codes which are not to be violated without penalty by fellow inmates. Those aspects of the "code" which reinforce the values of inmate solidarity apparently tend to be reinforced the most by inmates, but resented the most by administrators.

The Task Force Report: Corrections (1967:46-47), produced for the President's Crime Commission, discusses "inmate subcultures" and states:

Distance between staff and inmates is accentuated by forces that operate unofficially through inmates. Because staff have nearly absolute authority to punish or reward, inmates are especially concerned with keeping many of their activities covert. Accordingly, whenever an inmate communicates with staff, he runs the risk of being accused by his fellows of informing on them and thus of suffering violent reprisals.

It probably can be assumed that the kind of advice one prisoner gives to another (especially upon entry into the institution) is similar to the advice prison officials give to each other. As Sutherland and Cressey suggest (1974:534-535), this would include advice to be rational, stay "cool," and do not antagonize others. Glaser (1964: 98-100), in studying the federal prison system, asked inmates what kind of advice they most gave and most received. By and large, the most important piece of advice exchanged included: "Do your own time" and "Mind your own business."

Prison administrators depend upon the inmate code to maintain a quiet institution. In many ways, they support the various codes, help to develop and maintain inmate leadership, and "lean heavily" on those inmates who do not support the system. Inmate "elites" tend to have considerable power over fellow inmates, may receive "favored" treatment by correctional officers, may abuse fellow inmates more than guards or administrators do, and control the distribution of much of the "contraband" in the institution. Precisely how they operate depends upon the culture and tradition of the particular institution, the leadership and management abilities of the prison officials, the size of the institution, and the nature of the inmates (e.g., violent and/or in a maximum security facility).

Sutherland and Cressey summarize the situation in the contemporary large American prison (1974:536–537):

> One of the amazing things about prisons is that they "work" at all. Any prison is made up of the synchronized actions of hundreds of people, some of whom hate and distrust each other, love each other, fight each other physically and psychologically, think of each other as stupid or mentally disturbed, "manage" and "control" each other, and vie with each other for favors, prestige, power, and money. Often the personnel involved do not know with whom they are competing or cooperating and are not sure whether they are the managers or the managed . . . Somehow the personnel, including the prisoners, are bound together enough so that most conflicts and misunderstandings are not crucial . . . and the prison continues to "work." Viewed in this way, the prison is a microcosm of the larger society which has created it and which maintains it, for this larger society also is a unit which continues to "work" despite numerous individual disagreements, misunderstandings, antagonisms, and conflicts.

References

Alper, Benedict S.
  1974   Prisons Inside-Out: Alternatives in Correctional Reform. Cambridge: Ballinger.
American Correctional Association
  1973   Directory of Juvenile and Adult Correction Institutions and Agencies. College Park, Maryland: ACA.
  1966   Manual of Correctional Standards. 3rd ed. College Park, Maryland: ACA.
American Friends Service Committee
  1971   Struggle For Justice. New York: Hill and Wang.
Beaumont, Gustave de and Alexis de Tocqueville
  1964   On the Penitentiary System in the United States and Its Application in France. Carbondale: Southern Illinois University Press.
California Assembly
  1969   Report on the Economic Status and Rehabilitative Value of California Correctional Industries. Sacramento: California Legislature, Office of Research.
Carter, Robert M., Daniel Glaser, and Leslie T. Wilkins (eds.)
  1972   Correctional Institutions. Philadelphia: J.B. Lippincott Co.

Cloward, Richard A. *et al.*
  1960   Theoretical Studies in Social Organization of the Prison. New York: Social Science Research Council.
Cohn, Alvin W.
  1973   "Failure of Correctional Management." Crime and Delinquency 19 (July) 3:323-331.
Cohn, Alvin W. and Dennis Sullivan
  1972   "Halfway Houses: Panacea or Palliative?" Unpublished paper prepared for National Criminal Justice Reference Service, Law Enforcement Assistance Administration. Washington, D.C. (Mimeo).
Cressey, Donald R. (ed.)
  1966   The Prison: Studies in Institutional Organization and Change. New York: Holt, Rinehart and Winston.
Flynn, Edith Elizabeth
  1973   "Jails and Criminal Justice." In Lloyd E. Ohlin (ed.). Prisoners in America. Englewood Cliffs: Prentice-Hall: 49-85.
Fox, Vernon
  1972   Introduction to Corrections. Englewood Cliffs: Prentice-Hall.
Glaser, Daniel
  1964   The Effectiveness of a Prison and Parole System. Indianapolis: Bobbs-Merrill.
Goffman, Erving
  1961   Asylums: Essays on the Social Situation of Mental Patients and Other Inmates. New York: Doubleday.
Hindelang, Michael J., C.S. Dunn, L.P. Sutton, and A.L. Aumick
  1973   Sourcebook of Criminal Justice Statistics 1973. Washington, D.C.: Law Enforcement Assistance Administration.
Holbrook, Stewart H.
  1957   Dreamers of the American Dream. New York: Doubleday.
Irwin, John
  1970   The Felon. Englewood Cliffs: Prentice-Hall.
Keller, Oliver J., Jr. and Benedict S. Alper
  1970   Halfway Houses: Community-Centered Correction and Treatment. Lexington: Health Lexington Books.
Korn, Richard R. and Lloyd W. McCorkle
  1965   Criminology and Penology. New York: Holt, Rinehart & Winston.
Liepmann, Morris
  1928   "American Prisons and Reformatories; a Report." Mental Hygiene 12:231-232.
Lopez-Rey, Manuel
  1958   "Some Considerations on the Character and Organization of Prison Labor." Journal of Criminal Law, Criminology and Police Science 49:10-28.
McCartt, John M. and Thomas J. Mangogna
  1973   Guidelines and Standards for Halfway Houses and Community Treatment Centers. Washington, D.C.: Law Enforcement Assistance Administration.

McKelvey, Blake
> 1972   American Prisons. Montclair: Patterson Smith. (Original, 1936).

Morris, Norval
> 1974   The Future of Imprisonment. Chicago: University of Chicago Press.

National Advisory Commission on Criminal Justice Standards and Goals
> 1973   Corrections. Washington, D.C.: U.S. Government Printing Office.

National Jail Census: 1970
> 1971   A Report on the Nation's Local Jails and Types of Inmates. Washington, D.C.: Law Enforcement Assistance Administration.

President's Commission on Law Enforcement and Administration of Justice
Task Force Report
> 1967   Corrections. Washington, D.C.: U.S. Government Printing Office.

Prestbo, John A.
> 1972   "A Helping Hand: Halfway Houses Draw Both Praise, Criticism for Care of Ex-Cons." Wall Street Journal, March 3: 1.

Rothman, David J.
> 1971   The Discovery of the Asylum. Boston: Little, Brown & Co.

Sellin, Thorsten
> 1964   "Introduction." In Beaumont, Gustave de and Alexis de Tocqueville. On The Penitentiary System in the United States and Its Application in France. Carbondale: Southern Illinois University Press: xv–xl.

Sutherland, Edwin H. and Donald R. Cressey
> 1974   Criminology. 9th ed. Philadelphia: J.B. Lippincott Co.

Sykes, Gresham M.
> 1966   The Society of Captives: A Study of a Maximum Security Prison. New York: Atheneum.

Takagi, Paul
> 1974   "The Correctional System." Crime and Social Justice 2 (Fall–Winter): 82–89.

Tannenbaum, Frank
> 1938   Crime and the Community. New York: Columbia University Press.

U.S. Bureau of Prisons
> 1964   Annual Report. Washington, D.C.: U.S. Government Printing Office.

U.S. Department of Justice
> 1970   National Prisoner Statistics. Washington, D.C.: U.S. Government Printing Office.

CHAPTER 16

PAROLE

Early History

The classic definition of parole is provided in the Attorney General's Survey of Release Procedures in 1939 (Vol. IV:4): "release of an offender from a penal or correctional institution, after he has served a portion of his sentence, under the continued custody of the state and under conditions that permit his reincarceration in the event of misbehavior." As the National Advisory Commission on Criminal Justice Standards and Goals (*Corrections*, 1973:390) states, while some jurisdictions impose limitations on the use of parole, offenders throughout the country generally can be paroled, but repeatedly returned to confinement for parole violation "until the term of their original confinement has expired." In effect, parole can last as long as the original sentence would have lasted.

It is commonly thought that parole in the United States was developed in the 1840s as a direct result of European and Australian measures of ticket-of-leave and license. The former Chairman of the New York State Board of Parole, Frederick A. Moran, writing in the 1945 (71) *Yearbook of the National Probation Association*, states that this is a misconception:

> Parole did not develop from any specific source of experiment, but is an outgrowth of a number of independent measures, including the conditional pardon, apprenticeship by indenture, the transportation of criminals to America and Australia, the English and Irish experiences with the system of ticket of leave, and the work of American prison reformers during the nineteenth century.

According to Rubin (1973:620–622), some elements of contemporary parole as a method of conditional release are found in the model developed by Captain Alexander Maconochie in 1840 who was then head of England's penal colony at Norfolk Island. This was a system that was devised after the transportation system (sending convicted offenders off to other countries—especially colonies) proved to be a failure:

> Maconochie found that a man under a time sentence thinks only how he is to cheat that time, and while it away; he evades labor, because he has no interest in it whatever, and he has no desires to please the officers under whom he is placed, because they cannot serve him essentially; they cannot in any way promote his liberation.

Maconochie developed a system whereby prisoners would be awarded marks for industry, labor, and good conduct which could be used to earn their way out of confinement. The number of marks required for such release depended, in part, upon the original offense for which the offender had been convicted and was balanced by the loss of marks whenever the prisoner misbehaved. The Attorney General's Survey (1939:10) adds that a second feature of Maconochie's system was the series of four stages leading to freedom. The first stage was absolute confinement and adherence to rigid disciplinary rules. The second was participation in government chain gangs. The third was limited liberty within a confined area, while the last was a grant of ticket-of-leave for conditional freedom, followed finally by absolute freedom.

Rubin (1973:621) comments that despite Maconochie's optimism about the system of marks and progressive stages of freedom, the plan was neither widely followed, even at Norfolk, nor subsequently adopted in England to any great extent. It is assumed that its principal flaw was the lack of supervision over the released exconvicts which, apparently, was remedied to some extent first by Sir Joshua Jebb in 1846 and then by Sir Walter Crofton, who in 1854 became the director of the Irish prison system.

Crofton followed a plan of progressive stages of liberty for the convicts and upon being granted a ticket-of-leave, the convict was also given a list of specific and rather restrictive conditions of liberty. If any of the conditions were violated, the authorities would be able to revoke the liberty. In addition to being subject to reincarceration, the liberated prisoner also had to make periodic reports to police officials.

Giardini (1959:7–9) reports that Crofton made full use of the Penal Servitude Act, which provided three stages of penal treatment. The last of these was ticket-of-leave granted on the basis of visible evidence the inmate had been reformed in prison. The Act also provided for revocation of license upon failure to abide by the conditions, and return to prison. In spite of these advances in the conditional release of prisoners, there still remained the basic weakness of lack of supervision of the releasee—a weakness which apparently was recognized in the Australian experiment. Just as occurs today, this lack was brought to the attention of the public as a result of an outbreak of serious crimes shortly after the ticket-of-leave became widely used. As a consequence, the police were used for supervision. Later, the police were assisted in this process by prisoners' aid societies, which were partly subsidized by the government.

Some of the root concepts of what we call parole today, according to Giardini (1959:8), were introduced in some of the European penal codes of the 16th and 17th centuries. Commutation was first used as a sort of pardon. Later, it was used as an incentive for good behavior in prison enabling the prisoner to earn unconditional discharge before the expiration of the sentence. This is the origin of the "good time" concept, a device which was used in the Amsterdam Tuchthuys between 1599 and 1603, with juvenile offenders in France in 1832, besides being adopted in the 1805 Cadiz Code in Spain and in a general code in 1807, and later used by Maconochie and Crofton.

The indeterminate sentence, which serves in part as the forerunner of parole, goes as far back as the Middle Ages, where it was conceived as a means of securing social protection against habitual offenders. As a concept whereby offenders could be detained for as long as the authorities wished (without any fixed sentence), it was first introduced in the Code of 1532 under Charles V of Germany and again in the Code of 1768 of Maria Theresa. It appeared in similar form in the Colonial Law of Connecticut in 1769. Giardini comments on the future course of the indeterminate sentence and its relationship to parole (1959:8-9):

> The indeterminate sentence idea became quite widespread in Europe and especially in Germany, but disappeared in the middle of the 19th century. Montesinos in Spain . . . in 1835 and Obermaier in Germany between 1830 and 1862 not only made use of the indeterminate sentence, but also introduced vocational trades. Obermaier seems to have been far ahead of his time in the use of reformative treatment. Under his regime, release from prison was determined largely by evidence of reformation. He also introduced supervision after release by agencies other than the police. In 1837 he suggested the organization of prisoners' aid societies . . . These were sponsored by the government and were composed of volunteer workers who supervised and cared for released prisoners.

Parole in the United States

It is not possible to understand the development of parole in the United States apart from the development of prison societies and the indeterminate sentence. Although churches had been active in dealing with those who were "afflicted," sick, or in prison, it appears that in the United States the first secular organization to be developed to help people in prison was in 1776 and was known as the Philadelphia Society for Assisting Distressed Prisoners. Its purpose was to collect and distribute food and clothes for prisoners in the local jail. The American Revolution interrupted its program so it disbanded after only 19 months of work. However, it was reorganized in 1787 under the name of The Philadelphia Society for Alleviating the Miseries of Public Prisons and later became known as the Pennsylvania Prison Society. The work of the Society spread and provided impetus for the development of similar groups throughout the Northeast, including the Boston Prison Discipline Society, New Jersey Howard Society, the Prisoners' Friend Association of Boston, and the Prison Association of New York. These organizations were very active in prison reform and the amelioration of criminal procedures in general. Their growth also coincided with changes in penal laws and practices as Positive criminology developed. In 1870, representatives of many groups met in Cincinnati under the name of the American Prison Association (now known as the American Correctional Association) and adopted a set of "Principles" which were reaffirmed in 1970 at the Centennial meeting of the ACA.

An early principle of shortening the term of imprisonment as a reward for good conduct found legal recognition in the New York "good time" law of 1817. This is a concept which has been made legal in every political jurisdiction in the United States today, the last law having been passed in Maryland in 1916. The indeterminate sentence was first introduced with the establishment of the Houses of Refuge for children in New York City in 1825. "This furnished another pattern of shortening the time served in the institution on the basis of good conduct. The same means of motivating good conduct during incarceration had been used with adult offenders in England and on the continent" (Giardini, 1959:10).

These early forms of conditional release set a pattern which is still followed in corrections: if the prisoner will behave and not make trouble, the authorities will reward such behavior with reduced time in prison. Additionally, as a result of prior experiences, another pattern developed which demanded that prisoners agree to a contract with the releasing authority regarding postrelease behavior. Today it is called a *parole agreement* and most jurisdictions require the parolee actually to sign such an agreement. Among the conditions to which the released convict had to agree (and which is still practiced today) was the recognition that if the terms and conditions were violated or abridged in any way, the parolee would be returned to the institution to finish the original sentence.

To assist the ex-prisoner in adjusting to society and to avoid being returned to prison, most releasing authorities eventually provided some form of supervision, generally by volunteers. Children who had been released from Houses of Refuge tended to be supervised by their "masters," for they were in effect indentured. Adults generally were not indentured, but were "supervised" by volunteers in the community, who were usually members of prison societies. As early as 1822, the Philadelphia Society for Alleviating the Miseries of Public Prisons recognized the importance of caring for discharged prisoners, but it was not until 1851 that the Society appointed two agents actually to supervise men who had been released from the

Philadelphia County Prison and the Penitentiary. It was at this time, too, that the use of the word "parole" replaced "conditional liberation" as the process for shortening imprisonment. Dr. S.G. Howe of Boston is alleged to have been the first person to use the term. He wrote a letter to the Prison Association of New York in 1846 (Killinger, 1951:361) and said:

> I believe there are many prisoners who might be so trained as to be left upon their parole during the last period of their imprisonment with safety.

Killinger (1951:361) goes on to say that the word is derived from the French word *parole*, and is used in the sense of "word of honor," *parole d'honneur*. "The choice of the word as adopted in America was a very unfortunate one, and it is not surprising that the French prefer the term 'conditional liberation' to the one we have borrowed from them."

Massachusetts was the first state to arrange for a salaried public employee to supervise parolees, for it was in 1845 when the state appointed an agent to assist released prisoners in obtaining employment, tools, clothing, and transportation—and with the aid of public funds. However, the experiment in Massachusetts did not catch on and it was many years later before releasing authorities were able to depend upon public employees to supervise and otherwise "manage" those persons released early from imprisonment.

The first indeterminate sentence law was passed in Michigan in 1869 at the instigation of Zebulon R. Brockway, a well-known penologist. The law was declared unconstitutional, but after Brockway became Superintendent at the Elmira Reformatory in 1876, he was successful in having a similar law passed in New York which was upheld as constitutional. Thus, a complete correctional process was established for the first time. Giardini (1951:11) states:

> (The law) ... comprised not only the use of the indeterminate sentence, but also a system of grading the inmates, compulsory education, and a careful system of selection for parole. Supervision of the released prisoners was provided by volunteer citizens who were known as guardians. One of the conditions of parole was that the parolee must report to the guardian on the first of each month. Later, written reports were required and submitted to the institution after they had been countersigned by the employer and the guardian.

The basic principles of parole, as spelled out in the first law, have been carried through the years and serve as the basis of much of contemporary parole philosophy in the United States. Dressler (1959: 55–56) spells out these basic and original principles in considerable detail:

1. Offenders are reformable. This simple assertion is the core of parole philosophy. If people cannot be helped to change for the better, why spend money on parole?

2. Reformation is the right of every convict and the duty of the state. Revolutionary doctrine! Most people felt that criminals had no rights and the one duty of the state was to punish them.

3. Every prisoner must be individualized. The emphasis would be upon the offender, not the offense.

4. Time must be given the reformatory process to take effect. If faith in Elmira was justified, if it had something to offer, then the emphasis should not be upon rushing a man out, but on helping him get the maximum benefits while he is inside. Teaching a trade, schooling, treating attitudes—these would take time.

5. The prisoner's cure is always facilitated by his cooperation and often impossible without it. Today, we are chary of the word "cure" in this context, for we are not sure whether or when it has been effected. Nevertheless, contemporary penologists approve the general principle.

6. No other form of reward and punishment is so effective as transfer from one custodial class to another, with different privileges in each, but the most important agency for gaining a prisoner's cooperation is the power possessed by the administrators to lengthen or shorten the term of incarceration. That called for a program of parole. At Elmira, it was patterned on the Irish system.

7. Finally, the reformatory process is educational. That means more than instructional. It includes the concept of re-education of attitudes, motivation, behavior.

Although the indeterminate sentence served as the forerunner to parole as we know it today, especially as the reformatory movement developed, parole legislation in the United States spread much more rapidly than the indeterminate sentence. In fact, the latter did not regain its popularity until well into the 20th century and then mostly for youthful offenders. Most of the early parole laws empowered the governors of the states to attach conditions for early release from prison, with wardens authorized to technically violate parolees if the terms and conditions of such release were not followed. The first state-wide law relating to parole of adults by an agent or agency other than the governor was passed in Ohio in 1884.

By 1901, 20 states had parole laws while only 11 states had indeterminate sentence laws. Today, every state, the District of Columbia, and the federal government have parole laws for adults as well as for youths (generally known as aftercare procedures).

According to the Attorney General's Survey of Release Procedures, prior to 1939, when the Survey was completed, the United States could be divided into three geographic regions according to the extent to which parole was being utilized as a conditional release from prison: (1) the Eastern-Midwestern region, where parole was uniformly and widely used; (2) the Western-Pacific area, where parole was used intermittently; and (3) the Southern area, where parole was used hardly at all. Paradoxically, the Survey also revealed that wherever the indeterminate sentence prevailed, parole was used most widely.

Parole and Other Forms of Conditional Release

We have previously defined parole as the release of an offender from a penal or correctional institution after he has served a portion of his sentence, under the continued custody of the state, and under conditions that permit his reincarceration in the event of misbehavior. As developed by Brockway, Maconochie, and Crofton, parole is only one of several methods by which an offender can be released from an institution on a conditional basis. This is in addition to release upon expiration of sentence—that is, the offender remains incarcerated until the end of his term according to the sentence of the court, minus any "good time" which he may have obtained as a result of "good behavior."

Parole is different from *pardon*, according to Rubin (1973: 623), in that (1) it is usually administered by an executive board, whereas pardon is administered by the governor; (2) parole occurs only after imprisonment, whereas pardon can occur both before and after imprisonment; and (3) parole does not denote forgiveness or (usually) restore the prisoner to his civil rights, whereas a pardon forgives a prisoner.

> The granting of parole is merely permission to a prisoner to serve a portion of his sentence outside the walls of the prison. He continues to be in the custody of the authorities, both legally and actually, and is still under re-

straint. The sentence is in full force and at any time when he does not comply with the conditions upon which he was released, or does not conduct himself properly, he may be returned, for his own good, and in the public interest.

Parole legislation does not in any way infringe upon a governor's right to pardon, but in the early days of parole, the courts did not always distinguish so clearly between the two. In *People* v. *Cummings*, the Supreme Court of Michigan in 1891 struck down legislation creating a parole authority and said: "It is claimed that the pardoning power is not granted to the board of control by this statute, because there is no authority to discharge prisoners absolutely conferred upon the board . . . If they have the power to release on a condition, those conditions may be made so trifling as to be in fact no conditions at all."

Parole, which can occur only after an offender has served some time in a correctional facility, is always granted by a releasing authority, which is administratively housed in the executive branch of government, insofar as adults are concerned. Parole may be similar to *probation* in that the offender remains in the community under supervision. However, it differs from probation in that probation is always a form of sentence granted by a judge, under which the probationer does not serve any prison time if he successfully serves his probation term. In some jurisdictions, statutes enable judges to provide *split sentences* in which an offender is simultaneously sentenced to a term of imprisonment and probation. In Ohio, as we have discussed, recent legislation known as "Shock Parole" allows the release of an offender under sentence to prison, upon authorization by the paroling authorities, to a term of parole. The basis for this legislation is literally to "shock" an offender into recognition of the hardships of prison and to enable him to appreciate what freedom is. Hopefully it also provides, through this dramatic technique, sufficient "willingness" to want to be rehabilitated and live a law-abiding life in the community.

Clemency refers to the pardoning power of any chief of state (Governor or President) for a prisoner within the political jurisdiction. It may be initiated by the executive, but, more often, a prisoner files a formal petition with the executive, who then asks some member of his staff or a correctional authority to investigate the case and make appropriate recommendations. It is not a method commonly used for release in the United States, but is used to correct unduly severe sentences, for mitigating circumstances, where guilt is dubious, because of physical or mental conditions of the prisoner, for turning state's evidence, for political reasons, or to avert the death penalty. Where clemency is used, it frequently reduces the length of prison sentence and/or allows the prisoner to be released on parole.

Amnesty is viewed as a general pardon and is extended to groups of persons without regard to the nature of the individual case. It is generally granted for political purposes and may occur when a legislature passes a law covering specific groups of persons. Amnesty may also be used to release large numbers of prisoners and is more frequently utilized in other countries (especially for political purposes) than in the United States.

A *reprieve* is a respite or postponement of the execution of a sentence, "usually granted in order that time and opportunity may be had for final action on an application for pardon" (Rubin, 1973: 669). The main use of reprieve historically has been to stay execution of a death penalty, pending action on application for pardon or commutation or on allegations of newly discovered evidence. *Commutation* is another act of "mercy" which is available to a chief executive which lessens the punishment of the original sentence, usually where imprisonment has been ordered. It is not too different from pardon and has three main purposes (Rubin, 1973:670):

> ... (1) to make eligible for parole those who were excluded from eligibility under their original sentence, (2) to make immediately eligible for parole those who are not yet eligible, and (3) to avoid the death penalty. In some states, persons under life sentences are not eligible for parole, despite the fact that many "lifers" are good parole risks.

Rubin reports that one group for whom commutation has been sought in recent years, especially by some judges and United States Attorneys, are those who have been convicted under the federal narcotics control laws, given extraordinarily long sentences, and who are denied the possibility of parole. It is argued that in view of the changing values and beliefs about narcotics use, especially by youthful offenders, they should be eligible for parole in order to have greater rehabilitative opportunities. These efforts have not met with particular success, but it appears that some paroling authorities are taking such matters into greater consideration and releasing these youthful offenders at early dates, where possible and legal.

Organization of Parole Systems

There have been three, or perhaps four, basic stages of centralization of parole services in the United States. At the earliest, parole decision-making and administration was vested in the warden or superintendent of the correctional facility from which the inmate was released. As penal administration became more centralized, paroling power was transferred from individual institutions (which were themselves frequently autonomous) to state departments of correction. The third trend has been toward the creation of parole boards that are completely autonomous and independent of departments of correction and whose members are answerable only to the appointing authority, usually the governor of the state. In this kind of an organization, the paroling authority is responsible for decision-making and policy setting, but the actual delivery of parole services is generally administered by the department of correction. A possible fourth stage is one that overlaps the latter considerably, but is one in which a state authority, in the executive branch of government, combines both probation and parole services and actually delivers such community based services as well.

This trend toward centralization is both defended and attacked, according to Korn and McCorkle (1965:611), because of the two distinct functions which parole involves—selection and supervision:

> *Selection* of inmates to be paroled involves a range of decisions dealing not only with whom to parole and when to parole but with the effects of the release on the inmate, the institution and the community. *Supervision* of paroled inmates involves a different range of decisions and responsibilities and requires personnel who are trained to deal with the paroled offender in a looser, freer situation and who are equipped with knowledge of the local community to which he will return. These different responsibilities and functions must be recognized as underlying any discussion of parole administration.

Those who argue in favor of "local" parole decision-making assert that since the parolee is to return to a specific community and for a specific "treatment program," members of the institutional staff are best equipped to determine when the offender should be released. It is further argued that even if the paroling authority utilizes institutional reports to make its decision about the release of the offender, full knowledge and understanding of the offender's adjustment and behavior in the institution cannot possibly be recorded. Those who argue in favor of centralization of parole decision-making state that the institution should not have such complete power that they not only supervise an inmate's daily behavior during the period of his incarceration, but that they can also control when the inmate will be released from the institution. Further, it is argued, a centralized parole authority is better equipped to monitor the temper of the communities being served and thereby afford society a greater degree of protection in terms of who shall be released, and when, than could possibly occur if institutional staffs made release decisions.

This argument does not rage on as a full-fledged battle, since every state has some kind of centralized authority for adult parole. In the case of juveniles, the situation is quite the reverse, for even though many states have centralized authorities for dealing with juvenile aftercare (parole), decisions regarding when a youth will be released are generally made by institutional staffs (even though higher authorities may have to confirm the decisions). The President's Crime Commission, in fact, reports that 34 of 50 states use this form (institutional) of organization in the juvenile aftercare field. (For more discussion on juvenile aftercare, see Chapter 13.)

In the field of adult parole, every state has an identifiable and separate parole authority, although in four states the power of these authorities is limited to recommending a disposition to the governor. According to the President's Crime Commission (*Corrections*, 1967: 65), in 41 states the parole board is an independent agency; in 7 states it is a unit within a larger department within the state; and in 2 states it is the same agency that regulates correctional institutions. "In no jurisdiction in the adult field is the final power to grant or deny parole given to the staff directly involved in the operation of a correctional institution."

The Parole Board

Although all parole boards are concerned with making decisions about who shall be released from institutions and when this release should occur, most parole boards also have a number of other responsibilities assigned to them by governors or legislatures. Table 16.1 summarizes these responsibilities.

As Table 16.1 illustrates, only five parole boards are free of extramural responsibilities, while approximately one-half of all state

TABLE 16.1. Responsibilities of Adult Paroling Agencies
Other Than Parole, 1965.

Additional Responsibility	Number of Boards
Holds clemency hearings	28
Commutes sentences	24
Appoints parole supervision staff	24
Administers parole service	20
Paroles from local institutions	19
Grants or withholds "good time"	17
Supervises probation service	14
Grants pardons, restorations, and remissions	1
Fixes maximum sentence after 6 months	1
May discharge prior to sentence expiration	1
Sets standards for "good time"	1
Acts as advisory board on pardons	1
None	5

Source: National Council on Crime and Delinquency. Correction in the United States. New York: NCCD, 1967:215.

boards are concerned with clemency and commutation issues. In 43 states, the board has full and exclusive power to grant and revoke paroles; in the others, the board is advisory or has limited authority. As for the board's location within the governmental structure, the President's Crime Commission reports that in 41 states, the board is an independent state agency; in the other states, it is part of a larger state department except in one state where the board of institutions also serves as the parole board.

As is shown in Table 16.2, in 23 states the members of the parole boards serve in a full-time capacity, with the range in numbers of persons who sit on the board being 3 to 10. Table 16.3 illustrates the terms of office of parole board members in 51 jurisdictions (all states and the District of Columbia). While the range extends from the pleasure of the governor to life, most appointments are for six years—a term which tends to overlap the terms of the governors. All parole board members are appointed by the governor in 39 states, while in 4 states the appointment is made by a combination of the governor and other officials. In 1 state, 2 members of the board are appointed by the governor and 3 are ex-officio. In 3 states, the board consists entirely of ex-officio officials. In another 3 states, the board is appointed by the state correction agency and by the director of the state welfare department in 1 other state. According to the

TABLE 16.2. Number of Full-Time and Part-Time Boards and Number
of Members, According to Population

	Number of Boards			Range in Number of Board Members		
	Full[a] Time	Part Time	Combi- nation	Full Time	Part Time	Combi- nation
Largest States (10)	8	1	1	3–10	7	3
Medium States (20)	13	5	2	3– 5	3–6	5–7
Smallest States (21)	2	19	0	3– 5	3–7	–
Totals	23	25	3	3–10	3–7	5–7

[a]In a few instances, members are employed full time in the correctional system but devote only part of their time to board functions.

Source: National Council on Crime and Delinquency. Correction in the United States. New York: NCCD, 1967:215.

NCCD Survey (1967:217), the median salary for parole board members is in the $13,000 to $17,000 range, although in 1976 the average is thought to approximate $19,000.

Selection for Parole

It is estimated that approximately 60 percent of all adult felons in the United States are released on parole prior to the expiration of the maximum term of their sentences. There is considerable variation in the use of parole, however, for some states utilize parole less than 20 percent of the time (e.g., Oklahoma, South Carolina, and Wyoming), while others grant parole 100 percent of the time for those so eligible (e.g., New Hampshire and Washington), according to the President's Crime Commission, *Corrections*, 1967:60–61.

There is considerable variation in the process by which paroling authorities determine who shall be paroled, but two considerations, at least, affect the decision-making process. These include the offender's parole *eligibility* and his *suitability* for parole. The first consideration is affected by statutes which frequently govern minimum length of sentence, accumulated "good time," and parole board traditions which may dictate (unless specified by law) how much time an inmate must serve before being eligible for parole. Suitability,

TABLE 16.3. Term of Office of Parole Board Members, by Number of States

Term of Office	Number of States
Pleasure of Governor	2
During Term of Office*	1
2 Years	3
3 Years	2
4 Years	11
5 Years	4
6 Years	21
7 Years	1
12 Years	1
Life	5
	51

*Applies to board composed of elected officials.
Source: National Council on Crime and Delinquency. Correction in the United States. New York: NCCD, 1967:215.

on the other hand, is determined mostly by an assessment by the paroling authorities of the inmate's institutional performance, likelihood of adjusting to societal demands upon institutional release, and such other factors associated with the inmate's background and life style that might indicate the likelihood of continued criminal activity. The philosophies and kinds of information which are utilized in making parole decisions vary considerably among the jurisdictions.

Table 16.4 also points out the variation in use of parole, for, on a regional basis, the Southern states utilized parole only 44 percent of the time in 1964, while the Northeast utilized parole 82 percent of the time. Furthermore, as Table 16.5 illustrates, the average length of the parole period also varies, with the South imposing a relatively long period of parole (37 months) and the Midwest only an average of 20 months.

It is at a *hearing* that the parole decision-making process occurs, even though the final decision may be made at a later date. Typically, the parole board meets at the institution to conduct release (and revocation) hearings. At the institution hearing, the inmate generally makes a personal appearance before the board. In some jurisdictions, institutional staff and/or the parole officer may also be present. If a parole officer is present, the "pre-release" plan for the inmate is personally discussed. In only a few jurisdictions is the parole hearing open to the public. The extent to which parole boards engage in for-

TABLE 16.4. Prison Population and Number of Releases, in 1964, by Regions

Region	Prison Population	All Releases		Parole or Conditional Releases	
		Number	Percentage of Prison Population	Number	Percentage of All Releases
Northeast	35,141	16,374	47%	13,458	82%
North Central	48,844	23,459	48%	17,506	75%
South	68,711	36,123	53%	15,746	44%
West	39,951	15,577	39%	12,322	79%
Totals	192,647	91,533	47%	59,032	65%

Source: National Council on Crime and Delinquency. Correction in the United States. New York: NCCD, 1967:214.

TABLE 16.5. Average Length of Parole Period, 1965, by Regions

Region	Average Parole Period
East and Northeast	31 months
Midwest and Plains	20 months
Border South	28 months
South	37 months
West	24 months
Insular	39 months
National	29 months

Source: National Council on Crime and Delinquency. Correction in the United States. New York: NCCD, 1967:215.

mal or informal processes during the hearings also varies considerably. In some states, the board meets *en banc*, which means the entire board sits as a panel to make decisions. In others, it meets as a "panel," with members of the board working as teams. The panel may include from one to three members. Some jurisdictions now utilize *parole examiners* or *hearing officers* to assist in some aspects of the hearing and they may even make specific suggestions to the board regarding parole recommendations. These examiners or officers may interview inmates, collect pertinent information, and forward "findings" to the parole board, which then makes a final parole determination.

For the most part, paroling authorities must rely on others for information about the inmates being considered for parole. Assuming that the information about the background of the offender, criminal record, institutional adjustment, and potential for adjustment in the community upon release is accurate, parole officials must still face the task of evaluating the information and putting it all together. As the President's Crime Commission states (*Corrections*, 1967:63), "One method, by far the most common, is for the decision-maker to depend basically on his own judgment of the circumstances in an individual case."

Board Member Orientations

In designing a series of training programs for parole board members, O'Leary and Hall (1963) addressed this issue of personal judgment by utilizing an exercise known as "Frames of Reference in Parole." With information collected from a number of parole board members, the authors were able to construct an inventory describing five basic value systems or orientations which affect the decision-making process concerning the granting of parole. They include:

> *The Jurist Value System.* Emphasis from this orientation reflects an attitude that the parole process is part of the mainstream of American criminal justice. It is sensitive to concepts such as due process, appeal, rules of evidence, impartiality, and the protection of individual rights.
> *The Sanctionor Value System.* The emphasis from this orientation is upon exacting equitable penalties for criminal offenses. It also reflects itself in assuming a responsibility for exacting penalties for failure to adhere to acceptable behavior defined for inmates and parolees.
> *The Evaluator Value System.* This orientation focuses on the individual case and the determination of the risk and rehabilitative potential of a given individual. Its major premise involves a sensitivity to the various factors involved in assigning risks and maximizing potential success.
> *The Citizen Value System.* This orientation reflects itself in concern for the maintenance of community harmony and the preservation of social order. It also reflects itself in a special sensitivity to the desires of the citizenry and to their expectations regarding the handling of convicted persons.
> *The Regulator Value System.* This orientation reflects a concern about the effect of the parole board's decision on the prison system. It is also sensitive to the powerful influence of its decision on the treatment of inmates and the reaction of inmates to those decisions.

O'Leary (1966:162–163) also examined a number of considerations which "consciously and significantly" affect parole decision-makers in determining parole for inmates. As Table 16.6 indicates, parole board members' concern over potential criminal behavior is the most serious consideration, while colleague reaction to decisions appears to be the least influential factor.

Board Activities

How busy the parole boards are in conducting hearings varies from state to state, not only in terms of procedures, but in terms of the numbers of cases which must be handled. As Table 16.7 indicates, some parole boards hear an average of 40 cases per day, while others average less than 20.

The workload is also affected by the nature of the parole hearing itself. As Table 16.8 shows, some jurisdictions permit counsel to be present at the hearings, witnesses to present testimony, and some require a verbatim record of the proceedings be made.

When making a decision to grant or deny parole, the board generally has before it the complete file on the inmate. This usually includes the original pre-sentence investigation and some form of parole plan prepared by a parole officer in which details about the inmate's plans for living and working in a specific community are outlined and, frequently, assessed. Table 16.9 also illustrates that length of time served in prison has some effect on parole decisions, whether by tradition or statute.

In evaluating the pre-release plan, the drafters of the Model Penal Code (American Law Institute, 1962) proposed some criteria to serve as guidelines in parole decision-making:

Model Penal Code

(Proposed Official Draft, 1962)
Section 305.9 Criteria for Determining Date of First Release on Parole.

1. Whenever the Board of Parole considers the first release of a prisoner who is eligible for release on parole, it shall be the policy of the Board to order his release, unless the Board is of the opinion that his release should be deferred because:
a. there is substantial risk that he will not conform to the conditions of parole; or

TABLE 16.6. Considerations Affecting Parole Board Member Decisions
A. Estimates by 100 randomly selected parole board members of the percentage of cases that they heard in the past year in which various considerations affected "consciously and significantly" their decisions to grant or deny parole; B. Designations by these board members of "the five most important" of these considerations "for a parole board member," regardless of the frequency with which they were considered.

Considerations	A. Median percent of cases in which this consideration consciously and significantly influenced their decision	B. Percent of board members including it as one of the five most important considerations
1. My estimate of the chances that the prisoner would or would not commit a serious crime if paroled.	79.4	92.8
2. My judgment that the prisoner would become a worse risk if confined longer.	13.6	71.9
3. My judgment that the prisoner would benefit from further experience in the institution program, or at any rate, would become a better risk if confined longer.	27.6	87.1
4. My judgment that the prisoner had already been punished enough to "pay" for his crime.	13.3	43.2
5. What I thought the reaction of the local police might be if the prisoner were granted parole.	3.0	12.2
6. What I thought the reaction of the press, radio and TV might be if the prisoner were granted parole.	3.5	8.6
7. What I thought the reaction of the judge might be if the prisoner were granted parole.	7.5	20.9
8. What I thought the reaction of other prisoners might be to the policy which they might ascribe to me from my decision in a particular case.	3.7	12.2
9. What I thought the reaction of prison officials might be to my decision in a particular case.	3.1	5.0

TABLE 16.6, continued

	A. Median percent of cases in which this consideration consciously and significantly influenced their decision	B. Percent of board members including it as one of the five most important considerations
10. My feelings about how my decision in this case would affect the feelings or welfare of the prisoner's relatives or dependents.	9.2	33.8
11. What I thought the consequences of my decision policy might be in getting legislative support for the parole system's requests.	0*	7.9
12. What I thought the consequences of my decision policy might be for the governor or for other officials in the executive branch of government.	0.4†	8.6
13. What I thought would be the reactions of my colleagues on the parole board.	0‡	9.4
14. The probability that the prisoner would be a misdemeanant and a burden to his parole supervisors, even if he did not commit any serious offenses on parole.	8.9	35.3

*61 percent of the board members said this was not a consideration in any case.
†49 percent of the board members said this was not a consideration in any case.
‡58 percent of the board members said this was not a consideration in any case.
Source: O'Leary, Vincent. Selection for Parole. New York: National Parole Institutes, National Council on Crime and Delinquency, 1966:162–163.

TABLE 16.7. Average Number of Cases Heard Per Day During Parole Consideration Hearings: 51 Jurisdictions,* Felony Offenders

Average Number of Cases Heard Per Day	Number of Parole Boards
1–19	11
20–29	15
30–39	14
40 and over	11

*Excludes Georgia, Hawaii, and Texas, where no parole hearings are conducted.
Source: Vincent O'Leary and Joan Nuffield. The Organization of Parole Systems in the United States. 2nd ed. Hackensack, N.J.: National Council on Crime and Delinquency, 1972:xxx.

TABLE 16.8. Selected Parole Hearing Practices of 51* State
and Federal Parole Boards: Felony Offenders, January, 1972

| | Number of Boards | |
Selected Practice	Yes	No
Counsel permitted at hearing	21	30
Inmate permitted to present witnesses	17	34
Reasons for decision recorded	11	40
Verbatim record of proceedings made	20	31

*Georgia, Hawaii, and Texas not included since no hearings are conducted in these jurisdictions.

Source: Vincent O'Leary and Joan Nuffield. The Organization of Parole Systems in the United States. 2nd ed. Hackensack, N.J.: National Council on Crime and Delinquency, 1972:xxxiv.

     b. his release at that time would depreciate the seriousness of his crime or promote disrespect for law; or

     c. his release would have a substantially adverse effect on institutional discipline; or

     d. his continued correctional treatment, medical care or vocational or other training in the institution will substantially enhance his capacity to lead a law-abiding life when released at a later date.

     2. In making its determination regarding a prisoner's release on parole, it shall be the policy of the Board of Parole to take into account each of the following factors:

     a. the prisoner's personality, including his maturity, stability, sense of responsibility and any apparent development in his personality which may promote or hinder his conformity to law;

     b. the adequacy of the prisoner's parole plan;

     c. the prisoner's ability and readiness to assume obligations and undertake responsibilities;

     d. the prisoner's intelligence and training;

     e. the prisoner's family status and whether he has relatives who display an interest in him, or whether he has other close and constructive associations in the community;

     f. the prisoner's employment history, his occupational skills, and the stability of his past employment;

     g. the type of residence, neighborhood or community in which the prisoner plans to live;

     h. the prisoner's past use of narcotics, or past habitual and excessive use of alcohol;

     i. the prisoner's mental or physical makeup, including any disability or handicap which may affect his conformity to law;

     j. the prisoner's prior criminal record, including the nature and circumstances, recency and frequency of previous offenses;

TABLE 16.9. Sentence and Actual Time Served by First Releases*
from State Correctional Institutions in 1970

State	1† 1-5 Years (Percent) Sentenced	2 Served	3 5-10 Years (Percent) Sentenced	4 Served	5 10+ Years (Percent) Sentenced	6 Served
Arizona	34.56	88.54	42.44	9.22	23.00	2.44
California	15.21	81.32	66.51	16.13	9.49	2.55
Colorado	21.30	95.70	32.45	3.42	46.25	.88
Connecticut	51.59	97.86	42.39	1.58	6.02	.56
Delaware	87.00	98.65	10.31	.90	2.24	.45
Georgia	56.68	88.80	27.84	9.48	15.47	1.72
Hawaii	4.26	80.85	17.02	13.83	78.72	5.32
Idaho	47.26	94.56	32.88	3.40	19.86	2.04
Illinois	48.47	89.00	30.16	8.00	21.37	3.00
Kansas	8.50	91.51	39.44	6.73	52.05	1.76
Kentucky	72.55	94.14	12.20	5.28	15.25	.58
Louisiana	56.98	88.84	26.97	9.84	16.04	1.32
Maine	76.95	95.20	13.25	3.00	9.80	1.80
Maryland	78.97	97.17	15.12	2.14	5.91	.69
Massachusetts	14.66	92.30	65.43	6.47	19.91	1.23
Minnesota	21.94	5.81	39.35	31.61	38.71	62.58
Mississippi	63.38	87.36	19.89	6.69	16.73	5.95
Missouri	74.81	96.05	19.39	2.74	5.80	1.21
Montana	54.70	95.30	25.17	4.03	20.13	.67
Nevada	38.53	93.51	29.87	6.49	31.60	0.00
New Hampshire	54.44	97.78	34.44	2.22	11.11	0.00
New Mexico	8.54	86.65	47.49	10.83	43.97	2.52
New York	57.40	89.79	28.26	7.61	15.86	2.59
North Dakota	68.47	96.40	19.82	2.70	11.71	.90
Ohio	5.43	84.77	19.95	10.74	74.62	4.49
Oklahoma	73.80	95.57	17.82	3.61	8.37	.82
Oregon	65.90	95.62	25.09	4.26	9.01	.12
South Carolina	64.41	92.62	20.46	5.16	15.12	2.22
South Dakota	86.19	95.24	38.10	4.29	4.19	.48
Tennessee	61.69	90.20	19.46	8.33	18.84	1.47
Utah	10.55	90.45	21.11	9.55	68.34	0.00
Vermont	70.37	100.00	25.93	0.00	3.70	0.00
Washington	3.06	95.78	2.75	3.06	94.19	1.16
West Virginia	0.00	87.15	10.10	10.76	89.90	2.08
Wyoming	73.72	94.89	16.06	3.65	10.22	1.46

* A first release is a prisoner released for the first time on his current sentence.
† Explanation of Table:
    Column 1: Percent of first releases sentenced to 1 to 5 years.
    Column 2: Percent of first releases who actually served less than 6 months to 5 years.
    Column 3: Percent of first releases sentenced to 5 to 10 years.
    Column 4: Percent of first releases who actually served 5 to 10 years.
    Column 5: Percent of first releases sentenced to 10 or more years.
    Column 6: Percent of first releases who actually served 10 or more years.

Source: National Prisoner Statistics: State Prisoners, Admissions and Releases, 1970.
Washington: Federal Bureau of Prisons, 1971:45, 47–81.

k. the prisoner's attitude toward law and authority;

l. the prisoner's conduct in the institution, including particularly whether he has taken advantage of the opportunities for self-improvement afforded by the institutional program, whether he has been punished for misconduct within six months prior to his hearing or reconsideration for parole release, whether he has forfeited any reductions of term during his period of imprisonment, and whether such reductions have been restored at the time of hearing or reconsideration;

m. the prisoner's conduct and attitude during any previous experience of probation or parole and the recency of such experience.

Parole Hearings Standards

The National Advisory Commission on Criminal Justice Standards and Goals (*Corrections*, 1973:422), 10 years later, assessed the nature of parole hearings. While not measurably different from the Model Penal Code, the Commission published another set of standards which, perhaps, may have more force in bringing about changes in the parole hearings.

Each parole jurisdiction immediately should develop policies for parole release hearings that include opportunities for personal and adequate participation by the inmates concerned; procedural guidelines to insure proper, fair, and thorough consideration of every case; prompt decisions and personal notification of decisions to inmates; and provision for accurate records of deliberations and conclusions.

A proper parole grant process should have the following characteristics:

1. Hearings should be scheduled with inmates within one year after they are received in an institution. Inmates should appear personally at hearings.

2. At these hearings, decisions should be directed toward the quality and pertinence of program objectives agreed upon by the inmate and the institution staff.

3. Board representatives should monitor and approve programs that can have the effect of releasing the inmate without further board hearings.

4. Each jurisdiction should have a statutory requirement, patterned after the Model Penal Code, under which offenders must be released on parole when first eligible unless certain specific conditions exist.

5. When a release date is not agreed upon, a further hearing date within one year should be set.

6. A parole board member or hearing examiner should hold no more than 20 hearings in any full day.

7. One examiner or member should conduct hearings. His findings should be final unless appealed to the full parole board by the correctional authority or the inmate within 5 days.

8. Inmates should be notified of any decision directly and personally by the board member or representative before he leaves the institution.

9. The person hearing the case should specify in detail and in writing the reasons for his decision, whether to grant parole or to deny or defer it.

10. Parole procedures should permit disclosure or information on which the hearing examiner bases his decisions. Sensitive information may be withheld, but in such cases nondisclosure should be noted in the record so that subsequent reviewers will know what information was not available to the offender.

11. Parole procedures should permit representation of offenders under appropriate conditions, if required. Such representation should conform generally to Standard 2.2 on Access to Legal Services.

Parole Outcome

In recent years, considerable attention has been focused on studying parole outcome across the United States. In the past, this was an almost impossible task, for most paroling authorities either kept poor or no data on the recidivism rates of those inmates who had been paroled. The National Council on Crime and Delinquency, as a result of a grant from the National Institute of Mental Health, began to collect uniform nationwide data on parole outcomes through the Uniform Parole Reports. In a report on data collected from every adult parole jurisdiction in the United States between the years 1965 and 1970, Gottfredson et al. (1973:21-23) report that in a one-year follow-up period after release from prison on parole, offenders tend to have a much higher successful parole outcome than had been previously assumed. This is true for property as well as person offenders, for the rates of success reach a high of 97 percent (manslaughter) to a low of 59 percent (auto theft). Tables 16.10 and 16.11 depict the data.

In October, 1974, NCCD issued a report on a three-year follow-up study of selected parolees across the United States who were released from prison in 1969. An analysis of the sample of adult, male felons in terms of their parole behavior indicates that 63 percent

TABLE 16.10. Parole Outcome for 30,908 Offenders Convicted of Five Crimes Against Persons, According to Time Served[a] Before First Release and Prior Prison Record: Age Adjusted, One Year Follow-up

Offense Categories	Number	Percent Favorable Outcome By Time Served Pentiles				
		First	Second	Third	Fourth	Fifth
NO PRIOR NONPRISON SENTENCES						
ARMED ROBBERY (months served)	3,450	81.8 (0–14)	84.0 (15–23)	85.6 (24–35)	83.9 (36–58)	83.2 (59–449)
AGGRAVATED ASSAULT (months served)	1,812	86.8 (0–6)	87.5 (7–11)	87.0 (12–18)	84.3 (19–31)	85.7 (32–312)
FORCIBLE RAPE (months served)	886	90.3 (0–15)	87.2 (16–32)	87.3 (33–59)	90.5 (60–108)	86.0 (109–496)
MANSLAUGHTER (months served)	863	96.9 (0–9)	94.0 (10–15)	92.6 (16–23)	94.9 (24–39)	90.6 (40–278)
HOMICIDE (months served)	3,311	94.7 (0–21)	93.0 (22–44)	93.9 (45–79)	95.4 (80–124)	90.0 (125–637)
OVERALL*	10,322	88.8	88.6	89.2	89.1	86.7
PRIOR NONPRISON SENTENCES						
ARMED ROBBERY (months served)	8,851	73.2 (0–17)	71.8 (18–27)	73.6 (28–41)	75.0 (42–63)	75.1 (64–537)
AGGRAVATED ASSAULT (months served)	4,487	77.6 (0–6)	78.0 (7–12)	79.9 (13–19)	77.5 (20–30)	74.8 (31–396)
FORCIBLE RAPE (months served)	1,480	83.6 (0–23)	79.4 (24–40)	76.6 (41–62)	81.4 (63–105)	83.0 (106–455)
MANSLAUGHTER (months served)	1,030	86.5 (0–10)	84.6 (11–16)	86.7 (17–26)	84.2 (27–45)	80.9 (46–275)
HOMICIDE (months served)	4,738	88.3 (0–23)	87.9 (24–42)	87.3 (43–71)	89.6 (72–120)	86.5 (121–720)
OVERALL*	20,586	79.5	78.2	79.0	79.7	78.2

*The results reported in the rows labeled "Overall" were obtained by combining subjects from each offense category based on the time served pentile assignments for their respective offenses.

Source: Gottfredson, Don, M.G. Nethercutt, J. Nuffield, and V. O'Leary. Four Thousand Lifetimes: A Study of Time Served and Parole Outcome. Davis, California: National Council on Crime and Delinquency, 1973:21.

TABLE 16.11. Parole Outcome for 60,202 Offenders Convicted of Five Property Crimes, According to Time Served Before Release and Prior Prison Record: Age Adjusted, One Year Follow-up

Offense Categories	Number	Percent Favorable Outcome By Time Served Pentiles				
		First	Second	Third	Fourth	Fifth
NO PRIOR NONPRISON SENTENCES						
AUTO THEFT (months served)	1,454	76.1 (0-7)	73.6 (8-10)	73.8 (11-14)	68.4 (15-21)	64.1 (22-394)
CHECK OFFENSE (months served)	2,482	73.4 (0-7)	71.8 (8-10)	75.3 (11-14)	73.5 (15-21)	65.1 (22-230)
BURGLARY (months served)	8,487	81.5 (0-7)	79.7 (8-11)	79.1 (12-16)	75.2 (17-25)	75.9 (26-374)
LARCENY (months served)	2,755	81.7 (0-6)	81.1 (7-9)	81.1 (10-12)	79.7 (13-20)	76.2 (21-267)
FRAUD (months served)	335	88.6 (0-6)	84.7 (7-9)	85.6 (10-12)	86.6 (13-19)	76.8 (20-108)
OVERALL*	15,513	79.8	78.4	78.4	75.4	73.0
PRIOR NONPRISON SENTENCES						
AUTO THEFT (months served)	4,285	64.5 (0-7)	65.7 (8-11)	62.5 (12-16)	58.9 (17-24)	63.3 (25-231)
CHECK OFFENSE (months served)	8,493	66.3 (0-8)	66.1 (9-12)	66.3 (13-17)	62.8 (18-25)	60.4 (26-281)
BURGLARY (months served)	23,790	70.7 (0-9)	69.3 (10-13)	68.3 (14-19)	69.3 (20-30)	69.0 (31-494)
LARCENY (months served)	7,448	76.4 (0-7)	72.6 (8-11)	74.3 (12-15)	69.7 (16-23)	66.0 (24-362)
FRAUD (months served)	673	71.1 (0-7)	74.3 (8-10)	77.0 (11-14)	79.6 (15-22)	71.6 (23-241)
OVERALL*	44,689	70.2	68.9	68.5	67.3	66.3

*The results reported in the rows labeled "Overall" were obtained by combining subjects from each offense category based on the time served pentile assignments for their respective offenses.

Source: Gottfredson, Don, M.G. Nethercutt, J. Nuffield, and V. O'Leary. Four Thousand Lifetimes: A Study of Time Served and Parole Outcome. Davis, California: National Countil on Crime and Delinquency, 1973:21.

were continued on parole, regardless of original commitment offense or length of time served in prison. Table 16.12 presents the data. Of the 21,019 parolees in the study, less than 9 percent were returned to prison as a result of new major convictions and 20 percent were returned as technical violators.

Table 16.12 also points out that the least successful parolee is the vehicle thief, for slightly better than 50 percent are successful for at least three years after release from prison. Those who murder, either willfully or negligently, are among the most successful parolees, comparatively.

In 1975, NCCD released data describing the success rates of 27,567 adult, male, felon parolees who were released in 1972 and followed for one year. Vehicle thieves have a success rate of 72 percent and willful murderers' success rate jumps to 90 percent. The overall success rate for all those released in 1972 in the sample in a one-year follow-up is 79 percent, which is 16 percentage points higher than for those followed for three years (1969–1972).

Parole Conditions

Similar to probation, paroling authorities always attach conditions or establish specific rules which the parolee must follow if he or she hopes to remain in the community and not be returned to the institution to complete the term of sentence. As Kassebaum, Ward, and Wilner (1971:183) state:

> Theoretically, a man may be returned to prison for failure to abide by any *one* of the obligations of the parole contract; in fact, this is not done. The conditions are regarded as a means to an end—supervision and control —enforcement is not an end in and of itself. Parole rules are enforced and violations are actionable depending on the features of individual cases and the degree of significance which seems to be attached to the various conditions . . . (by the paroling authority).

They proceed to enumerate the various rules or conditions which the California Parole Division enforces, which can serve as an example of the kinds of rules other paroling authorities enforce (1971:183–196):

> 1. Upon release from the institution you are to go directly to the program approved by the Division of Adult Paroles and shall report to the Parole Agent.

TABLE 16.12. Parole Outcome in First Three Years for Persons Paroled in 1969

Parole Outcome	Total Part 1 & 2	Willful Homicide	Negligent Manslaughter	Armed Robbery	Unarmed Robbery	Aggravated Assault	Forcible Rape	Statutory Rape	All Other Sex Offenses
Continued on Parole — No difficulty or sentence less than 60 days	13,319 63%	1,248 78%	248 82%	1,337 60%	471 60%	839 72%	315 74%	109 75%	328 76%
With new minor conviction(s)	251 1%	22 1%	2 1%	21 1%	11 1%	17 1%	6 1%	7 5%	4 1%
New major conviction(s)	203 1%	4 ½%		22 1%	5 1%	9 1%	1 ½%	2 1%	4 1%
Absconder	1,275 6%	49 3%	9 3%	120 5%	42 5%	59 5%	14 3%	8 6%	28 6%
Return to Prison as Technical Violator									
No new conviction(s) and not in lieu of prosecution	2,780 13%	158 10%	25 8%	334 15%	118 15%	114 10%	41 10%	8 6%	30 7%
New minor or lesser conviction(s) or in lieu of prosecution	799 4%	52 3%	8 3%	71 3%	31 4%	52 4%	20 5%	4 3%	16 4%
In lieu of prosecution of new major offense(s)	718 3%	25 2%	3 1%	83 4%	35 4%	31 3%	11 3%	4 3%	7 2%
Return to prison no violation	7 ½%	1 ½%		2 ½%					
Recommitted to Prison With New Major Conviction(s)									

Commitment Offense

	Total	Burglary	Theft or Larceny	Vehicle Theft	Forgery Fraud or Larceny by Check	Other Fraud	Violations of Narcotic Drug Laws	Violations of Alcohol Laws	All Others
Same jurisdiction	1,323 6%	37 2%	5 2%	184 8%	53 7%	38 3%	12 3%	2 1%	12 3%
Any other jurisdiction	344 2%	7 ½%	1 ½%	55 2%	16 2%	9 1%	5 1%	1 1%	3 1%
Total	21,019*	1,603	301	2,227	784	1,168	425	145	432
Percentage of Total	100%	8%	1%	11%	4%	6%	2%	1%	2%

*32 subjects excluded: charges pending.

	Burglary	Theft or Larceny	Vehicle Theft	Forgery Fraud or Larceny by Check	Other Fraud	Violations of Narcotic Drug Laws	Violations of Alcohol Laws	All Others
Continued on Parole								
No difficulty or sentence less than 60 days	3,908 62%	1,214 63%	631 51%	1,160 56%	114 69%	522 62%	53 87%	822 63%
With new minor conviction(s)	66 1%	23 1%	19 2%	29 1%	3 2%	10 1%	1 2%	10 1%
New major conviction(s)	57 1%	19 1%	23 2%	16 1%		26 3%		15 1%
Absconder	336 5%	159 8%	86 7%	214 10%	7 4%	45 5%	1 2%	98 8%
Return to Prison as Technical Violator								
No new conviction(s) and not in lieu of prosecution	894 14%	222 12%	193 16%	338 16%	25 15%	105 12%	3 5%	172 13%
New minor or lesser conviction(s) or in lieu of prosecution	243 4%	74 4%	53 4%	78 4%	2 1%	43 5%	1 2%	51 4%
In lieu of prosecution	242	72	63	76	4	26		36

TABLE 16.12 Continued

| | Commitment Offense | | | | | | | |
	Burglary	Theft or Larceny	Vehicle Theft	Forgery Fraud or Larceny by Check	Other Fraud	Violations of Narcotic Drug Laws	Violations of Alcohol Laws	All Others
of new major offense(s)	4%	4%	5%	4%	2%	3%		3%
Return to prison no violation	2	1	1					
	½%	½%	½%					
Recommitted to Prison With New Major Conviction(s)								
Same jurisdiction	480	109	127	115	6	64	2	77
	8%	6%	10%	6%	4%	8%	3%	6%
Any other jurisdiction	100	27	32	59	4	4		21
	2%	1%	3%	3%	2%	½%		2%
Total	6,328	1,920	1,228	2,085	165	845	61	1,302
Percentage of Total	30%	9%	6%	10%	1%	4%	½%	6%

Source: Uniform Parole Reports. Davis, California: National Council on Crime and Delinquency. October, 1974: Table I.

2. Only with approval of your Parole Agent may you change your residence or leave the county of your residence.

3. It is necessary for you to maintain gainful employment. Any change of employment must be reported to, and approved by, your Parole Agent.

4. You must submit a written monthly report of your activities on forms supplied by the Division ... (It) shall be true, correct and complete in all respects.

5. The unwise use of alcoholic beverages and liquors causes more failures on parole than all other reasons combined. You shall not use alcoholic beverages or liquors to excess.

6. You may not possess, use or traffic in, any narcotic drug in violation of the law. If you have ever been convicted of possession or use of narcotic drugs or become suspect of being a user of narcotic drugs and are paroled to a section of California where an Anti-Narcotic Program is, or becomes available, you hereby agree to participate in such programs....

7. You shall not own, possess, use, sell, nor have under your control any deadly weapons or firearms.

8. You must avoid association with former inmates of penal institutions unless specifically approved by your Parole Agent; and you must avoid association with individuals of bad reputation.

9. Before operating any motor vehicle you must have permission from your Parole Agent and you must possess a valid operator's license.

10. At all times your cooperation with your Agent, and your good behavior and attitude must justify the opportunity granted you by this parole.

11. You are to obey all municipal, county, state, and federal laws, ordinances, and orders, and you are to conduct yourself as a good citizen.

12. Your Civil Rights have been suspended by law. You may not marry, engage in business nor sign contracts unless the Parole Agent recommends, and the Adult Authority approves, restoring such Civil Rights to you.... The following Civil Rights *only* are hereby restored to you at this time: You may make such purchases of clothing, food, transportation, household furnishings, tools, and rent such habitation as are necessary to maintain yourself and keep your employment. You shall not make any purchases relative to the above on credit except with the written approval of your Parole Agent. You are hereby restored all rights under any law, relating to employees such as rights under Workmen's Compensation, Unemployment Insurance laws, Social Security laws, etc.

13. *Special Conditions.* Registration with local police and participation in the Parole Outpatient Clinic (POC) represented the most frequently imposed special condition. Registration pertained to certain sex offenders, arsonists, and narcotic offenders. The parolee was required to report his registration number to his agent; departmental headquarters notified the agent if they did not receive notification of the parolee's registration. Failure to attend the POC could result in confinement in the county jail as a warning. Special conditions could be imposed by the Adult Authority during the parole period as well as prior to it.

In their study of California parolees, Kassebaum, Ward, and Wilner (1971:194) summarize the probable consequences of parolee violations of the various conditions. These are presented in Figure 16.1.

Parole Revocation and Due Process

As occurs in probation, the parole officer or agent has a responsibility to work with the parolee in order to enhance his or her adjustment upon release from the institution. Parole Officers assume many different styles and roles in providing this service (see Chapter 14 on Probation). Traditionally, it has been assumed that if a parolee fails on parole it is substantially due to his or her failure to comply with the terms and conditions of parole and/or to follow the recommendations of the worker. It generally has not been the case that the parole officer is held accountable for such failure. In the past, it tended to be relatively easy for a parole officer to arrange for the revocation of a parolee. The officer merely had to present a "case" against the parolee and the parole board generally went along with the revocation recommendation. In the case of probationers, this was also a relatively easy task, even though the final decision to revoke remains with the judge.

A great deal of attention has been focused on the revocation process in recent years, especially by the appellate courts. Since revocation can result in a parolee being returned to prison, it has been interpreted that this requires more "due process" than has occurred in the past. That is, since one's liberty is at stake, the offender should be entitled to protection of his or her constitutional rights. One of the reasons correctional authorities have not been so willing to provide due process centers around the belief that parole is a privilege and not a right; therefore, parole could be summarily revoked by legitimate authority—the parole board, in administrative action. The National Advisory Commission on Criminal Justice Standards and Goals (*Corrections,* 1973:426) expresses the opinion that ". . . there has been a growing consensus that the recommitment of a parolee represents a substantial denial of freedom and words like 'privilege,' 'grace,' and 'contract' cannot blur the loss of liberty so clearly at stake."

The appellate courts, which previously had a "hands-off" policy with regard to revocation have begun to change their position. In

FIGURE 16.1. Parole Behavior and the Probability of Return to
Prison in California

Parole Behavior	Retain on Parole	Return to Prison
Violations of Conditions 1 to 5, 7 to 10, 12 to 14	Usually	Rarely
		Parolee at large, once located often returned TFT*
Violation of Condition 6 First detection of narcotics use	NTCP* parolees placed in special confinement category	Rarely for NTCP parolees Often for regular parolees
Second detection	NTCP parolees seldom reconfined at special NTC Units	Usually for NTCP Certainly for regulars
Miscellaneous misbehavior though no crime is charged	Usually, though may be detained in jail on parole arrest	Seldom Suspicion of violence poten-tial or "bizarre" actions may result in return TFT
		The need for medical or psy-chiatric treatment may also result in technical violation
Misdemeanor arrest or fel-ony arrest reduced to mis-demeanor charge: No conviction	Usually	Seldom
Conviction	Maybe	Seldom on first conviction but not infrequent after second or third misdemeanor arrest or conviction In lieu of county jail time
Felony arrest: No conviction	Especially if other parole behavior has been stable	Sometimes, especially if sec-ond time, if division is con-vinced of his guilt, or deal with prosecution was made, or if parolee had been violator at large (PVAL)*
Conviction	Never	Automatic return with new term (WNT)*

TFT – To Finish Term
WNT – With New Term
NTCP – Narcotics Treatment Program
PVAL – Parole Violator At Large
    Source: Gene Kasselbaum, David Ward, and Daniel Wilner. *Prison Treatment and Parole Survival*. New York: John Wiley & Sons, 1971, p. 194.

such cases as *Gagnon* v. *Scarpelli* [411 U.S. 778 (1973)] and *Morrissey* v. *Brewer* [408 U.S. 471 (1972)], the courts began to require correctional authorities to protect the rights of parolees. That 'rights" were seen as important to parolees is best summarized in a statement contained in the decision in *Morrissey* v. *Brewer*:

> We see, therefore, that the liberty of a parolee, although indeterminate, includes many of the core values of unqualified liberty and its termination inflicts a "grievous loss" on the parolee and often on others. It is hardly useful any longer to try to deal with this problem in terms of whether the parolee's liberty is a "right" or a "privilege." By whatever name the liberty is valuable and must be seen as within the protection of the Fourteenth Amendment. Its termination calls for some orderly process, however informal.

To protect the rights of parolees and to ensure an orderly process for revocation hearings, the Standards Commission (*Corrections*, 1973:425–426) recommends the following:

> Each parole jurisdiction immediately should develop and implement a system of revocation procedures to permit the prompt confinement of parolees exhibiting behavior that poses a serious threat to others. At the same time, it should provide careful controls, methods of fact-finding, and possible alternatives to keep as many offenders as possible in the community. Return to the institution should be used as a last resort, even when a factual basis for revocation can be demonstrated.
>
> 1. Warrants to arrest and hold alleged parole violators should be issued and signed by parole board members. Tight control should be developed over the process of issuing such warrants. They should never be issued unless there is sufficient evidence of probable serious violation. In some instances, there may be a need to detain alleged parole violators. In general, however, detention is not required and is to be discouraged. Any parolee who is detained should be granted a prompt preliminary hearing. Administrative arrest and detention should never be used simply to permit investigation of possible violations.
>
> 2. Parolees alleged to have committed a new crime but without other violations of conditions sufficient to require parole revocation should be eligible for bail or other release pending the outcome of the new charges, as determined by the court.
>
> 3. A preliminary hearing conducted by an individual not previously directly involved in the case should be held promptly on all alleged parole violations, including convictions of new crimes, in or near the community in which the violation occurred unless waived by the parolee after due notification of his rights. The purpose' should be to determine whether

there is probable cause or reasonable grounds to believe that the arrested parolee has committed acts that would constitute a violation of parole conditions and a determination of the value question of whether the case should be carried further, even if probable cause exists. The parolee should be given notice that the hearing will take place and of what parole violations have been alleged. He should have the right to present evidence, to confront and cross-examine witnesses, and to be represented by counsel.

The person who conducts the hearing should make a summary of what transpired at the hearing and the information he used to determine whether probable cause existed to hold the parolee for the final decision of the parole board on revocation. If the evidence is insufficient to support a further hearing, or if it is otherwise determined that revocation would not be desirable, the offender should be released to the community immediately.

4. At parole revocation hearings, the parolee should have written notice of the alleged infractions of his rules or conditions; access to official records regarding his case; the right to be represented by counsel, including the right to appointed counsel if he is indigent; the opportunity to be heard in person; the right to subpoena witnesses in his own behalf; and the right to cross-examine witnesses or otherwise to challenge allegations or evidence held by the State. Hearing examiners should be empowered to hear and decide parole revocation cases under policies established by the parole board. Parole should not be revoked unless there is substantial evidence of a violation of one of the conditions of parole. The hearing examiner should provide a written statement of findings, the reasons for the decision, and the evidence relied upon.

5. Each jurisdiction should develop alternatives to parole revocation, such as warnings, short-time local confinement, special conditions of future parole, variations in intensity of supervision or surveillance, fines, and referral to other community resources. Such alternative measures should be utilized as often as is practicable.

6. If return to a correctional institution is warranted, the offender should be scheduled for subsequent appearances for parole considerations when appropriate. There should be no automatic prohibition against reparole of a parole violator.

References

American Law Institute
    1962   Model Penal Code. New York: ALI.
Attorney General
    1939   Attorney General's Survey of Release Procedures. Washington, D.C.: U.S. Government Printing Office. Vol. IV.
Dressler, David
    1959   Practice and Theory of Probation and Parole. New York: Columbia University Press.
Federal Bureau of Prisons

1964, 1971   National Prisoner Statistics. Washington, D.C.: U.S. Department of Justice.

Giardini, G.I.
1959   The Parole Process. Springfield: Charles C. Thomas.

Gottfredson, Don, M.G. Nethercutt, J. Nuffield, and V. O'Leary
1973   Four Thousand Lifetimes: A Study of Time Served and Parole Outcome. Davis, California: National Council on Crime and Delinquency.

Kassebaum, Gene, D. Ward, and D. Wilner
1971   Prison Treatment and Parole Survival. New York: John Wiley and Sons.

Killinger, George C.
1951   "Parole and Services to the Discharged Offender." In Paul W. Tappan (ed.). Contemporary Correction. New York: McGraw-Hill.

Korn, Richard R. and Lloyd W. McCorkle
1965   Criminology and Penology. New York: Holt, Rinehart & Winston.

Moran, Frederick A.
1945   "The Origins of Parole." In Bell, Marjorie (ed.). Yearbook: National Probation Association. New York: NPA:71-98.

National Advisory Commission on Criminal Justice Standards and Goals
1973   Corrections. Washington, D.C.: U.S. Government Printing Office.

National Council on Crime and Delinquency
1967   Correction in the United States. New York: NCCD.

O'Leary, Vincent
1966   Selection for Parole. New York: National Parole Institutes, National Council on Crime and Delinquency.

O'Leary, Vincent and Jay Hall
1963   "Frames of Reference in Parole." New York: National Parole Institutes, National Council on Crime and Delinquency. (Mimeo).

O'Leary, Vincent and Joan Nuffield
1972   The Organization of Parole Systems in the United States. 2nd ed. Hackensack, New Jersey: National Council on Crime and Delinquency.

President's Commission on Law Enforcement and Administration of Justice
1967   Task Force Report: Corrections. Washington, D.C.: U.S. Government Printing Office.

Rubin, Sol
1973   The Law of Criminal Correction. 2nd ed. St. Paul: West Publishing Co.

Uniform Parole Reports
1974   "Parole Outcome in First Three Years for Persons Paroled in 1969." Davis, California: UPR, National Council on Crime and Delinquency.

1975   "Parole Outcome in First Year for Persons Paroled in 1972." Davis, California: UPR, National Council on Crime and Delinquency.

index of subjects

Council on Crime and Delinquency)
naturalistic explanation of crime,
139
NCCD (*see* the National Council on
Crime and Delinquency)
NCP (*see* the National Crime Panel)
neoclassical criminology, 9, 146
night watches, 203
nonreporting of crime, 39–43, 76
NORC (*see* the National Opinion
Research Center)

organized crime, 70, 87, 88, 91, 93,
100, 105

pardon, 416–17
parens patriae, 272, 314
parole: conditions of, 435, 439–40;
and due process, 440, 442–43;
and the Elmira Reformatory, 414;
and "good time," 411, 413, 416;
organization of, 419–20; outcome
of, 432, 435; revocation of, 440,
442–43; and the Standard Probation and Parole Act, 359, 361;
standards for, 431–32; and the
ticket-of-leave, 411
parole agreement, the, 413
parole board, the, 420–22, 425–26,
431
Pennsylvania system of prisons, 377–
78, 397
personalistic approach to crime, 30–31
persons in need of supervision
(PINS), 315
Philadelphia Society for Alleviating
the Miseries of Public Prisons,
the, 412, 413
phrenology, 132, 150
physiognomy, 132
PINS (*see* persons in need of supervision)
plea bargaining, 107, 180–82, 251
pocket picking, 85
police: and the Bow Street Runners, 201; brutality, 227; costs
of, 212–13, 215; and discretionary
law enforcement, 227; evaluation
of, 227–31; and frontier law
enforcement, 206–7; goals of,
231–34; harassment, 227; and

"the hue and cry," 199; and lay
police organizations, 201–2; modernization of, 204–6; and night
watches, 203; operations of, 215,
223–24, 227; private, 90; productivity of, 230–31; and property protection, 200–1; racism of,
227; reform of, 204–6; and the
sheriff, 199; standards for, 231–
34; and urbanization, 207–10;
and vigilantes, 202, 207
"Police Training and Performance
Study" (McManus), 224
political crime, 107–9
positive criminology, 9, 11, 133, 146,
147–49, 272, 273, 347, 376, 380
preclassical criminology, 141–43
prerelease centers, 392
President's Commission on Law Enforcement and Administration of
Justice (*see Crime and Its Impact;
An Assessment*)
prevention, crime, 304–9, 342–43
prisoners, labor of, 397–99
prisons: administration of, 390–92;
and the Boston Prison Discipline Society, 378; and crime control, 8; and the criminal justice
system, 373–406; and criminal
punishment, 298, 299, 307, 309;
discipline in, 399–403; history of,
373–80; length of stay in, 385,
390; reform of, 274; social system in, 403–6; as "total institutions," 398, 403, 404; and
workhouses, 376–77
processing, prisoner, 174–92
productivity, police, 230–31
professional criminal, the, 104–6
property crime, 69–71, 81–87, 106
property protection, 200–1
prosecutor, the, 251, 254–55, 257–60
prostitution, 87, 88, 120, 121
probation, 188, 347–70, 417
probation officers, 359, 361–62,
365–68
public inebriation, 115–19, 120

Quaker doctrines in criminology, 378

race and crime, 63, 72, 81
racism, police, 227

index of NAMES

Adams, Stuart, 274
Adler, Freda, 186
Allen, Francis A., 273, 277
Amir, Menachem, 76

Bailey, Walter C., 274, 309
Bain, Read, 197
Balbus, Isaac D., 173
Barnes, Harry, 297, 299
——; Shalloo, J.P., 156
——; Teeters, Negley, 142, 151, 301
Beaumont, Gustave de; Tocqueville, Alexis de, 378
Becker, Howard S., 271, 272
Bers, Melvin K., 104
Best, Harry, 1
Bittner, Egon; Platt, Anthony M., 294, 301
Black, Donald J.; Reiss, Albert J., Jr., 39
Block, Herbert A.; Geis, Gilbert, 132
Bordua, David J., 163
Brown, Richard M., 207
Buckley, Walter, 169
Burgess, Ernest, 13

Caldwell, Robert G., 161, 162
Cargan, Leonard; Coates, Mary A., 189
Carleton, William, 206, 207
Carter, Robert M.; Glaser, Daniel; Wilkins, Leslie T., 404
Chute, Charles L.; Bell, Marjorie, 348, 351
Cicourel, Aaron V., 271, 274
Clinard, Marshal B., 129
——; Quinney, Richard, 31
Cloward, Richard A., 404
——; Ohlin, Lloyd E., 162
Cohen, Albert, 158
——; Short, James F., Jr., 273
Cohn, Alvin W., 173, 274, 279, 324, 359
——; Sullivan, Dennis, 392
——; Viano, E., 228
Conrad, John, 278
Cressey, Donald R., 278, 404
——; McDermott, Robert A., 327

Dash, Samuel, 275
Diamond, Bernard, 25, 26

Dressler, David, 348, 349, 350, 415
Dunn, Robert H., 306
Durkheim, Emile, 2, 95, 170

Elliott, Mabel A., 19, 134, 135, 154, 238
Empey, LaMar T., 314
Ennis, Philip H., 50, 78
Epstein, Irwin, 351
Erickson, Maynard L., Empey, LaMar T., 57

Fox, Vernon, 380, 397
Frank, Benjamin, 277, 278, 279
Frankfurter, Felix; Landis, James M., 239
Freed, Daniel J, 169
Friday, Paul C.; Petersen, D.M.; Allen, H.E., 188
Friesen, Ernest C., Jr.; Gallas, Edward C.; Gallas, Nesta M., 243

Gemignani, Robert, 334
Germann, A. C.; Day, F. D.; Gallati, R. R. S., 199, 203, 251
Giardini, G. I., 411, 413, 414
Gibbons, Don G., 34
Gillin, John, 145
Glaser, Daniel, 367
——; Cohen, F.; O'Leary, V., 187
Glueck, Sheldon, 24, 155
——; Glueck, Eleanor, 151
Goddard, Henry H., 154
Goffman, Erving, 403
Goldman, Nathan, 271
Goring, Charles, 154
Green, Milton D., 244, 245
Grinnell, Frank W., 348

Hall, Jerome, 200, 201, 202, 277
Henderson, Charles R., 134
Henslin, James M., 5
Hibbert, Christopher, 294, 298, 299
Hickey, William L.; Rubin, Sol, 110
Hindelang, Michael J., 65, 357
Holbrook, Stewart H., 378
Hood, Roger; Sparks, Richard, 57
Hooten, Earnest, 150
Hoover, J. Edgar, 211